MW00343677

Beginning PowerApps

The Non-Developers Guide to Building Business Mobile Applications

Tim Leung

Apress®

Beginning PowerApps

Tim Leung
Reading, United Kingdom

ISBN-13 (pbk): 978-1-4842-3002-2   ISBN-13 (electronic): 978-1-4842-3003-9
https://doi.org/10.1007/978-1-4842-3003-9

Library of Congress Control Number: 2017961125

Copyright © 2017 by Tim Leung

This work is subject to copyright. All rights are reserved by the Publisher, whether the whole or part of the material is concerned, specifically the rights of translation, reprinting, reuse of illustrations, recitation, broadcasting, reproduction on microfilms or in any other physical way, and transmission or information storage and retrieval, electronic adaptation, computer software, or by similar or dissimilar methodology now known or hereafter developed.

Trademarked names, logos, and images may appear in this book. Rather than use a trademark symbol with every occurrence of a trademarked name, logo, or image we use the names, logos, and images only in an editorial fashion and to the benefit of the trademark owner, with no intention of infringement of the trademark.

The use in this publication of trade names, trademarks, service marks, and similar terms, even if they are not identified as such, is not to be taken as an expression of opinion as to whether or not they are subject to proprietary rights.

While the advice and information in this book are believed to be true and accurate at the date of publication, neither the authors nor the editors nor the publisher can accept any legal responsibility for any errors or omissions that may be made. The publisher makes no warranty, express or implied, with respect to the material contained herein.

Cover image by Freepik (`www.freepik.com`)

Managing Director: Welmoed Spahr
Editorial Director: Todd Green
Acquisitions Editor: Joan Murray
Development Editor: Laura Berendson
Technical Reviewer: Jenefer Monroe
Coordinating Editor: Jill Balzano
Copy Editor: Karen Jameson

Distributed to the book trade worldwide by Springer Science+Business Media New York, 233 Spring Street, 6th Floor, New York, NY 10013. Phone 1-800-SPRINGER, fax (201) 348-4505, e-mail orders-ny@springer-sbm.com, or visit `www.springeronline.com`. Apress Media, LLC is a California LLC and the sole member (owner) is Springer Science + Business Media Finance Inc (SSBM Finance Inc). SSBM Finance Inc is a **Delaware** corporation.

For information on translations, please e-mail rights@apress.com, or visit `http://www.apress.com/rights-permissions`.

Apress titles may be purchased in bulk for academic, corporate, or promotional use. eBook versions and licenses are also available for most titles. For more information, reference our Print and eBook Bulk Sales web page at `http://www.apress.com/bulk-sales`.

Any source code or other supplementary material referenced by the author in this book is available to readers on GitHub via the book's product page, located at `www.apress.com/9781484230022`. For more detailed information, please visit `http://www.apress.com/source-code`.

Contents

About the Author xv

About the Technical Reviewer xvii

Foreword xix

Acknowledgments xxi

Introduction xxiii

■Part I: Getting Started 1

■Chapter 1: Introducing PowerApps... 3

What Is PowerApps? 3

Who Is the Typical Developer?.. 4

What Are the Typical Uses? 4

    Asset Checkout App.. 4

    Budget Tracker... 5

    Service Desk App... 6

    Site Inspection App.. 7

    Other Sample Apps 8

How Do You Build a PowerApp? 8

How Do Users Run PowerApp Applications? 9

What Data Can a PowerApps Consume? 10

    Connecting to On-Premises Data... 11

    Common Data Service 11

    Connecting to Other Data Sources 12

How Do You Write Code? 12

How Much Does It Cost? 13

Summary 14

■Chapter 2: Subscribing to PowerApps 15

How to Get PowerApps 15

Obtaining PowerApps via Office 365 15

What Is Office 365? 16

Consumer vs. Business Office 365 16

Understanding Work Accounts and Personal Accounts 16

What Office 365 Editions Support PowerApps? 18

Subscribing to a PowerApps Stand-Alone Plan 18

Registering for an Account 19

Obtaining a Suitable Email Address 20

Logging onto PowerApps 21

Configuring Environments 21

Installing PowerApps Studio 22

Summary 24

■Chapter 3: Creating Your First App 25

Preparing an Excel Data Source 25

Creating an App 26

Creating an Auto-Generated App 27

Creating Apps from SharePoint 28

Exploring the Designer 29

Running Your App 30

Examining the Screens at Runtime 30

Understanding the Auto-Generated App 32

Adding and Removing Data Sources 32

Adding, Deleting, and Rearranging Screens 33

Understanding How Screens Are Connected 34

Understanding Forms and Cards 39

Setting Project Properties 49

Saving Your Project 51

Opening a Project 51

Summary 52

▓**Chapter 4: Sharing Apps**.. **53**

Sharing Your App 53

Adding a User 55

Applying Permissions 57

Managing Environments.. 57

Moving an App to a New Environment.. 57

Updating a Data Source... 58

How Data Connections Work 59

Versioning an App... 60

Installing the Mobile Player 60

Running with Foreign Languages.. 61

Summary 64

▓**Part II: Refining Your Application** **65**

▓**Chapter 5: Exploring Data Sources**... **67**

Using the Common Data Service 67

Getting Started 68

Exploring the Common Data Model 70

Exploring a Standard Entity 71

Creating a Relationship 76

Using Field Groups... 77

Picklists 78

Deleting CDS Data 81

On-Premises Data Gateway.. 82

Installing the Gateway 82

Starting the Gateway Service 83

Connecting to a Data Source 84

Uninstalling a Gateway 86

Using a SharePoint Data Source 86

Creating a SharePoint List 87

Connecting to a SharePoint Data Source..88

Other Data Sources 89

Microsoft Translation Data Source...90

Microsoft MSN Weather Services 91

Summary...92

■Chapter 6: Using Formulas 95

Writing Formulas..95

Using the Function Tool 96

Working with Variables..98

Setting Screen Variables...98

Setting Property Values from Code 101

Setting Global Variables..102

Manipulating Data 102

Working with Text...103

Working with Numbers...107

Working with Dates...110

Working with Tables of Data..113

Defining Hard-Coded Sets of Values..113

Understanding Collections...113

Defining Tables 116

Working with Columns...116

Table Functions...117

Counting Records 118

Performing Aggregate Calculations 119

Conditional Statements and Logical Operations 120

Specifying Colors 121

Navigation Functions 121

    Launching Websites and Apps 123

    Retrieving Startup Parameters 124

    Exiting an App 125

Managing Errors 125

Summary 126

■ **Chapter 7: Customizing Screens** **129**

Using Predefined Layouts 129

    Laying Out Tablet Apps 134

Understanding Sample Screen Designs 135

    Building a List and Details Screen 135

    Updating the Details Section of a Screen 138

    Displaying a Delete Confirmation Screen 139

    Building a Tab Control Screen 140

Using Themes 142

Summary 143

■ **Chapter 8: Using Controls** **145**

Overview of Controls 146

Building Data Structures to Support Controls 146

Action Controls 147

    Displaying Geometric Shapes 148

Displaying Text with Label and HTML Text Controls 149

Using Simple Controls 150

    Text Input Control 150

    Radio Control 151

    Toggle and Checkbox Controls 152

    Slider Control 153

    Rating Control 154

Working with Dates 155

    Date Picker Control 155

Setting Lookup Values 160

    Limiting Input Values with a Drop-Down Control 160

    Setting Lookup Values with a Drop-Down Control 161

    Customizing the Drop-Down Display Value 162

    Nesting Drop-Down Controls 163

    List Box Control 164

Displaying Tables of Data 164

Using CDS-Specific Controls 165

    Using Entity Form Controls 166

    Drop-Down Controls with CDS 168

Working with Media Controls 170

    Playing Videos 172

    Playing Audio 173

    Image Controls 173

Using the Timer Control 174

Resetting Form Controls 175

Summary 176

▓Chapter 9: Working with Data 179

Basic Behavior 179

    Understanding Delegation 180

Searching Data 182

    Basic Search Functions 183

    Setting Multiple Sort Sequences 188

    Additional Search Criteria Options 189

Joining Data 191

    Joining Records - Showing Related Records 191

    Checking for Nonexistence 192

    Returning Distinct Records 193

Working with Data in Code 194

    Retrieving Single Records 194

    Updating Records 195

    Creating a New Record 196

    Deleting Data 200

Setting Default Screen Values 200

Validating Form Values 201

    Checking Validation Rules 202

Sending Notifications 203

Summary 206

▓Chapter 10: Working with Images 209

Choosing Where to Store Images 209

Setting Up a Data Source 210

    Storing Images in Excel 210

    Storing Images in CDS and SQL Server Databases 210

Creating an Image App 211

    Viewing Records in the CDS 212

    Using the Add Picture Control 213

Using the Camera Control 213

    Retrieving the Camera Data 215

    Switching Between Cameras 215

    Setting Brightness, Contrast, and Zoom Levels 216

Creating a Gallery 216

Using the Pen Control 221

    Erasing Text 221

    Converting Annotations to Text 222

Scanning Barcodes 223

Summary 224

▓Chapter 11: Mapping Data 227

Introduction to GPS 227

Retrieving Location Details 228

Introducing Signals 228

Freezing the Location Details 229

Obtaining Longitude and Latitude.Readings 229

Saving Location Details 230

Switching the Signal On/Off 231

Other Signals 232

Displaying Maps 232

Using Google Maps 233

Bing Maps 234

Summary 235

▓Chapter 12: Using Charts 237

Introduction 237

Aggregating Data 239

Column Chart 240

Creating a Chart 242

Setting Legends 244

Setting Label Orientation 244

Applying Colors and Styles 245

Pie Chart 246

Line Charts 247

Grouping Data by Month 247

Showing Chart Data Dynamically 248

Showing Multiple Series 249

Summary 252

▧**Chapter 13: Securing Apps** **253**

Authentication 253

Role-Based Security 255

Securing the CDS 255

Securing SharePoint Lists 257

Verifying Permissions Within an App 259

Configuring Record-Level Access 261

Setting Up the Data Source 261

Getting the Logged On User 262

Filtering Records by the Logged On User 263

Creating Data Loss Prevention Policies 264

Testing a DLP Policy 266

Summary 266

▧**Part III: Maintaining Your Application** **269**

▧**Chapter 14: Importing and Exporting Data** **271**

Using the Import and Export Controls 271

Exporting Data 272

Importing Data 273

Importing and Exporting Related Data 277

Importing and Exporting CDS Data 281

Importing Data 281

Exporting Data 283

Using the Excel Add-In 283

Importing Static Data 284

Summary 285

■**Chapter 15: Using Flow** **287**

What Is Flow 287

What Can We Do with Flow? 288

Creating a Flow 289

Copying Files 289

Calling Flows from Apps 292

Sending Notifications 293

Filtering Data 295

Working with Variables 297

Sending the Email 299

Manipulating Data 300

Constructing HTML Tables 300

Introducing Workflow Definition Language 301

Applying Workflow Definition Language 303

Using Output Values in Workflow Definition Commands 305

Referring to Items in Loops 306

Calling SQL Stored Procedures 306

Approving Actions 308

Managing Flows 309

Summary 311

■**Part IV: Extending Your Application** **313**

■**Chapter 16: Working Offline** **315**

What Happens Offline? 315

Techniques to Enable Offline Working 316

Saving and Retrieving Local Data 316

Making an App Available Offline 317

Setting the Data Source to a Local Collection 319

Handling Offline Deletions 321

Handling Offline Record Updates 322

Building the Synchronization Screen 325

Building the Conflict Resolution Screen 331

Summary 332

■Chapter 17: Creating Custom Data Connectors 335

What Can We Accomplish with Web Services? 335

Overview of Steps 336

Understanding How the Web Works 336

Making HTTP Web Requests 337

Understanding HTTP Responses 337

Documenting a Web Service 338

Creating a Web Service Description 339

Using Postman 340

Using Swagger 340

Examining an Open API Document 342

Creating a Custom Connector 343

Using the Custom Connector 348

Summary 351

■Appendix A: Data Models 353

Overview of CDS Entities 353

Foundation Entities 353

Person Entities 354

Group Entities 355

Sales Entities 355

Purchase Entities 358

Customer Service Entities 360

Human Resources Entities 361

CDS Field Names 362

Foundation Entities 362

Person Entities 362

Group Entities 364

Sales Entities 365

Customer Service Entities 368

Organization Entities 368

Purchase Entities 369

Human Resources Entities 370

Retail Entities 371

Data Structure of the Sample 'Journey' Application 371

Index **373**

About the Author

Tim Leung is a software developer with vast experience in designing and building large-scale commercial applications. He is a recognized expert in the field of rapid application development and his previous publication with Apress (*Professional Visual Studio LightSwitch*, 2015) covered this topic in depth.

Tim is a Microsoft certified developer, a chartered member of the British Computer Society, and holds a degree in Information Technology.

About the Technical Reviewer

 **Jenefer Monroe** is a Principle PM Manager at Microsoft, currently serving on the Customer Success Team for Power Apps, Microsoft Flow, and the Common Data Service. She previously served as Software Engineering Manager in the Excel team, and as a Software Engineer in SharePoint, Access, and Excel Online.

Foreword

Greetings readers! I am a program manager at Microsoft. I also served as the technical reviewer of Tim's *Beginning PowerApps* book. I would like to take a few minutes to share my insights on PowerApps, the role they play on meeting the business needs of Microsoft customers and partners, and what they can mean to you.

First, please allow me the opportunity to introduce myself. My role at Microsoft is that of a Customer Success program manager, which obviously means exactly that. I do everything in my power to make sure our customers succeed at meeting their unique business needs. Organizational-wise, I exist as a liaison between the customer and the product teams within engineering. Being here gives me the unusual perspective of being able to look from the outside in, as well as the inside out. My two primary objectives in this role are to work directly with customers to enroll them in the extensibility suite (otherwise known as the power suite), which refers to common data service, Microsoft Flow, PowerBI and PowerApps—the subject of this book. I hear firsthand about their challenges, be it the migration of InfoPath forms, the Access web app, or a brand new business still using paper. Sometimes I build pilots and proofs of concept... anything I can do to make their life easier. Wearing my other hat, I advocate for our customers and deliver stories to the internal team, sharing general and specific feedback including pain points, features that our customers love or hate, and anything in between.

I come from an engineering and development background. Prior to this role, I spent ten years (also with Microsoft) with Excel and five years prior on teams in Office, SharePoint, and Access. My most recent years with Excel were spent building the collaboration platform for Excel Desktop, which allows for the ability to have the rich desktop application edit a file at the same time as other rich desktop applications. Whew, talk about the hardest technical challenge of my life! So I stepped into this role in a similar fashion to other people on my team. We are very able to be technically knowledgeable about what is impeding customer success while keeping on top of what is getting rolled by the product team. It's an amazing role. I love it. I absolutely love it!

However, while I was head-down in collaboration, I looked up and I immediately recognized I had been so deeply entrenched in this singular technical problem for so long that I had some massive industry transformation. You know the cloud? Yes, that cloud. Well, I had somehow convinced myself that it was just for storing documents because that is how my product used it. Really? That was my wake up all. I began searching for the Holy Grail and found PowerApps.

I believe in PowerApps as an extensibility platform for business users. When I began scratching the surface of it, I realized that the myriad of opportunities it offers citizen developers (also referred to in many circles as the power user) is nothing short of mind blowing. It offers an opportunity to utilize existing skill sets to do something entirely new. Just as an example, say you have the tools to develop professional looking PowerPoint decks. Then, like magic, you can apply those exact same skills to PowerApps to develop beautiful professional-looking business applications. Or, if you are adept at making formulas in Excel, or mingling data with a look up, or excel at doing logic flows with if statements, or doing mathematical operations on data to summarize... all these skills transform to PowerApps and can be used to develop powerful logical flows within your business application. Giving power users the resources to create an application that can show up on Android, and iOS, and Windows and even in a browser, now that's life changing.

Let's talk about accessing data, and more specifically, connectors (160 available at time of writing) that allow power users to connect to things like SQL in SharePoint, and external applications like Twitter and Facebook as well. You cannot do that in PowerPoint and Excel. Now I can go into Active Directory and see who you are, and I can pull your picture through the Office 365 connector simply by learning a couple of interfaces that are readily available. You can build a really slick UI for your team that shows pictures and other information. These connectors are a key new tool for the power user. And, wait, that's not all! While we're doing all of this cool stuff with connectors and cross platform development in PowerApps, we are actually keeping our IT and admin colleagues in mind. Think about it. Massive user bases withstanding, the ability for IT Pros and admins to create governance models around the usage of Excel and Access never happened. Admins and IT departments hated Access and Excel because, in spite of them being user and business friendly, it left the governance of those IT needs completely out of the hands of IT. Not so with PowerApps! Right out of the starting gate, we are ensuring that IT and admins feel comfortable with data-loss policies and monitoring features. In fact, I would even go so far as to call it a pillar in PowerApps. You have to admit, the ability to see where the viral usage of this product is happening, and saying, "I have control over it," is pretty darn compelling.

PowerApps fits into the Microsoft business intelligence space as part of the new extensibility platform. We also sometimes refer to it as the power suite, and in true Microsoft style, we continue to "evolve" naming conventions. Greatly simplified, I ask you to think of it in three parts: Measure, Act, and Automate. PowerBI is the Measure. It is how we expect people to measure their data. For example, it works for small transactional style data (e.g. someone wants to see machine orders), but it also works for giant flows of data, like from IoT. Power Apps is the Act. So now that I know this data that I have pulled together, what is the human decision-maker going to do? If we refer back to the example of the hardware order app, it would be something like, "which machine shall I query?" Flow is the Automate part of the platform. It is how you go and take some of those processes for immediate action. Some don't actually require human intelligence; they're just automatic— like if you trigger an approval every time a new lead is found. Related, Common Data Services is a topic on its own. Underneath it all, that has to do with the extensibility of data. So it's essentially the data service, SQL for the Power User, and the focal point of data.

PowerApps has been evolving for the last couple of years. Many of you probably remember when PowerApps used "Sienna." Well Tim has been working with PowerApps since way back when. I believe he has more knowledge and context about this product than many of us on the team. He was one of the first people I met in my new role. I can say with confidence that the book you are holding in your hands is a phenomenal one. Tim, by nature, is such a detail-oriented and inquisitive person. But don't just take it from me; the proof is in pudding. Go ahead and take a quick look at the offline chapter— the one on how to utilize caching for offline scenarios. If you think about Power apps as a mobile interface for data, the ability to do small periods of offline reporting is really important. Let's say, for example, that you are inspecting oil rigs. You might not have constant access to the Internet. In order to sync the data in real time, you may need to cache it locally for small periods of time to submit later. Now this is not something Microsoft natively supports, but Tim's book offers a workaround. While a somewhat complex task, Tim has laid out the process in an intuitive and engaging manner. In fact, when I shared it with the team, they were notably impressed. Tim's book does not just impress in that one chapter. It also offers readers who are interested in learning PowerApps a means to do so from A to Z. He offers a comprehensive learning path for PowerApps not seen in depth or breadth in any articles, documentation, or sites anywhere, not even in the coursework that is available online. To me, *Beginning PowerApps* hands down has the best content available to get yourself to the 200 level. Read it, and by the time you are done, hopefully he will have a 300 level book in the queue ready for publication. Enjoy!

Jenefer Monroe
Microsoft
November 2017

Acknowledgments

First, I'd like to thank Apress for the opportunity to publish this work. I especially want to thank all the members of my editorial team for their hard work. This includes Todd Green, Joan Murray, Jill Balzano, and Laura Berendson.

Equally, I'd like to thank Jenefer Monroe, Darshan Desei, and all the other team members at Microsoft who have worked on my project behind the scenes.

Finally, I'd like to thank the PowerApps team for developing a great product and to acknowledge all of those who have contributed to the PowerApps community.

Introduction

Welcome, and thank you for choosing this book. Within its contents, you'll learn how to build functional apps and how to avoid the common mistakes that beginners often make. The contents of this book are organized into three logical sections:

- The first four chapters describe how to build and publish an app. This book assumes no prior knowledge and therefore, we'll start at the very beginning. This includes how to subscribe and to install the requisite software. Within these chapters, we'll cover elementary topics such as how to retrieve and update data from a data source, how to build screens, and how to configure the navigation linkages between screens.

- The main section of this book describes how to embellish our apps. We'll look at how to use a cloud-based data store called the common data service. We'll also cover practical tasks including how to use screen controls, how to capture photos, how to retrieve location details with GPS, and how to display data with charts. This section of the book also contains a reference guide of formulas. These are very important because they provide the means for us to program PowerApps.

- In the final section of this book, we'll cover some advanced techniques. This includes how to configure security, how to import and export data, and how to build apps that can work offline. We'll also examine how to use Flow, a workflow service that can carry out tasks outside of PowerApps. The final chapter describes how to expand the capabilities of PowerApps by calling third-party web services.

To provide some context to the concepts in this book, we'll refer frequently to demonstration app that records journey details. This typifies the sort of application that businesses use to record mileage expense claims. In technical terms, this app enables us to explore a wide range of data types. The data structure that supports this app stores user and vehicle details, and we can use this structure to explore techniques such as how to use drop-down controls, and how to assign lookup values.

Figure 1 illustrates the type of screen that we can build with this data structure.

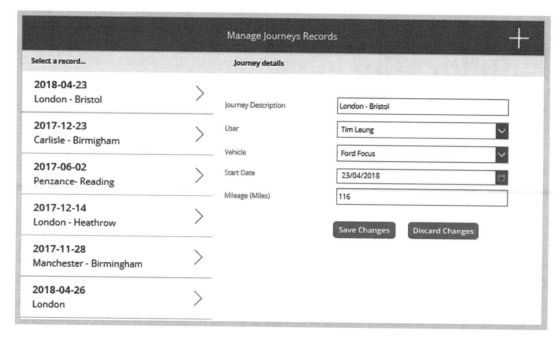

Figure 1. *Screen from example app*

Versioning

PowerApps benefits from frequent updates. Microsoft usually updates PowerApps on a three-week cycle. These updates include new features and bug fixes. Because of these frequent updates, menu item locations can change over time, and the screenshots in this book may quickly appear out of date. Please don't be too alarmed by this! The core concepts and principles in this book are likely to remain the same, despite any additions and cosmetic changes that take place afterward.

Erata

Although we take great care to verify the contents of this book, there is a slight chance that it might contain some errors. Therefore, the product page for this book contains an up-to-date list of any problems that we identify.

www.apress.com/9781484230022

Finally

We hope you find this book useful, and we wish you much success in building some great apps with PowerApps.

PART I

■ ■ ■

Getting Started

CHAPTER 1

■ ■ ■

Introducing PowerApps

Even if you are completely new to PowerApps, you probably know that PowerApps is a tool for building mobile device applications. Additionally, you'll understand that PowerApps is simple to use and allows you to build applications very quickly. But beyond these basic concepts, you might not fully understand the specific capabilities of PowerApps, or how, exactly, a PowerApps application looks or feels. In this chapter, we'll clarify the things that we can do with PowerApps by looking at the sample apps that Microsoft provides. The purpose of this is to clarify whether PowerApps can solve a specific business problem. Some of the basic topics that we'll explore in this first chapter will include the following:

- What we can accomplish with PowerApps
- Examples of applications
- How to get started with building apps

What Is PowerApps?

From a high-level perspective, PowerApps is a subscription-based service for building applications. The apps that we build can run through a web browser, and are therefore compatible with a wide range of devices. However, these apps work best on a mobile or tablet device. A typical app will connect to a data source and include screens to view and edit data. A typical app also includes functionality to help facilitate a business process.

Historically, PowerApps evolved from a Microsoft project called Siena. Microsoft developed Siena during the Windows 8 era. Siena provided a platform for programmers to build new style 'metro' apps that connected to data.

Microsoft provides sample applications you can use to learn PowerApps, and we'll look at these later in this chapter. These apps include service desk, budget tracking, and site inspection applications. One thing you quickly realize is that PowerApps is a business tool. It isn't a tool for building consumer grade applications – for example, apps or games that you want to sell via app stores.

A key characteristic of PowerApps is the way in which it embraces the cloud. Specifically, apps can access data from OneDrive, Dropbox, Salesforce, Dynamics 365, and many other cloud providers. Another characteristic is the product's ease of use. You don't need to be developer to use PowerApps. In fact, the product feels highly inspired by Microsoft Office. It includes a visual designer and we use Excel like formulas to build functionality. In terms of deployment, the concept is that we share PowerApps in the same way that we would share an Office document.

© Tim Leung 2017
T. Leung, *Beginning PowerApps*, https://doi.org/10.1007/978-1-4842-3003-9_1

Who Is the Typical Developer?

Microsoft designed PowerApps for non-developers – users who are not professionally trained software programmers. The target demographic includes managers or office workers who work regularly with Microsoft Office. Market research shows that demand for mobile applications will outstrip the availability of qualified programmers. Therefore, the goal of PowerApps is to address this problem by making it easier for users with basic IT literacy to build mobile apps.

At this early stage, the product seems to attract a large number of professional users from the Microsoft Office community. This includes users with Office 365, Access and Access Web Apps, and SharePoint experience. In part, this is because these users have easy access via SharePoint and Office 365.

The product is likely to attract Microsoft InfoPath users – a product that has been discontinued by Microsoft. InfoPath is a tool for adding forms over data. Personally, I chose PowerApps as a LightSwitch alternative – this was a Microsoft product for rapid application development.

For more complex applications, there may be tasks that require the skill of an experienced developer. Such tasks include connecting apps to data sources that are not natively supported, configuring application security, and building flows. A flow is a set of tasks that runs, following an event in an app. For example, you can use flows to send emails, copy files, or to add items to a SharePoint list.

What Are the Typical Uses?

What applications can you build with PowerApps and what tasks can those applications carry out? To help us better understand what PowerApps can do, let's look at some of the sample apps that Microsoft provides. These include the Asset Checkout, Budget Tracker, Cost Estimator, and Inventory Management apps.

Asset Checkout App

The Asset Checkout App enables users to check out items. However, this isn't the e-commerce tool that the 'checkout' part of the name suggests. It's more like a system that enables you to borrow hardware items from a library. That being said, the app demonstrates some useful features. The most noteworthy is the integration of product images into the application (Figure 1-1). The first screen contains UI features such as search, a horizontal scroll control, and a tab control. The product image strip on the home screen shows the most recently checked-out items. Therefore, logic exists in the application to perform this type of query.

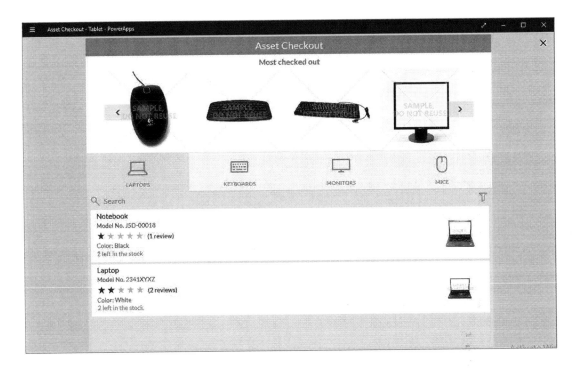

Figure 1-1. *Asset Checkout App*

Budget Tracker

The Budget Tracker App highlights the mathematical tasks that you can carry out in a PowerApps application. The home screen shows calculations that are conditionally formatted with red and green fonts. It also features a pie chart that illustrates a breakdown of expenses (Figure 1-2). With this app, users can add and delete expense records. Therefore, we can learn how to program data tasks such as adding or deleting records through this app.

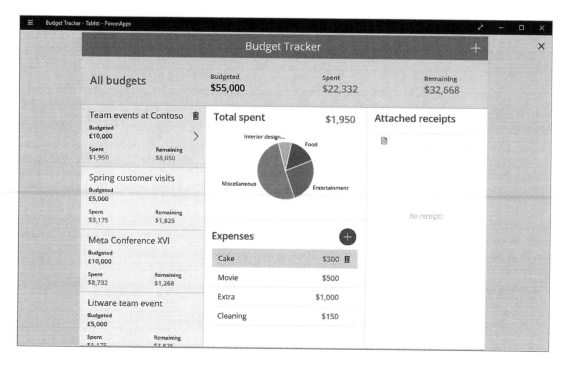

Figure 1-2. *Budget Tracker App*

A highlight of the budget tracker app is the ability for users to capture pictures of receipts, and to assign those receipts to an expense claim. This feature demonstrates how PowerApps can integrate natively with cameras that are built into mobile devices.

Service Desk App

The Service Desk App is a nice example of a data entry application. The purpose of this app is to manage the support tickets that arise through a help desk department. I like this application because it demonstrates the data structures that developers typically expect to see in database applications. For example, the application allows users to assign a priority rating, and an area (or department) to each support ticket, therefore illustrating the concept of one-to-many data structures. See Figure 1-3.

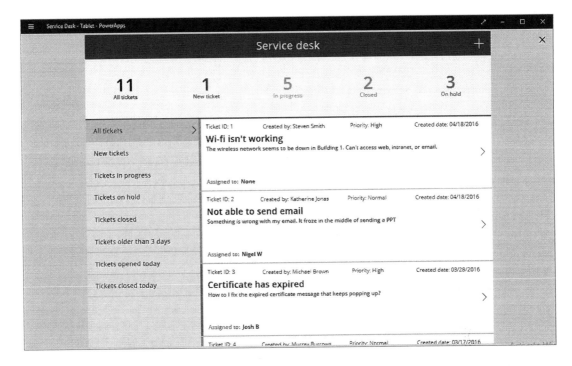

Figure 1-3. *Service Desk App*

Site Inspection App

The Site Inspection App demonstrates integration with location and mapping services. With each site inspection record, the user can use a device camera to capture multiple images. This one-to-many relationship of image data can be useful in the apps that you build. The Site Inspection app also enables users to record the current location using the GPS on the mobile device. For each record, the app can also integrate a map that shows the location. See Figure 1-4.

Figure 1-4. *Site Inspection App*

Other Sample Apps

The remaining sample applications are characterized by data features with a similar theme, namely, the ability to select a record from a list, and to view and edit the selected record. Other notable apps include the following:

- Product showcase app. – This is a well-presented app that looks great and demonstrates how to display videos in apps.

- PDF Reader App – This app allows users to view PDF documents from within the app.

- Suggestion App – This app implements some basic role maintenance. You can add users to an administrator role, and those users can carry out additional tasks in the application.

- Case Management App – A feature of this app is that it stores data using the Common Data Service (CDS). I'll describe this in more detail later in this book.

How Do You Build a PowerApp?

PowerApps Studio is the tool for building apps. There are two versions available – a version that runs on Microsoft Windows, and a version that runs through a web browser. The Windows version is a store app and requires Windows 8.1 or Windows 10. The web-based version is slightly more limited than the Windows version. Note that the Windows App doesn't support Windows 7. Therefore, Windows 7 users will need to use the web version of PowerApps Studio. There are currently three supported browsers – Microsoft IE11, Google Chrome, and Microsoft Edge. Firefox and Safari are not supported.

Figure 1-5 shows a screenshot of the Windows version of PowerApps Studio. This image highlights how we can design applications using a visual designer. At the top of the designer, there is a ribbon menu bar that looks like the ribbon bar that exists in Microsoft Office. Within the designer, we can see a visual representation of the screens and controls as we build our app.

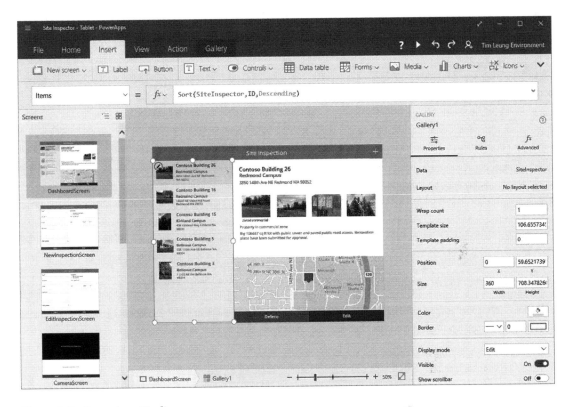

Figure 1-5. *PowerApps Studio*

■ **Tip**   The Windows version of PowerApps Studio is a Store App and therefore, we can only run one instance of the app at a time. To work around this limitation, we can use PowerApps Studio for Windows for our main project, and open an additional project in the web version of PowerApps Studio. While we're learning, we can use this technique to open a sample project in a separate window, and we can easily switch to the sample project to refer to formulas and layout.

How Do Users Run PowerApp Applications?

Once we build an app in PowerApps Studio, we can grant users access to our app. Users use a PowerApps 'runtime' app to run apps on mobile devices. These runtime apps are called 'players,' and players are available for Android, iOS, and Windows Mobile devices. Figure 1-6 shows the section on the PowerApps website where we can download the PowerApps software.

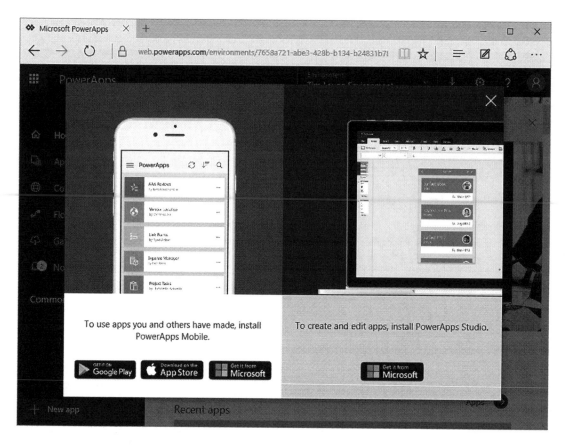

Figure 1-6. *PowerApps Mobile and PowerApps Studio*

Users can download the mobile player from the app store of the device. The system requirements at the time of writing are these:

- Android – version 5.0 (Lollipop)
- Apple iPhone / iPad – iOS 8.0
- Windows Mobile – Windows 10 Mobile

Desktop users can use PowerApps Studio to run apps. This method is particularly useful for desktop users. With the browser version of PowerApps Studio, any device that can run a web browser can run PowerApp apps.

What Data Can a PowerApps Consume?

The apps that we build with PowerApps can display and edit data from a wide range of data sources. The simplest data storage option is to store our data on an Excel spreadsheet. Most of sample apps that we can create with PowerApps templates work in this way. We must save the Excel spreadsheets onto cloud storage in order for PowerApps to access the data. The most popular cloud storage platforms that PowerApps supports include OneDrive, Dropbox, and Google Drive.

Connecting to On-Premises Data

Typically, many businesses store data in databases that reside within an internal company network. We can make this data available to PowerApps through a program called the 'On-premises data gateway'. Through the On-Premises data gateway, we can connect to various data sources. Two of the most common are SQL Server and SharePoint Server.

Common Data Service

When we're building an application from scratch, we can save time by using the Common Data Service (CDS). The CDS provides pre-built table definitions and saves us from having to design commonly used data structures.

For example, let's suppose that we want to build an app to store user details. With the CDS, we can simply add the 'Application User' entity to our application. The 'Application User' entity includes the data that we typically want to store for a user, such as name, address, and email address. Figure 1-7 shows some of the CDS entities that are available.

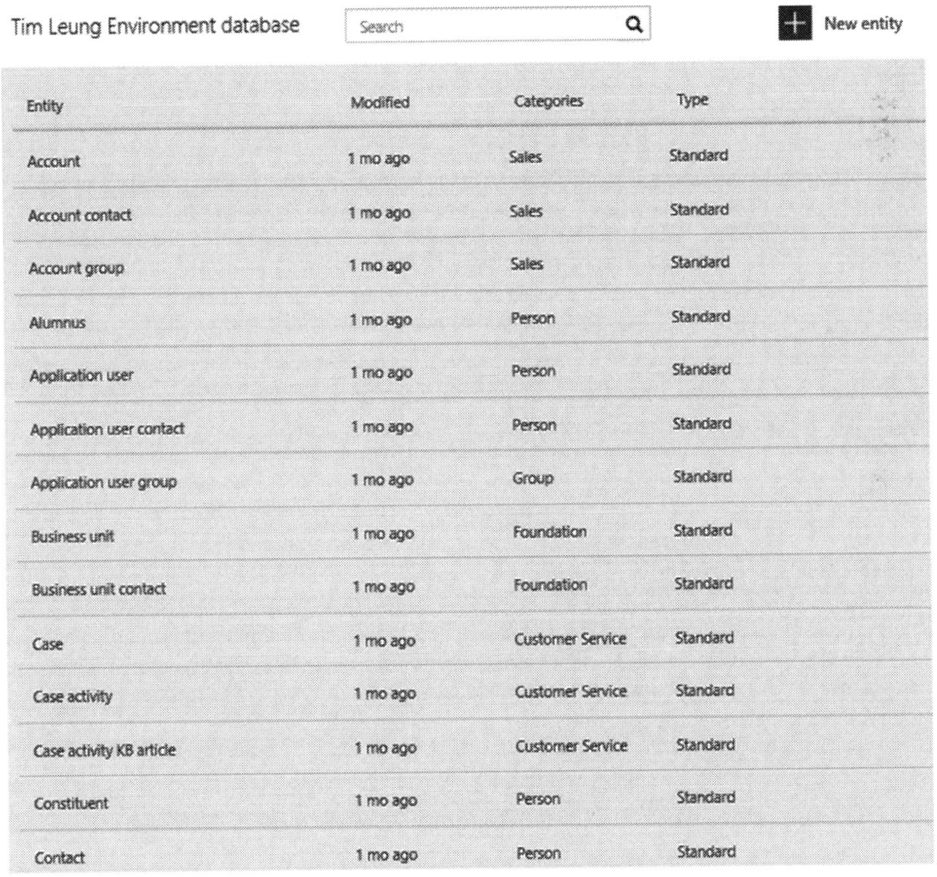

Tim Leung Environment database	Search				New entity
Entity	**Modified**	**Categories**	**Type**		
Account	1 mo ago	Sales	Standard		
Account contact	1 mo ago	Sales	Standard		
Account group	1 mo ago	Sales	Standard		
Alumnus	1 mo ago	Person	Standard		
Application user	1 mo ago	Person	Standard		
Application user contact	1 mo ago	Person	Standard		
Application user group	1 mo ago	Group	Standard		
Business unit	1 mo ago	Foundation	Standard		
Business unit contact	1 mo ago	Foundation	Standard		
Case	1 mo ago	Customer Service	Standard		
Case activity	1 mo ago	Customer Service	Standard		
Case activity KB article	1 mo ago	Customer Service	Standard		
Constituent	1 mo ago	Person	Standard		
Contact	1 mo ago	Person	Standard		

Figure 1-7. *CDS entities*

11

Connecting to Other Data Sources

Companies increasingly store corporate data in online, cloud-based systems. To support this growing trend, PowerApps can connect to a wide range of data sources. These include Dynamics 365, Sales Force, and Email services. Figure 1-8 highlights the screen to add a data source. This image illustrates a handful of the data sources that we can connect to.

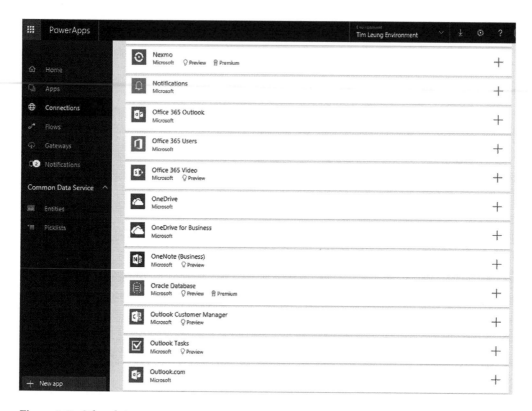

Figure 1-8. *Other data sources*

How Do You Write Code?

PowerApps has a strong resemblance to Microsoft Excel. We use formulas to add logic and functionality to an application, just like we would in Excel. This makes it easy for Microsoft Office users to transition to PowerApps. However, traditional programmers might find it a struggle to adjust to this way of working. To illustrate this, Figure 1-9 shows a typical formula.

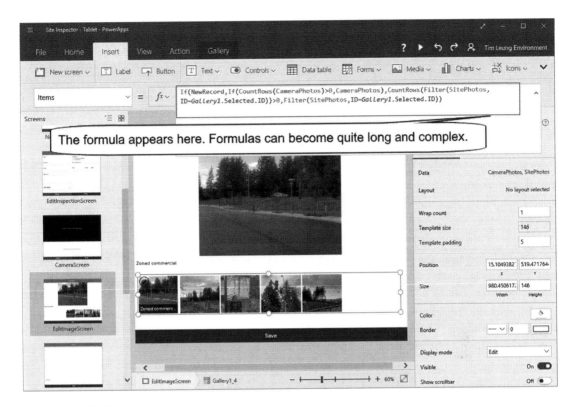

Figure 1-9. *Writing formulas*

The formula appears in the formula bar at the top of the screen, just like Excel. The purpose of the formula in the screenshot is to display a set of images. As you can see, it can take some skill to build the formula to carry out a task in PowerApps.

How Much Does It Cost?

An important consideration for any software solution is cost. PowerApps is a subscription-based service, and the typical way to obtain access to PowerApps is through an Office 365 or Microsoft Dynamics 365 subscription.

Without an Office 365 or Dynamics subscription, another way is to purchase a PowerApps plan. There are two plans available: PowerApps Plan 1 and PowerApps Plan 2. Plan 1 is the cheapest option and provides most of the features for building, running, and sharing apps. The additional features you get with Plan 2 are features to manage security policies, the ability to model data in the CDS, access to premium connectors like Salesforce, and more data storage in the CDS. For example, Plan 1 provides 20MB storage in the CDS whereas Plan 2 provides 200 MB.

Figure 1-10 shows the pricing from the official PowerApps website at `https://powerapps.microsoft.com/en-us/pricing/`. At the time of writing, the cost for Plan 1 is $7 USD per user per month, and the cost for Plan 2 is $40 USD. I mention these prices to give an indication of the costs and pricing of PowerApps. No doubt, these prices will change over time.

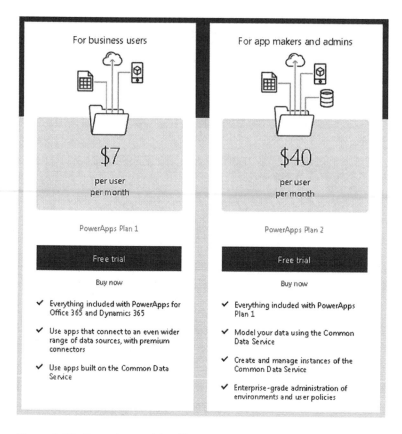

Figure 1-10. *PowerApps pricing illustration*

Within an organization, users do not need to all subscribe to the same plan. Therefore, an organization could license 2 users with plan 2, 20 users with plan 1, and 30 users with Office 365.

Summary

PowerApps is a tool for building mobile business apps. A perfect use of PowerApps is to build 'forms over data' apps. This tool is designed for power users.

Several sample applications are available, and we can use these to learn how to build apps with PowerApps. These include a budgeting app, a service desk app, and many other apps. These sample apps demonstrate how to use the camera, GPS, and how to access data and carry out calculations.

A PowerApp application can connect to wide range of data sources. This includes the CDS, cloud-based data sources such as Dropbox and One Drive, and on-premises data sources. The on-premises data source is very useful for corporate users who want to connect to data in their companies.

Users build apps with a tool called PowerApps Studio. This tool can run in Windows or in a browser. Mobile users would run applications on mobile devices using a runtime app. This is available in iOS, Android, and Windows Mobile.

PowerApps is a subscription-based service. We can use PowerApps by subscribing to Office 365 or by purchasing a PowerApps plan.

CHAPTER 2

■ ■ ■

Subscribing to PowerApps

In this chapter, we'll look at how to subscribe to PowerApps. This can be a challenge because several subscriptions exist with different usage rights and prices. You'll learn about the available subscription options, and we'll go through the steps to install the required software on a computer. What you will learn in this chapter will include the following:

- An overview of Microsoft Cloud Services. Microsoft provides different cloud services for consumers and businesses. This can be confusing, and it complicates the process of logging in. We'll examine these differences to help avoid any confusion moving forward.

- How to manage a subscription through the web-based portal. The portal is important because it enables us to manage some of the underlying PowerApps settings.

- How to install PowerApps Studio – the tool that we'll use throughout this book to build apps.

How to Get PowerApps

PowerApps is a subscription-based service, and there are two main ways to obtain access to PowerApps, which are the following:

- Through an Office 365 or Dynamics 365 subscription

- Through a PowerApps subscription

For learning purposes, Microsoft also provides a 'Community Edition' of PowerApps. This is a free edition of PowerApps that individuals can use to gain familiarity with the software. The limitation with this edition is that it's not possible to share the apps that we create with other users.

Obtaining PowerApps via Office 365

A common way for organizations to access PowerApps is through an Office 365 or Dynamics 365 subscription. To the uninitiated, the myriad of subscription offerings with Office 365 can be confusing. So to start this section, I'll provide an introduction to Office 365.

© Tim Leung 2017
T. Leung, *Beginning PowerApps*, https://doi.org/10.1007/978-1-4842-3003-9_2

What Is Office 365?

By now, you are likely familiar with the desktop versions of Word, Excel, Outlook, PowerPoint, and Access that run on Windows. In the past, many users would have purchased perpetual licenses to use these products. From a strategic point of view, Microsoft needed to move toward a cloud-based, subscription model. This business model would provide a more consistent revenue stream, and it would better position the company against competition such as Google Apps.

In 2011, Microsoft released Office 365 as a subscription service aimed at businesses. For small businesses, the service provided email hosting via hosted Exchange, SharePoint, and Lync (a tool for communication and conferencing). The service also provided access to Office Web Apps. These are online versions of Word, Excel, PowerPoint and OneNote that run through a web browser. At the same time, Microsoft also offered an Enterprise version that included desktop licenses.

Later in 2013, Microsoft introduced editions of Office 365 for consumers. To cater for this demographic, Microsoft sold prepaid subscriptions at shops and retail outlets.

Consumer vs. Business Office 365

There are two distinct 'flavors' of Office 365 that are targeted at business and retail users. Although both share the same Office 365 name, they are fundamentally very different. It's very important to understand this in order to avoid confusion. In truth, much of the Microsoft Office branding can be confusing. Let's examine some of the differences between the business and retail editions of Office 365.

The business editions of Office 365 provide email hosting through Microsoft Exchange. They also provide file storage though 'OneDrive for Business', and voice communications and instant messaging through 'Skype for Business'.

On the other hand, the retail editions of Office 365 provide email hosting through Outlook.com, the name for what used to be Hotmail. The retail editions also provide file storage through OneDrive, and voice communications through Skype.

Looking at online file storage, it's important to realize that the retail version of OneDrive is not the same as OneDrive for Business. The consumer version of OneDrive provides cloud storage, and users typically use this service to store music and videos. On the other hand, 'OneDrive for Business' is a storage system that is internally based on hosted Microsoft SharePoint. So as you can see, 'OneDrive for Business' and the consumer edition of OneDrive are primarily very different.

Likewise, the version of Skype that you would use to call your parents is not the same as 'Skype for Business'. Skype for Business was formally known as Microsoft Lync, which was formally called Microsoft Live Meeting.

The important thing to take away from this is that often, Microsoft Services are branded with similar names, but refer to completely different services.

Understanding Work Accounts and Personal Accounts

Another very important difference between the business and retail editions of Office 365 is that both services use completely separate authentication databases.

The business editions of Office 365 are based on Office 365 accounts. Users log on with credentials that consist of an email address and password. In general, the Office 365 administrator for an organization sets up the Office 365 accounts for users.

The retail editions of Office 365 are based on Microsoft accounts. Like most authentication methods, a Microsoft account consists of an email address and password. These are the same credentials you could use to log on to Windows 8 or 10 computers, or the credentials you would use to log in to the Hotmail or Outlook. com services.

Because each email address can be associated with two separate authentication databases at Microsoft, this can cause much confusion. For instance, if we log into a Microsoft website with a Microsoft account (e.g., Outlook.com) and then navigate to certain areas on the PowerApps portal, we might see the error message that's shown in Figure 2-1.

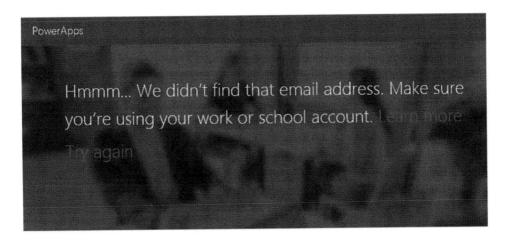

Figure 2-1. *Authentication error message*

One way to overcome this type of error is to log out from our Microsoft account, or to completely close and reopen our web browser.

Figure 2-2 shows the screen that appears when we log in with an email address that is associated with both an Office 365 and a Microsoft account.

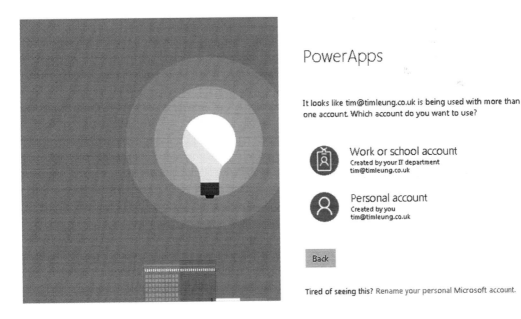

Figure 2-2. *PowerApps login screen*

To log in to PowerApps, we would choose the 'Work or school account' option. One thing to highlight here is the use of the word 'Work or school account'. This is the type of account that I call the 'Office 365 account'. Another name that refers to the same type of account is an 'Azure Active Directory' account, often abbreviated to 'AAD'. The most likely place that we'll encounter the term 'AAD' is on technical forums and help sites. The main thing to understand here is that 'Office 365 account', 'Work or school account', and 'AAD account' all refer to the same thing.

Once you begin developing apps, it's useful to relay this information to your end users, because those users may not be familiar with the differences between the Microsoft account types. Even for experienced users, it can be difficult to keep track of what account you need to log in to a specific Microsoft service. For example, I use my 'Personal account' to log into my Azure and VisualStudio.com accounts, and this choice of account isn't perhaps the most obvious for a work-based service.

When we use PowerApps, it's useful to have this clarity about the different account types to help avoid confusion. To give a relevant example, it's not uncommon to log into PowerApps with an Office 365 account, and to store application data in a personal OneDrive account.

What Office 365 Editions Support PowerApps?

The business editions of Office 365 provide access to PowerApps. It is not available through the retail editions of Office 365.

The business editions of Office 365 are further separated into Business and Enterprise plans. Only the Enterprise plans provide access to PowerApps. Figure 2-3 shows a screenshot of the Office 365 Enterprise plans. The purpose of this screenshot is to illustrate the tiers that make up the pricing structure, and the approximate costs. By the time you read this, the prices will have likely changed.

Figure 2-3. Office 365 Enterprise plans

Subscribing to a PowerApps Stand-Alone Plan

If we choose not to access PowerApps through an Office 365 subscription, the alternative is to subscribe to a PowerApps Stand-Alone plan. As Figure 2-4 illustrates, two plans are available – Plan 1 or Plan 2. To build apps, we need to subscribe to Plan 2. The cheaper Plan 1 is designed for app users, rather than app designers.

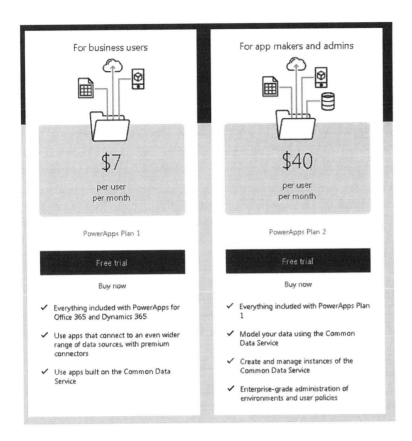

Figure 2-4. Stand-Alone Plans and features

It's possible to mix stand-alone and Office 365 plans. For example, if we build an app with a Plan 2 subscription, we can share our app with users that are licensed for PowerApps through Office 365.

If you're only interested in learning how to use PowerApps, you can subscribe to the free community plan. This plan still provides access to valuable features such as the Common Data Service and Microsoft Flow. The only limitation is that you can't share apps with other users. To sign up, you'll need a Microsoft work account.

Even if you subscribe to a paid-for plan, it's still worth subscribing to the community plan. This is because the community plan provides you with a separate environment that you can use for test purposes. At the time of writing, here's the address to register for the community plan.

```
https://powerapps.microsoft.com/communityplan/
```

Registering for an Account

To subscribe to PowerApps, visit `https://powerapps.microsoft.com/` and register with a corporate email address. It's necessary to use an email address that ends with a custom domain name. The registration process rejects personal email addresses that are hosted by ISPs, or companies like Gmail or Hotmail. It will also reject a government or military email address (that is, an email address that ends with .gov or .mil).

If you have a corporate email address and attempt to subscribe, you might receive the error in Figure 2-5 if your business is covered by an Office 365 subscription. In this case, you should speak to your company administrator and request access to the PowerApps.

Figure 2-5. *Registration error*

If you attempt to sign up for PowerApps, there are several things that can cause your attempt to fail. A common cause is if you attempt to register while still logged into a Microsoft personal account within the same browser session. In the case of a registration failure, the page usually offers a friendly error message like the one that's shown in Figure 2-5. In such instances, you should visit the visit the web page that's devoted to troubleshooting registration failures:

```
https://powerapps.microsoft.com/en-us/tutorials/signup-for-powerapps/#troubleshoot
```

Here, we can find a table that translates these friendly error messages into technical explanations that we can act on and resolve.

Obtaining a Suitable Email Address

If you want to sign up for PowerApps but don't have a suitable email address, there isn't any simple workaround to this problem. You must obtain a custom email address in order to subscribe to PowerApps.

A search on the web will reveal hundreds of companies that can sell you a custom domain name. The going rate seems to be around $2 for an initial 12-month registration. Once you purchase a domain name, you can link it with a free email hosting provider such as Zoho.com to provide a low-cost method to trial PowerApps.

If you work for a large bureaucratic organization, it may even be easier for you to trial PowerApps using this technique, rather than to go through any complicated internal channels.

Logging onto PowerApps

Once we subscribe successfully to PowerApps, we can access the PowerApps Portal, as shown in Figure 2-6. This is the website that helps us administer our PowerApps account. Through this portal, we can create apps, data connections, and Flows. We can also manage gateways, notifications, and manage the Common Data Service (CDS).

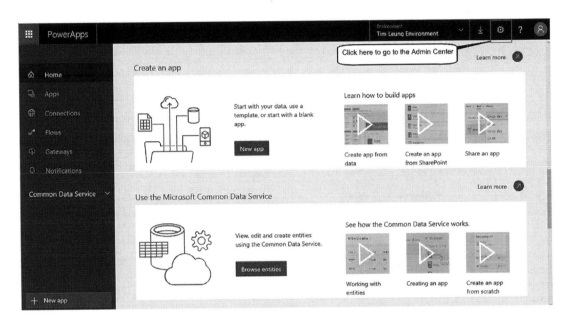

Figure 2-6. *PowerApps Web Portal*

By clicking the download icon at the top of the page, we can download PowerApps Studio and the mobile player apps. The cog icon opens the PowerApps Admin Center. Let's now open the Admin Center and see what features are available there.

Configuring Environments

From the Admin Center, there are two menu items: Environments and Data Policies. At this stage, the more important of the two is Environments. Data Policies are a feature to help us secure our data and I'll describe this topic more fully in Chapter 13.

Figure 2-7. *PowerApps Admin Center*

Environments are containers for apps and resources. Environments play a key role in security and access control. When we save an app to an Environment, we can control who can access our app based upon access control permissions at an Environment level. Furthermore, data connections, flows, and Common Data Model databases are entities that are specific to a single Environment. We can't share these items between Environments.

The reason to configure multiple Environments is to help compartmentalize apps and users. For example, we could create separate environments for apps in development and apps that are currently in live use.

Installing PowerApps Studio

In the final section of this chapter, we'll look at how to install PowerApps Studio. This is the Windows program that we use to build and run apps. To download the software, click the download link from the web portal, or visit the following link:

```
https://aka.ms/powerappswin
```

PowerApps Studio is a Microsoft Store App that works with Windows 8 or above. The links above will open the App Store on our computer. If you've never used the Store App, the first screen will prompt you to log in with a Microsoft account (as shown in Figure 2-8). As you'll recall, this is not the same as your PowerApps/Office 365 account.

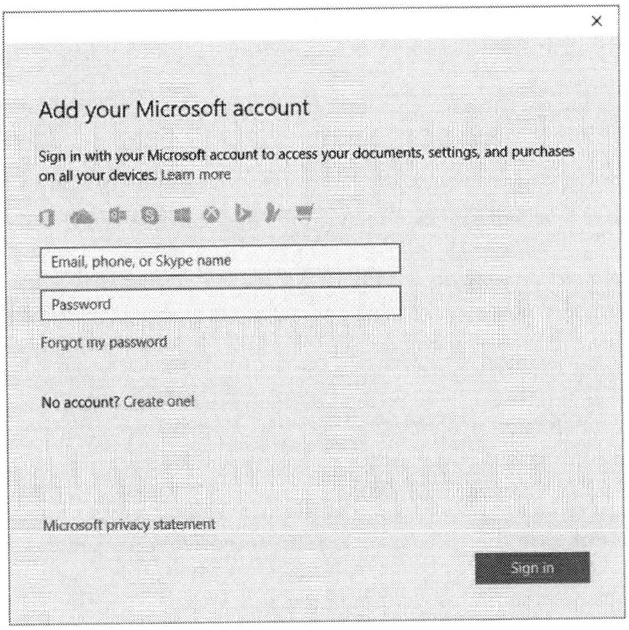

Figure 2-8. *Logging into the Windows Store App*

Once you log in to the Store App, you'll see the screen that's shown in Figure 2-9. From here, click the 'Install' button to download and install App Studio.

Figure 2-9. *Installing PowerApps via the Microsoft Store App*

When the installation process completes, we can start PowerApps Studio by searching for the app through the Windows start menu. When we run PowerApps Studio for the first time, it'll prompt us to log in with our Microsoft wok account.

Summary

In this chapter, we looked at how to subscribe to PowerApps. We can obtain PowerApps through an Office 365 or stand-alone PowerApps subscription.

There are separate versions of Office 365 for businesses and consumers. The business editions of Office 365 are further separated into business and enterprise plans. To gains access to PowerApps, we need to select one of the enterprise plans.

To register for a stand-alone subscription to PowerApps, it's necessary to use a custom email address. The registration process rejects Gmail, Hotmail, ISP, and government email addresses. There are two stand-alone plans that are offered: Plan 1 or Plan 2. To build apps, we need to subscribe to the more expensive Plan 2. Plan 1 subscriptions are designed for users who want to run the apps you build. For trial or test purposes, we can subscribe to the free community plan.

We use a Microsoft 'Work or School Account' to log into PowerApps. This type of account is also known as an 'Office 365 account, or an 'Azure Active Directory account'. Once we log into the portal, we can access the links to download PowerApps Studio, or the PowerApps players for mobile devices. PowerApps Studio is the Windows application that we use to build apps. It can only run on computers with Windows 8 or above.

From the Admin Center section of the PowerApps portal, we can create and manage environments. Environments allow us to compartmentalize apps and users for access control purposes. One use for environments is to configure separate environments for apps that are in development, and apps that are in live use.

CHAPTER 3

■ ■ ■

Creating Your First App

In this chapter, you'll learn how to create a basic app that connects to data. It's simple to build this type of app because we can point PowerApps at a data source and tell it to generate an app for us. Because PowerApps carries out all the hard work, the challenge is to understand the app that PowerApps builds. This is important because the knowledge enables us to further enhance and develop such 'auto-generated' apps. To demonstrate this process, we'll develop an app that connects to an Excel spreadsheet. The topics that we'll cover in this chapter will include the following:

- How to prepare an Excel spreadsheet for use in PowerApps. This step is important because PowerApps can only connect to spreadsheets that are set up in a certain way.

- How to use data forms and cards. These controls provide the ability to view and edit individual records. They are complex controls that are not easy to understand. In this chapter, we'll discover exactly how these controls work.

- How screen navigation works. We'll examine how to open an individual record when a user selects an item from a list of records, and how to change the screen that is visible. These techniques are applicable to almost all apps.

Preparing an Excel Data Source

PowerApps supports many data sources. This includes SharePoint, SQL Server, Salesforce, and many more. Of all the supported data sources, the easiest to understand is an Excel spreadsheet. Therefore, that's the data source that we'll use regularly throughout this book.

In this chapter, we'll work step by step toward building a simple app. The purpose of our app is to store names and addresses. So to begin, the first step is to create the spreadsheet that's shown in Figure 3-1.

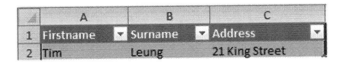

Figure 3-1. *Sample Spreadsheet*

© Tim Leung 2017

T. Leung, *Beginning PowerApps*, https://doi.org/10.1007/978-1-4842-3003-9_3

For PowerApps to recognize a spreadsheet, the first row must contain column headings and the data must be defined as a table. To do this, select the data and click Insert ➤ Table button from the menu in Excel.

The next step is to name our table by using the 'Table Tools' menu in Excel. Figure 3-2 outlines the steps to rename our table to *Users*.

Figure 3-2. *Use the 'Table Tools' ribbon option to name your table*

If we choose not to name our table, it inherits the default name of 'Table1.' If we retain the default name of 'Table1,' it makes it difficult to identify our data from within the PowerApps designer.

It's possible to add multiple tables to each Excel spreadsheet. But if we decide to do this, it's a good idea to add each table to a separate worksheet. When PowerApps connects to an Excel spreadsheet, it stores working data in the cells that are adjacent to the table. By adding each table to a separate worksheet, we prevent the possibility of any data corruption to occur.

Once we complete our spreadsheet, the final step is to upload it to a cloud storage location. Two of the most popular services that PowerApps supports are Microsoft OneDrive and Dropbox. For the purposes of this chapter, we'll upload our data to Microsoft OneDrive.

■ **Note**   We must define our data as a table for PowerApps to recognize the data in our spreadsheet.

Creating an App

Once we upload our spreadsheet to the cloud, we can start PowerApps Studio and begin to build our app. When we start PowerApps for the first time, it prompts us to log in with our Microsoft Work Account. After logging in, we can select the 'New' menu and view the choices for building a new app (Figure 3-3). An effective way to build an app is to choose the option to 'Start with data.' When we select this path, PowerApps builds an app that includes screens to display, create, update, and delete records. Throughout the remainder of this book, I'll refer to these apps as 'auto-generated apps.'

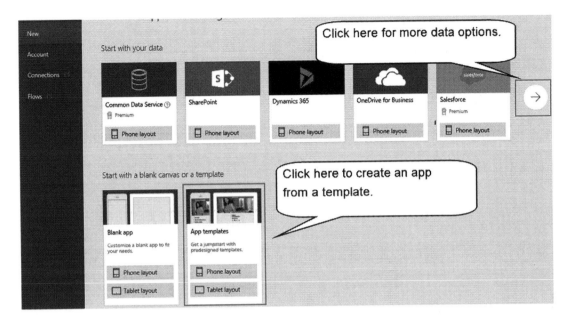

Figure 3-3. *Ways to create a new App*

Alternatively, we can create an app from a template. Microsoft provides some excellent templates and I recommend that you explore these. We can learn a great deal by examining the apps that we can build from templates.

Creating an Auto-Generated App

To create our first app, we'll choose the option to 'Start with your data'. The 'Start with your data' section offers a choice of five data sources that include Common Data Service, SharePoint, Dynamics 365, OneDrive for Business, and Salesforce. The right-pointing arrow icon opens the screen that's shown in Figure 3-4. From here, we can connect to a wider range of data sources.

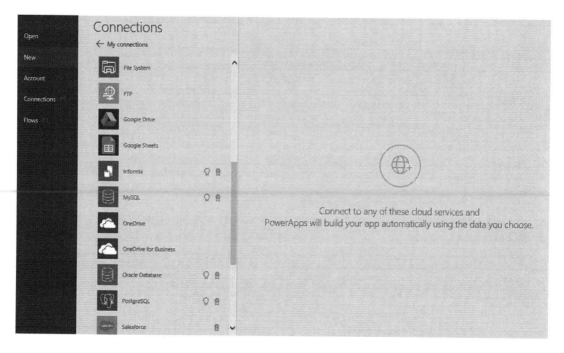

Figure 3-4. *Creating a new connection*

From the screen that's shown in Figure 3-4, add a connection to the cloud storage provider (in our example, OneDrive), and navigate to the spreadsheet location. Select the spreadsheet to show a list of available tables, as highlighted in Figure 3-5. Once we select a table from this list, PowerApps will create an app. Note that we can only select a single table from this list. It isn't possible to select more than one table as a basis for an auto-generated app.

Figure 3-5. *Choose a table from your spreadsheet*

Creating Apps from SharePoint

If we were to build an app from a SharePoint Online data source, there's another method to quickly build auto-generated apps. From a SharePoint list, select the menu item to create a new app, as shown in Figure 3-6.

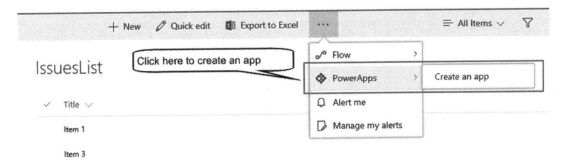

Figure 3-6. *Creating an app from a SharePoint list*

Exploring the Designer

When PowerApps opens, we'll see the screen that's shown in Figure 3-7. Here are the highlights of the sections that make up the designer:

- The top part of the designer contains a ribbon menu. The 'File' menu enables us to perform tasks that include opening and saving apps. The remaining menu items carry out design tasks, such as inserting controls on screens.

- The left part of the designer shows the screens in our app. We can edit a screen by selecting it from this part of the designer. The icons at the top switches the view between the 'screen explorer' and 'screen thumbnails' views. The 'screen explorer' view provides a tree view of all the controls on a screen, whereas the 'screen thumbnails' view provides a far more basic view.

- The central section of the screen houses the screen designer. From here, we can edit and position the controls on a screen. Furthermore, we can also delete controls, or add additional controls through the menu items in the Insert section of the ribbon menu bar.

- The right-hand side of the designer allows us to apply settings for the currently selected control.

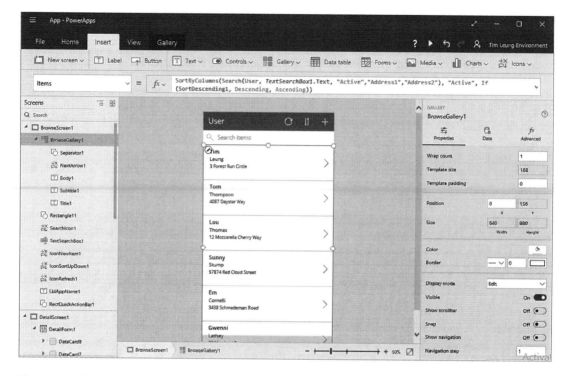

Figure 3-7. *PowerApps designer*

Running Your App

Without having to make any additional modifications to our project, we can run our app by selecting the first screen in the left pane (BrowseScreen1), and clicking the white 'play' button in the top-right part of the menu bar. We can also run our app by pressing the F5 button on our keyboard instead.

It's possible to run any screen in our project by selecting it via the left pane and clicking the play button. For example, to run the edit screen, we can simply select it and click the play button. There's no need to start the app from the initial startup screen and to navigate to the screen that we want to see.

To return to the designer, the simplest way is to click the escape key on the keyboard.

Examining the Screens at Runtime

Let's now examine the screens in our auto-generated app. The first screen that appears when we run the app is the browse screen, as shown in Figure 3-8. The name of this screen is BrowseScreen1.

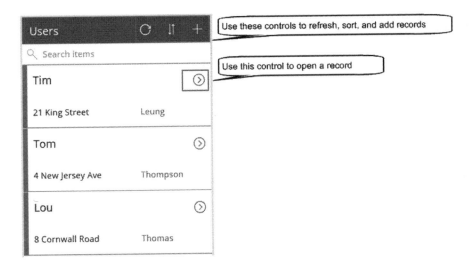

Figure 3-8. *Browse Screen*

The browse screen displays a list of records from the data source. The buttons to the right of the title bar refresh and sort the data that's shown in the list. There is also a button to add a new record. Beneath the title bar, the 'Search items' text box enables us to filter the results. Against each record, we can click the 'right arrow' icon to open the selected record in the details screen (Figure 3-9).

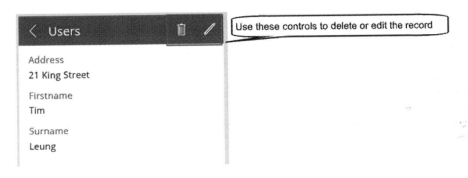

Figure 3-9. *Details screen*

The name of the details screen in our project is DetailScreen1. The main body of this screen shows the value of each field in the selected record. To the right of the screen title are two buttons. The first button deletes the record, and second button opens the edit screen as shown in Figure 3-10.

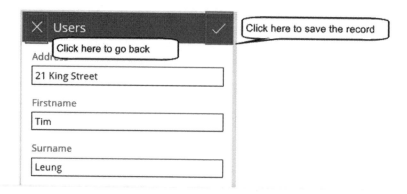

Figure 3-10. *Edit screen*

The name of this screen in our project is EditScreen1. From this screen, users can modify the selected record. The 'tick' icon to the right of the screen title saves the record, while the cross icon on the left returns the user to the detail screen.

The initial browse screen includes a button to add a new record. This button opens the same edit screen, but places the screen into 'add mode', rather than 'edit mode'.

Understanding the Auto-Generated App

Now that we've seen what an auto-generated app looks like, let's look at how it works technically.

Adding and Removing Data Sources

The data source for our app is an Excel spreadsheet. You can examine the data sources in a project by clicking the Data Sources button beneath the Content menu. When we click this button, the list of data sources in our project appears in the lower-right section of the screen, as shown in Figure 3-11. Here, we can see the data source in our app, which is called Users.

Figure 3-11. *Managing Data Sources*

The placement of the data sources panel in the screen designer might be confusing. Although the Data Sources panel appears beneath the BrowseScreen1 heading, data sources are not screen specific. In this case, Users is a data source that we can access from any screen in our project, and not just the BrowseScreen1 screen.

As Figure 3-11 illustrates, each data source includes a context menu that we can access through the button with three ellipses. Through this context menu, we can refresh or delete a data source.

The purpose of the refresh function is to update our project when a data source changes. For example, if we were to add additional columns to our Excel spreadsheet table, PowerApps would recognize the new columns only after we click the refresh button.

Frustratingly, there's no simple way to view the details of an Excel data source. In this example, there's no way to tell the exact location on OneDrive where our Excel file exists. To make it easier to remember the location of your Excel file, some app builders make a note of the OneDrive file path in the description setting of the app.

Let's suppose that we want to move our data source. For example, we might want to relocate our Excel file to different location on OneDrive, or to move our file from OneDrive to Dropbox. To move a data source, the best way is to delete our data source, and to re-add it. The good news is that when we delete a data source, PowerApps doesn't make any breaking changes to the project. For example, it won't automatically remove screens, controls, or objects that are associated with the data source.

■ **Note**   We can access data sources globally throughout an app. A data source is not specific to an individual screen.

Adding, Deleting, and Rearranging Screens

The left part of the screen designer enables us to manage the screens in our app. When a user runs an app, the first screen that opens is the screen at the top of this list. Therefore, the way to configure an app to show a different startup screen is to move the desired screen to the top of the list. We can move a screen by dragging it with the mouse or by using the context menu, as shown in Figure 3-12.

Figure 3-12. *Use the context menu to manage screens*

Through the context menu, we can add, delete, and duplicate screens. Each application must include at least one screen. Therefore, if only one screen exists in an application, the 'delete screen' item will not appear in the menu. To rename a screen, we can use the context menu or use the screen name text box in the properties pane, as shown in Figure 3-13.

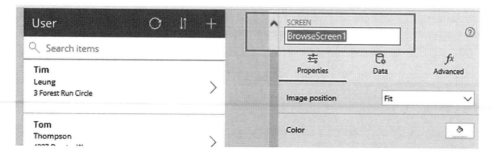

Figure 3-13. *Renaming a screen*

The good news is that when we rename a screen, the designer will change all formula references to use the new name. This makes it simple to rename screens because we don't need to worry about manually changing other parts of the app that refer to the screen.

Understanding How Screens Are Connected

The auto-generated app includes three screens that are all connected to data. It includes navigation links and buttons that connect all three screens. How exactly does this work? In this section, we'll find out how.

How the Browse Screen Works

Starting with the browse screen, the main body of the screen contains a control called a gallery control. The purpose of this control is to show a list of records. It includes a property called Items. This property specifies the data that appears.

The gallery control in the browse screen is called BrowseGallery1, and the screenshot in Figure 3-14 shows the value of the Items property. This property value contains a formula to support the search and sort features of the screen. But ultimately, BrowseGallery1 connects to the Users data source, which was shown in Figure 3-11.

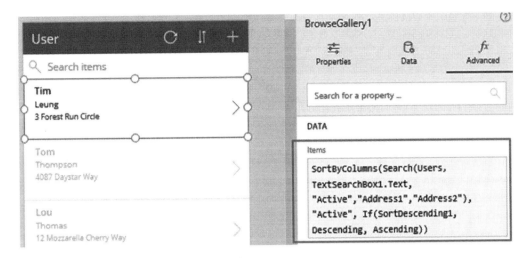

Figure 3-14. *The data source for the gallery control*

From the browse screen, the user can open an existing record or create a new record. Let's look at the formula that opens an existing record. From `BrowseGallery1`, select the icon with the right-pointing arrow, as shown in Figure 3-15.

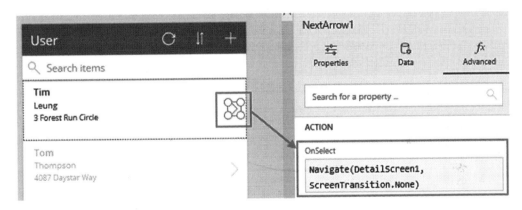

Figure 3-15. *Formula to open an existing record*

Because the gallery control shows multiple records, we can only select the first item in the control. This first item acts as a template for the repeating items in the gallery control.

The properties pane shows a property called `OnSelect`. This defines what happens when a user clicks a control.

The OnSelect formula calls a function called Navigate. The purpose of this function is to change the screen that is currently visible. This function accepts two arguments, the first being the screen that you want to show. The second argument specifies the screen transition effect and there are four that we can choose from – None, Fade, Cover, UnCover. The differences between these transition effects are these:

- Fade - The existing screen fades away to reveal the new screen.

- Cover - The new screen will slide into view, covering the existing screen.

- UnCover - The exiting screen will slide out of view, thereby uncovering the new screen.

You might be curious as to why the navigate function doesn't specify which record to open in the detail screen. Don't worry, you'll find out very soon.

Let's look at the formula to create a new record. Figure 3-16 shows the formula attached to the add icon at the top of the screen. This formula calls the Navigate function to open the edit screen (EditScreen1) but before it does so, it calls a function called NewForm.

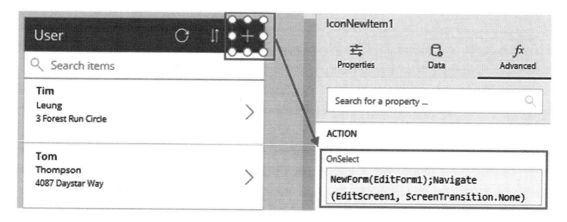

Figure 3-16. *The add record button calls the NewForm function*

The purpose of the NewForm function is to support the behavior of the edit screen. The edit screen serves two purposes. It enables users to modify existing records and it also enables users to add new records. The NewForm function prepares the form on the edit screen to receive the entry of a new record. A form is a control that houses data entry controls and in this example, the name of the form on the edit screen is EditForm1.

After the call to NewForm, the next command in the formula calls the Navigate function to open the edit screen.

How the Detail Screen Works

The screen that displays a single record is called DetailScreen1. The main body of this screen contains a form object called DetailForm1. See Figure 3-17.

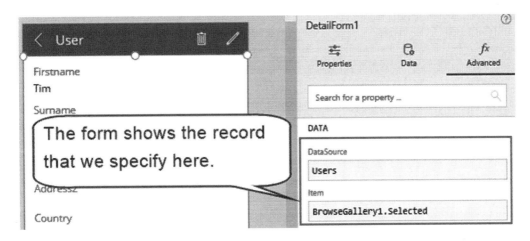

Figure 3-17. The data source for the detail form

Forms provide the framework to display a single record on a screen. The data source of DetailForm1 is set to Users. A form shows a single record and the Item property defines the record to display. In this case, the Item property is set to BrowseGallery1.Selected. This refers to the browse gallery control in BrowseScreen1. The browse gallery control keeps track of the selected item. When a user clicks an item in the gallery, we can access the selected record through the Selected property.

Because the Item property in DetailForm1 refers to BrowseGallery1, this explains why we don't need to provide a record when we open this screen with a call to the Navigate function. DetailForm1 is connected to BrowseGallery1 through the Item property of the DetailForm1.

Let's look at the formula that opens the selected record in the edit screen. Figure 3-18 shows the formula that is attached to the edit icon. The first command calls a function called EditForm. This function prepares the form on the edit screen by loading the record into the form. The next command in the formula calls the Navigate function to open the edit screen.

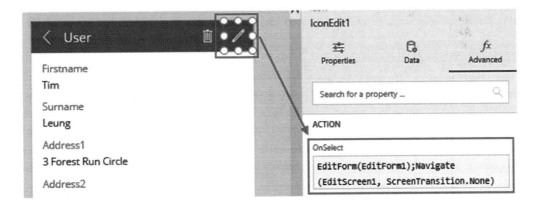

Figure 3-18. The edit button calls the EditForm function

Searching for Controls

At this stage, it's useful to clarify that control names are unique at an application level. For instance, we can only have one control named DisplayForm1 within an app. This can be a surprise because many other development platforms exist where controls are unique at a screen level, rather than at application level.

Because of the way that formulas can refer to controls on other screens, a very handy feature is the search facility. If we were looking at the application for the first time and saw a reference to BrowseGallery1, how would we know which screen to find BrowseGallery1? By using the search facility, we can search for objects throughout our project. The search facility is very useful because it makes it much easier to understand the complicated apps that we can build via the built-in templates.

To search for an item, use the search box at the top of the screen explorer. Figure 3-19 shows the result when we enter the search term BrowseGallery. The search feature returns the objects that contain the search term in the tree view.

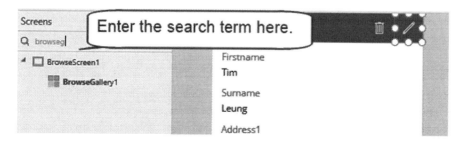

Figure 3-19. *Using the search facility*

■ **Note**   Control names in PowerApps are case sensitive and must be unique throughout a project.

How the Edit Screen Works

Let's now examine the last of our three screens – the screen to edit data. The name of this screen is EditScreen1 and the body of the screen contains the edit form that I mentioned earlier.

The edit form provides a framework to display, update, and add records. The data source of our edit form is set to Users. An edit form is designed to show a single record, and the Item property defines the record to show. Just like the form on the detail screen, the Item property of the form is set to BrowseGallery1.Selected (Figure 3-20).

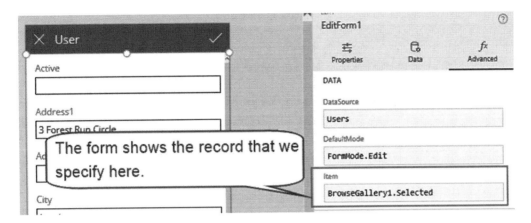

Figure 3-20. The data source of the edit form is connected to the gallery control

Figure 3-21 shows the formula that is attached to the save icon. This formula calls a function called SubmitForm. The SubmitForm function saves the data changes to the underlying data source. If we called the NewForm function before opening the screen, SubmitForm adds a new record to the data source. Whereas if we called the EditForm function, the SubmitForm function will update the existing record in the data source.

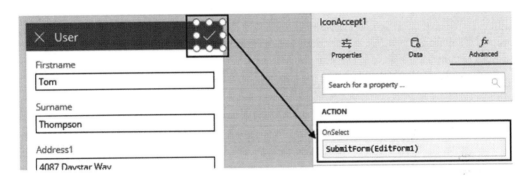

Figure 3-21. The save button calls the SubmitForm function

Understanding Forms and Cards

How exactly do forms retrieve and update data from a data source? In this section, we'll find out how. A form contains a series of card objects. Each card contains text boxes (or other controls) to display the data values. At the beginning, I struggled to understand the necessity of this hierarchy of controls. It's perfectly possible to add text boxes directly to a screen. So why introduce a complex structure that requires us to connect text boxes to cards, and cards to forms?

The main reason is that it provides a framework to retrieve and update data. It can make it quicker to build screens, and it reduces the amount of code we would otherwise need to write to perform data access tasks.

Figure 3-22 shows the design view of EditForm1. The items that appear beneath the Fields heading represent the *auto-generated* cards that appear in the form. The reason they are called auto-generated cards is because the designer creates the cards automatically based on the fields in the data source.

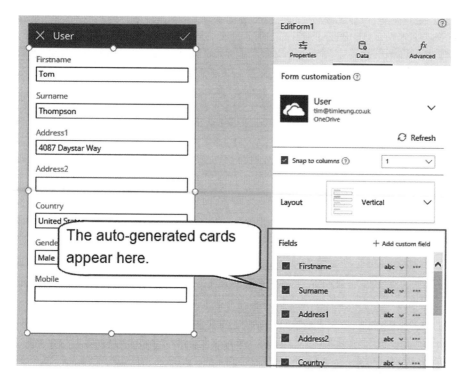

Figure 3-22. *Features of Cards*

The card list reacts dynamically to the data source. If we were to add a new field (for example, phone number) to our Excel table, the designer would generate a phone number card as soon as we refresh our data source.

To hide a card, untick the checkbox that corresponds to the card that you want to hide. Figure 3-23 illustrates the appearance of the form with the 'active' card hidden. As you can see, the designer shows a grayed-out version of the card when it is hidden. To reinstate the card, you can simply tick the checkbox to reenable the card.

Figure 3-23. *Hiding and Showing cards*

By default, the cards appear in alphabetical sequence. We can rearrange the sequence of the cards in a form by dragging the cards in the 'fields' list to the desired location.

To summarize why we can build screens more easily with forms and cards, here are three benefits. The first benefit is that forms react when a change to the underlying data source occurs and this behavior makes it easier for us to maintain our app.

The second benefit of the card system is that the auto-generated cards can retrieve validation rules from the data source. This doesn't apply to our Excel example but if we used a SharePoint data source instead, the cards would validate data type of the input data, and also enforce the entry of any mandatory fields. Figure 3-24 shows an example from a separate app based on a SharePoint source.

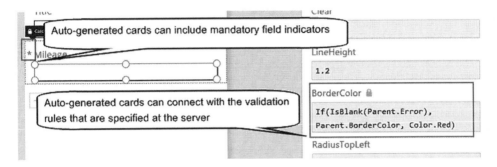

Figure 3-24. The cards can enforce validation rules

The third benefit of cards is that we can easily change the control type. If we click the 'abc' icon next to the card name, the designer provides a list of controls that we can use instead of a text input control (Figure 3-25). The choices include 'View Text', 'View Phone', 'View Email', 'Edit Text', 'Edit Multi-Line Text', and 'Allowed Values'.

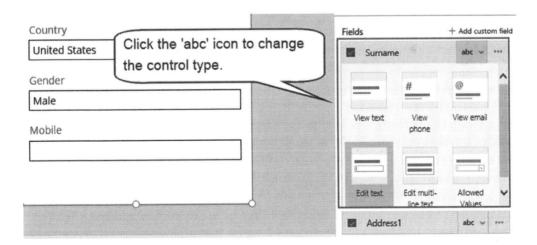

Figure 3-25. Changing the control type

It's possible to modify the appearance of an auto-generated card but we can only do so once we unlock it. To unlock a card, select the card and click the Advanced tab, as shown in Figure 3-26. From here, click the padlock icon to unlock the card.

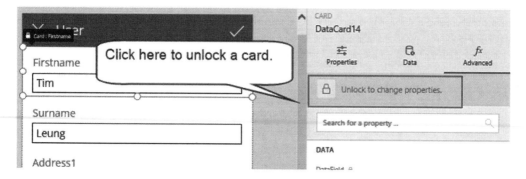

Figure 3-26. *Unlocking a card*

Let's suppose that we unlock the firstname card. As soon as we unlock the card, the designer auto-generates another firstname card, but the card will be in a disabled state. This allows us to revert to the default state of an auto-generated card if we want to discard our customizations.

■ **Caution**   If the designer fails to apply your changes, make sure that the card you want to edit is unlocked.

Reading Data into a Form

Here's how a form retrieves data from its data source. The form uses the data source and selected item properties to determine the record to load.

For each card, the Default property defines which field in the record to retrieve. Figure 3-27 shows the auto-generated card for the firstname field. As this screenshot shows, the Default property of this card is set to ThisItem.Firstname. The ThisItem keyword enables us to reference the fields in the record.

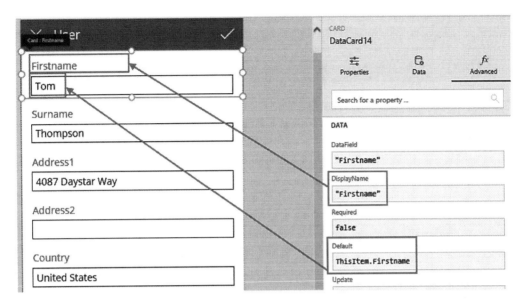

Figure 3-27. *The default property specifies the field that the card retrieves*

Another useful card property is `DisplayName`. PowerApps uses this value to set the label heading for the card.

■ **Tip** To configure a card to read data, the only property we need to set is the `Default` property. In an auto-generated card, we can clear all other property values and the data will still load.

How Card Controls Work

The card itself doesn't display any data directly, or provide any discernable functionality to the end user. It simply acts as a container for other controls. The content of the firstname card includes a text input control, as shown in Figure 3-28. For text input controls, the `Default` property specifies the text that the control displays. In this example, the value of this property is `Parent.Default`.

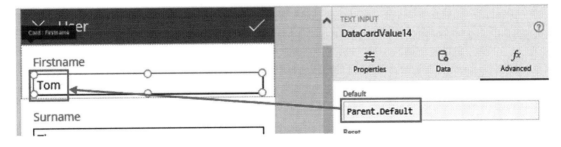

Figure 3-28. *specifying the text that appears in the text input control*

43

Because the text input control belongs inside a card control, the Parent keyword enables us to refer to the properties of the parent card control. In this case, `Parent.Default` will resolve to the default property of the card control, which in this case is `ThisItem.Firstname`.

Rather than set the default property of the text control to `Parent.Default`, everything would work the same if we were to set the default property of the text control to `ThisItem.Firstname`. So why use this parent syntax? The benefit of this pattern is that it encourages better encapsulation of the card. If a card were to contain multiple child controls that refer to the firstname field, it's better to use the `Parent.Default` syntax because if we want to change the card so that it displays a different field, we can apply this change in a single place at the card level, rather than apply the change in multiple places in child controls.

Notice that the label for the card also applies this same pattern. As Figure 3-29 shows, the `Text` property of the text box control is set to `Parent.DisplayName`.

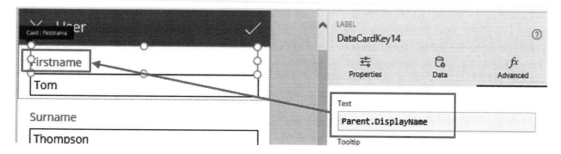

Figure 3-29. *Label control for a card*

When we work with forms and cards, a useful feature to mention is the cookie trail control that appears in the lower part of the screen designer (Figure 3-30). If we want to set the properties of an object such as a screen or a form, the cookie trail enables us to quickly select our desired object. When controls are placed closely together on a screen, it can be difficult to select the correct object with the mouse. Using the cookie trail makes this task simple. Another reason why the cookie control is useful is because it confirms that we've added a control to the right place. For example, to insert a control onto a card, we need to select the card with the mouse before choosing a control from the insert menu. If we forget to select the card, the designer adds the item that we insert onto the screen. Therefore, the cookie trail provides confirmation when we insert child items onto a control.

Figure 3-30. *Using the cookie control in the designer*

■ **Tip**   We can also use the screen explorer to view the hierarchy of controls on a screen. The screen explorer is especially useful because we can use this to view hidden controls.

Saving Form Data to a Data Source

How does PowerApps insert and update records? The insert or update operation begins when a user initiates a call to the SubmitForm function. The save icon in EditScreen1 calls this function and supplies the name of the edit form. The SubmitForm function retrieves the data that the user enters through the child controls on the cards, and updates the data store.

Figure 3-31 shows the firstname card on the edit form. The card properties that are pertinent to the save operation are the DataField and Update properties.

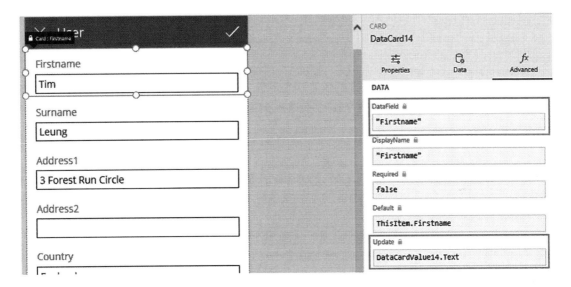

Figure 3-31. *Inserting or Updating a record*

The SubmitForm function works its way through each card on the form. For each card, it uses the DataField property to determine which field to update in the data store and then uses the Update property to work out the value to set. In this specific example, the SubmitForm function updates the Firstname field, and sets the value to the text that the user enters through a text input control. Just to clarify, DataCardValue14 is the name of the text input control inside the firstname card.

The SubmitForm function can update an existing record or it can insert a new record. This depends on the function that we called prior to opening the screen. If we called the EditForm function, SubmitForm will update an existing record in the data source. Whereas if we called the NewForm function, SubmitForm will add a new record to the data source.

If the SubmitForm completes the save operation successfully, it runs the formula that's defined in the OnSuccess property. In this case, it calls the Back function (Figure 3-32). This function navigates the user back to the screen that was previously open. In the event of a failure, the formula in the OnFailure property will run instead.

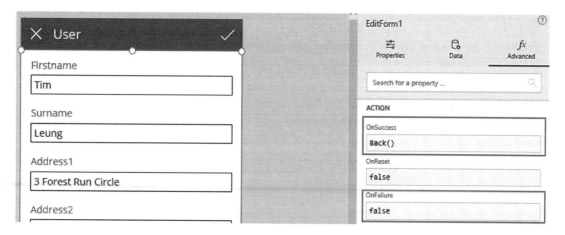

Figure 3-32. *Specifying the action that runs when the SubmitForm function succeeds or fails*

Choosing Not to Use Forms and Cards

Although there are benefits to using forms and cards to read and write data, it's possible to build data entry screens without the use of these controls. We could add custom text controls to a screen and call a function named Patch to update the data source.

One reason not to use forms and cards is the ability to build data entry screens with a greater level of customization. There may also be situations where we need to update more than one table. Edit forms are associated with single tables and in scenarios where we want to update more than one table, it can be easier to write custom formula, rather than build screens with multiple forms.

Recap of Concepts

We've covered a lot so here's a summary to reinforce some of the concepts that we've learned. Figure 3-33 illustrates how screen navigation works in an auto-generated app.

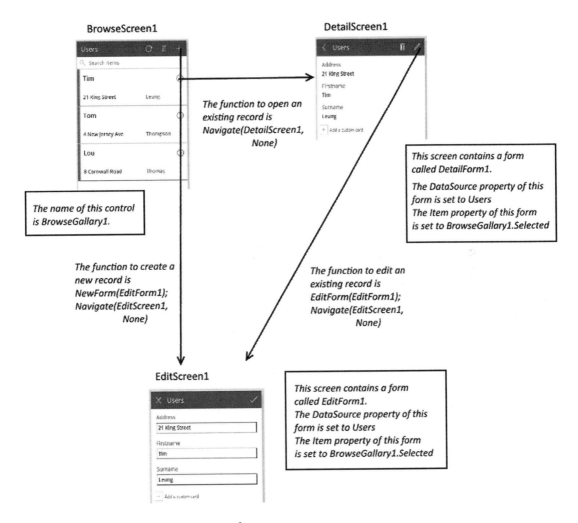

Figure 3-33. *How the screens are connected*

Figure 3-34 illustrates how the read process works in the form of a diagram, and it also describes the role that forms and cards play in this process.

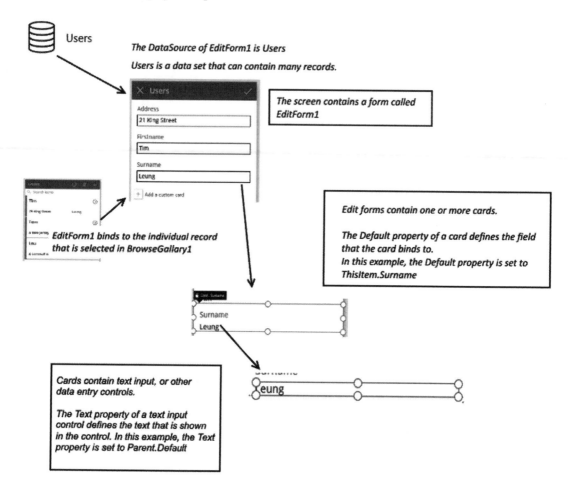

Figure 3-34. *How the data read process works*

Finally, Figure 3-35 illustrates how the save process works in the form of a diagram.

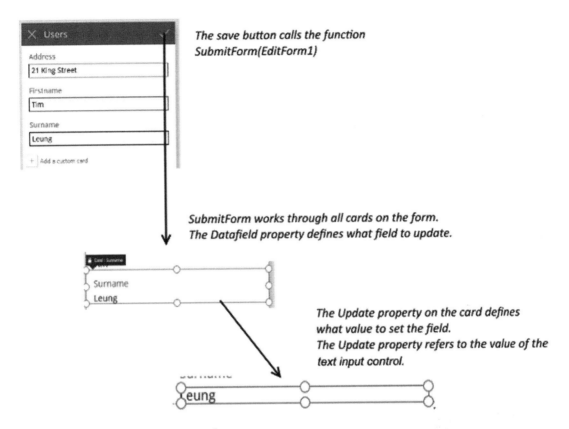

Figure 3-35. How the save process works

Setting Project Properties

For each application, there are project properties that we can set. Through the 'App settings' section of the designer, we can specify an app name, description, background color, and icon (Figure 3-36). When we share our app with other users, the app name and description help other users to identify our app.

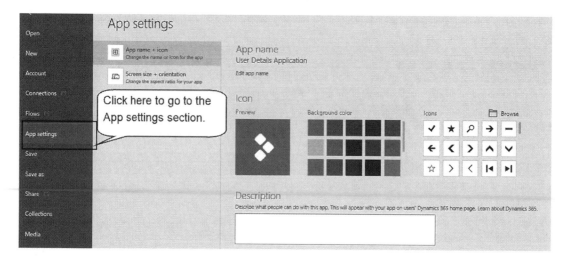

Figure 3-36. App settings

Through the 'App settings' screen, we can also configure the screen size and orientation settings, as shown in Figure 3-37. A notable setting is the lock orientation setting. By default, this is set to on. When we turn this off, our app will re-orientate itself when the user rotates the device.

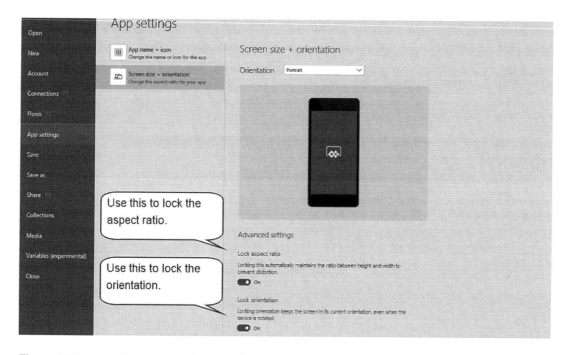

Figure 3-37. App settings – screen size and orientation

Saving Your Project

To save our work, use the File ➤ Save As menu item, as shown in Figure 3-38. There are two places where we can save our project – to the cloud, or to our local PC.

Figure 3-38. Saving your project

If we choose the cloud option, PowerApps will save our work to the current environment. We can switch environments though the account menu. However, we can't switch environments at the point at which we want to save because we'll be prompted to discard our changes.

If we save our project to our local computer, we won't be able to open it from the web version of PowerApps Studio. Saving work to the local computer can make it easier to manage backup copies of your work, if that is your preferred way of working. We can also share project files with other users by email when we save our work locally.

When we choose the option to save to our local computer, PowerApps Studio creates a file with a `.msapp` extension.

Opening a Project

To open a project, use the open menu, as shown in Figure 3-39. This is the default screen that appears when PowerApps opens. For projects that are saved locally, we can double-click the `.msapp` file in Windows Explorer to open the project directly.

Figure 3-39. Opening a project

We can use the ellipses button to access a context menu. Through this menu, we can view the details of an app. One useful feature of the details page is that it lists the data connections that an app uses.

Through this context menu, another useful option is the ability to delete a project. Note that only the app owner can delete an app. There is no administrative feature to delete an app that doesn't belong to you. Where this can be a problem is if the owner of an app leaves our organization. This can leave orphaned files in an environment that no one can delete.

Summary

In this chapter, we looked at how to build an auto-generated app based on an Excel spreadsheet. To use Excel as a data source, we must define the data as a table in order for PowerApps to recognize the data. Once we complete the spreadsheet, we need to save it to one of the cloud storage providers that PowerApps supports. This includes Microsoft OneDrive and Dropbox.

When we start PowerApps Studio, it offers several options to create a new app. The first is to build an app based on one of the built-in templates. These templates provide a great way to learn more about PowerApps.

Another option is to choose the 'start with data' option. This option builds an auto-generated app that enables users to create, update, and delete records from a data source.

Once we create an app, we can use a simple graphical designer to modify our project. The left part of the designer shows the screens in an app, and the menu options in the ribbon bar enables us to add content. Though the properties pane on the right, we can modify the settings of objects such as screens and controls.

Auto-generated apps contain three screens – a browse screen, detail screen, and an edit screen. The browse screen contains a gallery control. This control displays a list of data and a user can use this control to open a specific record in the detail screen. The detail screen shows the full details of a record, and includes a link that opens the record in the edit screen. The edit screen enables users to make modifications to a record.

To display an individual record, the display and edit screens utilize a control called a form control. A form connects to a record, and typically, we would configure a form to connect to the selected item in a gallery control. Forms are containers for cards. A card is an object that connects to a specific field in a record, and the purpose of a card is to retrieve and update fields from a data source. Cards are containers for data controls, which are controls that users interact with. Examples of these controls include text input controls or drop-down boxes. One benefit of this system is that PowerApps produces auto-generated cards that we can include in a form. These auto-generated cards reflect any subsequent changes that we make to the data source, and therefore provide a simple way for us to add additional fields to a data source.

Here's a summary of some the functions that we've covered in this chapter. The function that switches the visible screen is called `Navigate`. A form control can modify an existing record, or it can create a new record. To prepare a form to edit an existing record, we would call a function called `EditForm`. To prepare a form to create a new record, we would call a function called `NewForm`. To save the form changes to the data source, we would call a function called `SubmitForm`.

To round off an app, we can use the settings area to define the name, description, icon, and other properties of our app. Finally, we can save apps either to the cloud or to our local computer.

CHAPTER 4

Sharing Apps

The final step of developing an app is to make it available to users. In this chapter, we'll walk through the steps to publish an app. This enables named groups or users to enjoy the work that we created. Other useful topics that we'll cover will include the following:

- How to manage app versions. This feature is helpful because it enables us to restore a previous version of an app if we accidently publish updates that contain breaking changes.

- How to configure data connections when publishing apps. In some cases, PowerApps can share data connections with end users. It's important to understand how this works because this determines whether end users need to provide data source credentials when they start an app.

- How to move apps between environments or organizations. This can be a challenge because there's no direct way to carry out this task. In this chapter, we'll look at how to carry out this task.

Sharing Your App

To share an app with other users, the first step is to save our app to the cloud. To help users identify an app, it's a good idea to provide a meaningful name and description. When the save operation completes, click the link to 'publish this version', as shown in Figure 4-1. The publish option makes an app available to users. If we save an app without publishing it, our work will only be visible to users with sufficient permissions to edit the app.

© Tim Leung 2017
T. Leung, *Beginning PowerApps*, https://doi.org/10.1007/978-1-4842-3003-9_4

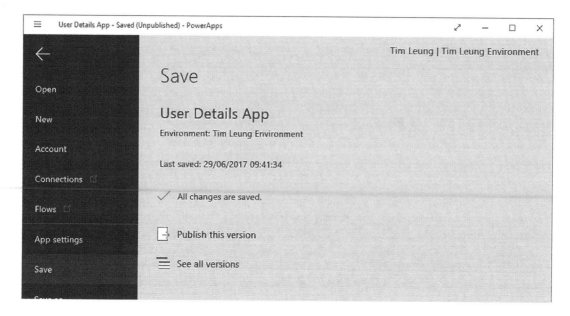

Figure 4-1. *Save your app to PowerApps*

The next step is to define the users with whom we want to share our app. To do this, click the Share menu to open the PowerApps web portal (Figure 4-2). From this section of the portal, we can specify the user with whom we want to share our app. We can also choose the option to share the app with an entire organization, or with a group of users. There is a checkbox option to notify our users by email. The email notification that the user receives will include a link to your app.

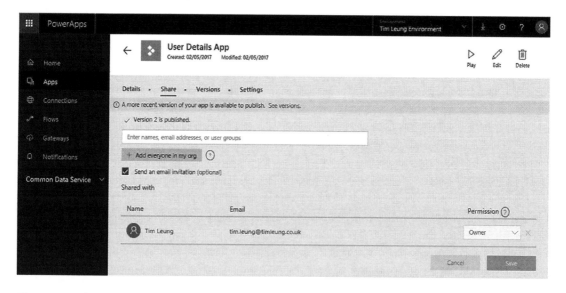

Figure 4-2. *Sharing an app with other users*

Note that we can only share apps with users from the same organization. It's not possible to share apps with users outside of our organization.

PowerApps will notify the users with whom we share our app. End users can view notifications by logging into the portal and opening the notifications section, as shown in Figure 4-3.

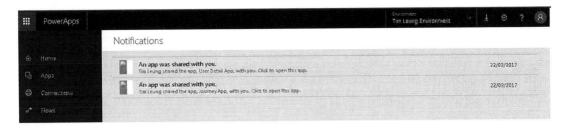

Figure 4-3. *Viewing notifications*

End users do not require any specific permissions on the environment that houses your app. However, without permissions to the underlying environment, it can be slightly more difficult for the user to find your app. This is because the user won't be able to select the environment in the portal and to view the page that shows the apps that belong in an environment.

Adding a User

To share an app with a new user, it's necessary to create a work account for the user. The place to do this is through the Office 365 Admin Portal, as shown in Figure 4-4. For the new user, we must enable the 'Microsoft PowerApps and Flow' setting in the product licenses section.

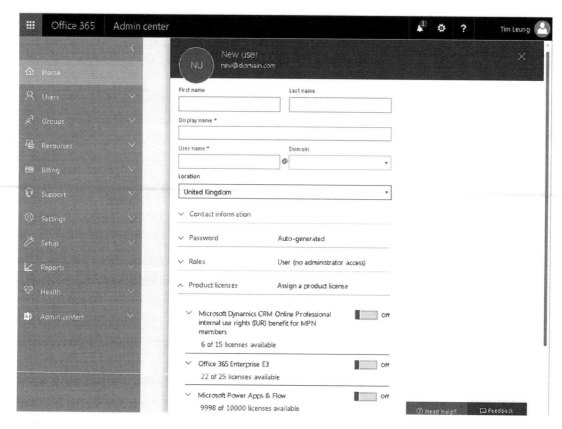

Figure 4-4. *Creating a new user in the Office 365 portal*

To make it easier to manage users, we can organize sets of users into groups. Figure 4-5 shows the section in the Admin center to add a new group.

Figure 4-5. *Creating a new group*

Applying Permissions

For each user or group that can access an app, we can assign one of two permissions: 'Can use' or 'Can edit'. Figure 4-6 shows the screen that's visible through the File ➤ Share menu item in PowerApps Studio. Users with the 'Can use' permission can run the app, and do nothing more. Users with the 'Can edit' permission have full access. These users can run the app, customize it further, and share the modified version with other users.

Figure 4-6. Specifying permissions for an app

Managing Environments

For development purposes, it can make sense to develop our app in a separate environment and to move our work to a 'live environment' once we're happy with our modifications. In this section, we'll look at how to move apps between environments.

Moving an App to a New Environment

The easiest way to move an app to a new environment is to save the app to our local computer. The next step is to change the environment and open the app from the local file that we saved.

Figure 4-7 shows the section in PowerApps Studio where we can switch environments. Once we open our app from the local file, we can save it to our new environment and publish it to our users.

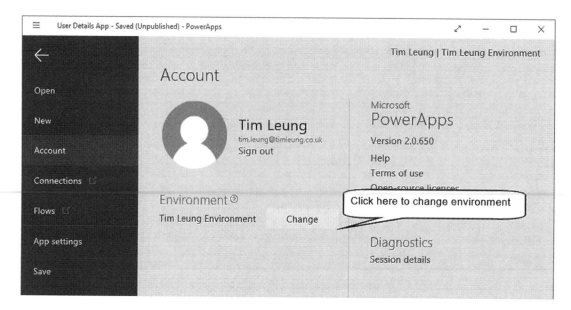

Figure 4-7. *Changing Environments*

This technique of saving our work to a local file can help us transfer projects between organizations, should the need arise.

Updating a Data Source

An important point to bear in mind is that data connections are defined at an environment level. If we move an app to a new environment and fail to reconfigure the data source, the application will fail to run. Users will receive an error that looks like the one that's shown in Figure 4-8. The text in this message is very generic (the specified record was not found), and it might not be obvious from this message that the cause is a missing data connection.

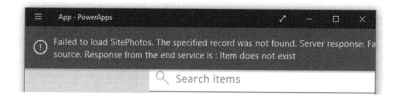

Figure 4-8. *The error that appears when the data connection is missing*

To update the data source in an app, go to the data sources section by clicking Content ➤ Data sources. The menu next to the data source shows two options: - Refresh and Remove.

Figure 4-9. *Updating a data source to use a new connection*

To update a data source so that it uses a new connection, remove the data source and re-add it with the 'Add data source' option.

How Data Connections Work

Data connections are always protected in some way. For instance, a username and password combination controls access to the data in a SQL Server data source. In the case of an Excel spreadsheet, access to the underlying file storage such as OneDrive or Dropbox controls access to the data. When we publish an app, how does the end user authenticate to the underlying data source at runtime?

With some data connections, users connect to the data source with the credentials that the app builder specified at design time. One example is an on-premise SQL Server data connection. We can determine the data connections that are shared by viewing the connection details in the portal. A share option will be visible against the data connections that are shared, as shown in Figure 4-10.

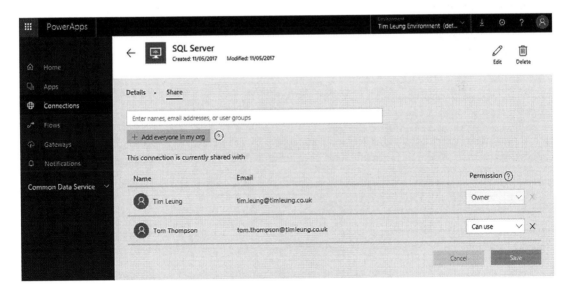

Figure 4-10. *The presence of a share tab indicates a shared connection*

PowerApps does not share Excel connections. To share an app that uses an Excel data source, it's necessary to grant each intended user edit permissions through the settings of the cloud storage provider (i.e., OneDrive, Dropbox, etc.).

For other non-shared connections that require authentication, the end user will need to enter credentials when the app starts.

Versioning an App

Each time we save an app to the cloud, PowerApps maintains a history of our changes. We can view the version history for each app through the PowerApps website. In the Apps section, click the information icon against an app to open the page that's shown in Figure 4-11.

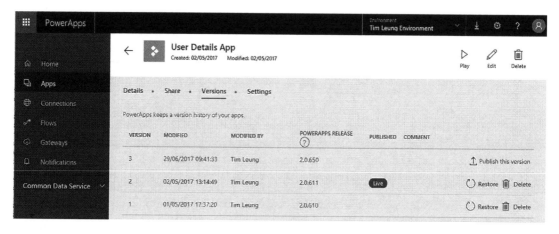

Figure 4-11. *Maintaining App versions*

Through this page, we can use the restore button to restore an app to a previous version. In the example shown in Figure 4-11, let's suppose we want to restore the app to version 1. When we click the restore button for version 1, the system will restore this version to a copy that is labeled version 4. This provides us with the ability to restore our app back to version 2 or 3, if we later change our mind.

Before restoring an app, we should consider any data schema changes that might have occurred following the version that we want to restore. If we renamed or removed data columns, it's important to revert these changes prior to restoring the app.

Another feature on this page is the option to delete copies of an app from the version history. We can use this feature to de-clutter this view and to remove any app versions that we no longer want.

Installing the Mobile Player

Mobile users need to install the PowerApps player to run apps on their phone or tablet devices. Users can do this by visiting the app store for their device. For example, an Android user would install PowerApps from the Play Store.

When the mobile player starts for the first time, it prompts the user to log in with the username and password for their Microsoft Work Account. The next screen shows a list of available apps. The mobile player caches the login credentials. Therefore if a user turns the device off and on again, it won't prompt for the login credentials again.

A useful feature in the details section of an app is the ability to 'pin to homescreen', as shown in Figure 4-12. When we click this option, the application creates a shortcut on the home screen of the mobile device, outside of the PowerApps player. This icon starts the specified app directly, and bypasses the app selection screen.

Figure 4-12. *Pinning an app to the home screen*

As is typical with mobile apps, we can move away from the PowerApps player and the app will continue in the background. For example, if we temporarily suspend what we're doing to take a phone call or read a text message, we can use the task switcher to return to the app and to resume from the screen that was last open.

In the case of a stock Android device, we can use the task switcher button in the bottom right-hand part of the device to resume a PowerApps session. If we were to click the PowerApps icon on the home screen, however, PowerApps would start from scratch and we would need to reload the app from the app selection screen.

Running with Foreign Languages

PowerApps can support languages other than English. To test an app under a different locale, we can achieve this by changing the language of our browser and then opening the app in this browser. Alternatively, we can open an app in PowerApps Studio for Windows by first changing the language of the Windows installation in Control Panel, as shown in Figure 4-13.

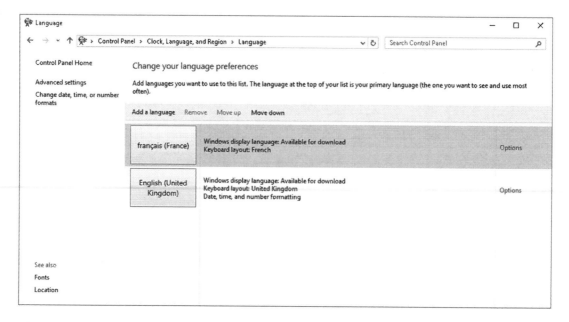

Figure 4-13. *Changing the language of PowerApps by changing the Windows language*

Once we add a language, click the Options button and download the supporting files. Once this is complete, it's necessary to restart our computer and at this point, the entire UI of Windows will appear in the new language. When we start PowerApps, all of the menu items will appear in the new language, as shown in Figure 4-14.

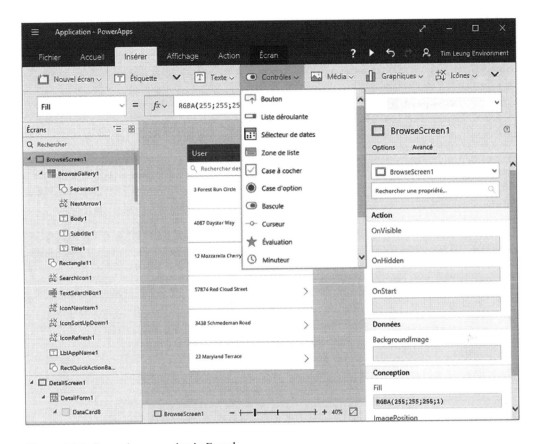

Figure 4-14. *PowerApps running in French*

French is an interesting language because it uses the comma character as a decimal point separator. Because of this difference, it uses double semicolons in formulas to denote the command termination command, rather than a single semicolon.

One final thing to be aware of is that we can change the language of the PowerApps Web portal by specifying the language in the address bar. For example, we can open the PowerApps portal in Spanish by logging into the PowerApps and website and then navigating to the address:

```
web.powerapps.com/?l=es-ES
```

The `es-ES` value in this address is a standard language tag. The first part denotes the language and the second part denotes the region. For example, to specify French Canadian, we would append the value `fr-CA`. To find a list of language tags we can use, the simplest way is to do an Internet search for the term 'IETF language tags'.

Summary

In this chapter, we looked at how to make an app available to other users. To share an app, the first step is to save the app to the cloud and to choose the option to publish the version. The next step is to visit the PowerApps portal and to select the users or groups with whom we want to share our app. For each user or group, we can assign one of two permissions – can use, or can edit. A user with the 'can use' permission can only run the app, whereas a user with the 'can edit' permission can make further modifications to the app.

The place to add new logins or groups is through the Office 365 admin center. Note that it's not possible to share an app with users outside of our organization.

When we build apps, it can be useful to set up a development and a production environment. This allows us to develop and test an app before releasing it to end users in the production environment. To move an app between environments, save the project to a file in the source environment, and then open that project file in the destination environment. When we move an app between environments, we need to re-create the data connections in the destination environment.

When we publish an app, PowerApps can share certain data connections. An example of a shared connection is SQL Server. Where connections are shared, PowerApps authenticates the user automatically to the data source using the credentials that the app builder specified at design time. In cases where the connection is not shared, the user will need to enter credentials when the app starts.

For apps that are stored in the cloud, PowerApps maintains a history of all changes. We can restore previous versions through the PowerApps portal. This feature can help us roll back mistakes or unwanted changes to an app.

PART II

Refining Your Application

CHAPTER 5

■ ■ ■

Exploring Data Sources

In the chapters so far, we've used Microsoft Excel as a data source. The benefit of Excel is that it's simple to use and understand. However, PowerApps supports many other data sources and in this chapter, we'll explore these in greater detail. The first section of this chapter focuses on the Common Data Service (CDS), a data store that works hand in hand with PowerApps. We'll also discover one the most outstanding features of PowerApps - the On-Premises Data Gateway. This feature enables us to connect to SQL Server and SharePoint servers that are inside internal company networks. For readers who are new to SharePoint, this chapter also contains a basic guide on how to set up a SharePoint list and how to configure choice items. This setup enables the basic storage of data in SharePoint. Useful topics that we'll cover in this chapter include the following:

- How to use the Common Data Service. We'll look at how to get the most out of the CDS, including how to configure lookup data and how to create hierarchical data models.

- How to use the On-Premises Data Gateway. This section guides you step by step toward setting up a gateway. Occasionally, unexpected errors may occur, but to help, we'll look at troubleshooting tips that you can apply.

- How to call external data services. We can add value to apps by utilizing data sources in innovative ways. To demonstrate this, we'll add translation capabilities to an app, and find out to display the current weather on a screen.

Using the Common Data Service

The Common Data Service (CDS) is a service that enables us to build and store structured data. We can access the CDS from the suite of Microsoft products that includes PowerApps, PowerBI, and Microsoft Flow. Of all the data sources, the CDS is the easiest to use because it is inherently linked to the environment where an app exists. Unlike other data sources, we don't need to specify any connection settings to connect to a CDS database.

There are several other benefits to using the CDS. The first is that we can use the web portal to build our data structure, so it's simple to use. The second benefit is that through the CDS, Microsoft provides common data models that we can utilize. By using these models, we can save time by not having to set up and design our data models. The third benefit is that if we want to use PowerBI or Microsoft Flow, we can more easily share data with these products.

The CDS is a platform that Microsoft promotes heavily. There are plenty of tech articles on the CDS, and Microsoft often applies new innovations to the CDS before other data sources.

© Tim Leung 2017
T. Leung, *Beginning PowerApps*, https://doi.org/10.1007/978-1-4842-3003-9_5

Despite these benefits, there are some drawbacks to using the CDS. First, it's difficult to access data from outside the suite of supported products. Second, there's no built-in backup mechanism for data. Third, there are plenty of included data models and if we choose to use these, it can be difficult to find a table to match a specific requirement. Finally, Microsoft reserves the right to share and reuse any of the schemas that we create. When we first provision a CDS database, Microsoft provides a prominent warning, as shown in Figure 5-1. Therefore, if you want build schemas that are commercially sensitive, the CDS isn't the best choice.

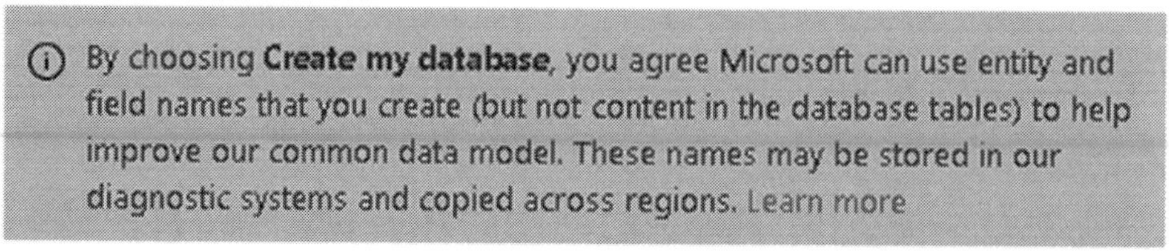

Figure 5-1. *Privacy warning when you create a CDS database*

One last point to consider is licensing. We can provision a maximum of one database per environment. At the time of writing, a 'Plan 1' subscription to PowerApps offers 20MB of data storage per user, while a 'Plan 2' subscription to PowerApps offers 200MB. To ensure that we don't incur excessive storage charges, it's important to have some idea of how much storage capacity we require before choosing the CDS. As a technical point, the maximum size of a CDS database is 10GB.

Getting Started

To get started with the CDS, the first step is to create a database. Databases are associated with environments and we can create a maximum of one database per environment. To create a database, log onto the PowerApps portal and select an environment. Next, select the *Entities* option from the Common Data Services menu in the left-hand menu. This opens the screen that's shown in Figure 5-2.

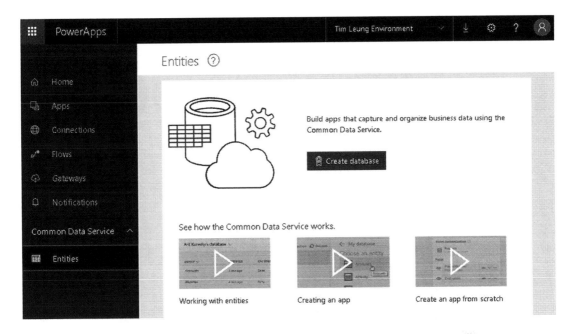

Figure 5-2. *Creating a database*

An entity defines a structure of data in the CDS. In SharePoint, we would store our data in lists. In Excel, we would store our data in tables. With the CDS, we would access a repository of data through entities.

When we create a new database, we can set the security of our database to one of two values: - open access, or restricted access. With open access, any user with access to the environment can access the database. It's important not to enable open access if we want to prevent certain users from accessing our data. In this situation, we should set our database to restricted access.

To modify the security setting of a database after creation, we can do this through the Admin Center, as shown in Figure 5-3.

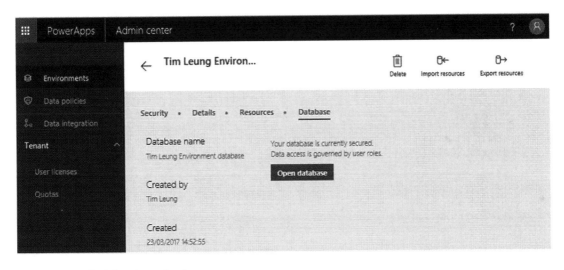

Figure 5-3. *Administering a database*

The Admin Center includes links at the top of the screen to import and export resources. We can use this feature to copy entities between databases. The 'export resources' function produces a file with a .pkg extension and we can use this file to import entities into our target database. Note that this only imports the definition of the entities; it won't import the data that is stored in the entities.

One limitation to be aware of is that the time of writing, there isn't an option in the Admin Center to delete a database. The reason this is important is because some Office 365 subscriptions provide a limit of two databases. In this situation, it's difficult to re-provision a database for use in a different environment. As a workaround, we can delete a database by deleting the host environment. But as you can imagine, this isn't convenient if our environment contains active users.

We can click the delete button at the top of the screen to delete an environment, and we can use the setting in the Details section to rename an environment.

Exploring the Common Data Model

Once we create a database, we can explore the entities that make up the Common Data Model. To see these entities, click the Entities menu in the PowerApps portal, as shown in Figure 5-4. As this screenshot shows, there are plenty of entities to choose from. Because there are so many entities, it can be difficult to find an entity that suits our intended requirement. For this reason, you can find a list of all the standard entities in Appendix A.

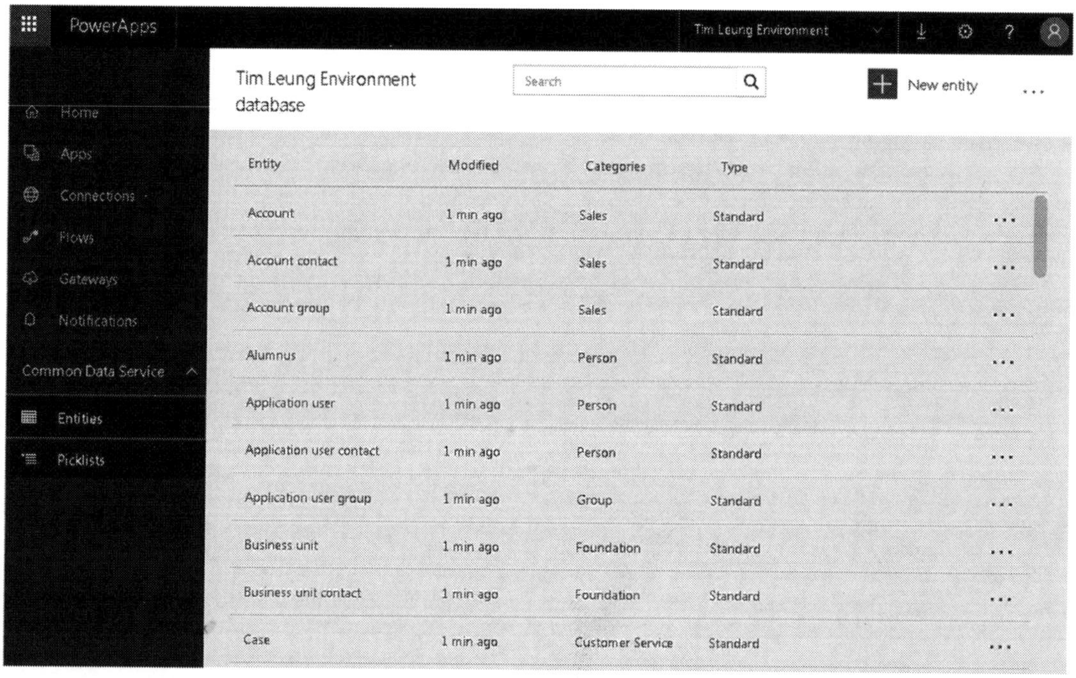

Figure 5-4. *Illustration of standard entities*

The system groups entities into categories that share a common purpose, as shown in Table 5-1. If, for example, we want to build a customer service app, we could potentially find all the entities we need in the customer service category.

Table 5-1. *CDM Categories*

Category	Description
Foundation	This category includes typical, generic entities such as Address and Currency.
Person	The entities in this category are designed to store people data. It includes entities such as Alumnus, Application User, Constituent, Tenant, and Worker entities.
Organizations	There are two entities in this group – Organization and Organization Contact.
Groups	The entities in this category are designed to store people data. It includes the Family, Fan, and Team Member entities.
Purchase	The entities in the Purchasing category are designed to build purchasing solutions. It includes entities to store orders, receipts, tax, and vendor data.
Project	The entities in the Project category store details of projects, and the contracts that are associated with a project.
Sales	The entities in the Sales category are designed to build sales solutions. It includes entities to store accounts, leads, opportunities, quotes, and sales orders.
Customer service	The entities in the Customer Service category are designed to build apps to manage customer complaints. It includes entities to store cases and help desk articles.

Here's a quick tip. The system assigns any entities we create into a category called custom. If we want to show just the entities we create, enter the word 'custom' into the search box. Note that the search feature matches search terms against entity names, but doesn't match against field names. For example, we can't use this feature to find all entities that include a field called 'surname'.

Exploring a Standard Entity

To learn more about the standard entities, let's look at the first entity in the list, the Account entity. Figure 5-5 shows the design view of this entity.

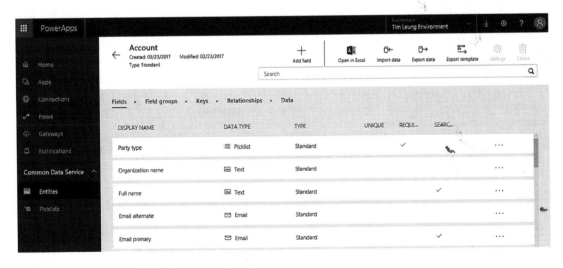

Figure 5-5. *Illustration of the Account entity*

The entity view includes five navigation links – Fields, Field Groups, Keys, Relationships, and Data. We can use the initial page to manage the fields in an entity. Fields define the individual pieces of data for each record. The fields in the Account entity include the common fields that we would like to store against an account, such as organization name and full name. Each field stores data that matches a specific data type. The data types that we can assign include numeric and text types, as well as specialized types such as email addresses and phone numbers. We can also specify pick lists to constrain the values that a user can enter.

Something that might not seem obvious is that we can add additional fields to standard entities. If we want to add a field called 'account manager' to the standard account entity, that's entirely possible. To do this, click the 'Add field' button.

Although we can add additional fields to a model, we can't modify any of the standard fields in an entity. So if we live in England and want to change the display name of the 'Organization name' field to 'Organisation name', that isn't possible.

■ **Tip**   We can add our own fields to the built-in, standard entities.

Creating a Custom Entity

To demonstrate how to create an entity, here's how to create an entity to store vehicle makes (or manufacturers). Select the Entities menu from the left-hand menu and click the 'new entity' button. This opens the pane that's shown in Figure 5-6. The mandatory fields here are Name and 'Display name'.

Figure 5-6. *Creating a new entity*

The name is the programmatic value that we use to refer to the entity in formula, whereas Display name is the value that appears in lists of entities.

Entity names must start with a character and can only include alphanumeric characters. The name cannot include spaces, but the underscore character is permissible. The maximum length we can enter is 50 characters. The standard convention is to use singular nouns for our entities such as Customer, rather than Customers. We can't modify an entity name, so it's important to choose a name that we want to keep.

Once we provide an entity name and description, the fields will appear as shown in Figure 5-7. Each custom entity includes built-in fields to record the date when the record was created and last modified, and the user that carried out those operations. These built-in fields cannot be deleted.

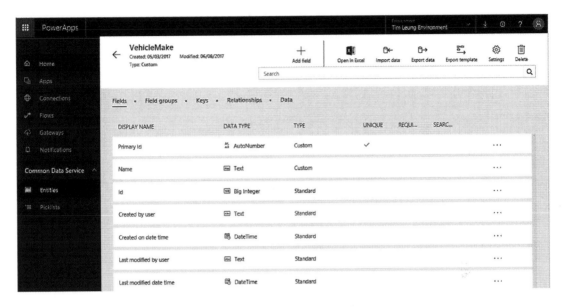

Figure 5-7. *Custom Entity with built-in fields*

By default, the designer also adds a unique Primary Id field to make each record identifiable. The data type of this field is AutoNumber. When we assign the AutoNumber type to a field, the database generates a unique, consecutive number to each record. If desired, we can prefix each number with a set of characters. The prefix cannot include spaces and must begin with a character. The prefix characters are stored with each record. Therefore, if we modify the prefix value at a later point in time, the new prefix will not apply retrospectively to existing records. The sequential numbering will still continue though.

Adding a New Field

To add a new field, click the Add field button at the top of the screen. This opens a panel to the right of the screen, as shown in Figure 5-8. From here, we must provide a name, display name, and data type.

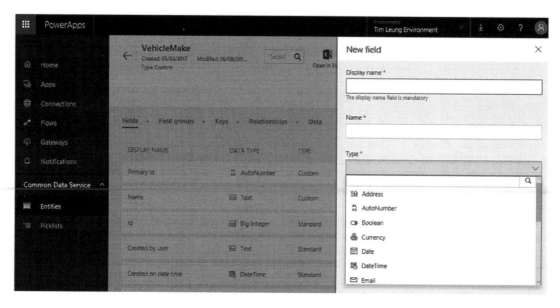

Figure 5-8. *Adding a new field*

Just like with entities, the name is the programmatic identifier that we use in formulas. The name must begin with a character and cannot contain spaces. The underscore character is acceptable. The type drop-down enables us to specify the data type of the field, and the data types are self-explanatory. The more notable points to be aware of are these:

- To store text values, we can use the Text or Multiline Text data types. The Text data type enforces a maximum of 128 characters whereas the Multiline Text data type enforces a maximum character length of 2048 characters. The CDS does not support text fields that exceed 2048 characters. The underlying storage for these data types is Unicode, which makes it possible to store non-Latin, foreign characters.

- To store numeric data, we can use the Quantity, Integer, or Number data types.

- The CDS provides no support for binary data, but it does provide an image data type.

In addition, the CDS offers three compound data types – Address, Currency, and PersonName. These data types enable a user to store multiple pieces of data in a single field. Here's a summary of these three types:

- The Address data type provides separate fields for the first line, second line, city, state/province, postal code, and country/region for an address.

- The Currency data type provides two fields – a decimal field to store the value, and a second field to store the currency code. The currency type provides a built-in list of three digit currency codes, such as USD or EUR.

- The PersonName data type provides three fields – first name, middle name, and surname.

In terms of storing text, there are three special data types that are based on the string data type. These are Email, Phone, and WebsiteUrl. The benefit of using these data types is that PowerApps provides controls that are specially designed for these data types. Just like the other text types, PowerApps stores the data in Unicode.

Finally, there are two data types that are related to dates: Date and DateTime. The DateTime data type stores both the date and time components down to fractional seconds, whereas the Date data type stores only the date component.

One important thing to stress is that we should never use the DateTime data type for fields where we only want to store the date component (for example, birthdays). The reason is because screen controls can carry out time zone conversions on DateTime fields and if we're not careful, our screens may display incorrect values. For example, if we store birthdays in a DateTime field, users in different time zones may end up seeing values that are one day earlier or one day later than the correct value.

Storing Numbers

There are three data types that store numeric data: Integer, Number, and Quantity. But what exactly are the differences between these three types?

The Integer data type stores whole numbers between -2,147,483,648 and 2,147,483,647. To store a number with fractional units, we can use either the Number or Quantity data types. Both these types store decimal numbers but the difference between these two types is that the quantity type is a compound type. The quantity data type stores a decimal value and also stores the unit of measurement. Figure 5-9 shows the appearance of an auto-generated app that's based on an entity with a quantity field. As you can see, the auto-generated card includes a drop-down that enables the user to select the unit of measurement.

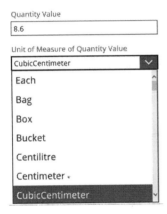

Figure 5-9. *The quantity type enables users to specify the unit of measure*

According to the CDS documentation, the number data type can store up to 32 digits, with a maximum of 6 digits to the right of the decimal point. But in practice, the values that we can store with PowerApps are far lower than this. PowerApps has a dependency on JavaScript and the maximum number that JavaScript supports is 9,007,199,254,740,991. So by extension, this is the maximum number that we can use with PowerApps.

■ **Tip** Microsoft provides documentation that includes much more detail about how the CDS works. However, you won't find this through the usual PowerApps website: `http://powerapps.microsoft.com`. Instead, you should visit the dedicated CDS website, which you can find here: `https://docs.microsoft.com/en-us/common-data-service/entity-reference/introduction`.

Creating a Relationship

The relationship section in the entity designer enables us to define lookups. For example, to create an entity that stores vehicle models and to allow users to assign a vehicle make to each vehicle model record, we would need to define a relationship between the two separate entities.

To build this example structure, create an entity to store vehicle makes. Next, create an entity to store vehicle models. In the Relationships section for the vehicle model entity, we can define a lookup to the vehicle make entity, as shown in Figure 5-10.

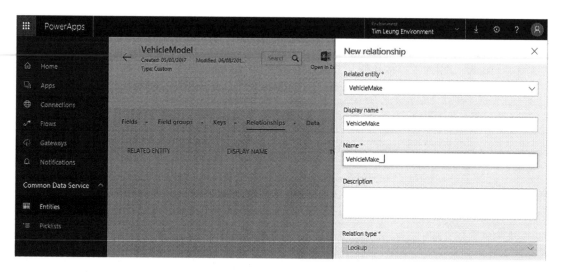

Figure 5-10. *Defining a relationship*

It's possible to define a relationship that references the same entity. In database terminology, this is called a self-join. A common use of this structure is to model hierarchical data, such as organizational charts. We can see an example of this in the standard Account entity, as shown in Figure 5-11. In this example, the entity uses a self-join to store the parent account for each account record.

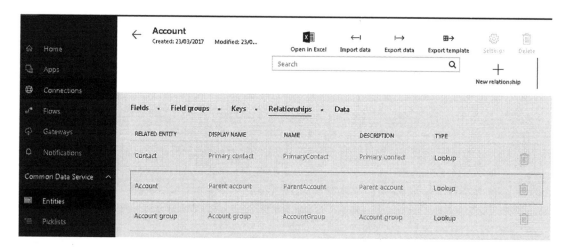

Figure 5-11. *An example of a self-join*

Deletion Behavior

To help maintain data integrity, the CDS prevents users from deleting parent records if related child records exist. So in this example, the CDS would prevent a user from deleting a 'vehicle make' record if vehicle model records exist that refer to the vehicle make record.

One important thing to be aware is how auto-generated apps behave when record deletion fails. If a user attempts to delete a record and the process fails because of related records, the app doesn't report this failure to the user.

Although PowerApps includes an errors collection to report data source errors, it won't report this particular type of error, and this can make it difficult to identify these types of errors.

Using Field Groups

We can organize fields with field groups. PowerApps includes a predefined set of field groups, and it uses these groups when we create an auto-generated app. Figure 5-12 shows the designer.

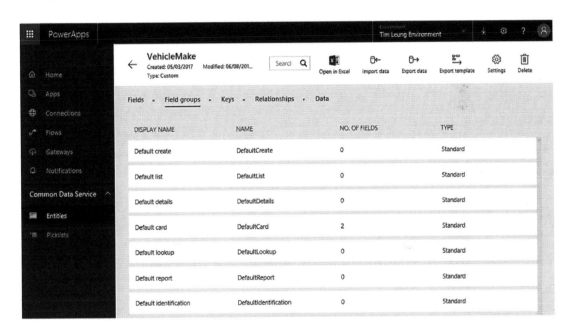

Figure 5-12. *Using Field Groups*

Two of the more useful groups are the 'default details' and 'default lookup' groups. What exactly are these field groups and how can they help us?

The 'default details' group helps us better manage entities that contain many fields. Take the standard Account entity as an example. This entity contains an enormous number of fields - 71 in total. It's unlikely that we would want to utilize all the fields in this entity. For example, the freight terms, Twitter identity, and stock ticker fields might be irrelevant for our needs. By adding only the fields we want to use to the 'default details' group, we can subsequently create an auto-generated app and PowerApps will create active card controls only for those fields that belong to the group.

The 'default lookup' group is also very useful because it defines which fields will appear in a drop-down control, if the entity were used as a lookup from a related entity.

Although field groups are useful, there are some limiting characteristics. We can only use the standard field groups that exist, and we can't create our own custom field groups. This means that when we create an auto-generated app, we can't choose which field group to use. The designer will always use the 'default details' field group.

Picklists

Picklists are lists of static data of that we can apply to fields in a CDS data source. When we add a field that is associated with a picklist to an app, we can limit the data values that a user can enter.

Picklists are ideal for common lists of data that we can apply to multiple entities. Examples include lists of colors, currency codes, or titles.

The common data model includes many predefined picklists, and some of these are illustrated in Figure 5-13. If a suitable picklist doesn't exist, we can create our own picklist.

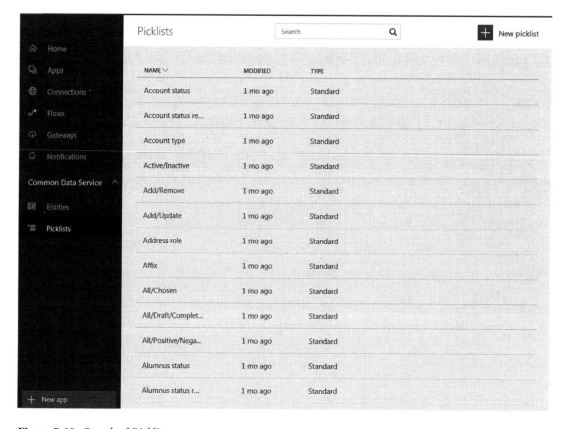

Figure 5-13. *Standard Picklists*

Here are some comments about picklist items. We can't add additional items to any of the standard picklists. For example, the account status picklist includes two values: Active and Inactive. If we want to add the value 'pending' to the list, this wouldn't be possible.

With a custom picklist, we have free reign to add whatever data values we choose. An administrator can add items to a picklist through the PowerApps web portal. End users cannot add picklist items through an app. Therefore, we should only use picklists to store static lists of data that are unlikely to change.

It is also not possible to sort the items that appear in a picklist. Therefore, if we want users to be able to add and sort list items, we should create custom entities for lookup values, rather than picklists.

■ **Note**   Use picklists to define static lists of data that will not change.

Creating a Picklist

To create a picklist, click the 'new picklist' button from the top of the page. This opens the new picklist panel, as shown in Figure 5-14.

Figure 5-14. *Adding a new picklist*

From this panel, we can enter a picklist name, display name, and description. The Name of a picklist cannot start with a number, and it cannot include spaces. The maximum length of a picklist name is 50 characters.

Adding Picklist Items

To add items to a picklist, click the Add item button that appears at the top of the picklist page. For each picklist item, we can enter a name, display name, and description (Figure 5-15). The name must start with a letter, and it cannot contain any spaces.

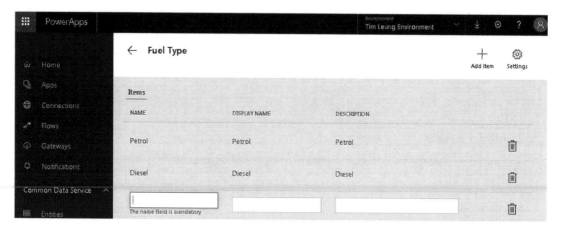

Figure 5-15. *Adding items to a picklist*

So what exactly is the difference between the name and display name for a picklist item? When we add a drop-down control to a screen in our app with the data source for the drop-down set to a picklist, the name values will appear as items in the drop-down. Also, if we were to export the data for an entity through the web portal, the output would include the picklist name value. This behavior seems unusual and may well be a bug in PowerApps. One would expect drop-down list items to show the display name value, rather than the name value.

However if we were to view the data for an entity through the data page in the entity designer, this output would show the picklist display name value against each row.

Applying Picklists to Fields

Once we define a picklist, we can apply our picklist to the fields in our entities. To do this, we would set the data type of our field to Picklist, as shown in Figure 5-16. Through the properties pane, we can then select our desired picklist.

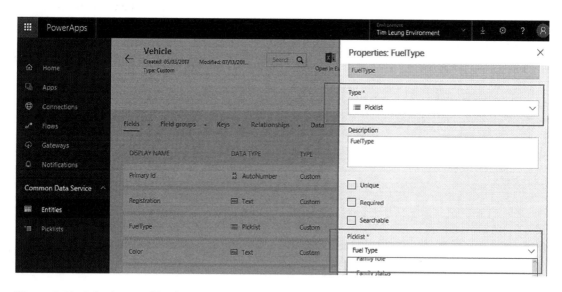

Figure 5-16. *Selecting a Picklist for use*

One final thing to mention about picklist data items is that unlike entity data, there isn't the option to export picklist values to an Excel spreadsheet. This may cause difficulties if we want to back up our picklist values, or to move data to a different environment.

Deleting a Picklist

To delete a custom picklist, click the garbage icon that appears in the top right of the picklist designer. To protect the integrity of our data, the CDS will prevent us from deleting a picklist if it is in use. In this scenario, the designer will display an error like the one that's shown in Figure 5-17.

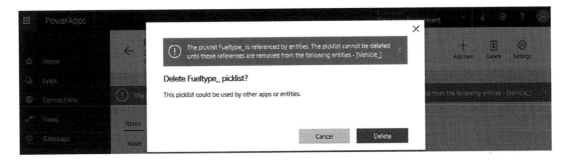

Figure 5-17. *Deleting a Picklist*

Deleting CDS Data

While on the topic of data deletion, the model database is preloaded with sample data. This sample data is really helpful for test purposes and for learning how to use the CDS. However, when we deploy an app that uses standard entities, we don't want our live application to be littered with dummy data. It can be difficult to delete this sample data because we need to delete any related data first in the correct sequence. As a tip, the quickest way to purge the database of sample data is to select the clear all data option from the top of the entity list, as shown in Figure 5-18.

Figure 5-18. *Deleting CDS data*

On-Premises Data Gateway

One of the most appealing features of PowerApps is the ability to build apps that can connect to SQL Server databases or SharePoint servers that are inside our internal network. The tool that enables us to do this is the on-premises data gateway.

Technically, here's how the gateway works. When an app queries an on-premises data source, the app passes the request to a cloud service called the Azure Data Bus. The on-premises gateway polls the Azure Data Bus regularly and responds to any requests that it finds. The on-premises gateway doesn't require any incoming ports. In most cases, it doesn't require any special firewall configuration. But if we install the gateway in a more secure environment, the online help provides the specific ports we need to open on our firewall.

One limitation is that the gateway works only with the default environment. This can be awkward because it prevents us from connecting to on-premises data from other environments, such as a test environment.

Installing the Gateway

To install the on-premises data gateway, the first step is to download the installer from the following web site: https://powerapps.microsoft.com/en-us/downloads/

Ideally, we should install the gateway on a computer with a fast Internet connection that is permanently switched on. We don't need to install the gateway on the same computer that runs SQL Server or SharePoint server. It's even possible to install the gateway on a workstation. The gateway is compatible with 64-bit versions of Windows only, and the minimum supported operating system is Windows 7.

During the installation, the installer prompts us to sign in with our Microsoft work account. Next, it prompts us to specify a gateway name and recovery key, as shown in Figure 5-19.

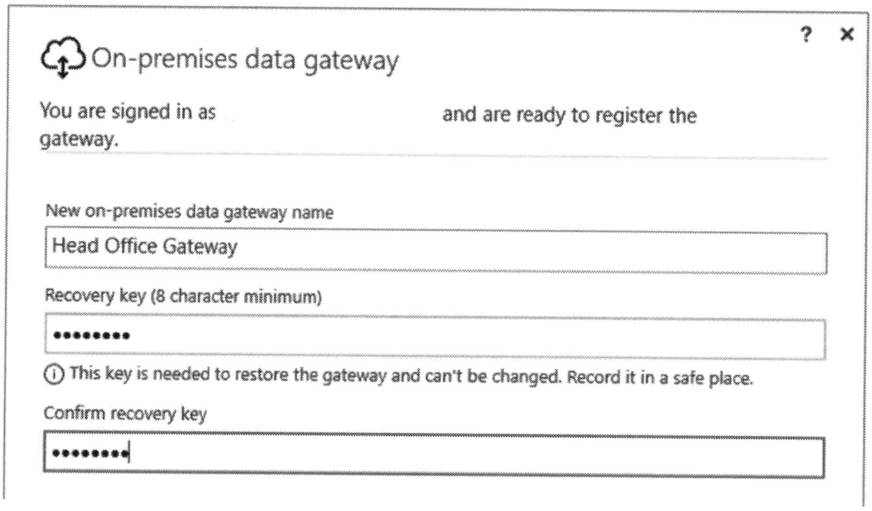

Figure 5-19. Configuring the gateway server

We can install multiple instances of the on-premises data gateway on different networks, so the gateway name enables us to identify the gateway when we make a connection from an app. The recovery key enables us to restore the gateway, and it's important to remember what we enter here. The reasons why we might need to restore the gateway service include hardware or operating system failure on the gateway computer. Microsoft also provides occasional bug fixes and updates to the gateway service. The recovery key would enable us to reinstall the gateway in this scenario.

Once we install the on-premise gateway, we can log onto the PowerApps portal and see the status of the gateway, as shown in Figure 5-20. We can use the status to determine if the gateway is operational. If the gateway computer were to lose Internet connectivity, we could detect this from the status page. From this page, we can also see the users and apps that are connected to the gateway, and we can also delete the gateway.

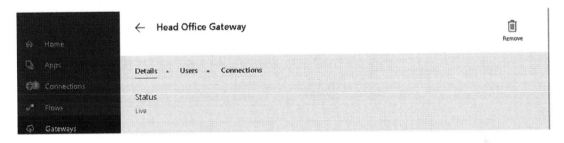

Figure 5-20. *Configuring the gateway server*

▓ **Note**   The on-premises data gateway works only with the default environment.

Starting the Gateway Service

The gateway runs as a Windows service and therefore, there is no specific program to manage the service. The place to manage the service is through the Services Snap-in, which we can find through the Windows Control Panel. The exact name of the service is the 'On-premises data gateway service', as shown in Figure 5-21.

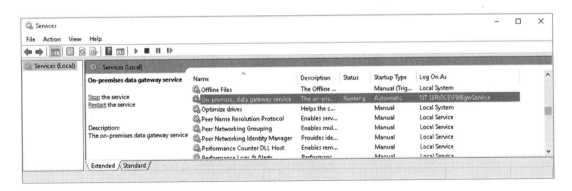

Figure 5-21. *Configuring the gateway service via Control Panel*

If the gateway fails to work, the first thing to check is that the service is running. By default, this service runs under an account called NT SERVICE\PBIEgwService. If the service fails to start with a logon failure, we can reset the service account password by clearing the password fields and applying the change (Figure 5-22). Alternatively, we can change the logon option to use a different account.

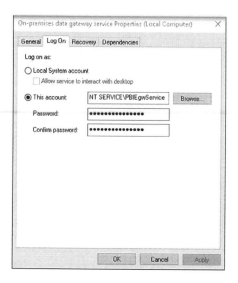

Figure 5-22. *Resetting the service account*

Connecting to a Data Source

Once we install the on-premises gateway, we can connect to an on-premises SQL Server or SharePoint data sources by simply adding a connection in our project, just like we would for any other data source.

Connecting to SQL Server

When we add a connection to a SQL server data source, PowerApps prompts us to enter the name of our SQL Server, as shown in Figure 5-23. If we want to connect to a named instance of SQL Server, we should provide the instance name in the box in the format 'MyServerServer\SQLInstanceName.'

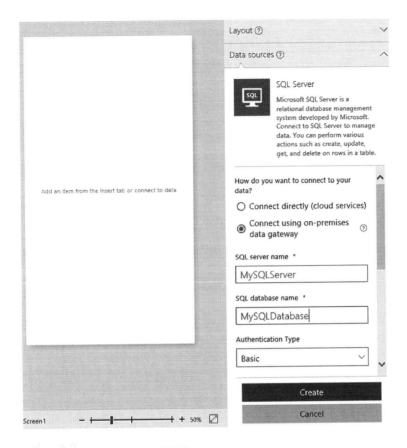

***Figure 5-23.** Connecting to SQL Server*

On this screen, we need to specify the login credentials to the SQL Server. Depending on how our target SQL Server is set up, we can connect either using Windows authentication, or SQL Server authentication (which is labeled Basic in the authentication type drop-down). Note that the credentials we enter here are encrypted and stored in the PowerApps gateway cloud service. The credentials are decrypted on the local computer that runs the gateway service.

Provided that all goes well, we should see the screen that's shown in Figure 5-24. This screen enables us to connect to a SQL table. Note that we can only connect to tables. The gateway doesn't support views, stored procedures, or functions. If we want to call a stored procedure, we can use Flow to do this. Also, there is a limit to the number of tables that the screen will show. If we connect to a database that contains approximately more than 1600 tables, not all the tables will appear. This is mostly a problem for users who want to connect to a Microsoft Dynamics SQL database, because it's not uncommon for these databases to contain several thousand tables.

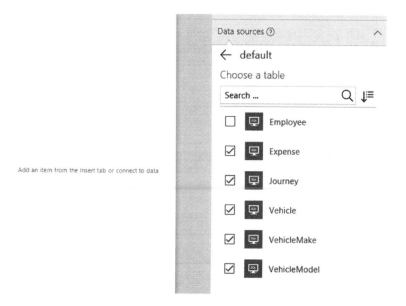

Figure 5-24. *Selecting SQL Server tables to use*

If the connection fails and you can't see the screen that's shown in Figure 5-24, try to use a different authentication type. If you used Windows authentication, try using SQL authentication instead. You can also try to use the IP address of the server, rather than the server name. If this fails, the next thing to do is to examine the gateway log files and the Windows event log.

One thing to be aware of is that the gateway doesn't support SQL Server tables with triggers. If we attempt to update data in a table where triggers are defined, the save operation will fail.

■ **Note**　The on-premises data gateway does not support tables with triggers, or SQL 2016 / SQL Azure temporal tables.

Uninstalling a Gateway

To uninstall the gateway, choose the uninstall option from the Programs and Features section of the Control Panel on the machine where the gateway is installed. When we uninstall the gateway service, the gateway will still appear in the Gateways section of the PowerApps web portal. This provides us with the option to install the gateway service on a new computer.

If we want to completely delete the gateway registration, we can do this from the web portal. Deleting a gateway won't delete any connections that use the gateway.

Using a SharePoint Data Source

A very common data source for PowerApps is SharePoint. We can easily connect to SharePoint Online in the cloud, or we can connect to an on-premises version of SharePoint via the on-premises Data Gateway. If you're completely new to SharePoint, this section provides a basic overview of how to set up a SharePoint list that works with PowerApps.

Creating a SharePoint List

Users with sufficient permissions in SharePoint can add a new list. A SharePoint list contains columns and Figure 5-25 shows the screen for creating new columns. The purpose of this screenshot is to illustrate the type of information we can store in a SharePoint list.

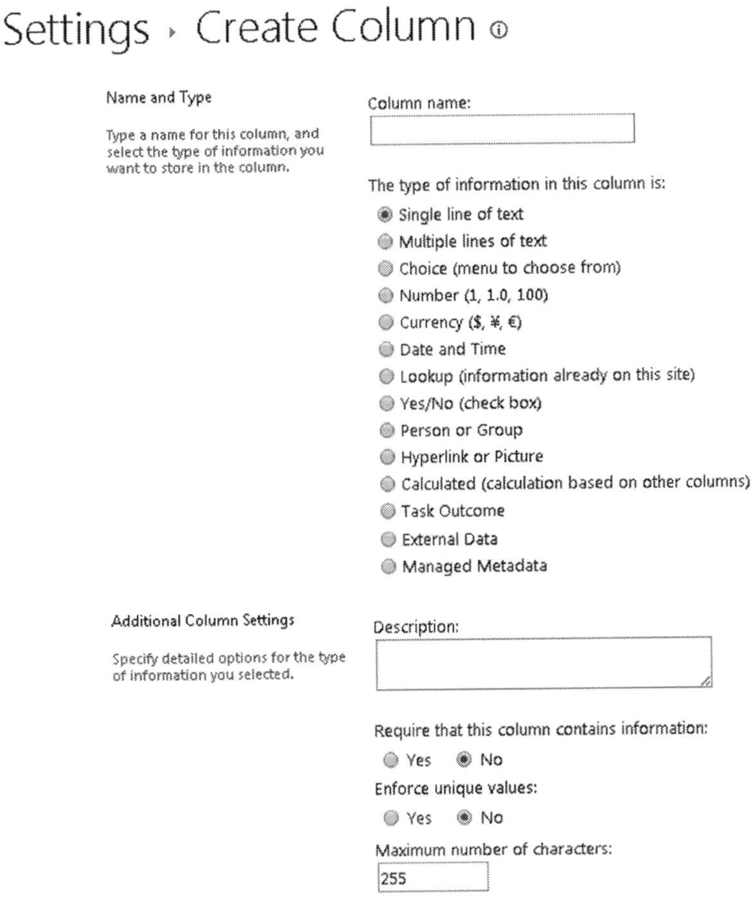

Figure 5-25. Creating a SharePoint Column

SharePoint can apply validation rules to columns, such as whether the data is mandatory, and the maximum number of characters that the field can store. PowerApps will honor the validation rules that are defined within SharePoint.

Apps work well with all the standard data types, including calculated types. However, one data type to be aware of is the 'Multiple lines of text' data type. With this data type, we can set the text type to rich text. Although PowerApps can display the rich text content without any difficulty, it doesn't include a rich text editor. This makes it very difficult for users to author rich text content.

Choice Items

We can limit the data that users can enter by defining Choice or Lookup columns. When we create an app that connects to one of these columns, PowerApps can populate drop-down boxes with the choice values to limit the values that a user can enter.

One thing to be aware of is that PowerApps doesn't support multiple selection choice columns, like the setup that's shown in Figure 5-26. On forms that bind to a data source with a multiple selection choice column, the screen designer won't create an auto-generated card for the column.

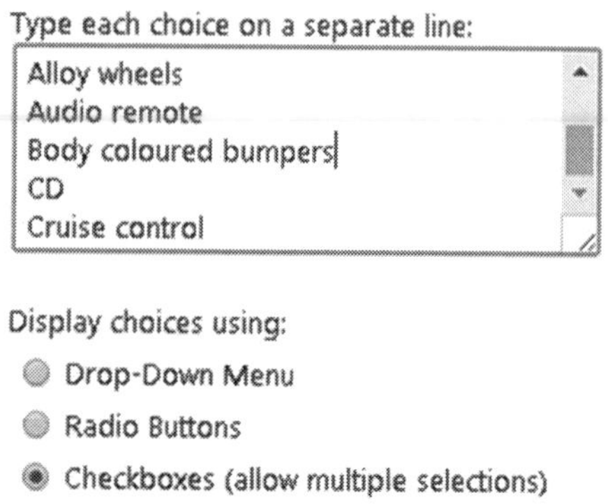

Type each choice on a separate line:

```
Alloy wheels
Audio remote
Body coloured bumpers|
CD
Cruise control
```

Display choices using:

○ Drop-Down Menu

○ Radio Buttons

◉ Checkboxes (allow multiple selections)

Figure 5-26. *SharePoint multiselection choice columns*

Connecting to a SharePoint Data Source

Just like all data sources, we can easily connect to SharePoint by adding a connection in our project. The first screen enables us to choose whether to connect to SharePoint online, or to connect to an on-premises instance of SharePoint, as shown in Figure 5-27. The next screen prompts us to enter the address of our SharePoint site and we should enter this in the format:

```
http://mysharepointserver.com/MySharePointSite
```

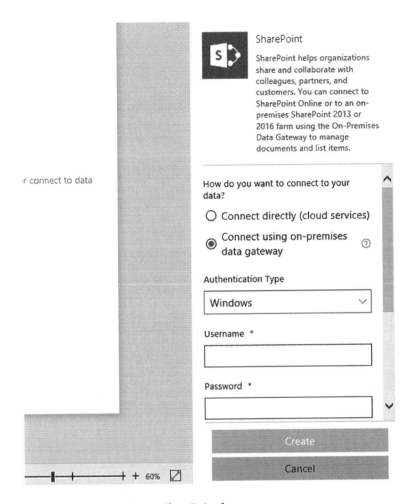

Figure 5-27. *Connecting to SharePoint from an app*

The next screen shows the lists in our site that we can connect to.

As you might recall, another way to create an auto-generated app from SharePoint Online is to use the PowerApps button that appears in the list page. This saves us from having to manually create a data connection. One thing to be aware of is that this feature can only create apps in the default environment. There isn't the option to choose which environment to use.

Other Data Sources

PowerApps supports a wide range of data sources and in the final part of this chapter, we'll look at two slightly unusual data sources – the Microsoft translator data source, and the MSN Weather data source.

Microsoft Translation Data Source

The Microsoft Translation service enables us to build multilingual apps. With this service, we can translate the data in our apps, as well the static user interface elements that make up the screens in our app. Here's a simple demonstration of how to translate the contents of a text input control from English to Spanish.

To use the Microsoft Translator service, the first step is to add a connection, as shown in Figure 5-28. Once we do this, we can write formula to carry out translations.

Figure 5-28. *Adding a connection to the Microsoft Translator service*

Figure 5-29 shows a screen with two text input controls called TextInputEnglish and TextInputSpanish. To configure the TextInputSpanish text input control so that it translates the English text that a user enters into the TextInputEnglish text input control, set the Text value of TextInputSpanish to:

```
MicrosoftTranslator.Translate(TextInputEnglish.Text, "ES")
```

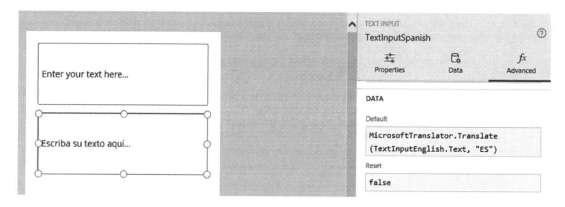

Figure 5-29. *Translating text from English to Spanish*

The Translate method accepts two arguments – the text to translate, and the target language. In this example, "ES" denotes the language code for Spanish.

If you were unfamiliar with this data source, how would you know the capabilities of the data source, and know what syntax to use? The key is to rely on the IntelliSense that the formula bar provides. When we type the name of the data source into the formula bar followed by the period symbol, the formula bar will show us a list of methods and provide a description of the arguments that we need to supply.

Microsoft MSN Weather Services

To demonstrate the capabilities of the MSN Weather Service, here's how to add a label that shows the current weather in London.

Unfortunately, many of the more unusual data connections are not well documented. Therefore, this example emphasizes the importance of using IntelliSense to determine the capabilities of the service and the correct syntax to use.

To create this example, add a label to a screen. Next, select the Text property and type the name of the data source MSNWeather into formula bar. At this point, IntelliSense reveals a method called CurrentWeather (Figure 5-30), in addition to methods to obtain forecasts for today and tomorrow. If we choose the CurrentWeather method, IntelliSense prompts us to provide a location and to specify the measurement units for our results. We can choose either metric or imperial.

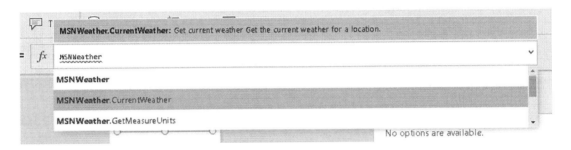

Figure 5-30. *Determining the method names*

If we leave the formula bar at this point, we'll discover that this syntax isn't complete. The designer underlines the formula with a red line, and shows the exact error when we hover the mouse over the exclamation point icon, as shown in Figure 5-31.

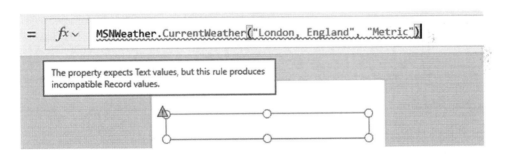

Figure 5-31. *Hover the mouse over the exclamation point icon to see the exact error*

To resolve these problems, the trick is to add a full stop character to the end of the formula to see what IntelliSense suggests (Figure 5-32). By using this technique, we can discover that the correct syntax is:

```
MSNWeather.CurrentWeather("London, England", "Metric").responses.weather.current.temp
```

Figure 5-32. *Use IntelliSense to determine the correct syntax*

When we enter the correct formula, PowerApps immediately calls the weather service and displays the temperature in the design view of the screen.

To summarize the MSN Weather service, we can obtain the current weather by calling a function called CurrentWeather. This function expects two arguments – the location and our preferred weather units. We can provide our location in the format "city, country," or we can specify our location with longitude and latitude values.

■ **Tip**   If the designer underlines a formula with a scribbly red line and you don't understand why, try adding a period to the end of the formula to see if IntelliSense can provide any additional suggestions.

Summary

With PowerApps, we can connect to a wide range of data sources. In this chapter, we looked at how to connect to some of the most common data sources – the Common Data Service, SQL Server, and SharePoint.

The Common Data Service provides cloud-based database storage. Databases are connected to environments, and each environment can have a maximum of one database. Of all the data sources, the CDS is the easiest to connect to because it forms an integral part of the environment. Therefore, there's no need to specify database names or to provide additional authentication details to create a connection to a CDS data source. A feature of the CDS is that it provides pre-built data models that we can utilize. Say if we want to build a sales or customer service app, the data structures to support those types of app are already there.

With the CDS, we define entities to store our data. Conceptually, an entity is equivalent to a database table. For each entity, we can create fields to define the pieces of data to store for each row of data. Some points to be aware of is that the CDS doesn't support text fields that exceed 2048 characters. Also, it doesn't support the storage of binary data. With CDS entities, we can define lookup fields by defining relationships between entities, or by creating picklists.

We can easily connect to a CDS database from PowerBI and Flow. However, it's difficult to connect to our data from other products, and there is no built-in backup mechanism for our data. The amount of storage space is connected to the number of licenses we have. Therefore, we need to consider whether the CDS provides sufficient storage capacity before we choose to use it.

Another popular data storage choice is SharePoint. SharePoint is simple to use because users can easily define lists through the web-based SharePoint interface. SharePoint provides storage for a wide range of data types, including text and numeric types. The benefit of SharePoint over the CDS is that we can store text data that exceeds 2048 characters. The text columns in SharePoint support rich text. This is text that users can format with different colors, sizes, or styles. Although PowerApps can display rich text from a SharePoint data source, it doesn't include a control for users to edit rich text. With both SharePoint and the CDS, we can limit the data values that user can enter by defining choice lists.

A great feature of PowerApps is the ability to connect to SQL Server or SharePoint data sources from internal company networks. The tool that enables this is the on-premises data gateway. This is a service that runs on a computer inside a local network. The on-premises data gateway is the perfect choice if we need to connect to existing company data. One slight limitation is that service only works with the default environment. Therefore, we cannot connect to SQL Server or other internal data sources from apps in other environments.

In the final part of this chapter, we looked at two slightly unusual data sources – the Microsoft Translator and MSN weather data sources. With these two data sources, we can translate data and obtain the current weather. The point of this section is to emphasize the range of data sources that we can use. Many of these data connectors are not well documented. Therefore, a helpful tip is to use IntelliSense to determine the capabilities of the data source and to work out the correct syntax to use.

CHAPTER 6

Using Formulas

PowerApps is similar to Excel because it uses formulas to carry out tasks. Formulas are the lifeblood of an app that enables us to add features to an app. One challenge is that many functions exist and it's difficult to appreciate how these functions apply in practical terms. Therefore, this chapter provides usage examples of the most useful functions in PowerApps.

The layout of this chapter is split into three main sections. In the first part of this chapter, we'll look at how to write formulas and how to use variables. Variables are crucial because they enable us to assign property values in PowerApps. The next part of the chapter provides a reference guide that lists the most useful functions, along with usage examples. In the final part of this chapter, we'll find out how to configure the startup behavior of an app, and we'll look at techniques that we can use to provide screen navigation. The useful topics that we'll cover will include the following:

- How to call functions that apply to text, number, and date values. We'll look at pattern matching techniques to help verify the format of input data. This technique enables us to validate social security numbers, postal codes, phone numbers, and more. We'll also cover text formatting and mathematical tasks, including date arithmetic and trigonometric functions.

- How to work with collections and tables of data. To illustrate how to apply bulk operations to multiple rows, we'll convert a table of mileages from miles to kilometers with just a single formula. For more complex tasks, we'll look at how to carry out row-by-row processing. We'll also find out how to calculate the average, minimum, maximum, and other aggregate values from a set of data.

- How to build navigation features. We'll find out how to build custom screen navigation menus. We'll look at how to launch websites, compose emails, send SMS messages, and much more from within PowerApps. We'll also build an app that can optionally show a specified record at startup, and we'll examine what happens when PowerApps encounters errors in formulas.

Writing Formulas

The first part of this chapter covers some elementary characteristics that are related to formulas. To illustrate these points, let's examine the formula from the `OnSelect` property of the edit icon from the details screen in an auto-generated app (Figure 6-1). The purpose of this formula is set the edit form on the edit screen to edit mode, and to navigate the user to the edit screen.

© Tim Leung 2017
T. Leung, *Beginning PowerApps*, https://doi.org/10.1007/978-1-4842-3003-9_6

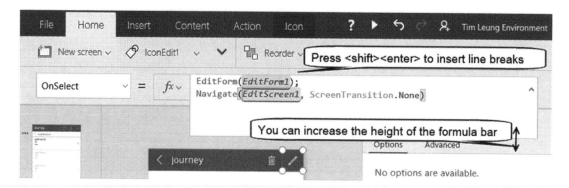

Figure 6-1. *Formula bar*

As this example highlights, formulas can include calls to several functions and each function is separated by a semicolon. Each function executes synchronously. That is, PowerApps will complete the execution of a single command before it moves onto the next command.

Often, it can be difficult to read and interpret very long formulas. As Figure 6-1 shows, we can use the mouse to extend the height of the formula bar. We can also insert line breaks by typing <shift><enter>. Both techniques can make it easier to edit and read formulas.

The standard Windows shortcuts also work in the formula bar. We can use <ctrl><c> to copy formulas into the Windows clipboard, and <ctrl><v> to paste the text from the clipboard. To edit very long formula, it's sometimes easier to copy the contents into Microsoft Notepad, make the modifications outside of the formula bar, and to paste the completed formula back into the formula bar. This is because the formula bar can react slowly as it tries to offer inline help, and this can make it difficult to select specific parts of a formula.

There are two important points to be aware of when writing formula. The first is that all function names and objects are case sensitive.

The second is that certain languages (for example, French) use the comma symbol as the decimal point separation character. To enable these non-English users to specify decimal values in formulas, PowerApps requires these users to use semicolons in places where we would normally use a comma. The knock-on effect is that PowerApps requires multiple functions in a formula to be separated by two semicolons, rather than a single semicolon. This behavior is important for non-English readers because most articles and code samples on the Web follow the English convention, and non-English users will encounter errors if they follow such code samples exactly.

Using the Function Tool

The designer provides a drop-down panel that provides additional assistance (Figure 6-2). This panel makes it easier to locate functions by grouping sets of related functions together. The formula bar also includes code coloration and offers help through IntelliSense. IntelliSense provides inline help and suggests the arguments that a function expects.

Figure 6-2. *Using the function tool*

ThisItem/Parent Syntax

Two useful keywords that don't appear in the drop-down panel are ThisItem and Parent. These keywords are applicable from inside the form control, as shown in Figure 6-3.

For controls that are nested inside cards, the Parent keyword references the properties of the card that contains the control.

The ThisItem keyword is particularly useful because it enables us to retrieve the field values from the record that is bound to the form.

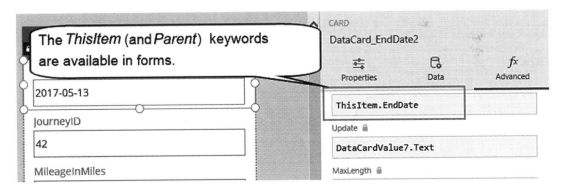

Figure 6-3. *Use the ThisItem keyword to refer to data values in form controls*

Working with Variables

Variables are a core component of all programming languages. They help us build functionality by storing working copies of data. With PowerApps, variables are very important because they enable us to set property values. You'll understand what this means exactly by the end of this section.

Variables have a *scope*. This defines the boundary from which we can access a variable. We can create variables that are accessible from individual screens only, or variables that are accessible throughout an app.

Unlike other systems, PowerApps is relaxed in the way that it deals with variables. We don't need to declare variables beforehand, nor do we need to specify the data type of a variable.

Setting Screen Variables

Screen-level variables are called *context variables*. This name derives from the fact that we can access these variables only within the context of a screen. Here's how to create a context variable called RecordCount and to set the value to 0:

```
UpdateContext({ RecordCount: 0 })
```

UpdateContext is the function that sets the value of a variable. Readers with the experience of using other programming languages might be tempted to use syntax that looks like this:

```
RecordCount = 0
```

With PowerApps, this syntax is not valid. The UpdateContext function is the only way to set the value of a context variable.

When this function first runs, the UpdateContext function creates the RecordCount variable if it doesn't exist. A very interesting and useful characteristic is that context variables can store more than just simple numbers and strings. We can store records and tables in context variables and this can be very powerful.

Once we run our app and call the UpdateContext function, the variable will appear in the variables section of the app, as shown in Figure 6-4. This screen is very helpful because it summarizes all the places that set or retrieve the variable.

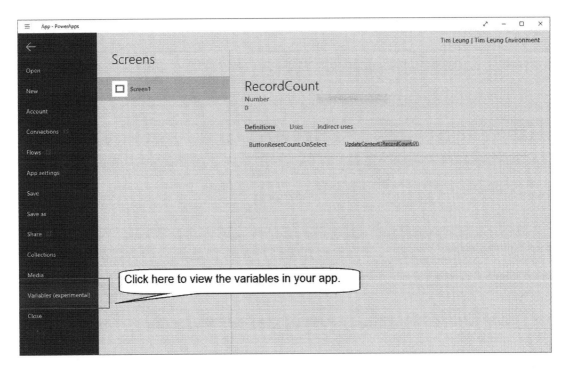

Figure 6-4. *Viewing the variables in an application*

Passing Values to Screens

Another way to set context variables is through the Navigate function. We can use this technique to supply values to a screen when it opens. The syntax we would use looks like this:

```
Navigate(BrowseScreen1, ScreenTransition.Fade, {RecordCount:0})
```

In this example, the Navigate function opens a screen called BrowseScreen1 and sets the value of the RecordCount context variable to 0.

When we build apps with screen navigation and context variables, there's an important piece of behavior to be aware of. When PowerApps switches the currently visible screen, it doesn't completely close the existing screen. Instead, the existing screen becomes invisible and remains active in the background. If a user opens other screens and returns to a screen that was previously open, the screen will retain the context variable values that were previously set. This might result in some unexpected behavior and is something to be aware of.

Example of Context Variables

So why would we want to use context variables? To better understand the capabilities of context variables, let's examine the sort button on a browse screen, as shown in Figure 6-5.

Figure 6-5. *The sort button on a browse screen updates a variable*

The purpose of this button is to toggle the sort order of the data. The OnSelect action of this button calls the following function:

```
UpdateContext({SortDescending1: !SortDescending1})
```

This code sets the value of the SortDescending1 variable to the logical negative of the current value. The initial state of the SortDescending1 variable is false. The ! operator returns true if its argument is false, and returns false if its argument is true. Therefore, the effect of this code is to toggle the value of the SortDescending1 variable.

Now that we see how the SortDescending1 variable is set, how exactly does the screen use this variable? The Items property of the gallery control refers to the SortDescending1 variable, as shown in Figure 6-6.

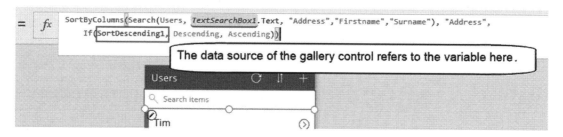

Figure 6-6. *The Items property of the gallery control*

As this screenshot shows, a function called SortByColumns populates the items of the gallery control. This function expects three arguments - a data source, the column to sort by, and the sort direction.

The data source for the SortByColumns function is the result of a function called Search. This function accepts a data source, a search term, and the columns to match against. The second argument to the SortByColumns function defines the column to a sort by - address, in this example. The final argument specifies the sort direction. This can be one of two values - Descending or Ascending.

The sort direction argument refers to the function called If. This function enables us to run commands conditionally. The syntax of the If function is this:

```
If ( logical test, action(s) to run if true, action(s) to run if false)
```

In this example, the If function checks the value of the SortDescending1 variable. If the value of this is true, it returns the result Descending. Otherwise, it returns the result Ascending.

■ **Note**   Context variables and the If function are two essential features that enable us to build apps with any reasonable functionality. Even the simplest apps rely heavily on these structures, and we can see evidence of this throughout all the sample apps that Microsoft provides.

Setting Property Values from Code

What we're about to cover here is a very important concept, perhaps the most important concept in this book. With PowerApps, we can't use formulas to assign property values from other objects. To illustrate this, let's build a simple *Hello World* program - a program that teaches programmers the very basics of a language.

To build this feature, we'll create a screen and add two controls: a label called LabelHello and a button called ButtonSayHello. The aim of this program is to show the text "Hello World" in the label when a user clicks the button. Let's attempt to build this feature by setting the OnSelect property of the button to the following formula:

```
LabelHello.Text = "Hello World"
```

As Figure 6-7 shows, this code looks OK. The designer doesn't underline the formula with a squiggly red line, and it doesn't show a warning icon next to the control. What do you think will happen when we click the button? Will the text "Hello Word" appear in the label?

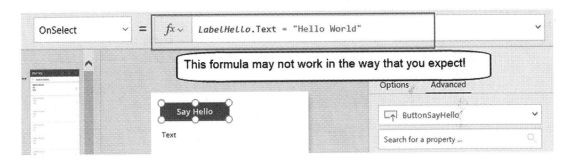

Figure 6-7. *Screen with a button and label*

The answer to this question is no. When we run this app and click the button, nothing happens. The reason for this is that we cannot assign property values in this way. This syntax is not valid.

So how do we overcome this problem? The answer is to use variables. To fix this example, we would write formula in the OnSelect property of the button that sets the value of a variable. The code would look like this:

```
UpdateContext({LabelText:"Hello World"})
```

We would then set the text property of the label to the name of this variable (LabelText in this example).

This is one of the most useful techniques in PowerApps because it enables us to make property assignments. When I began using PowerApps, I found it curious why we couldn't assign property values with formulas. To make sense of why PowerApps behaves like this, it can help to recognize that Excel behaves in exactly the same way. To illustrate this point, in Excel, we can't write a formula in the A2 cell to set the value of the A1 cell, using the type of formula that's shown in Figure 6-8.

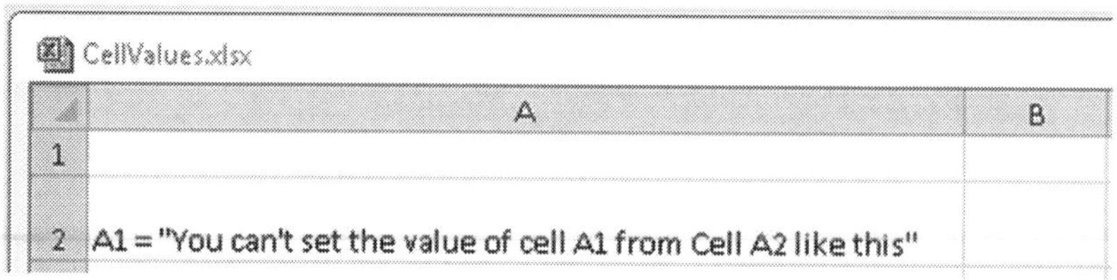

Figure 6-8. *In Excel, we can't assign cell values from other cells*

Setting Global Variables

In addition to context variables, we can store values in global variables. The main difference between a global variable and a context variable is that we can access global variables throughout an app rather than only on the screen where we define the variable. In addition to simple strings and numbers, we can store records, tables, and object references in global variables. Compared to context variables, the syntax to set a variable value is much simpler. Here's how to define a global variable called RecordCount, and to set the value to 8:

```
Set(RecordCount, 8)
```

Unlike the UpdateContext function, notice that there's no need to enclose the variable name and value within curly brackets. Once we define a global variable, we can refer to it by name in the formula.

The name of a global variable cannot match the name of an existing data source or collection. However, it can share the same name as a context variable on a screen. To clarify how to distinguish between variables that are named identically, let's suppose that we declare a context variable on the same screen using the following syntax:

```
UpdateContext({RecordCount:5})
```

In this scenario, RecordCount will refer to the context variable. To refer to the global variable with the same name, we would use the syntax: [@RecordCount].

A final point is that in cases where we set a global variable in multiple places, we must always assign values with matching data types. The designer will show a warning if we attempt to assign a value to a global variable that doesn't match the data type of a value that we assigned elsewhere. In these cases, it may help to pass the value that we want to store through a data type conversion function such as Value or Text. This ensures that we consistently store values of the same type in the global variable. The Value function converts an input value to a number whereas the Text function converts an input value to text.

Manipulating Data

In this section of the book, we'll examine the most helpful functions in PowerApps. We'll cover functions that help us manipulate text, numbers, and collections of data. This section serves a useful reference guide that we can refer to throughout the rest of this book. We'll begin by looking at how to work with text.

Working with Text

A fundamental part of building an app involves working with text data (also known as string data). The elementary things to know about this topic are the following:

- Defining strings - To specify a piece of text in a formula, we must enclose the text inside double quotes. To include a double quote within a string, we can use a double set of double quotes instead.

- New lines - To introduce a new line into a string, type <Shift><Enter> into the formula bar. Alternatively, we can use the Char function. Char(10) represents a carriage return and Char(13) represents a line feed.

- String concatenation – To combine strings, use the & operator.

- Char function – We can call this function to obtain a character by ASCII code.

To highlight these techniques, Figure 6-9 shows a formula that sets the text of a label. This formula illustrates the basic concepts that are described here.

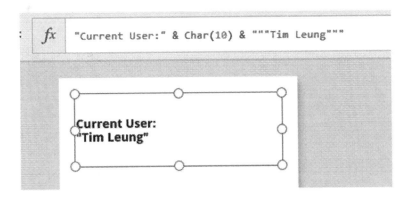

Figure 6-9. *Using the Char function, and escaping double quote characters*

▓ **Tip**   To display richly formatted text on a screen, construct HTML and display it with the HTML text control, rather than use the label control.

Text Manipulation Functions

Here are the functions we can use to manipulate text:

- Text – Use this to convert numbers, dates, and other data types to text

- PlainText – Call this function to strip the HTML and XML tags from an input string

- HashTags - Call this function to extract the hashtags (#hashtag) from a string

The Text function is extremely useful because we can use it to convert numbers to text. To build a string that includes numbers (for example, to display in a label), we would need to call this function to convert the numbers to text.

The HashTags function is useful for social media scenarios. It extracts the hashtags from a string, and returns the result in a single column table. This table will contain one row for each hashtag.

Text Extraction Functions

PowerApps provides functions to extract characters from an input string. The Left and Right functions return portions of a string, starting from the left or the right. The Mid function returns a portion from the middle of the string, and the Len function returns the length of a string. Table 6-1 shows the output of these functions when provided with the input string: "The quick brown fox jumps over the lazy dog".

Table 6-1. *Text manipulation functions*

Function	Output
Left("The quick brown fox",5)	The q
Right("The quick brown fox",5)	n fox
Mid("The quick brown fox",5,5)	quick
Len("The quick brown fox")	19

To clarify how these functions work, the Mid function expects three arguments: an input string, a start position, and number of characters to extract. The start position refers to the number of characters from the left. This number is 1 based, rather than 0 based. Therefore, 1 represents the position at the very start of the string. If we supply a start position that exceeds the length of the string, the Mid function returns an empty string and will not cause any exceptions. This behavior is useful to know because if the input string comes from the user, the length of the input string may be unknown.

The Len function returns the length of a string. The return value includes any leading or trailing spaces. If we provide either a null value or an empty string, the function will return 0.

A useful tip is that with all these functions, we can supply a single value, or we can supply a single column table. The ability to pass a single column table to a function is very powerful because it enables us to carry out bulk operations on multiple values. When we pass a single column table to a function, the output from the function will be a single column table.

PowerApps provides a couple of functions to remove spaces from an input string. These two functions are called Trim and TrimEnds. The difference between these two functions is that Trim removes extra spaces from the start, end, and throughout the content of a string, whereas TrimEnds removes trailing spaces from the end of a string only.

Modifying the Casing of Sentences

The three functions that modify the casing of sentences are Upper, Lower, and Proper. The Upper function coverts all the characters from an input string to upper case. Conversely, the Lower function coverts all the characters from an input string to lower case.

The Proper function converts the first letter of every word in a sentence to uppercase, and converts the remaining characters to lowercase. Here's an example of how to call this function:

```
Proper ("tim leung")
```

The result of this function returns "Tim Leung". As this example highlights, a perfect use of this function is to clean up the names and addresses that users enter on data input screens. On mobile devices, users often enter data all in lower case because of the awkwardness of using a soft keyboard.

Searching Within Strings

There are two functions we can call to search the contents of a string: Find and StartsWith. The Find function checks if one string appears within another and we can optionally provide a start position. The call beneath returns the value 5.

```
Find("quick", "The quick brown fox", 1)
```

In this example, the function searches for the word "quick" within the sentence "The quick brown fox". The call to this function includes the optional starting position of 1. The search that the Find function carries out is case sensitive. If it fails to find the search string, it returns an empty string.

The StartsWith function checks if a string begins with a specified piece of text. This function expects two arguments: - the text to search, and the starting piece of text. This function returns true or false. Unlike the Find function, the search that StartsWith carries out is not case sensitive. In the call shown beneath, the function will return true.

```
StartsWith("The quick brown fox","THE")
```

Matching with Regular Expressions

In addition to the Find and StartsWith functions, PowerApps enables us to carry out advanced pattern matching searches with regular expressions. A question that you might have is, what are regular expressions? You've probably encountered search systems where you specify wildcard characters in the search criteria. Regular expressions enable us to carry out this type of matching, but in a much more powerful way.

Regular expressions offer a perfect way to validate user input, such as email addresses, telephone numbers, and social security numbers. The function that provides regular expression matching is called IsMatch.

It can be difficult to learn how to build regular expressions. Therefore, a simple method is to visit websites that contain libraries of regular expressions that we can reuse. One such website is www.regexlib.com.

To demonstrate the use of regular expression matching, here's how to confirm that a social security number is valid. The first step is to find a regular expression, and Figure 6-10 shows one of the search results from www.regexlib.com.

▣	**Title**	**US SSN pattern match**	Details	Test
▣	**Expression**	\b(?!000)(?!666)(?!9)[0-9]{3}[-]?(?!00)[0-9]{2}[-]?(?!0000)[0-9]{4}\b		

Description	Finds 9 digit numbers within word boundaries, not separated or separated by - or space, not starting with 000, 666, or 900-999, not containing 00 or 0000 in the middle or at the end of SSN (in compliance with current SSN rules).	
Matches	123-45-6789, 123 45 6789, 123456789, 123-45 6789, 123-456789, 123 456789, etc.	
Non-Matches	000-45-6789, 666-45-6789, 123-00-6789, 123-45-0000, 900-45-6789 through 999-45-6789	
▣ **Author**	**Jeff Pentz**	Rating: ▭▭▭▭▭

Figure 6-10. *Use the Web to find regular expressions*

Once we find a suitable regular expression, we can pass this to the IsMatch function to validate social security numbers. Here's how to call this function to validate the social security number "123-45-6789":

```
IsMatch("123-45-6789",
        "\b(?!000)(?!666)(?!9)[0-9]{3}[ -]?(?!00)[0-9]{2}[ -]?(?!0000)[0-9]{4}\b")
```

The first argument in this example defines the social security number to check. The second argument contains the regular expression from www.regexlib.com. The result from this example returns true because the social security number matches a valid format.

Note that for simpler matching, we can call the IsMatch function and build an expression with one of the predefined patterns from the Match namespace. Figure 6-11 shows some of these predefined patterns.

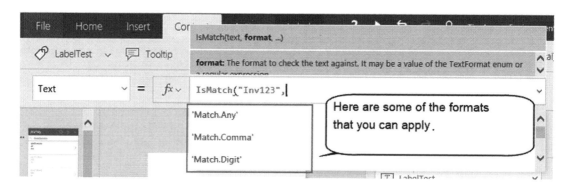

Figure 6-11. *Using a predefined expression*

As an example, if we want to confirm that the input text "Inv123" contains three letters followed by three numbers, we could use the formula that's shown beneath. In this example, the function would return true.

```
IsMatch("Inv123", Match.Letter & Match.Letter & Match.Letter & Match.Digit & Match.Digit & Match.Digit)
```

Replacing Text

PowerApps provides two functions to carry out text replacements - `Replace` and `Substitute`. These functions sound similar, so what are the differences between these functions?

The `Replace` function performs a single replacement and requires us to provide a numeric start position, and the numeric length of the text that we want to replace. The example beneath would return the string "The quick red fox".

```
Replace("The quick brown fox", 11, 5, "red")
```

To clarify the usage of this function, the first argument defines the input string. The second argument defines the start position for the text we want to replace, and the third argument specifies the length of the text that we want to replace. The final argument specifies the replacement text.

If we were to provide a start position that exceeds the length of the string, how do you think this function would behave? The answer is that the function would return the input string with the replacement text appended to the end.

The Substitute function enables us to substitute characters from an input string with a different set of characters. Unlike the replace function, we don't need to provide numeric positions. By default, the function substitutes every instance of the old text value with the new text value. The example below would return the string "The quick brown fox jumped over a lazy dog".

Substitute("The quick brown fox jumped over the lazy dog", "the", "a")

The first argument to the Substitute function defines the input string. The second argument defines the text to replace, and the third argument specifies the replacement text. If the input string contains more than one instance of the text that we want to replace, we can specify which instance to replace by optionally supplying a fourth argument that defines the instance number.

An important point this example highlights is that the `Substitute` function is case sensitive. Notice how the function doesn't replace the first instance of the word "The" in the sentence.

Working with Numbers

PowerApps provides a wide range of mathematical functions and in this section, we'll look at how to work with numbers. Starting with the basics, PowerApps provides basic arithmetic operators that include add (+), subtract (-), multiply (*), and divide (/).

To demonstrate a simple mathematical task, here's a simple screen that converts miles to kilometers. This screen contains a text input control that accepts a value in miles. When the user enters a value, the result in kilometers will appear instantly in a label. Figure 6-12 illustrates this screen. The name of the text input control is `TextInputMiles`, and the name of the label that displays the result is `LabelResult`.

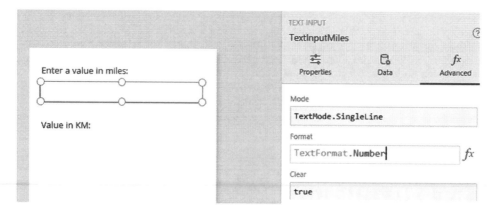

Figure 6-12. *An example screen to convert Miles to kilometers*

To implement this functionality, set the text property of LabelResult to the following formula:

```
"Value in KM: " & Value(TextInputMiles.Text) * 1.60934
```

This formula calculates the value in kilometers by multiplying the input value by 1.60934. The formula prefixes this result with the text: "Value in KM: "

This example highlights two useful points about using user input for calculations. The first is the use of the Value function. The data that we retrieve from the text input control is of type text. It's not possible to perform mathematical operations on text data, so we must convert the input data to the numeric representation. This is what the Value function does.

The second point is that with the text input control, we can set the format property to TextFormat. Number. This setting prevents users from entering non-numeric figures by configuring the control to accept only numbers.

Formatting Numbers

A common requirement is to format numbers in a certain way. We can accomplish this by calling the Text function. This function accepts two arguments - an input value, and a format string. Taking the example from the previous section, we can format the result to two decimal places by using the formula shown beneath:

```
"Value in KM: " & Text(Value(TextInputMiles.Text) * 1.60934, "#.##")
```

In this example, the string to format a number to two decimal places is "#.##". The # character defines a numeric placeholder. If the input value contains a number that maps to the position where the # character appears, the output will include the value. If not, nothing will appear. As an example, if we were to format the value 8.5 using the same format string, the output would be 8.5, and not 8.50.

In cases where we want to display preceding or trailing zeros, we would use the placeholder symbol 0, rather than #. We can also the use the comma symbol to format a number that includes thousand value separators. Here's an example:

```
Text(60934.2, "#,#.000")
```

In this example, the output of the function would be 6,0934.200. One other useful point is that we can add currency symbols to a format string. We can also specify a language tag to format a result for a particular region. Take the following example:

```
Text(60934.2, "[$-en-GB]#,#.00", "fr-FR")
```

This example would produce the result "60 934,20". To clarify how this works, the second argument specifies a region for the format specification, and the third argument defines the output region. So in this example, we are asking the Text function to return the French equivalent of the British format string "#,#.00". As the result shows, the function produces a result with a space character as the thousand separator, and a comma as the decimal point separator.

Rounding Functions

There are three functions to carry out rounding operations. These are Round, RoundUp, and RoundDown. These functions accept an input value, and the number of decimal places to round to. The RoundUp function rounds up the input value to the specified number of decimal place, whereas the RoundDown function rounds down the input value to the specified number of decimal place. The Round function performs arithmetic rounding on the input value. Here's an example:

```
Round(85.665,2)
```

This example rounds the value 85.665 to two decimal places. The result of this function is 85.67. One thing to be aware of is that unlike rounding functions that we might find in other systems, the round function performs arithmetic rounding rather than bankers rounding. Bankers rounding prevents the upward bias that occurs when rounding up as soon the minor fractional unit reaches 5. It does this by rounding to the nearest even number.

If we were to perform the same calculation in an Excel macro using the VBA (Visual Basic for Applications) version of the Round function, the return value would be 85.66, compared to the 85.67 value that PowerApps returns. If you're familiar with using Excel macros to round numbers, it's useful to understand that the result in Excel may be different to the result in PowerApps.

Trigonometric Functions

PowerApps provides the standard trigonometric functions Cos, Cot, Sin, and Tan. These functions accept an input angle in radians, and return the result of the trigonometric operation.

We can also call the inverse trigonometric functions, which are Acos, Acot, Asin, and Atan. With these functions, we can calculate arccosine, arccotangent, arcsine, and arctangent values. These functions accept an input value, and return the result of the function in radians. With all these trigonometric functions, we can supply a single value, or we can supply a single column table.

There are two functions to covert values between degrees and radians. The Degrees function converts an angle in radians to degrees, and the Radians function converts an angle in degrees to radians.

Finally, the Pi function returns the value of π – the number that begins with 3.14159.

Other Mathematical Functions

Other mathematical functions that are available are shown in Table 6-2. This table provides a description of the functions, and provides us with examples of how to call the functions, and the expected output.

Table 6-2. *Mathematical functions*

Example Function Call	Function Description	Example Output Value
Abs(-80)	Absolute positive value	80
Exp (5)	e raised to the power of 5	148.41315910
Ln(50)	Natural logarithm (base e) of 50	3.91202301
Power(8, 3)	8 raised to the power of 3 (8*8*8)	512
Sqrt(3)	Square root of 3	1.73205081

Working with Dates

PowerApps provides functions to help us work with dates and times. Here are the functions that retrieve the current date and time:

- Now – this function returns the current date and time

- Today – this function returns the current date with the time set to midnight

To create a date, we would call the Date function. This function accepts year, month, and day arguments, and returns a date with the time set to midnight. Here's an example of how to create a date set to the value of July 12th 2017:

```
Date(2017,7,12)
```

To create a time object, we would call the Time function. This function accepts hour, minute, second, and millisecond arguments. Here's an example of how to create a time object, set to the value of 2:15PM

```
Time(14,15,0,0)
```

Notice how the Date function doesn't allow us to specify a time element. It will always create a date with the time set to midnight. If we want to create a date object with specific date and time values, we can call the DateTimeValue function. This function accepts a string argument and returns a date object. Here's an example of how to create a date object with the value set to July 12th 2017, 12:15 PM:

```
DateTimeValue ("12/07/2017 12:15 PM",  "en-GB")
```

In this example, we provide a language code to specify that the input date is in British format (that is, day/month/year). This language code argument is optional. If we don't specify a language code, the function will use the locale of the current user.

Two other useful conversion functions are DateValue and TimeValue. The DateValue function accepts an input string and returns a date object. The TimeValue function accepts an input string and returns a time object.

One reason why these string to date and time functions are useful is because PowerApps doesn't include a stand-alone time picker control. Therefore, these functions help us convert the text representation of dates and times that users enter, into objects that we can use to perform date arithmetic, or to save into a database.

Formatting Dates Times

To format dates and times, we would call the Text function. We can format dates using predefined formats, or we can specify our own custom format.

Starting with the predefined formats, PowerApps offers a choice of date and time formats, in long and short formats. A long date format includes the full month name, whereas the short format includes an abbreviation of the month name. Table 6-3 shows a list of the predefined formats that we can use.

Table 6-3. *Predefined Date and Time formats*

Function Call	Example Output Value
Text(Now(), DateTimeFormat.LongDate)	17 December 2017
Text(Now(), DateTimeFormat.LongDateTime)	17 December 2017 02:00:00
Text(Now(), DateTimeFormat.LongDateTime24)	17 December 2017 14:00:00
Text(Now(), DateTimeFormat.LongTime)	02:00:00
Text(Now(), DateTimeFormat.LongTime24)	14:00:00
Text(Now(), DateTimeFormat.ShortDate)	12/17/2017
Text(Now(), DateTimeFormat.ShortDateTime)	12/17/2017 02:00:00
Text(Now(), DateTimeFormat.ShortDateTime24)	12/17/2017 14:00:00
Text(Now(), DateTimeFormat.ShortTime)	02:00
Text(Now(), DateTimeFormat.ShortTime24)	14:00
Text(Now(), DateTimeFormat.UTC)	2017-12-17T14:00:00.000Z

With these predefined formats, we can optionally provide a language code like so:

```
Text( Now(), DateTimeFormat.ShortDate, "en-GB" )
```

This function formats the date in British format (day/month/year) and produces the output "17/07/2017". If the predefined formats are too rigid and we want to customize our output further, we can provide a custom format string. Here's an example.

```
Text( Now(), "dddd dd-mmmm-yyyy mm:hh ss f ", "es-ES")
```

This example specifies a Spanish language code, and the result from this formula would produce output in the format - "domingo 17-diciembre-2017 14:00 00 0".

Looking more closely at this format string, the initial four characters "dddd" denote the day of the week in long format. The format "ddd" would return the day of the week in short format, that is, "dom" in Spanish, or "Sun" in English. The "mmmm" section of the string returns the full month name, whereas "mmm" would return a three-character representation of the month (for example, "dic" in Spanish, or "Dec" in English). The format string "mm" returns a two-digit numeric representation of the month.

One important point about custom formats is that the "mm" placeholder can represent the month number, or the minute component of the time. When we specify a custom format that includes the "mm" placeholder, the first instance of "mm" will always output the month component. Therefore, it isn't possible to construct a custom format that shows the minute component of the time prior to the month. To do this, we would need to format the times and dates separately and then concatenate the results.

Performing Date Arithmetic

PowerApps provides functions to carry out date arithmetic. The two main functions are DateAdd and DateDiff. The DateAdd function adds or subtracts durations from a date. The DateDiff function returns the number of days, months, quarters, or years between two dates.

To demonstrate the DateAdd function, here's the formula to retrieve yesterday's date:

```
DateAdd(Today(), -1, Days)
```

The first argument specifies the input date. The second argument defines the number of units to add. This can be a positive or a negative value. The third argument defines the units, and the possible options include days, months, quarters, or years. The third argument is optional. If we don't specify the units, the DateAdd function uses days as the unit for calculation.

To demonstrate the use of the DateDiff function, the formula beneath returns the number of days between January 1st 2017 and January 14th 2017.

```
DateDiff(Date(2017, 01, 01),Date(2017, 01, 14), Days)
```

The return value from this formula is 14. The first argument specifies the start date, the second argument specifies the end date, and the third argument specifies the number of units.

Although DateDiff appears easy to use, don't let this fool you into thinking that calculating date differences is a trivial task. A challenging task for developers is to calculate a person's age (or any time duration) expressed in years, months and days. Part of the challenge is that it's not possible to carry out the base calculation by taking the difference in days and dividing by 365. The reason for this is because the time span may include leap years. The second challenge is that date difference functions can often return ambiguous results. As an illustration, the formula below calculates the difference in months between December 30th 2016, and January 2nd 2017.

```
DateDiff(Date(2016, 12, 30),Date(2017, 01, 02), Months)
```

What do you think this call to DateDiff returns, given these dates? In this example, DateDiff reports a one-month difference for a time span of three days. In fact, it would even return a time difference of one year if we were to specify the unit as years. The lesson from this is that it's important to be aware of this behavior, especially if, for example, we were building apps for billing purposes.

Calendar Functions

PowerApps provides functions to retrieve a list of month names or weekday names in the language of the logged-in user. The results from these functions are ideal for use in drop-down boxes, or for date selection scenarios.

The Calendar.MonthsLong and Calendar.MonthsShort functions return a table that contains month names. The MonthsLong function returns a table that begins 'January', 'February', 'March' and so on, whereas the MonthsShort function returns a table that begins 'Jan', 'Feb', 'Mar' and so on.

The Calendar.WeekdaysLong and Calendar.WeekdayShort functions return a table that contains weekday names. The WeekdaysLong function returns a table that begins 'Sunday', 'Monday', 'Tuesday', and so on, whereas the MonthsShort function returns a table that begins 'Sun', 'Mon', 'Tue', and so on.

Working with Tables of Data

With PowerApps, there are several ways to build table like structures of data that can contain multiple rows. In this section, we'll examine these structures in more detail, and we'll examine the functions that work against tables of data.

Defining Hard-Coded Sets of Values

The basic way to define a list of data is to specify the items in a hard-coded array. We can use this technique to populate the items in a drop-down box. As an example, here's the syntax to define an array that contains two values: - male and female.

```
["male", "female"]
```

The items in an array are enclosed in square brackets. The comma symbol separates each item in the array. Figure 6-13 illustrates a drop-down box that contains a list of hours. In this example, PowerApps is set to French.

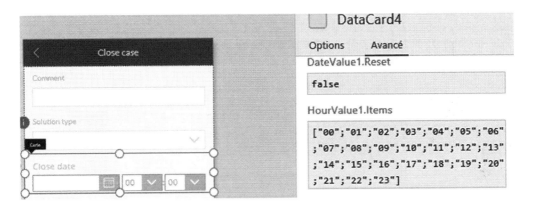

Figure 6-13. *Setting the data source of an item*

The purpose of this screenshot is to illustrate two points. The first is how to set the Items property of a drop-down to an array. The second is a reminder that because the comma symbol denotes the decimal point separator in French, French users must use the semicolon character to separate the items in an array.

With PowerApps set to English, you'll recall that the semicolon is the symbol that separates each function in a formula.

Understanding Collections

Collections provide an in-memory store for data. We can access the data in a collection from any screen in an app. This is useful because it gives us the ability to share working data between screens.

In practical terms, here are a couple of ways that we can use collections in an app. Supposing that we want to transpose or to aggregate data, we can use collections to store our working data, while we carry out a series of steps to shape our data.

Another use for collections is to cache data. If we were to perform a time-consuming data operation, we can store the results in a collection for later use. Because collections are held in memory, we can load frequently used data in collections to speed up an app.

To store an item in a collection, call the Collect function like so:

```
Collect(<CollectionName>, <DataToCollect>)
```

The first argument to this function specifies the collection name. Like context variables, we don't need to declare, or define a collection before use. The Collect function creates the collection for us if it doesn't exist.

The second argument specifies the data to add to the collection. This can include simple pieces of data such as numbers or strings, rows of data, or even entire tables of data.

We can clear all the items in a collection by calling the Clear function like so:

```
Clear(<CollectionName>)
```

PowerApps provides a function that combines the functionality of Collect and Clear. The name of this function is ClearCollect. ClearCollect removes all the data that is in the collection prior to collecting it, whereas Collect will append data to the collection. Here's how to call the ClearCollect function:

```
ClearCollect(<CollectionName>, <DataToCollect>)
```

ClearCollect is perhaps one of the most widely used functions. You'll find plenty of references to it in technical articles and blog posts.

Collecting Data

To demonstrate the use of collections, here's how to build a screen to collect data. Imagine a screen that contains many records. The functionality that we'll build will enable users to mark records for review. When a user marks a record, we'll add the record to a collection. At the end of this process, the user can navigate to a separate screen and view the records that have been collected.

To build this screen, create an auto-generated app. On the browse screen, add an icon to the item template. Select the icon, click the Action menu and select the collect option. When the collect dialog opens, select Collection1 and select ThisItem from the second drop-down, as shown in Figure 6-14.

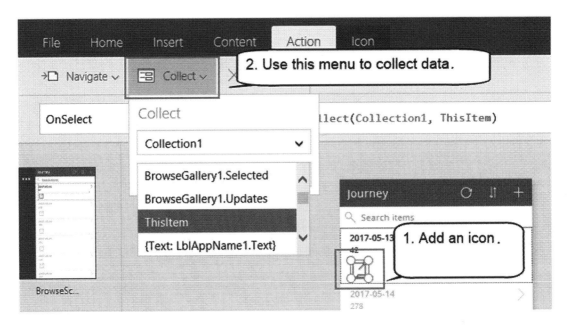

Figure 6-14. Adding an item to a collection

At this point, we can run our app. When the browse screen opens, click the icon to add some records to the collection. Now stop the app and return to the designer. The designer includes a special place where we can view the collections and the data in an app. Click the File ➤ Collections menu item, and you'll see the collections and data, as shown in Figure 6-15.

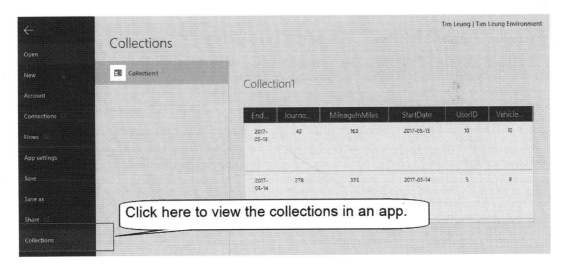

Figure 6-15. Items in the collection

At design time, any data that we add to a collection will available, even after we close and reopen our app. If we were to add some data to collection and then call `ClearCollect` to add a different type of data to the collection, the column headings from the initial collect operation will remain. To remove additional columns from the design time view, you'll need to call the `DeleteColumn` function. At run time, any data that is held in a collection will be lost when the user closes the app.

To complete this example, we can add a screen with a gallery control. We can then set the Items property of this control to `Collection1` to enable the user to view the records that have been marked.

Chapter 12 includes another example of how to use collections. This chapter describes how to use collections to aggregate data for the purposes of building a chart.

Defining Tables

Another way to define a structure that stores row data is to call the `Table` function. This function creates a temporary table. Here's an example of how to use this function.

```
Table({Desc:"Tomorrow", Date: DateAdd(Today(),1, Days) },
        {Desc:"Today", Date: Today()},
        {Desc:"Yesterday", Date: DateAdd(Today(), -1, Days) }
)
```

This formula creates a table with three rows of data. The items that we add to a table defines the columns. In this example, the table contains two columns - a column called `Desc`, and a column called `Date`.

Just like collections, we can use tables as the data source for a drop-down, or a gallery control. To do this, we can directly assign the table formula to the Items property of the control.

Here are a few useful tips about tables. We can only access tables from the screen where we define the table. We should use a collection instead if we want to share data between screens.

In terms of the data that we can store in a table, we can store tables within tables, and we can even store objects such as screens. This technique is especially useful for building screen navigation functions in an app.

Working with Columns

PowerApps provides functions to add, drop, or rename columns from data sources, collections, and tables. These functions are particularly useful when we work with collections. A common pattern in PowerApps is to gradually shape the data to suit our needs, especially in scenarios where we want to group or summarize values. These functions can help carry out this task. In this section, we'll look at these column-shaping functions in greater detail.

Adding Columns

The `AddColumns` function adds columns to a data source, collection, or table. Once reason why this function is useful is because it enables us to carry out operations that affect multiple rows with a single function call. To demonstrate, here's how to take a data source that contains journey data, and to add a column that shows the mileage traveled in kilometers. The data source includes a column called `MileageInMiles` that stores the mileage in miles.

```
AddColumns( Journey, "MileageInKM", MileageInMiles * 1.60934 )
```

This function accepts three arguments - a data source, the name of the column to add, and the value for each row. To define the value for each record, we can specify a formula that refers to other columns in the same data source.

An interesting thing is that the AddColumns function returns a table. This enables us to set the items property of a control such as a gallery control, directly to the output of the AddColumns function.

Dropping Columns

The DropColumns function takes a data source and column name. It then returns a table of data with the specified column removed. Here's an example of how to return the journey data source with the MileageInMiles column removed:

```
DropColumns (Journey, "MileageInMiles")
```

To clarify, the DropColumns function returns a table without the specified column. It does not delete any data from the data source that we provide. Like the AddColumns function, we can set the items property of a gallery or data control to the result of this function.

Renaming Columns

The function to rename a column is called RenameColumns. This function accepts three arguments - a data source, the column to rename, and the new name for the column. Here's how to return the journey data source with the MileageInMiles renamed:

```
RenameColumns(Journey, "MileageInMiles", "Mileage (miles)")
```

Like the previous functions in this section, the RenameColumns function returns a table with the specified column renamed. It does not modify the column name in the actual source data.

On reason why this function is useful is because we can use it to provide more meaningful column names to the controls that use the data. For example, when we set the data source for a chart, the chart control displays the column name in the legend. As this example shows, we can improve the readability of a chart legend by changing the column name to something that is more human readable.

Showing Columns

A useful function is the ShowColumns function. This function returns a subset of columns from a table. Here's how to return only the JourneyDate and MileageInMiles columns from the journey data source:

```
ShowColumns( Journey, JourneyDate, MileageInMiles)
```

The reason why this function is useful is because certain functions are designed to operate against a single column table. Examples include the aggregate functions such as Min, Max, and Avg. By using the ShowColumns function, we could return just the MileageInMiles column, and provide this to the Avg function to calculate the mean average of the mileage.

Table Functions

In this section, we'll look at how to work through the rows in a table, and how to perform aggregate calculations. This includes functions to retrieve the row count, minimum, maximum, or average values from a set of data.

Performing Actions Row by Row

The ForAll function enables us to calculate values or to perform actions for all records in a table. This function is perhaps the closest thing to carrying out a loop in PowerApps. The actions that we can call for each record in a table include Collect and Patch. As you'll recall, the Collect function adds data to a collection. Patch is a function that can update data in a data source, and I'll describe this later in the book.

To demonstrate the ForAll function, here's the syntax to copy rows from the journey table into a collection. This example includes a conditional clause, so that it only copies journeys that exceed 100 miles.

```
ForAll (Journey, If(MileageInMiles > 100, Collect(HighMileageCollection, JourneyUser))
```

The ForAll function accepts two arguments - a data source, and the action to carry out for each row in the data source. If the action that we want to carry out for each row in the data source consists of more than one function, we can specify additional functions by separating each one with a semicolon.

Because the ForAll function carries out row by row processing, it performs slower compared to other functions that operate directly on tables. Therefore, it's good practice to consider alternative ways of carrying out a task before we decide to use the ForAll function. In the given example, we could use a combination of the Filter, ClearCollect, and ShowColumns functions to accomplish the same task. Here's how this would look:

```
ClearCollect(HighMileageCollection, ShowColumns(Filter(Journey, MileageInMiles > 100), JourneyUser))
```

In the previous ForAll example, another thing to point out is that the Collect function returns a table that contains the contents of the collection. Therefore, calling Collect inside the ForAll function can result in high memory usage, which can cause your app to run more slowly.

An interesting point is that PowerApps can speed up this task by processing the actions inside the ForAll function in parallel. This means that we can't rely on the function processing the records sequentially. The side effect of this behavior is that PowerApps prohibits us from calling the UpdateContext, Clear, and ClearCollect functions from within the ForAll function.

Concatenating Data

A very useful function is the Concat function. This function enables us to combine the data from columns in a table. We can use this function to flatten columns of data into a comma-separated list. Here's the syntax we would use to carry out this task:

```
Concat(UsersDataSource, Firstname & " " & Surname & ",")
```

Counting Records

There are four functions we can use to count the number of records in a table. These are shown in Table 6-4.

Table 6-4. *Counting Records*

Function Call	Provides a count of...
Count(<SingleColumnTable>)	Records that contain a single number
CountRows(<Table>)	Records in a table
CountA(<SingleColumnTable>)	Records that are not blank, including ""
CountIf(<SingleColumnTable>)	Records that match a logical condition

At first glance, these functions look very similar. In particular, the `Count` and `CountRows` functions appear to do the same thing, because they provide a total count of records. The main difference is that the `Count` function accepts a single column table, whereas `CountRows` can accept a table with multiple columns. As an example of how to use the `CountRows` function, we could apply the `CountRows` function directly against a data source and show the count of records in a label.

The `CountA` function provides a count of records that are not null. A tip we might find useful is to combine the `CountA` and `Table` functions to check if a scalar value is null. For example, the following function will resolve to true if the input value is not null.

```
CountA(Table({ValueToCheck: YourInputValue })) = 1
```

In this example, `YourInputValue` could be a variable, or it could be an expression that that uses the `ThisItem` function to refer to data field in a form.

The CountIf function accepts an input table and returns a count of the records that match the condition. For example, here's how to retrieve the number of records in the journey table where the mileage value exceeds 100.

```
CountIf(Journey, MileageInMiles > 100)
```

An important point to mention is that all these functions are not delegable. This means that an app will download all the data to carry out the count, which can be a slow process.

▓ **Tip**   PowerApps does not provide an `IsNull` function, but we can use the `CountA` function instead to check for null values.

Performing Aggregate Calculations

PowerApps provides functions to aggregate tables of data. These are shown in Table 6-5.

Table 6-5. *Returning Aggregate Values*

Function	Returns the...
Average (<Table>, Expression)	Mean average
Max(<Table>, Expression)	Maximum value
Min(<Table>, Expression)	Minimum value
Sum(<Table>, Expression)	Sum of the arguments
VarP (<Table>, Expression)	Variance
StdevP (<Table>, Expression)	Standard deviation

All of these functions accept two arguments - a data source and an expression. The expression could consist of a single column, or a mathematical expression. Here's a demonstration of how to use the Sum function with an expression.

```
Sum(Journey, MileageInMiles * 0.45)
```

In this example, the Sum function returns the total mileage multiplied by 0.45, to mimic the type of calculation that carries out a mileage expense claim. With all these functions, we can use the Filter function against the data source to limit the aggregation to a subset of records.

To provide a brief mathematical explanation, variance is a measurement of how spread out a set of numbers are, and standard deviation is the square root of the variance.

A big warning is that in most cases, these functions are not delegable. In such instances, the result from these functions may be inaccurate because PowerApps will operate against the first 500 rows only. At the time of writing, PowerApps provides delegation support for aggregation tasks against SQL Server data sources only. The functions that PowerApps can delegate are Sum, Average, Min, and Max only.

Finally, these functions can work against a comma-separated list of expressions, instead of an input table. For example, the formula beneath would return the result 88.

```
Max(1, 14,  5 * 0.45, 50, 88. -5)
```

■ **Caution**   SQL Server is the only data source that supports delegation, and therefore the only data source where we can perform aggregate calculations quickly and accurately.

Conditional Statements and Logical Operations

So far, we've seen how to use the If function. This is one of the most useful and widely used functions in PowerApps. The way to call this function is as follows:

```
If( logical test, functions to run if true, functions to run if false)
```

In addition to the If functions, PowerApps provides other conditional functions. These include CountIf, RemoveIf, and UpdateIf.

■ **Note**   Because the If function is so widely used, here's a quick reminder that in French and other languages that use commas as a decimal point character, we should use semicolons to separate the arguments inside the If statement.

To build the conditional tests for use with the If function, PowerApps provides all the logical operators that we would expect to find. These include basic operators such as equals (=), greater than (>), less than (<), greater than or equal to (>=), and less than or equal to (<=).

There are two keywords we can use to carry out a logical and operation These are And and &&. We can use the && operator to combine sets of conditions. The And function accepts a comma-separated list of arguments and returns a Boolean result to indicate whether all the arguments resolve to true.

Likewise, there are two keywords we can use to carry out a logical or operation - Or and ||. The || operator enables us to supply sets of conditions and it returns true if any of the conditions resolve to true. The Or function accepts a comma-separated list of arguments and returns true if any of the arguments resolve to true.

Specifying Colors

To specify a color, we can call one of several functions. The ability to specify colors is important because it enables us to set control properties, such as the foreground color of a piece of text. The functions that we can call are shown in Table 6-6.

Table 6-6. *Obtaining a color value*

Method	Example Call...
Use predefined color	Color.Red
Obtain color from hex code	ColorValue("#ff0000")
Obtain color from red/green/blue/alpha values	RGBA(255, 0, 0, 1)
Obtain a lighter/darker shade of color	ColorFade(Color.Red, -0.2)

The simplest way to specify a color is to use one of the built-in colors in the Color enumeration. This provides access all the most popular colors.

The ColorValue function returns a color value from a hex code. This is perfect if you're familiar with HTML and CSS (Cascading Style Sheets) color codes.

The ColorFade function returns a brighter or darker version of a color. This function requires us to provide two arguments - a base color, and a fade value that ranges from -1 to 1. A fade value of -1 fully darkens the color to black, whereas a fade value of 1 fully lightens a color to white. By using this function, we can improve the appearance of an app by applying subtle offsets of colors to borders or adjacent controls.

Navigation Functions

We'll now look at functions to carry out navigation tasks. First, we'll explore a technique that we can use to provide screen navigation menus in apps. Next, we'll look at how to launch websites, compose emails, send SMS messages, and much more. To complete this section, we'll build an app that can optionally show a specified record at startup.

The two functions that provide navigation functionality are the Navigate and Back functions. The Navigate function changes the visible screen. With this function, we can pass values to the target screen by providing context variables in the call. The Back function returns the user to the previous screen. Both of these functions return true or false, depending on the outcome. Here's a formula that demonstrates how to use the return value.

```
If(Back(), true, Navigate(BrowseScreen1,ScreenTransition.Cover))
```

This formula calls the Back function. If the call to this function fails, the code navigates the user to a screen called BrowseScreen1 instead. A call to the Back function could fail if we run a specific screen in the designer and there isn't a screen that we can return to. The Back and Navigate functions could also fail if an error exists on the screen that we want to navigate to.

To make it easier to write the navigate code, we can select a control and use the navigate item in the toolbar. This feature inserts the correct formula and saves us from having to type out the formula manually, as shown in Figure 6-16.

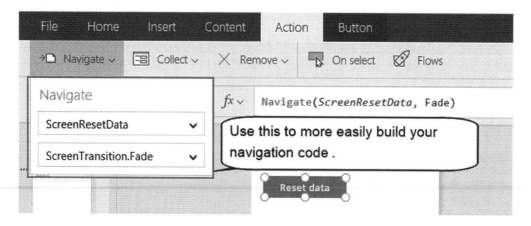

***Figure 6-16.** Setting the navigate action with the designer*

When building apps, we might want to open screens conditionally, or to add gallery or drop-down controls to navigate the user to a different screen. One challenge we face is that the navigate function expects us to provide a screen object, rather than the string representation of the screen name. This prevents us from constructing a screen name with formula and opening the result with the Navigate function. This limitation also makes it difficult to store unique startup screens for each user in a database because it's not possible to call the Navigate function and to supply a textual screen name from the database. The technique to work around this limitation is to store the screen references in a table.

As an example, let's imagine that we want to add a gallery control that shows a list of browse screens in our application. When a user selects an item from the control, the app should navigate to the selected screen. To build this function, add a gallery control to a screen. Set the items property of the control to the following formula:

```
Table({Desc:"View Journeys", ScreenObject: BrowseJourneys},
      {Desc:"View Users", ScreenObject: BrowseUsers}
)
```

This code is based on the assumption that we have two screens in our app - one called BrowseJourneys, and the other called BrowseUsers. Now add an icon to the template and set the OnAction property to the following

```
Navigate(GalleryControl1.Selected.ScreenObject, ScreenTransition.Fade)
```

Figure 6-17 illustrates how this feature appears in the screen designer.

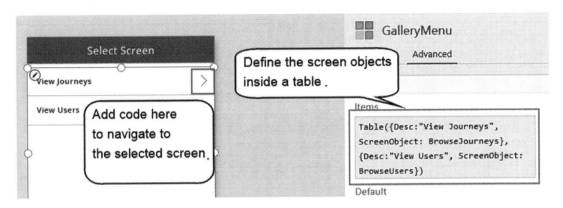

Figure 6-17. *Using a Gallery control to provide screen navigation*

Launching Websites and Apps

PowerApps provides a function called Launch that enables us to launch websites in a browser. To demonstrate this function, we'll create a button that opens a currency conversion web page from Google.

The first step is to determine the web address to use. If we open the currency conversion web page in Google and convert 50 US dollars to Euros, the page would display an address that looks like this:

```
https://www.google.com/finance/converter?a=50&from=USD&to=EUR
```

The a parameter specifies the amount to convert. The from parameter specifies the source currency type, and the to parameter specifies the target currency type.

To open this web page from a screen, add a button to your screen. Next, set the OnSelect property to the following value:

```
Launch( "https://www.google.com/finance/converter", "a","50","from","USD","to","EUR")
```

The Launch function requires us to provide the address of the webpage to open. We can optionally provide a list of parameters and in this example, we provide the a, to, and from arguments to specify our search terms.

A handy tip is to take advantage of the Launch function and to use it to open the telephone dialer, email client, SMS, or message apps. Table 6-7 provides highlights of the syntax that we could use.

Table 6-7. *Launching apps*

Description	Launch Function Syntax
Send an email	Launch("mailto:recipient@emailaddress.com")
Open the telephone dialer	Launch("tel:07876987656")
Send SMS	Launch("sms:07876987656", "body", "Our SMS message")
Initiate Skype call	Launch("skype:skypeRecipient?call")
Send WhatsApp message	Launch("whatsapp://send/07876987656", "text", "our message")

Retrieving Startup Parameters

For web-based users of PowerApps, we can call the Param function to retrieve parameter values from the web address. This feature is very useful because it enables us to configure the behavior when a user starts an app. For example, we could open a specific screen that shows a specific record based on a value that a user supplies. This feature is useful for workflow type apps. For instance, if the status of a record changes, we could send an email to a user with a link that directly opens the specified record in PowerApps.

To demonstrate this technique, we'll adapt an auto-generated app to optionally open a record on startup. Our auto-generated app will be based on a table of journeys. The URL parameter that signals the app to open a journey record will be called JourneyID.

We can find the web address for an app through the details page for the app in the web portal. The address will look something like this:

```
https://web.powerapps.com/apps/c354bf49-7618-4ee8-8603-4f29d484af33
```

To help build this feature, we'll utilize a property called OnStart. This useful property enables us to run formula when an app starts. The OnStart property is a perfect place to carry out initialization tasks. An example of the type of functionality we could carry out here might include formula that caches records into local collections to help improve application performance.

To build this feature, the first step is to build an auto-generated app. The data source for our example app will be called Journey. In the browse screen, set the OnStart property to the following value:

```
If(Not(IsBlank(Param("JourneyID"))),
    Set(RecordSeen, false); Navigate(DetailScreen1,ScreenTransition.Fade),
    Set(RecordSeen, true)
)
```

On DetailScreen1, set the Item property of the form, DetailForm1, to the following:

```
If(RecordSeen=true,
    BrowseGallery1.Selected,
    LookUp(Journey, JourneyID= Param("JourneyID"))
)
```

On DetailScreen1, set the OnHidden property to the following:

```
If(RecordSeen=false, Set(RecordSeen, true))
```

We can now test our app by opening a browser and appending a journey id argument to the end of the address, like so.

```
https://web.powerapps.com/apps/c354bf49-7618-4ee8-8603-4f29d484af33?JourneyID=12
```

This link opens the app and shows the record that matches journey id 12 in the detail screen. Note that the JourneyID parameter name is case sensitive. From this screen, the user can click the back icon to open the browse screen.

To clarify how this works, the formula that runs when the app starts checks whether the user has provided a JourneyID value. If so, the formula sets a global variable called RecordSeen to false, and navigates the user to the details screen. On the details screen, the formula that determines the record to show on the form checks the value of the RecordSeen variable. If this is false, the formula calls the Lookup function to retrieve the record that matches the JourneyID value that the user provides. Otherwise, it reverts to the its default behavior and shows the record that is selected on the browse screen. When the user leaves the details screen, the formula sets the value of the RecordSeen variable to true. This prevents the form from showing the startup record when a user subsequently opens the details screen.

■ **Tip**   The `OnStart` property is a very useful property because it enables us to customize the startup behavior of an app.

Exiting an App

Finally, PowerApps provides a function to close an app called Exit. This function accepts a single argument that controls whether to log the user out of PowerApps.

In the mobile versions of PowerApps, the Exit function closes the app and the user will remain in the PowerApps app. If we were to call the Exit function while previewing our app in the PowerApps Studio designer, the function will not exit our session.

Managing Errors

PowerApps deals with errors in a relaxed way. In most cases, PowerApps continues when it encounters an error and it won't crash, or grind to a halt.

Here's a screen that demonstrate how PowerApps copes with errors. This screen contains a button that calls the formula that's shown in Figure 6-18. The screen contains a label control, and the text property of this is set to a context variable called LabelText.

Figure 6-18. Forumulas with errors

This formula contains two errors. The second line in the formula contains the nonsense text BlahBlah. A subsequent command in this formula divides the number 80 by zero. This is a classic type of error that often crashes other types of application.

How do you think PowerApps behaves when this formula runs? Following the error, will it still execute the functions that are that are syntactically correct? The answer is that the whole block of code fails to run due to the unknown expression BlahBlah. If we were to remove this offending line, the code would run, despite the divide by zero error, and the label would display the text "Task Completed".

Another place where errors can occur is during data operations. Errors can occur when an app tries to read, or to save data to a data source. When these errors occur, we can retrieve a list of error messages by calling a function called Errors. This function accepts the name of a data source and here's the syntax we would use to call this function:

```
Errors(Journeys)
```

This function returns a table. Therefore, we can set the items property of a gallery control to this function to show a list of errors that have been generated for a specific data source.

Summary

Just like Microsoft Excel, we can write formula to add functionality to our apps. A formula bar at the top of the screen enables us to enter formula, and we can write formula to respond to control clicks and taps, and to set data sources and property values. In fact, we can assign formula in almost all the places where we can enter a property value.

Any nontrivial app will rely on variables and collections to store working copies of data. An important use of variables is to help set property values. Variables are necessary because it's not possible to assign property values through formula that is attached to a different object. To demonstrate this concept, we learned how to show a message on a label in response to a click of a button. To build this functionality, we configure the OnSelect property of a button to store the message text in a variable. We then set the text property of the label to this variable.

PowerApps offers two types of variable: global variables and context variables. The difference between these two types of variables is that global variables are accessible throughout an app whereas context variables are accessible from a single screen only. We can store all types of data in variables, including simple numeric and text values, as well as rows and tables. The UpdateContext function defines and sets the value of a context variable, while the Set function defines and sets the value of a global variable.

Collections provide local storage for rows of data. Just like variables, PowerApps clears all the data in a collection when a user exits an app. Collections are useful because they can store working data while we carry out data transformation tasks. We can also cache data in collections to help speed up apps. ClearCollect is the function that defines and adds data to a collection.

PowerApps provides functions that work with text, numbers, and dates. This includes functions to modify the case of text, and functions that search for the existence of a text value within another piece of text. A particularly useful feature is support for regular expressions. We can use this to match a piece of text against a predefined format, and this enables us to validate whether a piece of text matches the format of an email address, telephone number, or social security number. To extract parts of an input string, PowerApps provides string manipulation functions that include Mid, Left, Right, and Trim.

The mathematical functions that PowerApps provides include arithmetic operators, rounding operators, trigonometric functions, and many more. It also provides functions to carry out date arithmetic and to display dates in a format of our choice. Two useful functions are Text and Value. Text converts an input value to its text representation. This is useful because it allows us to covert data values into a format that we can display in labels. We can also call this function to format date values in a specified format. The Value function converts a text value to its numeric representation. This function is important because it allows us to convert user input into actual numbers that we use in mathematical calculations.

PowerApps provides helpful functions that can work against tables of data. This includes functions to add, remove, or rename columns. These functions allow us to extract specific columns that we can provide as inputs to other functions.

PowerApps provides aggregate functions to count, sum, or to calculate the average value from a set of data. An important point to be aware of is that SQL Server is the only data source that can delegate aggregate calculations. When we perform aggregate calculations against data sources that don't support delegation, PowerApps carries out the operation against the first 500 rows only and this can result in inaccurate calculations.

A useful function is the CountA function. This function is designed to count the numbers of rows in a single column table that are not null. However, we can also use this function to determine whether a single value is null. The is useful because the IsBlank function returns true for both empty string and null values. The CountA function enables us to specifically check for null values.

We looked at how to build custom screen navigation menus. The challenge here is that the Navigate function requires us to provide a screen object. This makes it difficult for us to navigate to a screen name that we construct through formula. The way to work around this is to create a lookup list of screen objects with the Table function, and to use this in conjunction with the Navigate function.

Another useful function is the Lanuch function. We can call this function to launch websites, initiate phone calls, compose SMS messages, or launch other mobile apps such as Skype or WhatsApp.

Finally, we can call the Param function to retrieve the arguments that a user provides to an app when it runs in a browser. This is useful because we can use these values with the OnStart property to specify the startup behavior of an app. The example in this chapter showed how to build an app that displays a user-specified record at startup.

CHAPTER 7

■ ■ ■

Customizing Screens

Many users, including myself, learned how to use PowerApps by studying the built-in template apps. These apps provide sophisticated and good-looking examples of what we can achieve with PowerApps. However, it can be a challenge for beginners to make sense of how they work. These apps are complex, and it's difficult to decipher how all the different parts fit together. Therefore, the main theme of this chapter is to document the interesting features within these apps. We can apply the lessons that we learn from this to help improve the presentation of our own apps. The topics that we'll cover in this chapter will include the following:

- Applying predefined layouts. The screen designer offers pre-built layouts that apply to screens, gallery controls, and forms. We'll examine the effect these layouts have on the appearance of an app, and we'll also find out how to apply a consistent color scheme to an app through themes.

- Building single screen layouts. By examining the template apps, we'll discover how to build a layout that contains two sections: a section that shows a list of records, and a section that shows the details of the selected record. The user can change the selected record by clicking a record from the list. We'll also find out how to implement a tab control. This enables the user to change the details that are shown in a predefined section of a screen.

- Building features. We'll find out how to add features to help improve the user experience. This will include how to show a confirmation screen when a user attempts to delete a record and how to display summary data when a user selects a record from a list. This summary data can include counts of child records, or totals and summaries of financial values.

Using Predefined Layouts

To begin, let's examine some of the predefined layouts in the designer. When we use the menu to add a new screen, the menu provides a choice of four screen types, as shown in Figure 7-1. These include blank, scrollable screen, list screen, and form screen layouts. What exactly are the characteristics of these four layout types?

Figure 7-1. The new screen option

The blank screen layout is the simplest layout, and adds an empty screen to your app. The 'scrollable screen' layout is very useful because it extends the usable area of a screen. With this layout, we can add cards to the bottom of the layout. A card is a container for controls and we can add as many cards as we want to a screen. The cards stack on top of each other and at runtime, a user can scroll down to view the cards that are lower down in the stack, outside of the visible area.

The form screen layout adds a screen with a title bar, a save icon, and a form control. When we connect the form to a data source, the layout drop-down offers a choice of vertical or horizontal layouts. The default is the vertical layout and in this layout, field labels appear above the data entry controls. If we choose the horizontal layout, the field labels appear to the left of the data entry controls, as shown in Figure 7-2.

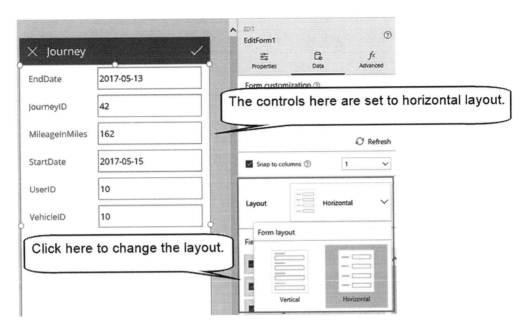

Figure 7-2. *Selecting either the Vertical or Horizontal layouts*

With the 'list screen' layout, we can use the layout drop-down to apply one of the many built-in layouts. The available layouts are grouped into lists and gallery layouts, as shown in Figure 7-3. The list layouts are designed to display a combination of text and images, whereas the gallery layouts are predominantly designed to show images.

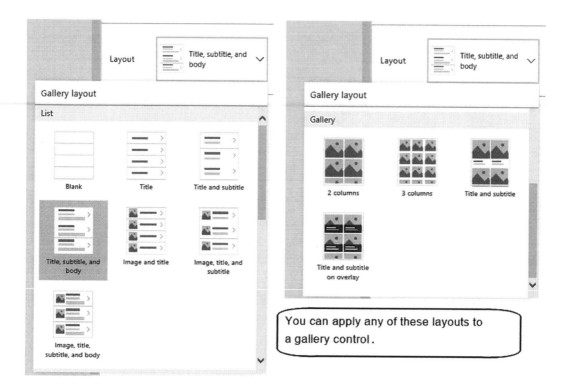

Figure 7-3. *Gallery control layouts*

Figure 7-4 shows the appearance of a screen when we select the 'image, title, subtitle, and body' layout. The template includes placeholders for all of these items. By default, the gallery control on a new screen shows sample data. We can change the Items property of the gallery control so that it references an actual data source. We can then use the controls in the properties panel to set the data fields that you want to show in each placeholder control.

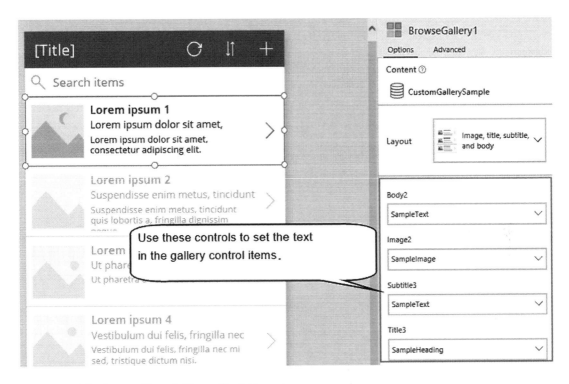

Figure 7-4. *The 'image,title, subtitle, and body' layout*

The remaining layouts in the list group are a subset of the 'image,title, subtitle, and body'. For instance, the 'title and subtitle' layout contains a gallery template with two placeholder controls only.

The layouts in the list group show one record per row. However, the gallery group control includes layouts that show multiple records per row. For gallery controls, the property that controls the number of records per row is the 'wrap count' property, as shown in Figure 7-5.

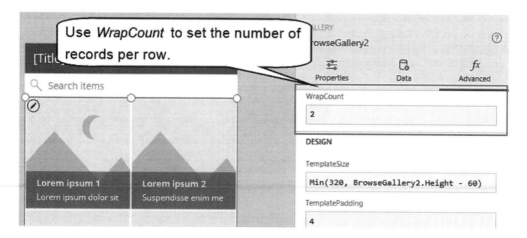

Figure 7-5. *By default, the 'title and subtitle' gallery layout shows two records per row*

Laying Out Tablet Apps

So far, we've focused on phone apps because the designer builds this type of app when we create an auto-generated app. With tablet apps, the horizontal gallery control fits the landscape orientation of tablet devices much better. The predefined layouts with horizontal gallery controls include carousel layouts, as shown in Figure 7-6.

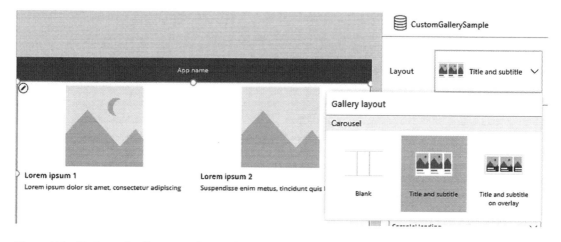

Figure 7-6. *Horizontal gallery control in a tablet application*

With such layouts, the records are arranged horizontally and a user would swipe left to view additional records. To configure other gallery controls to behave like this, we would set the Layout property to Layout.Horizontal.

When we build a tablet app, we can configure the aspect ratio through the File ➤ App settings menu. Figure 7-7 shows the available aspect ratios. Note that it's not possible to convert a phone app to a tablet app, and vice versa.

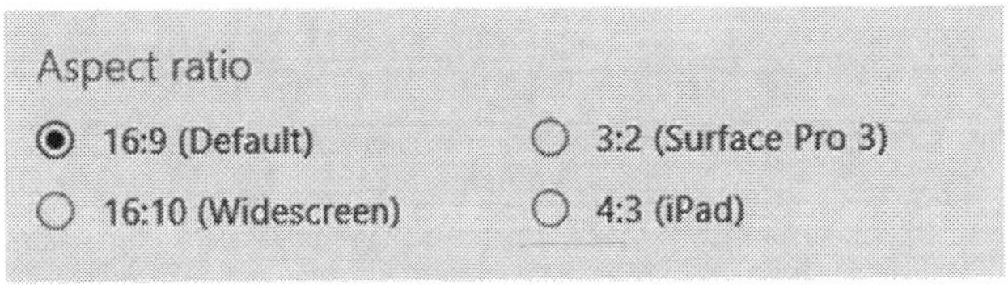

Figure 7-7. *Setting the aspect ratio of an app*

Understanding Sample Screen Designs

In this section, we'll examine some of the layouts from the template apps. By examining these apps, we can discover useful techniques that we can apply to our own apps. This includes how to construct list and detail screen layouts, how to show summary values, how to display delete confirmation messages, and how to build a tab control.

Building a List and Details Screen

The first layout we'll examine is the tablet version of the budget tracker track. This layout shows a list of budgets in a left-hand pane, as shown in Figure 7-8. When a user selects a budget item from the list, the other sections of the screen update themselves with the data that relates to the selected budget. The details section includes a pie chart that shows the total amount spent, a list of expenses, and summary values at the top of the screen that apply to the selected budget record. What ties all of this together? What is it that links the various controls on the screen with the list of budget records?

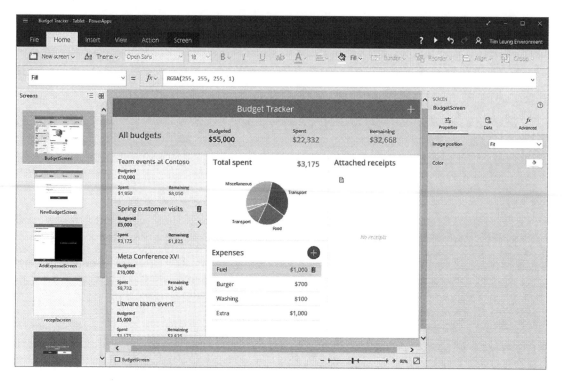

Figure 7-8. *List and details screen*

To explain this layout, let's begin by examining the structure of the source data, and the control that shows the list of budget records.

The data source for this app is an Excel spreadsheet held in OneDrive. This spreadsheet contains five tables, and the details of these are shown in Table 7-1.

Table 7-1. *Data source for the budget tracker application*

Table Name	Table Columns
Budgets	BudgetTitle, BudgetAmount, BudgetID
Expenses	Id, ExpenseName, BudgetTitle, Category, Expense, BudgetId
Categories	CategoryName
Receipts	Id, BudgetId, ExpenseId, ReceiptList[image], ReceiptName
ExpenseByCategory	Category, BudgetId, Expense

On the main screen of the app, the control that shows the list of budgets is a gallery control named Gallery1. The Items property of this control is set to the Excel table Budgets.

If we take a closer look at this gallery control, each row includes the budget amount, the amount of money that has been spent, and the amount of money remaining, as shown in Figure 7-9.

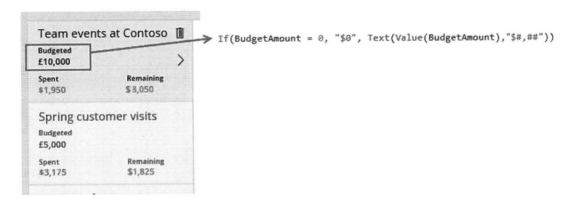

Figure 7-9. *The formula for the budgeted value*

Figure 7-9 illustrates the formula that displays the total budgeted amount. This formula formats the BudgetAmount value with thousand comma separators, and a preceding currency symbol. You might be curious to understand why the formula includes a conditional statement to display the literal text "$0" if the BudgetAmount is 0. Could we not just apply the following formula without the If function, like so?

```
Text(Value(BudgetAmount),"$#,##")
```

The reason why the formula conditionally tests for zero is to fix a piece of behavior with the Text function. If we were to format the value zero with the format string as shown below, the result of this function would return an empty string.

```
Text(0,"$#,##")
```

Therefore, the purpose of the If statement is to display the value "$0" when the budgeted amount is zero, rather than an empty string.

Let's now look at the formulas that calculate the spent and remaining amounts. The amount of money that has been spent against a budget is stored in the expenses table, and not in the budget table. Therefore, the formula that carries out the amount spent and the amount remaining are slightly more complex. Listing 7-1 shows the formula that carries out the spent calculation.

Listing 7-1. Formula for spent amount

```
If
(
        Text(
                Sum(
                        Filter(Expenses,BudgetTitle = ThisItem.BudgetTitle &&
                                        BudgetId=ThisItem.BudgetId),
                        Value(Expense)
                        ),
                "[$-en-US]$#,##")="$",
        "$0",
```

```
Text(
        Sum(
                Filter(Expenses,BudgetId = ThisItem.BudgetId ),
                Value(Expense)
                ),
        "[$-en-US]$#,##"
        )
)
```

The first thing you'll notice is that this formula begins with an If function. Just like before, the purpose of this conditional test is to format zero values as "$0". The pertinent code that calculates the sum of the expenses resides in the true part of the If function.

This formula calls the Sum function to calculate the sum of the expense column in the expenses table where the budget id matches the selected budget id in the gallery control.

Listing 7-2 shows the code that calculates the remaining budget amount. This code is mostly identical to the code that calculates the spent amount. The primary difference is that it subtracts the spent amount from the budget amount.

Listing 7-2. Formula to calculate the remaining amount

```
If (
        Text(ThisItem.BudgetAmount-Sum(
        Filter(
                Expenses,BudgetTitle = ThisItem.BudgetTitle && BudgetId=ThisItem.BudgetId),
                Value(Expense)
                ),
                "[$-en-US]$#,##")="$"
        ,"$0",
        Text(ThisItem.BudgetAmount-Sum(
            Filter(
                Expenses,BudgetId = ThisItem.BudgetId),
                Value(Expense)
                ),
        "[$-en-US]$#,##")
)
```

In conclusion, this section illustrates the code we would use to calculate sums and highlights how this code might be more complex than we first expect.

Updating the Details Section of a Screen

When a user clicks an item in the gallery control, the central part of the screen updates itself to show the budget record that the user selects. This central part of the screen shows a list of expenses that are related to the selected budget record. The controls that are linked to the selected budget work by referencing the selected item in the gallery control for the budget records. These controls are illustrated in Figure 7-10.

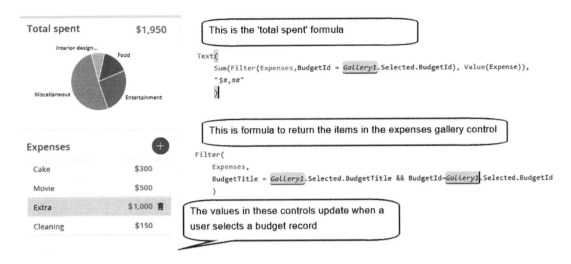

Figure 7-10. *Controls in central part of the screen*

The control that shows the list of expenses is a gallery control. The control that shows the 'total spent' is a label control. Note that the actual formula includes a call to the If statement to correctly format the zero values but the code in Figure 7-10 omits this for brevity.

Displaying a Delete Confirmation Screen

To prevent users from accidently deleting records, a common technique is to show a delete confirmation screen. The budget tracker app provides this feature, and in this section, we'll look at how this works.

In the gallery control of budget records, each row includes a trash icon, as shown in Figure 7-11.

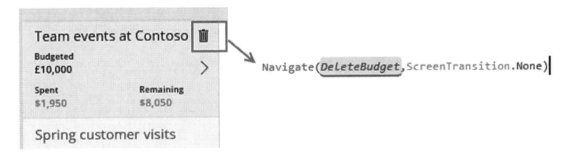

Figure 7-11. *The trash icon navigates the user to a new custom delete screen*

This icon navigates the user to a screen called DeleteBudget, as shown in Figure 7-12. This screen includes two buttons - a delete button, and a cancel button.

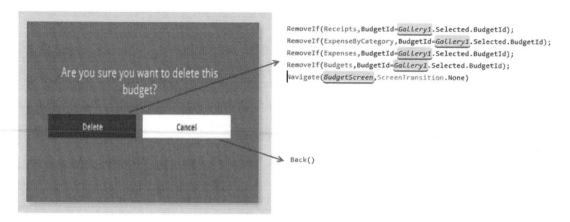

Figure 7-12. *Deleting a budget record*

As Figure 7-12 shows, the OnSelect property of the delete button calls the RemoveIf function five times. The RemoveIf function deletes data from a data source based on a condition. This code deletes the records in the four related tables that match the selected Budget Id of the record in Gallery1 (the gallery control that shows the list of budget records). Finally, the formula navigates the user back to the main budget screen.

The Cancel button simply returns the user to the previous screen by calling the Back function.

Building a Tab Control Screen

To organize the layout of a screen, we can group your controls into tabs. The asset checkout app includes such an example, as shown in Figure 7-13. In this screen, the main screen contains four groups - laptops, keyboards, monitors, and mice. When a user selects one of these items, the background color of the selected item turns gray, and the gallery control at the bottom of the screen updates and displays the products that belong to the group.

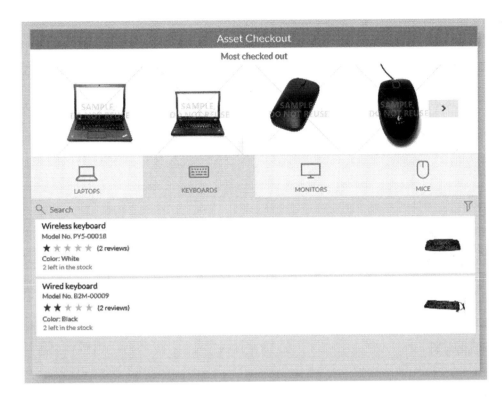

Figure 7-13. *The 'Asset Checkout' app includes a tab type control*

Let's take a look at how this screen is constructed. The strip that shows the groups is actually a gallery control. The reason why the gallery control resembles a tab strip is because the layout property is set to vertical. This configures the control so that the items sit side to side, rather than top to bottom. Additionally, the 'show navigation' setting is set to false to hide the navigation controls that would usually appear.

The background color of the gallery control is a light orange color. The Fill and TemplateFill properties of the gallery control help to define this.

The item template for the gallery control includes a gray color rectangle control. This rectangle control provides the canvas for the icon and text that appears in the template. The setting that makes this control behave like a tab control is the visibility setting of the rectangle control, which is set to the following formula:

```
If(ThisItem.IsSelected,true,false)
```

This formula hides the gray rectangle when the item is not selected. The final touch that rounds off the appearance of this control is that the strip at the bottom of the control is set to the same gray color. Figure 7-14 illustrates the settings that we looked at.

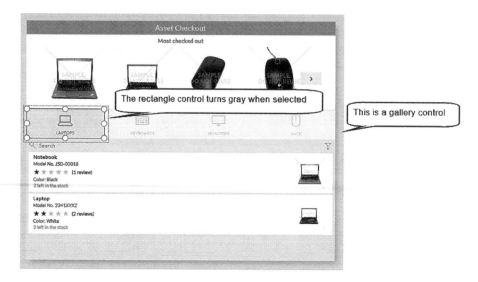

Figure 7-14. *How the tab control works*

Using Themes

We can use themes to apply a fresh new look to an app. The purpose of a theme is to apply a consistent color scheme to all the screens and controls in an app. There are 12 predefined themes that we can access through the home menu, as shown in Figure 7-15.

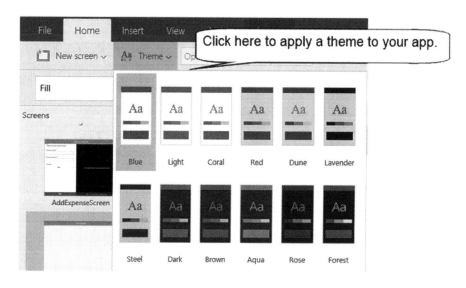

Figure 7-15. *Applying a theme*

When we apply a theme, the designer changes the control and background colors in every screen in the app. To prevent you from losing custom changes, the designer will not update any controls where you've modified the colors.

There are themes that consist of a light background and themes that consist of a dark background. A useful tip is that dark themes can help preserve the battery life of mobile devices. This is because a device requires less power to light up a screen that is predominantly dark.

Summary

In this chapter, we examined various screen design techniques that we can apply to our apps. PowerApps provides predefined layouts that we can apply to a screen. The most basic is the scrollable screen layout. This layout applies a colored title bar and a card control in the body of the screen. Cards are containers for child controls, and we can add multiple cards to a screen. The cards stack on top of each other, and the user can scroll down to reveal the cards that are beneath the visible area. The remaining layouts apply to screens that contain a gallery control.

The template apps provide a great way to learn more about PowerApps. Many of these templates follow a similar pattern. They consist of a principal screen with a gallery control. When a user selects a record from the gallery control, other labels and gallery controls update themselves to show data that pertains to the selected record.

The design principle is that the selected item in the gallery control is the object that drives everything in the application. If child records are associated with the main record, the data source of any child gallery controls are filtered by selected item in the main gallery control, therefore producing the correct data.

The budget tracker app includes a delete confirmation screen. This screen appears when a user triggers the deletion of a record. The confirmation screen contains two buttons - a delete button and a cancel button. The delete button calls the RemoveIf function to delete the specified record. If there are related records, the formula removes all child records before removing the main record.

To better organize the layout of a screen, we can group our controls into a tab structure. We can implement this feature by adding a gallery control to a screen and setting the layout property to vertical. We would set a different background color for the selected item in the gallery control to achieve the look of a tab strip.

Finally, we can skin an app through the help of a theme. A theme applies consistent colors to all the screens and controls in an app.

CHAPTER 8

■ ■ ■

Using Controls

Controls provide the means for users to interact with apps and play a crucial role in app design. In this chapter, we'll cover this important topic through four sections: how to work with simple controls, how to set lookup values, how to work with CDS-specific controls, and how to show media content on screens.

The overriding characteristic of simple controls is the ability to work against single values. Examples of these controls include the text input, radio, checkbox, and many more. Afterwards, we'll look at how to use the drop-down control and how to set lookup values. We'll also find out how to use the list box and table controls in this section.

There are some differences that exist when we work with CDS data sources. This includes a new type of form control, and different behavior with drop-down controls. We'll explore these topics and then move on to look at media controls. This will include how to display images, videos, and audio in apps.

In the final part of this chapter, we'll explore some practical techniques that we can apply. This includes how to use the timer control to run formula at timed intervals, and how to utilize the control reset feature. This feature restores control values back to their initial states, and we'll find out how to use this to allow users to undo changes to a record. Some valuable highlights in this chapter include the following:

- How to map data values to controls. It's common for data sources to store codified or abbreviated data values. Examples can include country code abbreviations, or letters such as 'Y' and 'N' to denote true or false. It can be a challenge to configure controls such as radio or list box controls to display meaningful options to the user, yet store and retrieve codified values from the data store. We'll find out exactly how to carry out the mapping task.

- How to work with dates and times. Surprisingly, displaying and editing dates can be quite complex. First, it's not straightforward to configure the controls on a default card to allow just the entry of the date without the time component. Secondly, PowerApps performs time zone conversions to allow users in different regions to work with times in their local time zones. The difficulty is that if we misconfigure our apps, we can store incorrect time values in the data source. In this chapter, we'll find out how to avoid these problems.

- How to use the drop-down control. To address the common task of setting lookup values, we'll examine some tricky yet important topics that relate to this control. This includes how to customize the text that appears in each row, and how to build a set of nested drop-down controls. This is where the data items in one drop-down will depend on the selected item of another drop-down.

© Tim Leung 2017
T. Leung, *Beginning PowerApps*, https://doi.org/10.1007/978-1-4842-3003-9_8

Overview of Controls

To explore the controls that PowerApps offers, we'll build an auto-generated app that's based on a table of vehicle records. We'll then replace the text input controls on the edit form with alternative controls. Figure 8-1 shows the end result of this exercise. The controls that we'll explore will include the drop-down, date picker, radio, rating, and slider controls. We'll fit the replacement controls into the existing card and form structure to ensure that the form continues to save and retrieve data correctly.

Figure 8-1. *The screen that we'll build in this chapter*

Before we begin, here are some elementary points to mention. First, the Insert menu in the designer enables us to add controls to screens. Second, we can only use the controls that PowerApps provides. There is no way to create our own custom controls.

■ **Tip**   We can arrange the cards on a form to span across multiple columns (as shown in Figure 8-1) by selecting the 'Snap to columns' checkbox on the form and entering the number of columns to display.

Building Data Structures to Support Controls

Here's the data structure of the Excel spreadsheet that supports the example in this chapter. The main table stores vehicle details, as shown in Figure 8-2. This spreadsheet stores common vehicle details such as the registration number, color, and model.

	A	B	C	D	E	F	G	H	I
1	VehicleID	ModelID	Registration	Color	FuelType	Seats	InsuranceEnd	Transmission	ComfortLevel
2	1	3	DA12 CJM	Green	P	4	22/05/2018 10:00	A	5
3	2	5	OX14 ACU	Red	P	4	08/05/2018 11:00	A	5
4	3	8	GV60 YAH	Blue	P	2	21/04/2018 12:00	M	4
5	4	12	HV55 REF	White	D	4	04/05/2018 11:00	M	3
6	5	4	NI17 HTA	Black	D	7	08/05/2018 11:00	M	3

Figure 8-2. *Vehicle Spreadsheet*

146

The model id field stores a numeric model number that corresponds to a value that's held in a model table, as shown in Figure 8-3. This table stores the model name and the year of the model. The table also includes a field called MakeID. This is a numeric field that references a Make table, which is also shown in Figure 8-3.

	A	B	C	D
1	ModelID	MakeID	Name	Year
2	1	1	A4	2008-2015
3	2	1	A5	2007-2015
4	3	2	Fiesta	2002-2008
5	4	2	Grand C-Max	2010-2017
6	5	2	Modeo	2014-2017
7	6	3	GS	2012-2017
8	7	3	IS	2013-2017
9	8	4	SLK	2004–2010
10	9	4	C Class	2007–2014
11	10	4	E Class	2009–2016
12	11	5	1 Series	2004 – 2011
13	12	5	3 Series	2011-2017
14	13	5	5 Series	2003–2010

	A	B
1	MakeID	Name
2	1	Audi
3	2	Ford
4	3	Lexus
5	4	Mercedes-Benz
6	5	BMW

Figure 8-3. *The Model and Make tables*

These sets of tables represent a typical data structure that we would find in a relational database. Later in this chapter, these tables provide a structure that we can use to learn how to set look up values with drop-down controls.

Action Controls

Before we look at data controls, let's find out how to configure a control to respond to user taps or clicks. The obvious control that provides this function is the button control. However, almost all controls in PowerApps can also respond to this type of interaction. To configure a control to respond to a user tap or click, we would add formula to the OnSelect property of the control. The buttons in the Action menu provide a simple way to build the OnSelect formula, as shown in Figure 8-4. We can use the options in this menu to navigate to a new screen, or to add and remove items from a collection.

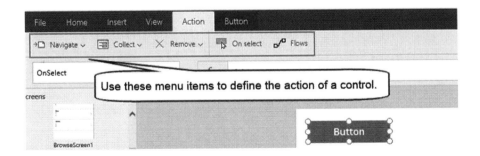

Figure 8-4. *Configuring the action of a button*

A common design technique is to use icons to respond to user interactions. We can insert icons through the Icon button in the Insert menu. Figure 8-5 shows the available icons.

Figure 8-5. *Icons that we can add to a screen*

Displaying Geometric Shapes

The geometric shapes we can add to a screen include all the common shapes such as circles, rectangles, and triangles. The menu item to add shapes is slightly hidden away. It appears beneath the icon menu in a shapes group, rather than a separate menu. Figure 8-6 shows the shapes that are available.

Figure 8-6. *Geometric shapes that we can add to a screen*

These shape controls are useful because they can serve as a background for other controls. For example, we could add a rectangle control and add child controls over the control. We could then apply background colors and borders to group controls together and to improve the appearance of your screen.

Another useful tip is to apply formula to the OnSelect property of a shape. This makes the shape react to a screen tap and we can use this technique to create custom buttons. For example, we could enable users to set the priority value of a record by clicking red, yellow, or green rectangles on a screen.

Displaying Text with Label and HTML Text Controls

There are two controls to display text: the label control and the HTML text control. The label control displays simple text and the Home menu provides options to format the contents of the control. As Figure 8-7 shows, we can set the font type, size, and color of a label. We can also apply text styles such as bold, italics, underline, and strikethrough. We can better align our label with adjacent controls by adjusting the vertical and horizontal text alignment.

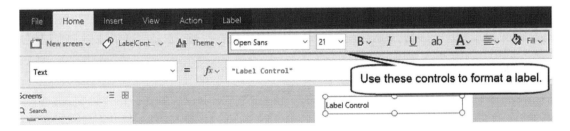

Figure 8-7. *Formatting the contents of a label*

The Text property defines the text that appears in the label, which can include display multiline text. To enter a line break, we can type <shift><enter> into the formula bar.

We can configure the label height to adapt automatically to its content. The AutoHeight property enables this behavior. We can also configure the label to show scrollbars by setting the Overflow property to true.

The fonts that we can use are limited. For example, the Wingdings font isn't available, which would enable us enter symbols that could include checkmarks, crosses, or emoticons.

The HTML text control enables us to display HTML content. HTML provides far greater control over the formatting of text. Unlike the label control, we can set the colors and styles of individual words in a sentence with HTML.

When we add an HTML text control to our screen, the HtmlText property provides example markup to help us author basic HTML, as shown in Figure 8-8. This includes how to set the text style to bold with the `<b>` tag, and how to set the text color to blue with the tag `<font color=blue>`.

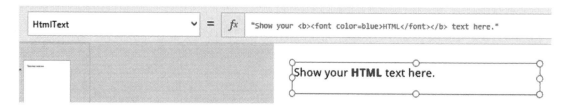

Figure 8-8. *The HTML text control provides example markup.*

The HTML text control is particularly useful when we want to display characters that are unavailable with plain text. This could include the superscript characters in chemical symbols, mathematical symbols, or even musical characters. Example symbols and the corresponding HTML tags include CO^2 (CO²) (CO<sup>2</sup>),∞ (∞), or B♭ (B ♭).

Using Simple Controls

Let's now look at how to use simple data controls - controls that bind to a single value. We'll use the edit form in our auto-generated app to help describe how these controls work. The controls that we'll examine in this section will include the Text Input, Radio, Slider, Toggle, and Rating controls.

Text Input Control

The default control that appears in the edit form is the text input control. This control receives text input from the user, and it offers many useful features that we can take advantage of.

To restrict the data that users can enter, the control provides a mode property that we can set to one of three values: MultiLine, SingleLine, or Password. The MultiLine and SingleLine properties control the entry of multiline text. In password mode, the control masks each character that the user enters with asterisk characters.

To restrict the amount of text that a user can enter, we can set the 'max length' property. The control also provides a format property that we can set to one of two values: text or number. If we set the format property to number, the control will only accept numeric input from the user.

To provide users with additional help, there are two properties we can set - the tooltip property and the hint text property. A tooltip is a piece of help text that appears when a user hovers the mouse over the control. Since there is no concept of a mouse for mobile devices, this is where the hint property comes into play. The text input control shows the hint text when the control is empty, as shown in Figure 8-9. As soon as the user enters some text into the control, the hint text disappears and the control shows the text that the user has entered.

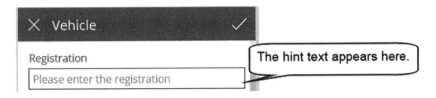

Figure 8-9. *Setting the hint text on the text input control*

The text input control also includes a property called Clear. When this is set to true, a cross icon appears in the far right of the control and the user can click this icon to clear the contents of the control.

On Windows, the official browsers that support this feature are IE and Edge. The clear feature does not work in the Windows version of PowerApps Studio.

■ **Tip** Use the hint text property to provide help for smartphone or tablet users. Tooltips do not appear on devices without a mouse.

Radio Control

The radio control permits a user to make a single selection from a list of choices. To demonstrate how to use this control, we'll replace the fuel type text input control in our edit form with a radio control. In our example, we'll set up the radio control to store one of three values in the spreadsheet. The values that we'll store in the 'fuel type' field will be P, D, or E (to denote petrol, diesel, or electric).

To replace the default text input control, the first step is to unlock the 'fuel type' card and to delete the text input control.

When we delete a text input control from a card, the designer will display two warnings. The first relates to the Update property of the card that is now invalid, and the second refers to a formula that calculates the y-position coordinate of an error warning label. We need to change this formula so that it refers to our new control, rather than the old text input control name. The other examples in this section follow the same pattern, and therefore, these steps will apply to those examples too.

The next step is to insert a radio control and to name it RadioFuelType. To define the items that appear in the radio control, set the Items property to the following value:

```
Table({FuelId:"P", FuelDesc:"Petrol"}, {FuelId:"D", FuelDesc:"Diesel"},
{FuelId:"E", FuelDesc:"Electric"})
```

This formula defines a table that includes the columns FuelID and FuelDesc. The FuelID field denotes a single character code, and the FuelDesc field contains a friendly description of the fuel type. To configure the radio control to show the friendly description, set the value property to FuelDesc.

The next step is to configure the card to use the selected radio item to update the 'fuel type' field when a user saves a record. To do this, select the parent card control, and set the Update property to the formula beneath:

```
RadioFuelType.Selected.FuelId
```

To complete this example, the final step is to configure the radio control to display the correct item when a user opens an existing record. The default property defines the selected radio option, and in our example, we need to provide the friendly description, because this is what the control shows. Therefore, we need a formula that converts the values P to Petrol, D to Diesel, and E to Electric. Here's the formula we would use to set the `Default` property:

```
If(Parent.Default="P", "Petrol",If(Parent.Default="D", "Diesel",If(Parent.Default="E",
"Electric","")))
```

Figure 8-10 shows our screen in the designer and highlights the appropriate formula. We can now run our app and the set the fuel type using the radio control.

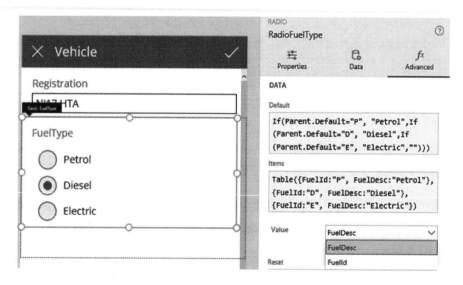

Figure 8-10. *Configuring a radio control*

A useful point to be aware of is that we cannot change the orientation of the radio items. The radio items always stack on top of each other, and it's not possible to amend the layout so that the items flow from left to right.

Toggle and Checkbox Controls

There are two controls that can accept yes/no, or true/false values from the user. These are the toggle control, and the checkbox control. Both of these controls function similarly so for brevity, we'll examine the use of the toggle control only. The toggle control is identical to the checkbox, except that the user changes the state of the control by sliding a button, rather than clicking a checkbox with a mouse.

To demonstrate this control, we'll add a toggle control to our screen to allow users to set the transmission type of a vehicle. The transmission field in the spreadsheet will contain the values A or M (to denote automatic or manual transmission). The state of a toggle control can be true or false. In our app, we'll use true to denote an automatic vehicle, and false to denote a manual vehicle.

The first step is to unlock the fuel type card and to delete the text box. Just like the previous example, we need to resolve any errors that might arise. Next, insert a toggle control and name it `ToggleTransmission`. Add a label next to the toggle control and set the text to "Is automatic".

The next step is to set up the card to use the toggle control to update the transmission field when a user saves the record. To do this, select the parent card control and set the Update property to:

```
If(ToggleTransmission.Value, "A","M")
```

To complete this example, the final step is to show the correct value in the toggle control when a user opens an existing record. This requires a formula that converts the value "A" to true, and "M" to false. The formula we would use to set the Default property of the toggle control is shown beneath:

```
If(Parent.Default="A", true, false)
```

A helpful point to mention about this formula is that the equality operator is case sensitive. Therefore Parent.Default="A" is not the same as Parent.Default="a".

Figure 8-11 shows this control in the designer. We can now run our app and then set the transmission type of a vehicle with the toggle control.

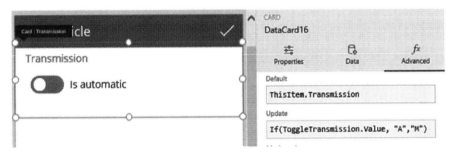

Figure 8-11. *Configuring toggle control*

Slider Control

The slider control provides a simple way for a user to enter a numeric value between a minimum and maximum value. To demonstrate this control, we'll provide a slider control on the edit form to set the number of seats in a vehicle.

The first step is to unlock the seat card and to delete the text box. Just like the earlier example, resolve any errors that occur. Insert a slider control and name it SliderSeats.

Some useful properties that we can set on the slider control are the minimum and maximum values, as shown in Figure 8-12. The minimum value can be negative, and the maximum value can be as large as the maximum number that JavaScript permits. Other useful settings include the size of the slider bar and button.

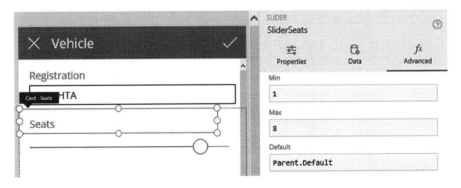

Figure 8-12. *Configuring the slider control*

The next step is to configure the card to use the slider value to update the seat field when a user saves a record. To do this, select the parent card control, and set the Update property to:

```
SliderSeats.Value
```

The final step is to display the correct value when a user opens an existing record. To do this, set the Default property to:

```
Parent.Default
```

We can now run our app and set the number of seats with the slider control.

Rating Control

The final control that we'll look at in this section is the rating control. This is a control that can set and retrieve numeric values. This control displays a number of stars and users can assign a rating by clicking on a star.

To demonstrate this control, we'll configure the rating control to store the comfort level of a vehicle. The first step is to unlock the comfort level card and to delete the text input control. Insert a rating control and name it RatingComfort.

We can set the maximum value that the control can accept, as shown in Figure 8-13. Like the slider control, the maximum value can be as large as the maximum number that JavaScript permits.

Figure 8-13. *Configuring the rating control*

The next step is to configure the card to use the rating control to update the comfort rating field when a user saves a record. Select the parent card control and set the Update property to:

```
RatingComfort.Value
```

The final step is to display the correct value in the rating control when a user opens an existing record. To do this, set the Default property to:

```
Parent.Default
```

We can now run our app and set the comfort level of a vehicle with the rating control. One thing to note is that some iOS users have reported problems with this control. In some circumstances, users may have to carry out a long press of a star before the control registers the selection.

Working with Dates

We'll now look at how to work with date values and how to use the date picker control. The biggest challenge is that due to time zone conversions, it's possible for apps to store and display incorrect time values. With the help of this section, we can take steps to avoid this problem.

Date Picker Control

PowerApps provides a date picker that users can use to enter dates. Figure 8-14 shows the date picker control at runtime. The highlights of this control are as follows. Initially, the control appears on a single line and shows the date in short date format. The control applies the short date format that is associated with the regional settings of the device or browser and there is no way to specify a different format. When a user clicks the control, it provides the ability to make a date selection through a calendar view.

Figure 8-14. *Date picker control*

This calendar view provides forward and backward icons to navigate thought the months. Something that might not be obvious is that users can quickly change the year and month values by clicking on these labels. Users who are unaware of this feature can easily become frustrated when they set a date that is significantly earlier or greater than the current date with the backward and forward navigation icons.

An important property to be aware of is the 'start year' property. This defaults to 1970 and users cannot select a year earlier than this. It's necessary to reduce this value if we want to accept earlier dates.

With Excel data sources, it's important to add sample data to a spreadsheet before we attempt to build an auto-generated app. If we create an auto-generated app with a spreadsheet that contains only table headings, the designer cannot determine the data types of any of the fields. In this instance, all the auto-generated cards will contain text input controls.

Showing Dates Only

For auto-generated apps, PowerApps provides auto-generated cards that include both date and time entry controls for the date fields in a data source. A common question from app builders is how to modify a card to accept date entries only. The answer is straightforward; we can simply remove the hour and minute drop-down controls. To demonstrate, this technique, we'll modify a date on the edit form of our sample app to accept date entries only. The name of the field that we'll modify is the 'insurance end date' field to accept only date entries.

Once we open the edit form in the designer, the first step is to unlock the card. Within the card, there are three controls that relate to the time component: an hour drop-down, a minute drop-down, and a label control that displays a colon between these two drop-downs. Select these three controls and delete them from the card. If the delete key on the keyboard fails to work, try using the delete option in the right-click context menu.

When we delete these time controls, the designer reports several errors, and we can review these by clicking the exclamation point icons, as shown in Figure 8-15. Several of these occur because X and Y coordinates of adjacent controls refer to the controls that we deleted. For the purposes of this demonstration, we can hide these errors by setting the incorrect values to 0.

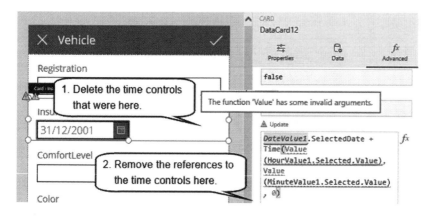

Figure 8-15. *The Update property is no longer valid when we delete the hour and minute controls*

The most importing setting to change is the update property. One of the exclamation point icons will take us to the update formula, and we can remove the references to the time controls. At this point, we can run our app and use the date picker to save just the date value.

Here's a useful tip. The designer does not provide an option to insert the time picker controls through the inset menu. If we want to add hour and minute drop-down controls to other parts of an app, we can copy and paste these controls from an auto-generated card.

Understanding How Date Values Are Stored

Let's now examine one of the biggest challenges that some app builders face. Because users from different parts of the world can run the same app at the same time, PowerApps is designed to accommodate users from different time zones. To display times values that are appropriate for the time zone for the user, PowerApps stores the UTC (Universal Time Coordinated) value of dates and times in the underlying data store. UTC shares the same time as GMT (Greenwich Mean Time), the time zone for England, and all time zones in the world are expressed as positive or negative offsets against UTC. This support for multiple time zones can lead to some unexpected behavior and we'll now explore this in more detail.

Let's assume that we're in London and that the current month is June. At this location, the current time zone is BST (British Summer Time), which equates to UTC+ 1hr. If we set the insurance end date value of a record in our example app to the 10th May 2017, the record handling will appear to work correctly. We can open the record and view the insurance end date value as expected.

However, things become more interesting when we start to delve into the underlying data. Figure 8-16 shows the record that PowerApps saves to Excel and as we can see, the date doesn't appear to be correct. It shows up as the 9th December 2017 23:00. This is because PowerApps converts the input date to UTC by subtracting one hour. When a user opens this record, PowerApps converts the value back to BST by adding one hour. Therefore, the user can enter and retrieve date values consistently because PowerApps carries out the UTC conversions during the save and retrieval operations.

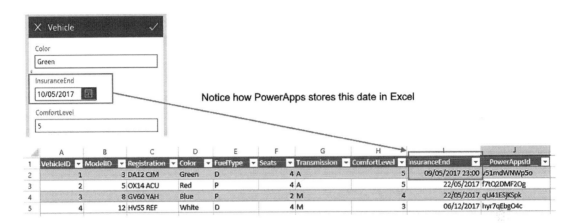

Figure 8-16. *PowerApps saves UTC times to the underlying data source*

This behavior causes a problem for other users who want to work directly with the data in Excel (or the underlying data source). The date values here will be one hour out of sync and will not be an accurate reflection of what the user intended.

Is there a fix for this? The answer is 'kind-of.' The date picker control provides a property called TimeZone. This property defines the time zone of the selected date in the control and we can set this to one of two values: local or UTC. The default value is local, and this is the reason why PowerApps subtracts one hour when it saves the date to Excel.

If we were to change this setting to UTC, PowerApps assumes that the input date is in UTC and will not carry out any conversions when it saves the data to Excel. By changing the TimeZone setting to UTC, the data in the Excel spreadsheet will appear more accurate, as shown in Figure 8-17.

	A	B	C	D	E	F	G	H	I		J	
1	VehicleID	ModelID	Registration	Color	FuelType	Seats	Transmission	ComfortLevel	InsuranceEnd		PowerAppsId	
2	1	3	DA12 CJM	Green	P	4	A	5	09/05/2017		v51mdWNWp5o	
3	2	5	OX14 ACU	Red	P	4	A	5	22/05/2017		f7tQ2DMF2Og	
4	3	8	GV60 YAH	Blue	P	2	M	4	22/05/2017		qU41ESjKSpk	
5	4	12	HV55 REF	White	D	4	M	3	06/12/2017		hyr7qEbgO4c	

Figure 8-17. *Excel data appears correct when we set the TimeZone to UTC*

However, there is one side effect of changing the time zone to UTC. When PowerApps retrieves the record, it still converts the source date to the local time zone, and therefore adds one hour. So although dates now appear correctly in Excel, the dates that appear in an app will be one hour greater than the correct time, as shown in Figure 8-18.

Figure 8-18. *The date that PowerApps retrieves is incorrect when we set the TimeZone to UTC*

So to make sure that users can consistently save and retrieve dates, we would need to find all the places where an app displays the date, and convert the value back to UTC like so:

```
Text(ThisItem.InsuranceEnd, "UTC")
```

The disadvantage of setting the TimeZone to UTC is that we now need to change all the places where the date appears and this can involve a lot of work. If we've built screens to search data based on date criteria, we would need to make sure to convert the input date to UTC.

Saving Dates in year-month-day Format

As you can see, creating apps that can read and write time values consistently throughout an app and the underlying data source can be a challenge. With the automated UTC time adjustments, the potential for incorrect data to enter a system is greater because dependencies exist that are outside of our control.

A typical problem that app builders report is that with apps that connect to SharePoint, the times that users enter through an app fail to match the values that appear in SharePoint. There are several possible causes for this. The regional settings on the client device or browser might be incorrect. Or alternatively, the administrator may never have set up the regional settings for the SharePoint site.

These problems are guaranteed to be difficult to diagnose. Therefore, one simple solution to maintain consistent dates is to store our date and time values as strings in the format yyyymmddhhmm. When we want to display a date in an app, we would format the date as required. Another benefit of this approach is that we can still sort our date values in ascending or descending order.

Here's how to amend our app to store the 'insurance end date' values in yyyymmddhhmm format. Open the edit form and modify the Update command for the 'insurance end date' card. Use the formula below to convert the input date in the date picker to yyyymmddhhmm format. In this formula, DateValue1 refers to the date picker control.

```
Text(DateValue1.SelectedDate, "yyyymmddhhmm")
```

Now modify the Default property of the date picker control to provide it with a valid date when a user opens an existing record. We need to call the DateTimeValue function and to provide an input string in the format "yyyy-mm-dd hh:mm", like so:

```
DateTimeValue(Left(Parent.Default, 4) & "-" & Mid(Parent.Default, 5,2) & "-" & Mid(Parent.
Default, 7,2) & " " &
                    Mid(Parent.Default, 9,2) & ":" & Mid(Parent.Default, 11,2)
)
```

This formula will produce an error (as shown in Figure 8-19) because in the initial spreadsheet, the data type of the insurance end field was a date and we've now modified this field to store text values instead.

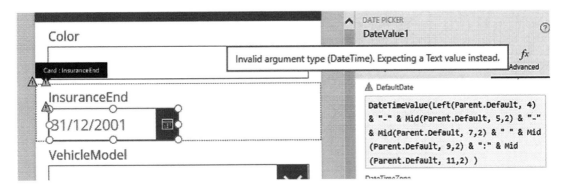

Figure 8-19. *Converting a field to yyyymmddhhmm*

To resolve this error, change the date values in the Excel spreadsheet to be in the format yyyymmddhhmm. In Excel, it's necessary to precede the values we enter with a single quote to force Excel to recognize the data as a string like so:

'201705090000

Next, change the format of the cells to Text, as shown in Figure 8-20. At this point, return to PowerApps and refresh your data source by clicking the Insert ➤ Data sources menu and choosing the right-click refresh option against the data source. Once we refresh our data source, the error will disappear.

	A	B	C	D	E	F	G	H	I
1	VehicleID	ModelID	Registration	Color	FuelType	Seats	Transmission	ComfortLevel	InsuranceEnd
2	1	3	DA12 CJM	Green	P		4 A	5	201705220000
3	2	5	OX14 ACU	Red	P		4 A	5	201705220000
4	3							4	201705220000
5	4							3	201705220000
6	5							3	201705220000
7									
8									
9									
10									
11									

Format Cells ? ×

Number | Alignment | Font | Border | Fill | Protection

Category:
General
Number
Currency
Accounting
Date
Time

Sample
InsuranceEnd

Text format cells are treated as text even when a number is in the cell. The cell is displayed exactly as entered.

Figure 8-20. *Changing the data type in the source data*

The final step is to apply a more readable format to any controls that display the 'insurance end date' field. In the auto-generated app, we would need to do this on the detail form. We can use a formula to display the date in long date time format, like so:

```
Text(DateValue(Left(Parent.Default, 4) & "-" & Mid(Parent.Default, 5,2) & "-" & Mid(Parent.
Default, 7,2) & " " & Mid(Parent.Default, 9,2) & ":" & Mid(Parent.Default, 11,2)),
DateTimeFormat.LongDateTime)
```

At this stage, we can run our app. The app will function as before, but the date values will be stored in yyyymmddhhmm format in the underlying Excel spreadsheet.

Setting Lookup Values

In this section, we'll examine the use of the drop-down and list box controls. These controls are important because they enable us to limit the values that a user can enter, or to set lookup values.

To demonstrate the drop-down control, we'll apply this control to two fields in the edit form of our auto-generated app - the color field, and the model id field. You can refer to Figure 8-2 and Figure 8-3 to review the structure of our data.

In the first example, we'll find out how to use a drop-down control to limit the colors that a user can enter to a set of predefined values. In the second example, we'll find out how to populate a drop-down control with vehicle model names, and how to store the numeric model id in the vehicle spreadsheet.

Limiting Input Values with a Drop-Down Control

Starting with the color field, let's replace the text input control with a drop-down list of hard-coded color values. The first step is to open the edit form and to find the card that relates to the color field. Change the control type to 'Allowed Values' and then unlock the card, as shown in Figure 8-21.

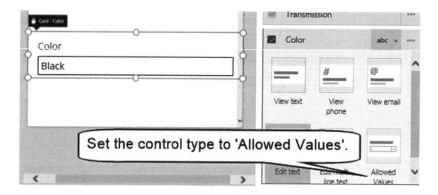

Figure 8-21. *Changing the control type to 'Allowed Values'*

Select the drop-down control in the card and set the Items property to the following formula:

```
["Red", "Green", "Blue", "Yellow", "Orange", "Purple", "Pink", " Brown" ," White"," Black"]
```

Figure 8-22 shows how this setting appears in the designer. We can now run our app and use the drop-down to set the color field of vehicle record.

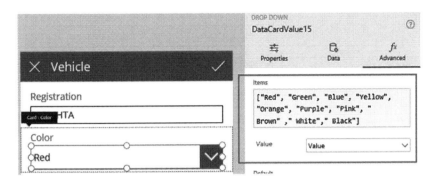

Figure 8-22. *Setting up drop-downs with static items*

An interesting question you might ask is this. If we open an existing record with a color value that doesn't exist in the drop-down, what would happen? The answer is that the drop-down would show a blank value. In this scenario, PowerApps will not display any error messages to the user, and it will not crash or stop working entirely.

Setting Lookup Values with a Drop-Down Control

We'll now look at the more complex scenario, which is how to set up a drop-down to assign a vehicle model to a vehicle record. Our drop-down control will display the vehicle model details from the model table, and we'll configure the form to save the numeric model id to the vehicle table.

The first step is to open the edit form and to select the card that relates to the model id field. Change the control type to 'Allowed Values' and unlock the card.

Set the Items property to the data source of the vehicle model spreadsheet, as shown in Figure 8-23. Because the vehicle models table includes several columns, we can use the value property to specify the field that appears in the drop-down. Set the value property to the Name field.

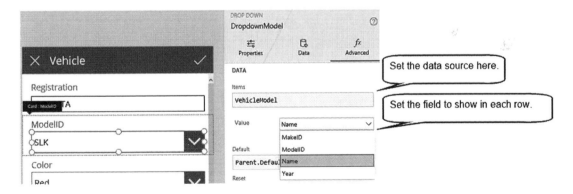

Figure 8-23. *Setting up Drop-Downs*

The default name of the drop-down will be something like `DataCardValue18`. To make this control easier to identify, rename it to `DropdownModel`.

The next step is to configure the card to save the numeric model id value when a user saves the record. To do this, select the parent card control, and set the Update property to the following formula:

```
DropdownModel.Selected.ModelID
```

To complete this example, the final step is to setup the drop-down box to show the correct item when a user opens an existing record. To configure this, set the Default property of the drop-down to the following formula:

```
LookUp(VehicleModel, ModelID = Parent.Default).Name
```

We can now run our app and then set the model using a drop-down box control.

Customizing the Drop-Down Display Value

A common task is to customize and display multiple fields in each row of a drop-down. In our example so far, the drop-down shows just the model name. How can we modify the drop-down to display both the model name and year of the model? The answer is to set the Items property of the drop-down to a formula that combines the fields that we want to display. Here's the formula we would use to display both the model name and the year:

```
AddColumns(VehicleModel, "ModelAndYear", Name  & " (" & Year & ")")
```

The purpose of the AddColumns function is to add columns to a data source, collection, or table. This function accepts three arguments - a data source, the name of the column to add, and the value for each row. Chapter 6 provides more details about these data-shaping functions. Once we add this function, we can set the value property of the drop-down to ModelAndYear.

The next step is to modify the formula for the Default property so that it selects the correct item in the drop-down for existing records. Here's the formula we would use:

```
LookUp(AddColumns(VehicleModel, "ModelAndYear", Name  & " (" & Year & ")"),
       ModelID = Parent.Default).ModelAndYear
```

The purpose of the Lookup function is to return the first record from a data source that matches a formula that we provide. The formula that we use here looks up the record in the data source where the ModelID value in VehicleModel table matches the ModelID value of the vehicle record.

Figure 8-24 shows the appearance of this code in the designer. We can now run our app, and each row in the vehicle model drop-down will show the name and the year fields.

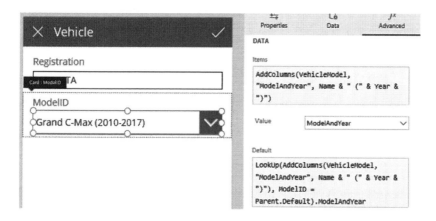

Figure 8-24. *Edit the Items, Value, and Default properties to customize the drop-down text*

Nesting Drop-Down Controls

To make it easier for users to enter data, we can nest together sets of drop-down controls. As a logical extension of the previous example, we'll add a vehicle make drop-down to the edit form and configure the vehicle model drop-down so that it shows records that match the selected vehicle make.

Figure 8-25 shows the vehicle makes table, and the formula in this section will refer to this data source as VehicleMake.

	A	B
1	MakeID	Name
2	1	Audi
3	2	Ford
4	3	Lexus
5	4	Mercedes-Benz
6	5	BMW

Figure 8-25. *The VehicleMakes table*

To build this feature, select the card that displays the vehicle model and insert a drop-down control above the 'vehicle model' drop-down. Name this control DropdownMakes and set the Items property to VehicleMake, as shown in Figure 8-26.

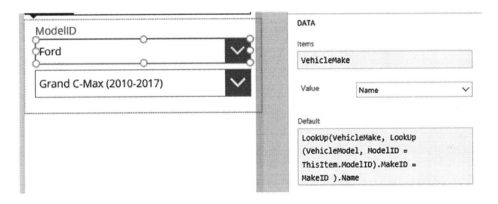

Figure 8-26. *The 'vehicle makes' drop-down*

When the card loads an existing vehicle record, it needs to show the vehicle make that corresponds to the vehicle model of the record. To configure this, set the Default property of the DropdownMakes control to the following formula:

```
LookUp(VehicleMake,
            LookUp(VehicleModel, ModelID = ThisItem.ModelID).MakeID = MakeID
        ).Name
```

This formula contains a set of nested lookups. The innermost lookup retrieves the MakeID that corresponds to the ModelID of the vehicle record. It uses the VehicleModel table to carry out the lookup. The outermost lookup retrieves the name field of the make record that matches the MakeID value from the inner lookup.

We can now configure the 'vehicle models' drop-down to filter the items according to the 'vehicle make' that the user chooses. To make this change, set the Items property of the 'vehicle models' drop-down to the formula below:

```
Filter(AddColumns(VehicleModel, "ModelAndYear", Name  & " (" & Year & ")"),
        MakeID =DropdownMakes.Selected.MakeID)
```

We can now run our screen and select a vehicle make. As soon as this happens, the vehicle model drop-down will show only those vehicle models that are associated with the selected vehicle make.

List Box Control

The list box control provides the ability for a user to select one or more items from a list. For practical purposes, this control works identically to the drop-down control, and the only difference is that the data items are always on display. Figure 8-27 shows the list box control in the designer.

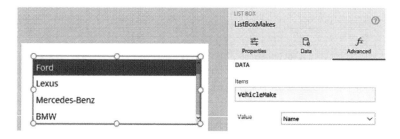

Figure 8-27. *The list box control*

The Items property defines the data source for the control. If the data source contains multiple columns, the value property will specify the field to display.

The SelectMultiple property controls whether the user can select multiple items, or whether the user can select a single item only.

We can use the SelectedItems property to retrieve the selected items with formula. Here's a useful tip. To show all the selected items in a label, we can call the Concat function to build a string that shows the selected items. Here's the syntax we would use.

```
Concat(ListBoxDefects.SelectedItems, Description & " ")
```

The Concat function accepts a data source and a formula. This function applies the formula to each row in the data source and combines all the results into a single output value.

The default property of the list box control specifies the selected item. We would set this to the text of the item to select. However, a major limitation is that we can preselect a maximum of one item only and this prevents us from using this control to display multiple items that are associated with a record.

Displaying Tables of Data

We'll now look at a control that displays data in a tabular format - the Table control. To add this control to a screen, click the 'data table' button in the insert menu. Next, use the Items property to set the data source. We can then define the columns in the table by enabling cards, as shown in Figure 8-28.

Figure 8-28. *Using the Table Control*

The table control is read only, and doesn't provide cell-level editing like Excel. This control behaves similarly to the gallery control because it keeps track of the selected row. A typical design pattern is to place an edit form next to the table control, and to set the data source of the edit form to the selected item in the data table. This provides the ability for users to select and edit a record on the same screen, as shown in Figure 8-29.

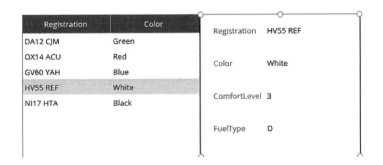

Figure 8-29. *Creating a List and Details screen*

Using CDS-Specific Controls

In this section of the chapter, we'll look at control features that are unique to CDS data sources. This includes a different type of form control called the 'entity form control', and differences in behavior with the drop-down control.

Using Entity Form Controls

In addition to the form and card controls that we've seen in auto-generated apps, we can utilize another type of form control with CDS data sources - the Entity Form control. This control allows us to quickly set up forms to display and edit data, and a key feature is the ability to show data in a tabular format.

To use this control, use the Insert menu to add the control to a screen and set the DataSource property to a CDS table, as shown in Figure 8-30. This control requires more screen space to fit all the data, and therefore works best on tablet applications.

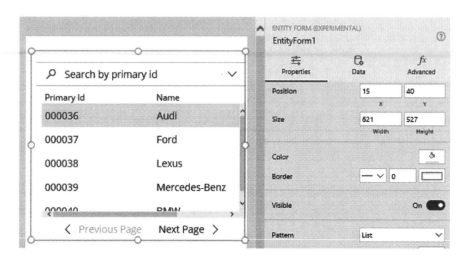

Figure 8-30. *Using the Entity Form Control - the List pattern displays data in tabular format*

The Pattern property provides one of four predefined formats: CardList, Details, List, None. The List pattern displays a tabular view of the data, the CardList pattern applies a format that resembles a tiled view of the data, and the Details pattern displays an individual record, rather than a list of records (as shown in Figure 8-31).

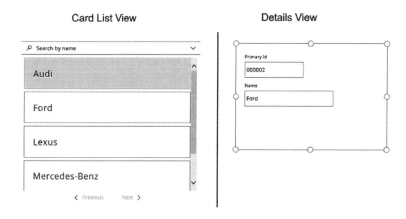

Figure 8-31. *The CardList and Details patterns*

An interesting characteristic is that there are no properties to define the fields or columns that appear in the form. Instead, we define the fields through 'field groups' in the entities section of the web portal, as shown in Figure 8-32.

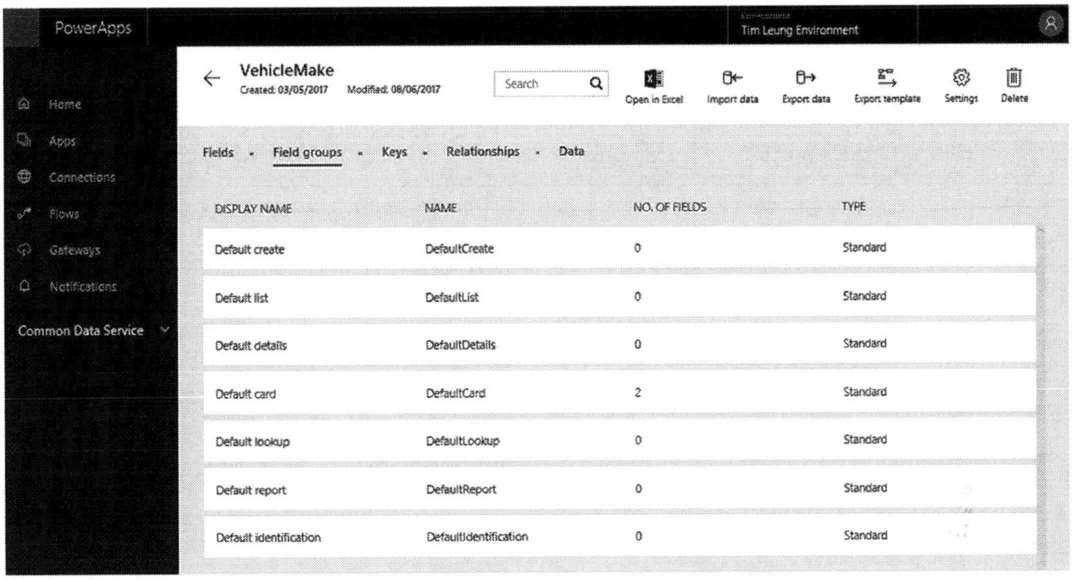

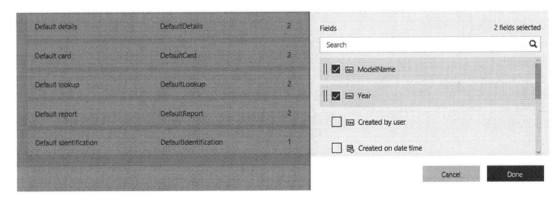

Figure 8-32. *The Field Groups for an entity*

This provides a centralized method to specify the fields that appear in a form, and any fields that we subsequently add or remove from the field group will affect all instances of the entity form control in all our applications.

The field group that applies to the entity form control depends on the pattern setting. With the pattern set to list, the DefaultList field group defines the columns that appear in the control. For the CardList pattern, the DefaultCard field group defines the visible fields. And for the Details pattern, it's the DefaultDetails field group that we need to set.

To define the fields that belong to a field group, select a field group to display the properties pane in the right-hand section of the screen. From here, we can select the fields for the group, as shown in Figure 8-33.

Figure 8-33. *Selecting the fields that belong to a field group*

In the data section of the properties pane, we can configure fields in the form to navigate the user to a different screen. When a user navigates away from an entity form control, the control automatically sets a context variable called `NavigationContext`. This variable stores the selected item in the form control, and we can use this to set the data source of data controls on any child controls that we choose to add to a screen.

Drop-Down Controls with CDS

Earlier in this chapter, we looked at how to set up a drop-down control to allow users to assign lookup values. With SharePoint and CDS data sources, the drop-down box controls work differently. The auto-generated cards recognize the existence of related data and include drop-down boxes for related data. This is great because it simplifies the task of building forms with lookup data.

To demonstrate how this works, here's a re-creation of the Excel example, but with a CDS data source. The CDS database contains two related entities - a vehicle entity and a 'vehicle model' entity. The vehicle entity includes a lookup to a vehicle model entity. Figure 8-34 shows the design of these two entities.

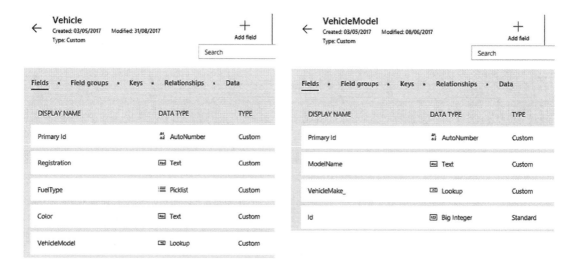

Figure 8-34. *Vehicle and Vehicle Model entities*

Figure 8-35 shows the edit screen from an auto-generated app that's based on the vehicle entity. The default card for the model field includes a drop-down box. Unlike the Excel example, there's no need to add a separate data source for vehicle models or to carry out any additional configuration. Everything works as it should by default!

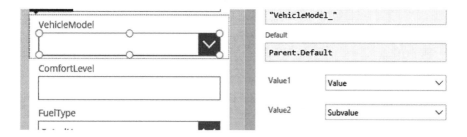

Figure 8-35. *Drop-down control for a CDS lookup field - notice the Value1 and Value2 properties*

Unlike the drop-down control that we added through the Insert menu of the toolbar, the drop-down controls on auto-generated cards for CDS and SharePoint data sources are different. As we can see in Figure 8-35, they include two slightly obscure options: Value1 and Value2. What exactly do these options do?

To explain this behavior, Figure 8-36 shows the appearance of the drop-down at runtime. Notice that the control shows the numeric id of the model number rather than the descriptive text.

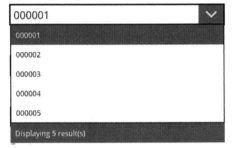

Figure 8-36. *At runtime, the drop-down shows the numeric id - this isn't much help for the user!*

This view of the data isn't very meaningful, so how do we change the drop-down so that it shows the model name rather than the model id?

The answer lies not in the designer, but in the entity designer. The 'default lookup' field group defines the fields that appear in drop-downs. To make additional fields available, we first need to add those fields to the 'default lookup' field group. Once we do this, we can return to the screen designer and set Value1 to the field name that we want to show in the drop-down. In our example, this would be ModelName, as shown in Figure 8-37. Note that it's necessary to set the Value1 property at the card level. At the time of writing, the drop-down does not show the correct field when we set the Value1 or Value2 property at the control level.

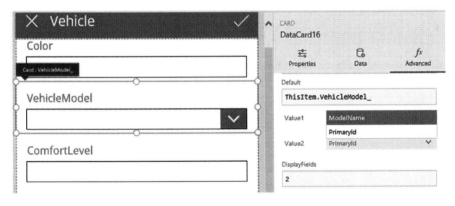

Figure 8-37. *Setting the display values of a CDS lookup field*

Another property we can set is the 'display fields' setting. This setting controls the number of fields to show in each row of the drop-down. By setting this to two, we can use the Value2 property to define the second field that appears in the drop-down. At runtime, both fields will appear one on top of each other, as shown in Figure 8-38.

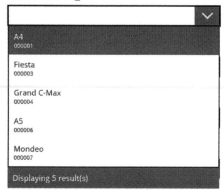

Figure 8-38. *Displaying two fields for each row in a drop-down*

Although we can more easily add drop-downs against lookup fields in CDS or SharePoint data sources, there are some limitations. First, we can't filter the items in the drop-down. For instance, if we want to restrict the items in a drop-down box of employees to show only active employees, this isn't possible. Second, we can't show multiple fields in each row of a drop-down box. If we need any of these features, we should add a custom card and insert a drop-down control manually. This would allow us to set the items property of the drop-down to a filtered data source, or a data source that combines multiple fields.

Finally, it's important to be aware that there is a limit on the number of items in a drop-down. In the case of a SharePoint data source, the maximum number of rows that a drop-down can display is 100 records.

Working with Media Controls

Let's now look at media controls. We can make applications more attractive by incorporating sounds, images, and videos. To make media content available in our apps, use the File ➤ Media menu to upload files, as shown in Figure 8-39.

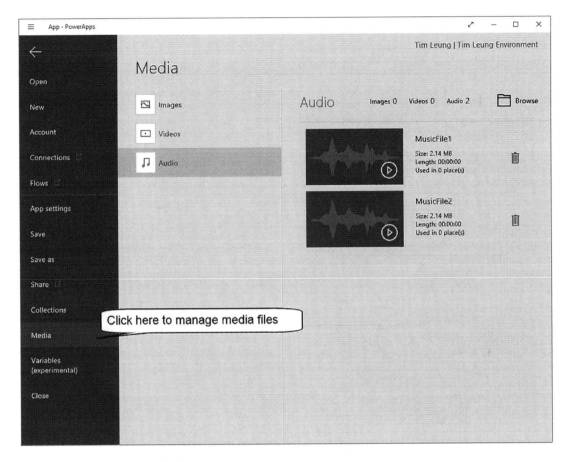

Figure 8-39. *Uploading media files into a project*

One important point is that that media files can easily bloat the size of an app. If we were to upload a 15MB video into an app, this would result in a corresponding increase in the size of the project. This would cause the app to load more slowly because the initial download of the app onto the device would take longer.

We can use the file name to refer to a file that we uploaded in formulas. Therefore, it makes good sense to provide files with meaningful names before we upload them into an app. Table 8-1 shows the file types that PowerApps supports. We'll now examine the controls that we can use to display images, and to play back video and audio files.

Table 8-1. *Supported media types*

Media	Supported file types
Images	.jpg, .jpeg, .gif, .png, .bmp, .tif,, .tiff, .svg
Videos	.mp4, .wmv
Audio	.wav, .mp3, .wma

Playing Videos

The video control can play videos that we've uploaded or videos from the Web or YouTube. Figure 8-40 shows the appearance of this control in the designer.

Figure 8-40. *The video control*

The Media property specifies the video to play. To specify a YouTube video, it's necessary to enclose the URL with double quotes. To specify a file that we uploaded, set the Media property to the file name. If the file name includes spaces, we would need to enclose the file with single quotes.

There are two properties that relate to the playback of videos: Start and AutoStart. The Start property specifies whether the video plays. The AutoStart property defines whether the video plays as soon the screen becomes visible.

A typical user requirement is to provide a button that starts and stops the playback of a video. To build this functionality, we would insert a button to the screen and set the OnSelect property value to the following formula:

```
UpdateContext({PlayVideo:true})
```

This code toggles the value of a variable called PlayVideo. The value of this when the screen first opens will be false. We would then set the Start property of the video control to the variable PlayVideo.

Other useful properties that we can set include the auto pause, start time, and loop properties. The auto pause property controls whether video playback pauses automatically when a user navigates away from the screen. The 'start time' property specifies the position in the video to begin playback, specified in milliseconds. Finally, the control can restart playback when the video ends when we set the loop property to true.

Playing Audio

The audio control plays sound files. Just like the video control, the Media property specifies the file or URL to play.

With all media content, a useful feature is to provide a list of content and to play back the item that that the user selects. We can accomplish this by adding a list box control to our screen, and setting the Media property of the audio control to the selected item in the control.

For example, if we uploaded the audio files MusicFile1.mp3 and MusicFile2.mp3 into an app, we can set the Items property of the list box control to:

```
Table({Description:"Music File 1", AudioFile:MusicFile1},
       {Description:"Music File 2", AudioFile:MusicFile2}
)
```

Assuming that the name of the list box is ListBoxAudio, we would then set the Media property of the audio control to:

```
First(ListBoxAudio.SelectedItems).AudioFile
```

Figure 8-41 illustrates this setup. This is a useful feature, and we can also apply this same technique to the video control example.

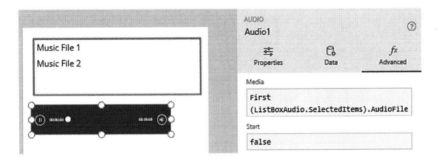

Figure 8-41. *A screen with the audio control*

Image Controls

The image control displays an image on a screen. The Image property specifies the image that the control shows. This could be a file that we upload to an app or an image URL. Useful properties of this control include the image position and transparency settings, as shown in Figure 8-42.

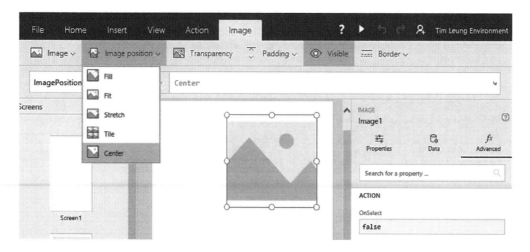

Figure 8-42. *A screen with an image control*

Here's a tip that might be useful. The image control shows rectangular images. We can make the image placeholder circular and the typical places where we see this design are in screens that display a profile picture of an individual. The way to set up a circular image is to set Height and Width to equal values. Next, there are four radius settings and we would set the each of these equal to the height value. These four settings are RadiusTopLeft, RadiusTopRight, RadiusBottomLeft, and RadiusBottomRight. For the radius settings, we can reference the height of the control by using the syntax ImageControl.Height, rather than the actual numeric values.

Using the Timer Control

The timer control runs formula after a predetermined time. We can configure the timer to reset itself after the elapsed time and this enables us to repeat an action at regular intervals. The timer control can be useful for many reasons. We can use the timer control to refresh data, update caches of data, or even carry out animations. One way to do this would be to change the background color of a shape control at rapid intervals to give the appearance of an animation.

The most important properties of this control include the duration, repeat, start, and auto start properties. The duration property is measured in milliseconds. The start property controls whether the timer is working and counting down. The auto start property defines whether the timer begins counting down immediately when the screen becomes visible. To retrieve the elapsed time, we can refer to the Value property. This returns the elapsed time in milliseconds.

To demonstrate this control, here's how to build a screen that refreshes every 60 seconds and displays the details of the last journey record in the data source.

The first step is to add a timer control to a screen. Set the Duration property to 60000, which is equivalent to 60 seconds. To configure the timer to start when the screen becomes visible and to restart every 60 seconds, set the AutoStart and Repeat properties to true.

To specify the behavior when the timer elapses, add formula to the OnTimerEnd property. Here's the formula to add:

```
UpdateContext({LatestJourney: "Latest record: " & Text(Last(Journey).StartTime) })
```

The purpose of this formula is to retrieve the latest journey record and to store the details into a variable called LatestJourney. To show these details, add a label and set the Text property to LatestJourney. We can now run our app and Figure 8-43 shows the appearance of this screen.

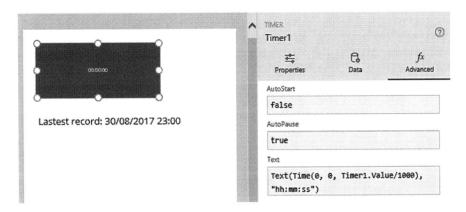

Figure 8-43. *Using the timer control*

The timer control is visible to the user and by default, the text on the control shows the elapsed time. When the timer is visible, users can click the control to start and to pause the timer. To hide the timer control, set the Visible property to false.

One point to be aware of is that the timer control isn't guaranteed to be precise. If we set the duration of a timer to five minutes, the time that it takes for the timer to complete may take more than five minutes. One possible way to re-create this behavior is to use a slower device where the JavaScript in the browser may run more slowly. If we were to build a measurement app that takes readings at specified intervals, we should be cautious of the impact that this has on the accuracy of the solution.

Another useful point to be aware of is that we can configure a timer to continue to run when a user navigates away from a screen. The way to enable this is to set the AutoPause property to false.

Resetting Form Controls

PowerApps provides a framework to reset control values back to their default states. This feature serves a very useful purpose because we can use it to allow users to undo their changes. We'll demonstrate this feature by adding a discard feature to the vehicle edit form. If a user starts to edit a record and decides not to continue, the discard button will restore the control values back to their initial state.

Every control includes a property called Reset and all controls will respond to a change in this property. When the reset property for a control changes to true, it triggers the control to restore its value back to its initial state. The pattern to build a discard feature is to set the Reset property of all controls to a context variable. To trigger the reset operation, we would set the value of the variable to true. Next, we would immediately set the value back to false to allow the user to discard changes at a later point in time.

To build this feature, the first step is to create an auto-generated app. Next, open the edit form and add a control to trigger the reset operation. A natural place is to add an icon to the top of the edit screen, as shown in Figure 8-44.

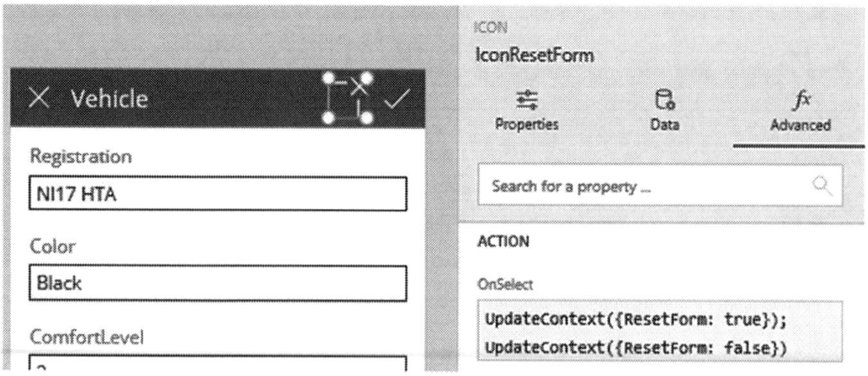

Figure 8-44. *Adding a discard button*

Here's the formula to add to the reset icon.

```
UpdateContext({ResetForm: true});  UpdateContext({ResetForm: false})
```

Now set the Reset property on all the data entry controls to the variable ResetForm. We can now run our screen. If we change the values on a form and click the reset icon, the controls will revert to their initial values.

Summary

This chapter covered the important topic of screen controls through four sections: how to work with simple controls, how to set lookup values, how to work with CDS-specific controls, and how to show media content on screens.

Starting with simple controls, we learned how to configure buttons and icons to respond to mouse clicks or taps. Almost all controls can respond to this type of interaction and the settings in the action menu enable us to define the behavior of a control.

Controls that display text include the Label and HTML text controls. The more powerful of these two controls is the HTML Text control because this provides the ability to format text with different styles. Therefore, useful applications of this control include the ability to show subscript and superscript characters, mathematical symbols, and many more.

The text input control receives text from the user. We can encourage users to enter valid data by specifying a maximum length, and we can also configure the control to accept numeric input only.

Other simple controls include the radio, slider, toggle, and rating controls. On the edit form of an auto-generated app, we can delete the default text input control on a card and replace it with an alternate control. To maintain the ability of the form to save and retrieve data, there are two settings we need to modify. First, it's necessary to set the Default property of the new control to show the existing data value when the form loads. In general, we would specify the Parent.Default property to retrieve the data value from the containing card, and we can also apply formula to carry out any data transformations. For example, with a checkbox or slider control, we could apply a formula to transform an underlying data value of 'T' or 'F' to the Boolean values true or false respectively. The second step is to modify the Update property of the containing card. This configures the card to retrieve the input value from the new control when the user saves the record. We can apply formula in the Update property to carry out any reverse transformations. For example, we could convert the Boolean value of a checkbox or slider control to the values 'T' or 'F' for storage in the underlying data source.

Next, we looked at the drop-down box control. This control is especially important because we can use it to restrict the values that a user can enter, and we can also use it to set lookup values. We can set the items of a drop-down to a static list or a data source. It's possible to filter the items in a drop-down and we can use this technique to build nested drop-down controls.

A typical way to configure a drop-down control is to set the data source to a two-column table that contains descriptive text and a corresponding code or numeric value. The drop-down would display the descriptive text and store the corresponding code in the data source. This technique relies on the use of the selected property of the drop-down to retrieve the code value. A common requirement is to customize the text in each row of the drop-down control, in order to present more meaningful details to the user. One way to accomplish this is to call the AddColumns function to build a data source that contains the customized text, and to then set the data source of the drop-down to the result of this function.

When we build auto-generated apps against SharePoint lists or CDS entities with lookup fields, the edit form provides drop-down controls to set the lookup fields. Compared to other data sources where we have to manually set up a drop-down control, there is less work to carry out with SharePoint or CDS data sources.

In auto-generated apps that are based on tables with datetime fields, the card on the edit form will include a date picker and time entry controls. A common requirement is to accept date entries without the time component, for example, to store birthdays. We can apply this change by deleting the time and minute controls and modifying the Update property of the parent card to remove any references to the time controls.

Outside of the form control, PowerApps doesn't provide a combined date and time entry control. To accept date and time entries on screens outside of forms, a quick way to implement this is to copy and paste the date and time entry controls from an auto-generated app.

To support multiple users in different time zones, the date picker control can automatically carry out time zone conversions. At the time of writing, this feature does not work completely reliably. In the meantime, a reliable workaround is to store the text representation of the date and time in the format yyyymmddmmss.

There are two controls that can display tabular data - the table control and the entity form control. Of these two controls, the table control is more flexible because it can display data from any data source. The entity form control works against CDS data sources only. The main characteristic of the entity form control is that the display fields are defined centrally through the CDS designer. Therefore, every instance of an entity form control across all apps displays the same fields.

We can use the media controls to display images, view videos, or to play audio. These controls can work against Internet-based resources such as YouTube for video files, or they can work against resources that we upload into the app.

To run formula at set intervals, we can use the timer control. We can specify the timer duration and configure the control to reset itself when the time elapses. This allows us to run formula repetitively, or for one time only. By default, this control is visible on a screen and shows the elapsed time.

Finally, we looked at how to restore control values back to their initial states. Each control includes a property called reset. When this value is true, the control will reset itself to its initial state. A typical way to build a reset or undo feature on a screen is to set the reset property on all participating controls to a Boolean variable. We would then add a button that sets the variable to true, and then back to false. This would trigger all participating controls to revert to their initial values.

CHAPTER 9

■ ■ ■

Working with Data

In this chapter, we'll find out to perform data-related tasks with formula. This is an important topic because it opens many new possibilities. By accessing data with formula, we can build better search capabilities, show more pertinent information, and provide better data entry screens.

This chapter describes how to build features to improve the usability of our apps. This includes how to set default values on new records and how to show alerts in the notifications section of mobile devices. The main topics that we'll cover in this chapter will include the following:

- How to build search screens. The auto-generated apps provide basic search capabilities. But what if we want to filter records by date, drop-down values, or show records that match a list of items? In this chapter, we'll find out how.

- How to carry out common data tasks on multiple sets of tables. Taking the typical example of an order processing app with two tables, customers and orders, how do we join these tables to show the customer detail that's associated with an order? How can we show customers who have not made orders, or show the distinct customers who have made orders? With the techniques from this chapter, you'll be able to answer these questions. In addition, we'll also discover how to group, ungroup, and to combine (or union) sets of tables together.

- How to retrieve, add, update, and delete records. We can apply the techniques in this section to update a field without showing or loading the entire record. We'll also discover how to create records in multiple related tables in one go. We'll address the complex task of how to retrieve server-generated primary key values prior to inserting child records.

Basic Behavior

To begin, there is one important data handling characteristic to be aware of. PowerApps limits the number of records that it retrieves to 500 records. It enforces this limit for performance reasons. By limiting the number of records that it returns, we're less likely to build features that can slow down our app.

The major disadvantage of this limit is that it prevents us from performing certain tasks. This applies particularly when we attempt to sum, or to count, fields from a data source. In these circumstances, the operation will apply to the first 500 records only and can therefore produce incorrect results. One exception, however, is SQL Server, which provides proper support for functions that include Sum, Min, Max, and Average.

To overcome this limit, we can load records 500 rows at a time into a local collection. Because there are no limits to the number of records you can store and retrieve from a collection, you can use collections to carry out more accurate aggregate calculations.

© Tim Leung 2017
T. Leung, *Beginning PowerApps*, https://doi.org/10.1007/978-1-4842-3003-9_9

Understanding Delegation

Delegation is a feature that speeds up data retrieval. Not all data sources support delegation, but SharePoint and SQL Server are two popular data sources that do support delegation.

What exactly does the term delegation mean? When we search data from a delegable source, the data source performs the search and returns the result. If we carry out the same operation against a non-delegable data source, the data source returns all the data and PowerApps then carries out the search on the local device. The non-delegable search works inefficiently because PowerApps needs to download more data than is necessary. Because the network connection is often the slowest link in any computerized system, non-delegable searches perform far more slowly. Additionally, mobile devices generally contain slower hardware compared to servers; and therefore, filtering data on a mobile device will be slower. Figure 9-1 illustrates this concept in the form of a diagram.

Without delegation, the data source returns all the data to the client. The client filters the data.

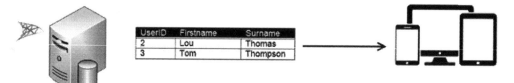

With delegation, the data source returns only the records that are required.

Figure 9-1. *How delegation works*

When we call the filter and lookup functions to search for data, the commands that support delegation include the following:

- And (including &&), Or (including ||), Not (including !), In

- =, <>, >=, <=, >, <

- +, -

- String functions including TrimEnds, IsBlank, and StartsWith

These operators depend on the data source, and not all delegable data sources will support the operators that are shown here. Most of the remaining functions do not support delegation .

Because it's preferable to write formula that is delegable, the designer shows a warning when we write data access formulas that are non-delegable. To demonstrate the type of warning we would receive, let's take the SQL server table that's shown in Figure 9-2.

	UserID	Firstname	Surname	Gender	Address1	Address2	City	Postcode	Country	Telephone	Mobile	Active
1	1	Tim	Leung	Male	3 Forest Run Circle	NULL	London	NULL	England	20-(915)361-6099	NULL	NULL
2	2	Tom	Thompson	Male	4087 Daystar Way	NULL	New York	NULL	United States	358-(866)328-8478	NULL	NULL
3	3	Lou	Thomas	Female	12 Mozzarella Cherry Way	NULL	Penzance	NULL	England	44-(731)100-0291	NULL	NULL
4	4	Sunny	Stump	Male	57874 Red Cloud Street	NULL	Surenavan	NULL	Finland	374-(344)829-6202	NULL	NULL
5	5	Em	Comelli	Male	3438 Schmedeman Road	NULL	Geoktschai	NULL	Mongolia	994-(116)563-3094	NULL	NULL
6	6	Gwenni	Lathey	Female	22 Maryland Terrace	NULL	Chikushino-shi	NULL	Egypt	81-(336)169-7418	NULL	NULL
7	7	Marget	MacKimm	Female	6101 Sloan Lane	NULL	Antsohihy	NULL	China	261-(227)802-7827	NULL	NULL
8	8	Trever	Haddrell	Male	54 Moose Lane	NULL	Dumaguete	NULL	Russia	63-(724)494-9134	NULL	NULL
9	9	Templeton	Ashworth	Male	308 Monica Drive	NULL	Pudong	NULL	South Korea	86-(890)912-6090	NULL	NULL
10	10	Tymothy	Shakshaft	Male	5836 Merchant Avenue	NULL	Stráni	NULL	Poland	420-(470)660-4399	NULL	NULL
11	11	Jessi	Lloyd	Female	2695 Messerschmidt Drive	NULL	Ninomiya	NULL	Philippines	81-(584)754-3518	NULL	NULL
12	12	Kenon	Blanch	Male	97 Golden Leaf Lane	NULL	Guaíba	NULL	Indonesia	55-(309)359-6154	NULL	NULL

Figure 9-2. *Table structure for search examples*

Let's suppose we want to show records where the country field matches the value 'United States' or England. If we implement this search by calling the in function, the designer shows the warning in Figure 9-3.

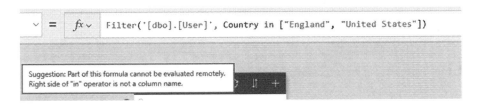

Figure 9-3. *Delegation warning*

Is there any way for us to avoid this problem? One way is to rewrite our formula using operators that are delegable. Here's an example of how to express the same query with the || operator.

```
Filter('[dbo].[User]', Country="England" || Country="United States")
```

With this expression, the designer will not show a warning. One useful thing to be aware of is that the || and Or functions do not function identically. With SQL Server data sources, the designer warns that the Or function is not delegable and underlines the operator with a blue line, as shown in in Figure 9-4.

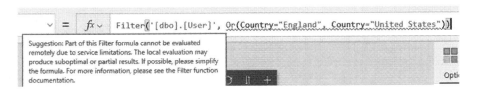

Figure 9-4. *The Or function is not delegable with SQL Server data sources*

Searching Data

An important feature in all applications is the ability to search for data. In this section, we'll look at how to provide users with the ability to search for records in an app. We'll develop a custom search screen that enables users to filter data more precisely by search criteria. Figure 9-5 shows the screens that we'll work toward building in this section. The first screen enables users to search journey records by a drop-down list of users. The user can also filter the records by date. We'll then adapt the screen to provide the ability to select more than one user.

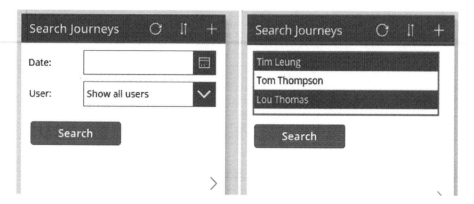

Figure 9-5. *The example screens that we'll build*

Developing these types of screens isn't as easy as it first appears. There are several complexities that we need to cover. The first is to configure the screen to not filter by date if the user leaves the date field blank. Additionally, we'll also look at a difficulty that can arise when we attempt to apply date filters. If the underlying data field contains both date and time components and we want to filter just by the date component, we need to customize our search formula to take this into account.

The user can also choose not to filter by user by selecting the 'Show all users' option from the drop-down. However, this presents another challenge - how to add a 'Show all users' row to the top of the drop-down control.

The final challenge is to initiate the search operation from a search button. We'll find out to conduct the search, only when the user clicks the search button.

The prerequisite to this section is to create an auto-generated app based on the journey table shown in Figure 9-6. This is a SQL Server table and the code in this section will refer this data source as '[dbo]. [Journey]'. If you don't have access to an SQL Server, you can easily substitute this with any other data source of your choice. The reason why we use an SQL Server in this chapter is because it allows us to better examine delegation characteristics, and it also enables us to explore how to retrieve server-generated validation rules and identity values.

	JourneyID	StartDate	UserID	VehicleID	MileageInMiles	EndDate	Text
1	1	2018-04-23 00:00:00.000	10	10	116	2018-04-23 00:00:00.000	NULL
2	2	2017-12-23 00:00:00.000	7	8	189	2017-12-23 00:00:00.000	NULL
3	3	2017-06-02 00:00:00.000	8	6	219	2017-06-02 00:00:00.000	NULL
4	4	2017-12-14 00:00:00.000	10	6	9	2017-12-14 00:00:00.000	NULL
5	5	2017-11-28 00:00:00.000	1	4	105	2017-11-28 00:00:00.000	NULL
6	6	2018-04-26 00:00:00.000	2	2	237	2018-04-26 00:00:00.000	NULL
7	7	2018-02-14 00:00:00.000	2	2	33	2018-02-14 00:00:00.000	NULL
8	8	2018-03-02 00:00:00.000	10	3	185	2018-03-02 00:00:00.000	NULL
9	9	2017-09-27 00:00:00.000	7	10	172	2017-09-27 00:00:00.000	NULL
10	10	2018-03-26 00:00:00.000	7	2	313	2018-03-26 00:00:00.000	NULL
11	11	2018-02-26 00:00:00.000	8	2	5	2018-02-26 00:00:00.000	NULL
12	12	2017-07-03 00:00:00.000	4	8	316	2017-07-03 00:00:00.000	NULL

Figure 9-6. Journey table

Basic Search Functions

To begin, let's review some of the search functions that enable us to build a search function. The key functions that we can call include search, filter, and lookup. These functions all sound very similar, so what are the differences? Here's a brief overview:

- Search - this function matches input *text* against the data in one or more columns

- Filter - this function matches records based on a *formula* that you provide

- Lookup - this function matches records based on a *formula* that you provide and returns the first record only

In the remainder of this section, we'll examine how to use these functions in greater detail.

Filtering by Drop-Down Values

To begin our sample search screen, the first step is to build an auto-generated app that's based on the journey table. The next step is to add the user tables to the app. The code in this section will refer to this table as '[dbo].[User]'. Figure 9-2 shows the structure of this table.

Next, add a drop-down control to the browse screen of the auto-generated app and name it DropdownUsers. Set the Items property of the control to the following formula:

AddColumns('[dbo].[User]', "FullName", Firstname & " " & Surname)

The purpose of this formula is to combine the first name and surname fields in order to show the full name in the drop-down. The final step to configure is the value property. Set this to Fullname, as shown in Figure 9-7.

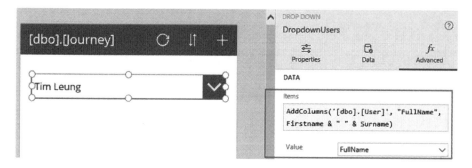

Figure 9-7. *Setting the data source of a drop-down control*

The next step is to modify the gallery control so that it filters records by selected item in the drop-down. To accomplish this, modify the Items property for the gallery control to the formula that's shown beneath:

```
SortByColumns(
            Filter('[dbo].[Journey]',
                UserID=DropdownUsers.Selected.UserID
            ),
            "StartDate",
            If(SortDescending1, Descending, Ascending)
)
```

This formula filters the journey table to return only those records where the UserID value matches selected a UserID in the drop-down box. The Filter function is the pertinent part of this formula, but for completeness, this code retains the default functionality that allows users to sort the records, which is implemented through the call to the SortByColumns function.

We can now review the fields that appear in the gallery control and at this point, we can run our app.

Adding a 'Show All' Option

Let's now extend our drop-down to include a 'Show all users' option at the top of the control. To help identify this row, we'll set the numeric ID value that's associated with this option to -1.

To add the 'Show all users' row to the top of the drop-down, set the items property of the DropdownUsers control to the following formula:

```
AddColumns (
    Ungroup(Table({TableSet: Table({UserID:-1,
                                Firstname:"Show all users", Surname:""})},
                {TableSet: ShowColumns('[dbo].[User]',
                                    "UserID", "Firstname", "Surname")}),
                                "TableSet")
    ,"FullName", Firstname & " " & Surname
)
```

If we now run our app, the 'Show all users' row will appear at the top of the drop-down, as shown in Figure 9-8.

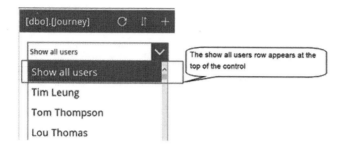

Figure 9-8. Adding an item to the top of the drop-down

The next step is to configure the Items property of the gallery control to stop it from filtering by user if the user selects the 'Show all users' row. The formula to do this is shown below:

```
If(DropdownUsers.Selected.UserID > 0,
   SortByColumns(Filter('[dbo].[Journey]',
                        UserID=DropdownUsers.Selected.UserID
                       ),
              "StartDate",
              If(SortDescending1, Descending, Ascending)
              ),
   SortByColumns('[dbo].[Journey]',
              "StartDate",
              If(SortDescending1, Descending, Ascending)
              )
)
```

This formula checks if the selected row in the drop-down has a user id value greater than 0. If so, the formula filters the records by the selected user. If not, it returns all records.

Grouping, Ungrouping, and Combining Data

The formula that we used to add 'Show all users' row is particularly helpful because we can use this same technique to union, or merge, sets of rows together. The syntax that we used isn't particularly straightforward, so let's take a closer look at how this formula works. The pertinent part of the formula is shown beneath:

```
Ungroup(Table({TableSet: Table({UserID:-1,
                               Firstname:"Show all users", Surname:""})},
              {TableSet: ShowColumns('[dbo].[User]',
                                     "UserID", "Firstname", "Surname")}
       ),
       "TableSet"
)
```

PowerApps provides no direct union operator, so instead, we need to perform this task with the help of a function called Ungroup. The primary purpose of this function is to expand a set of grouped data. To understand how this function works, let's begin by examining the simple usage of the Group and Ungroup functions.

The Group function groups data by columns. As an example, here's how to group user records by the country field.

GroupBy('[dbo].[User]', "Country", "UserRecords")

This code groups the data into the format that's shown in Figure 9-9. The result of this function is a two-column table. The first column contains the group value, and the second column contains the data rows that belong to the group.

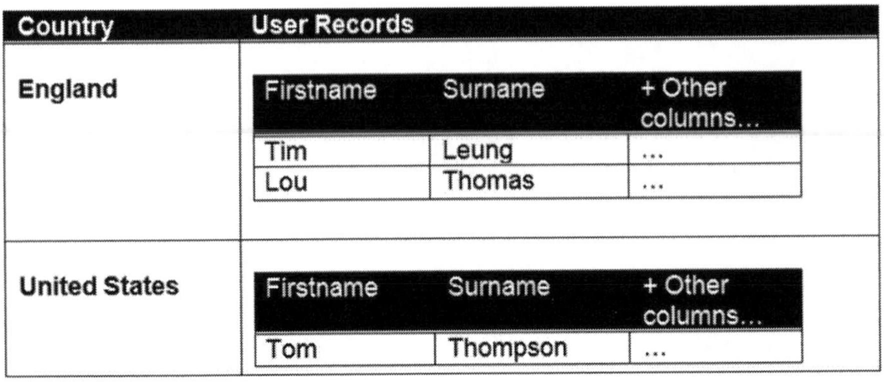
Country
User Records
England
Firstname
Surname
+ Other columns...
Tim
Leung
...
Lou
Thomas
...
United States
Firstname
Surname
+ Other columns...
Tom
Thompson
...

Figure 9-9. *The result of a GroupBy operation*

It can be useful to store the results in a collection. If it's necessary to refer to the results often, it's more efficient to store the results in a collection because the process of grouping data can be intensive. Here's how to store the result of this GroupBy operation into a collection called UsersByCountry.

ClearCollect(UsersByCountry , GroupBy('[dbo].[User]', "Country", "UserRecords"))

Now that we've seen how the GroupBy function works, let's look at the Ungroup function. To ungroup the UsersByCountry collection and return the data to its initial state, here's the formula we would use:

Ungroup(UsersByCountry, "Country")

This formula expands the data in the UserByCountry collection by the country column, as illustrated in Figure 9-10.

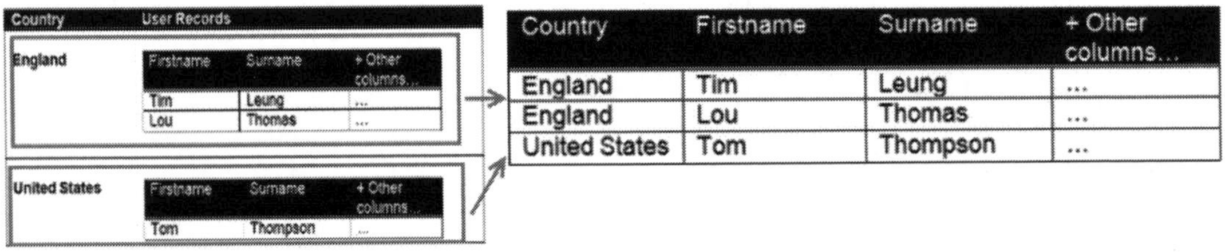
Country
User Records
England
Firstname
Surname
+ Other columns...
Tim
Leung
...
Lou
Thomas
...
United States
Firstname
Surname
+ Other columns...
Tom
Thompson
...
Country
Firstname
Surname
+ Other columns...
England
Tim
Leung
...
England
Lou
Thomas
...
United States
Tom
Thompson
...

Figure 9-10. *Ungrouping data*

Now that we can see how the ungroup function works, let's look at how this applies to the task of adding a 'show all users' row to a drop-drown. Our code calls the table function to define a two row, single column table. The column name of the outermost table is TableSet and the first row in this table contains a single row table that contains the record 'Show all Users'. The second row in the table contains user records from the data source.

Ungrouping this data by the TableSet column provides the same effect as combining the table data in each row, as shown in Figure 9-11.

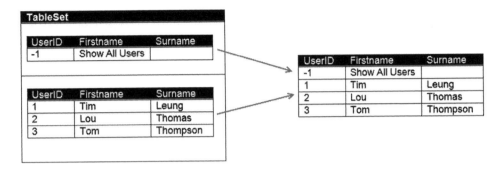

Figure 9-11. *Combining a set of data*

Searching by Date Criteria

Returning to our search example, let's now adapt our search screen to allow users to filter the records by the journey date.

First, add a date picker control to the browse screen and name it DatePickerJourney. Next, clear the DefaultDate property so that by default, the date picker control shows a blank value.

To highlight a slightly nontrivial example, the start date column in our journey table stores both the date and time. To match a single input date against date and time values, we need to filter for records that fall between midnight and 23:59 of the target date. For most data sources, the formula we would add to the items property of the gallery control is shown below:

```
Filter('[dbo].[Journey]',
          StartDate >= DatePickerJourney.SelectedDate &&
          StartDate < DateAdd(DatePickerJourney.SelectedDate, 1, Days))
```

However, if we were to run this screen against our SQL server data source, we would discover that this formula returns zero records. Therefore, this example also highlights a bug where the PowerApps connector fails to filter date and time fields properly. The workaround is to force PowerApps to filter the data locally by introducing a non-delegable clause in the filter operation. Here's how the formula would look:

```
Filter('[dbo].[Journey]',
          StartDate >= DatePickerJourney.SelectedDate &&
          StartDate < DateAdd(DatePickerJourney.SelectedDate, 1, Days)
          Day(StartDate) > 0)
```

The unfortunate effect of this workaround is that our screen will experience the problems of a non-delegable query, which includes slower performance and inaccurate results if the data source data exceeds 500 rows.

In terms of our custom search screen, we can adapt the call to the filter function so that it that filters by both the date picker and the user drop-down control.

■ **Note** The date filtering bug applies only to SQL Server data sources. You can find out more about this problem here:

https://powerusers.microsoft.com/t5/PowerApps-Forum/Filtering-on-prem-SQL-data-source-by-date/m-p/6151

Searching by Numeric Criteria

To search by numeric input values, an important step is to convert the input string to a numeric value by calling the Value function. Suppose we want to return journey records where the mileage exceeds a value that the user enters into a text input control, then here's the formula that we would use.

```
Filter('[dbo].[Journey]', MileageInMiles >= Value(TextInputMinMileage.Text))
```

Adding a Search Button

In the screen that we adapted, the gallery control refers directly to the data entry controls. This causes the gallery control to refresh as soon as a user enters any data into any of the controls. This behavior is not ideal because the gallery control will refresh more than it needs to. To address this issue, we'll add a search button to the screen to trigger the search operation.

To build this feature, we would amend the Items property of the gallery control so that it filters the data by variables, rather than by control values. We would then set the context variables on the click of the search button.

To clarify the exact formula that carries out this task and to avoid any extraneous logic, we'll apply this technique to the initial screen that contains a drop-down control of users only. The first step is to add a button to the screen and set the OnSelect property like so:

```
UpdateContext({SearchUserId: DropdownUsers.Selected.UserID })
```

Now set the Items property of the gallery control to the formula below:

```
SortByColumns(
        Filter('[dbo].[Journey]', UserID= SearchUserId),
        "StartDate",
        If(SortDescending1, Descending, Ascending)
)
```

⁕ We can now run our screen and initiate a search by clicking the button. To complete this example, we would extend the UpdateContext function to store all the criteria that user enters into variables. We would then reference these variables in the call to the filter function, rather than reference the user controls.

Setting Multiple Sort Sequences

To help users more easily find data, we can sort the items in gallery and other data controls by multiple fields. The browse screen in an auto-generated app sorts the records by single field, as shown in Figure 9-12.

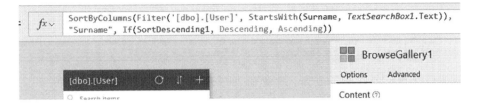

Figure 9-12. *The default sort formula in an auto-generated app*

We can sort by additional fields by providing additional sets of field names and sort sequences to the SortByColumns function. Here's the formula to sort the user table by surname, followed by first name.

```
SortByColumns(Filter('[dbo].[User]', StartsWith(Surname, TextSearchBox1.Text)),
    "Surname", If(SortDescending1, Descending, Ascending),
    "Firstname",If(SortDescending1, Descending, Ascending))
```

Additional Search Criteria Options

Other useful search capabilities that we can add to an app include the ability to match records against a list, or to find fields that contain null or empty data.

Matching Against Lists of Data

To match records against a user-defined list, we can provide a list box control that enables users to select one or more items to match against. To demonstrate this technique, we'll modify our search screen to return journey records that match a list of selected users.

To begin, add a list box control to our search screen and call it ListBoxUsers. Set the Items property to the formula that we used in our drop-down box earlier in this chapter, as shown beneath.

```
AddColumns('[dbo].[User]', "FullName", Firstname & " " & Surname)
```

Next, set the value property to FullName and confirm that the SelectMultiple property is set to true. The SelectMultiple enables users to select more than one item from the list. Figure 9-13 shows the appearance of this control in the designer.

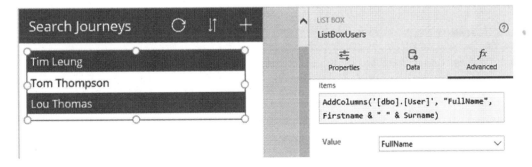

Figure 9-13. *Configuring the drop-down control*

The next step is to modify the gallery control to filter the records by the selected items in the list box. To accomplish this, set the Items property of the gallery control to the formula that's shown beneath:

```
Filter('[dbo].[Journey]', UserID in ListBoxUsers.SelectedItems.UserID)
```

This formula calls the in function. This function tests if a value belongs in a table or collection. At this point, we can run the screen and filter the journey records by one or more users.

It's important to apply some caution when you use this technique against SQL Server data sources. The in operator is not delegable and therefore, this technique will suffer from the usual limitations that apply with non-delegable queries.

Matching Blank Fields

It can be a challenge to search for empty fields because the matching functions behave differently when they encounter empty string or null values. To help highlight the techniques that we can use, Figure 9-14 shows an excerpt from the journey table. The journey description column contains records that are null, contain an empty string, and records that are not blank.

	JourneyID	StartDate	UserID	VehicleID	MileageInMiles	EndDate	JourneyDesc
1	1	2018-04-23 00:00:00.000	10	10	116	2018-04-23 00:00:00.000	NULL
2	2	2017-12-23 00:00:00.000	7	8	189	2017-12-23 00:00:00.000	
3	3	2017-06-02 00:00:00.000	8	6	219	2017-06-02 00:00:00.000	London to Manchester
4	4	2017-12-14 00:00:00.000	10	6	105	2017-12-14 00:00:00.000	London to Birmingham

Figure 9-14. *Example data in the journey table*

PowerApps provides a function called IsBlank This function accepts an input value and returns true if the input is empty string or null. If we set the items property of a gallery control to the formula shown below, the control would show the records with the JourneyIDs 1 and 2.

```
Filter('[dbo].[Journey]', IsBlank(JourneyDesc) )
```

In other words, the IsBlank function matches both null and empty string values. However, a disadvantage of this function is that it is not delegable. So if we intend to return records where the journey description field contains an empty string, a faster approach is to use the formula shown beneath. PowerApps can delegate the operation of matching against an empty string, and in this example, the formula would return the record for JourneyID 2 only.

```
Filter('[dbo].[Journey]', JourneyDesc="")
```

The inverse operation is to return records that are not blank. To do this, we can use the delegable expression that's shown beneath. This formula returns the records that match JourneyID 3 and 4.

```
Filter('[dbo].[Journey]', JourneyDesc<>"")
```

Finally, the expression below returns only the records that are null, excluding records that contain an empty string. This expression will return the record for JourneyID 1 only. Note that this expression is not delegable because it includes a call to the IsBlank function.

```
Filter('[dbo].[Journey]', IsBlank(JourneyDesc) && JourneyDesc <>"")
```

Joining Data

With any sizable app, a common and essential task is to display data from related tables. Unlike typical relational database systems, PowerApps provides no specific join command. Therefore, we'll now look at the techniques that we can use to display related data.

Joining Records - Showing Related Records

One technique we can use to show related records is to apply the lookup function. To highlight the use of this method, here's how to configure the gallery control in our auto-generated app to show a list of journey records combined with the associated user details. To accomplish this, set the items property of the gallery control to the following formula:

```
AddColumns('[dbo].[Journey]',
        "UserRecord",
        LookUp('[dbo].[User]',
            '[dbo].[User]'[@UserID] = '[dbo].[Journey]'[@UserID]
            )
)
```

This formula calls the `AddColumns` function to append the associated user record to the journey data source. The interesting thing this demonstrates is how we can create a structure of nested tables. Figure 9-15 illustrates the output of this function.

JourneyID	StartDate	Mileage	Other Columns...	UserRecord			
1	2018-04-23	116	...	UserID	Firstname	Surname	Other Columns
				10	Keith	Higgs	...
2	2017-12-23	189	...	UserID	Firstname	Surname	Other Columns
				7	Saheera	Hagedorn	...
3	2017-06-02	219	...	UserID	Firstname	Surname	Other Columns
				8	Anthony	Frost	...
4	2017-12-14	105	...	UserID	Firstname	Surname	Other Columns
				10	Keith	Higgs	...

Figure 9-15. *Nested data source*

This formula also illustrates an important learning point. It demonstrates how to fully qualify field names when we nest data with functions such as `AddColumns`, `Filter`, and `Lookup`. In this example, both the journey and user tables include a field called `UserID`. In formula, how would we distinguish between these two fields? Specifically, from the inner `Lookup` function, we need some way to distinguish between the `UserID` field in the journey table, and the `UserID` field in the user table. When we nest functions, any field name that we specify will refer to the innermost data source. So in this example, when we specify

UserID from inside the Lookup function, UserID will refer to the UserID field in the user table. To refer to the UserID field from the journey table, we need to prefix the UserID field with the table name in the format TableName[@Fieldname]. Therefore, we would refer to the UserID field in the journey table with the following syntax:

'[dbo].[Journey]'[@UserID]

The name for the @ operator is the *disambiguation* operator. Another scenario where this operator applies is in situations where a variable, collection, or data source that matches a field name. In this case, you would specify the variable, collection, or data source in the format [@ObjectName] to distinguish it from the field name.

Now that we've set the items property for our gallery control, we can access all the fields in the user record for each journey record through the UserRecord column, as shown in Figure 9-16.

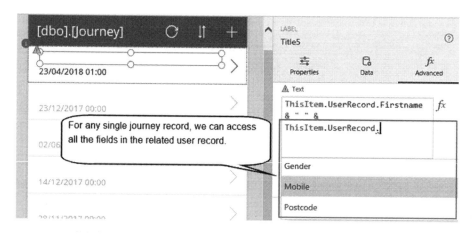

Figure 9-16. *Showing related records*

A word of caution is that the Lookup function is not delegable. Therefore, this technique will suffer from the usual limitations that are associated with non-delegated queries.

Checking for Nonexistence

A useful task that we occasionally need to carry out is to check for the nonexistence of a group of data within another data set. As an example, traditional order processing systems would use this technique to find customers who have not placed any orders. To highlight this technique, here's how to show the names of users who have not completed any journeys.

To show these users, add a gallery control to a screen and set the items property to the following formula:

```
Filter('[dbo].[User]',
        Not(UserID in ShowColumns('[dbo].[Journey]', "UserID"))
)
```

This formula filters the user table to show the records where a matching user id doesn't exist in the journey table. Just like the previous example, the syntax that we use here is not delegable, and therefore, the code here may perform slowly.

Returning Distinct Records

Sometimes, there may be the requirement to return a list of distinct records. To demonstrate this technique, here's how to return a distinct list of users who have carried out a journey in a specified month.

The underlying formula we would use to carry out this task is the GroupBy function. This function allows us to group data by a column. The formula shown below would return a list of journeys grouped by user id.

```
GroupBy('[dbo].[Journey]', "UserID", "JourneyRecordsForUser")
```

Figure 9-17 shows how this data looks after the GroupBy operation.

UserID	JourneyRecordsForUser					
10						
	JourneyID	StartDate	VehicleID	MileageInMiles	EndDate	JourneyDesc
	1	2018-04-23	10	116	2018-04-23	NULL
	4	2017-12-14	6	105	2017-12-14	London to Birmingham
	8	2018-03-02	3	185	2018-03-02	NULL
	21	2018-01-02	9	283	2018-01-02	NULL
7						
	JourneyID	StartDate	VehicleID	MileageInMiles	EndDate	JourneyDesc
	2	2017-12-23	8	189	2017-12-23	
	9	2017-09-27	10	172	2017-09-27	NULL
	10	2018-03-26	2	313	2018-03-26	NULL
8						
	JourneyID	StartDate	VehicleID	MileageInMiles	EndDate	JourneyDesc
	3	2017-06-02	6	219	2017-06-02	London to Manchester
	11	2018-02-26	2	5	2018-02-26	NULL
	51	2018-03-20	8	369	2018-03-20	NULL

Figure 9-17. Grouped data

The UserID column shows the distinct data. Once we apply this formula to a gallery control, we can add a label and call the LookUp function to retrieve the user details that are associated with the user id, as shown in Figure 9-18.

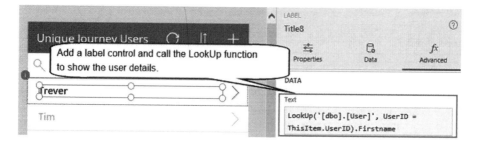

Figure 9-18. *LookUp in the label*

A typical use of this type of query is to return distinct records that are filtered by date. So to extend this formula, here's how to filter the source data by a specific month.

```
GroupBy(Filter('[dbo].[Journey]',
            StartDate >= Date(2017,6,1) &&
            StartDate < Date(2017,7,1)
            ),
        "UserID", "JourneyRecordsForUser"
)
```

This formula filters the data source to return journeys with a start date of June 2017. As a reminder, the Filter function does not filter by dates properly against SQL Server data sources. Like we saw earlier in this chapter, we can overcome this problem by adding the criteria && Day(StartDate) >0 to force the filter operation to run on the local device

Working with Data in Code

In this section, we'll find out how to perform data access tasks with formula. The specific tasks that we'll examine include how to write formula to create, retrieve, update, and delete data.

Retrieving Single Records

We can retrieve multiple records by writing formula that refers to the data source name. To retrieve an individual record by unique id, we could call the LookUp function. For example, to retrieve a user record with a user id of 8 and to show the surname value in a label control, here's the formula that we would add to the text property of the label:

```
LookUp('[dbo].[User]', UserID = 8).Surname
```

If a record with a UserID of 8 does not exist in the data source, the lookup function returns an empty string. This might not be very useful to the user, so therefore, we can test for this condition and show a meaningful message if the record doesn't exist. The syntax we would use would look like this:

```
If (CountIf('[dbo].[User]', UserID = 8) > 0,
    LookUp('[dbo].[User]', UserID = 8).Surname ,
    "User not found"
)
```

Updating Records

The function that creates and updates records is called a patch. This function can update data in data sources as well as data in a local collection.

Updating a Single Record

Just like its name suggests, we can call the patch function to make small lightweight patches to data. This is ideal in cases where we want to make small one-off changes, and don't want to load and display an entire record.

To demonstrate this method, Figure 9-19 shows an example screen to deactivate users. In businesses, this represents the typical screen that a manager would use to mark ex-employees. In other apps, we could use this same technique to change the status or to set the closure date of a record, especially for workflow type apps.

Figure 9-19. *Layout of example screen to update data*

The example screen here contains a gallery control called GalleryUsers. This control shows records from the users table, and the item template of the control contains a button with the text "Deactivate user". The OnSelect property of the button contains the following formula:

```
Patch ('[dbo].[User]', GalleryUsers.Selected, {Active:false})
```

When this screen runs, we can click the button to set the active field of the record to false.

Here's an explanation of how the patch function works. This function expects three arguments. The first is the data source, the second is the record to update, and the third argument specifies the field values to update.

When we call this function, it returns the newly updated record. In the event of an error, we can access the details by calling the Error function.

A useful piece of built-in behavior is that after the call to the patch function, the gallery control will automatically refresh and show the up-to-date data values.

Updating Multiple Records

We can call the UpdateIf function to update multiple records. For example, to update the journey data to set the mileage value to 5 for records lower than 5, we can use the formula that's shown beneath:

```
UpdateIf( '[dbo].[Journey]', MileageInMiles < 5, { MileageInMiles: 5 } )
```

An important point is that this function isn't delegable. Because of this, the formula here will process the first 500 records only. Another thing to be aware of is that updating records in bulk like this can be slow. In the tests that I conducted, this formula took around 20 minutes to process 500 records.

Creating a New Record

We can call the Patch function to add a new record, as well as update an existing record. We saw earlier how the patch function requires us to provide a source record to patch. In the case where we want to add a new record, there won't be an existing record. Therefore, PowerApps provides a function called Defaults that returns a default record that we can supply to the patch function.

Here's a formula we can use to create a new record in the users table.

```
Patch('[dbo].[User]',
    Defaults( '[dbo].[User]'),
    { Firstname: Joe, Surname: Smith }
)
```

■ **Tip**   We can call the Collect function to insert multiple new records. The data import example in Chapter 14 demonstrates the use of this technique.

Retrieving Auto-Generated Numbers

When we call the Patch function to add a record, the result of this function includes all server-generated data. This includes calculated fields, or auto-generated numbers from databases.

To demonstrate how to retrieve auto-generated data, Figure 9-20 shows the definition of the user table in SQL Server. The primary key is an identity column called UserID. Identity columns contain sequential numbers that are auto-generated by SQL Server.

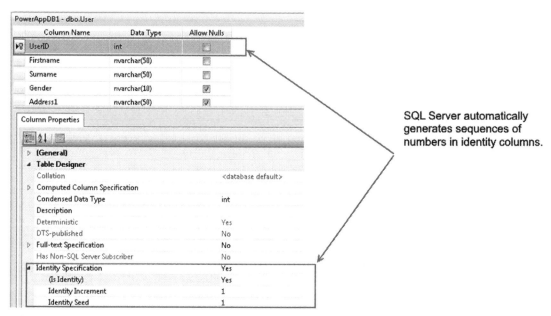

Figure 9-20. *The definition of an identity column*

In this example, each journey record stores the UserID of the user that is associated with the journey. If we were to build a screen to create both the user and journey records at the same time, we would need to retrieve the auto-generated UserID value before we add the journey record.

Let's look at how to build this feature. The first step is to build a screen with data entry controls that correspond to the fields in both tables, as shown in Figure 9-21. This screen includes a save button that saves the data into both tables.

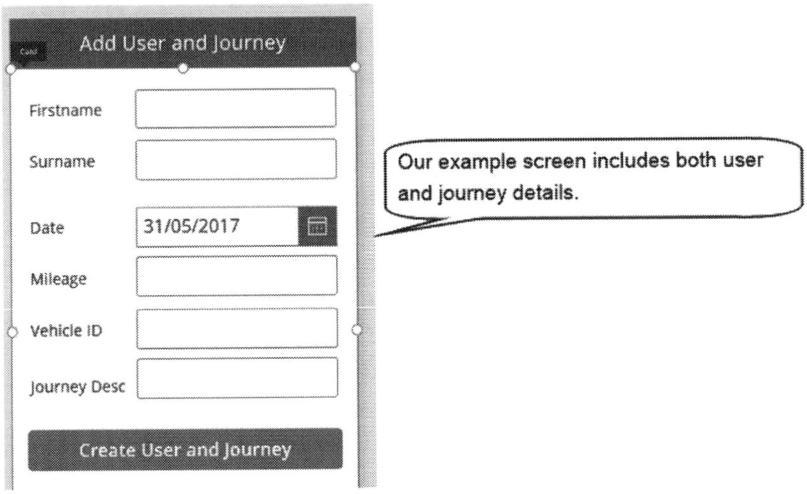

Figure 9-21. *Inserting data into two tables at the same time*

Here's the formula we would add to the OnSelect property of the button:

```
ClearCollect(AffectedRecords,
        Patch('[dbo].[User]',
            Defaults('[dbo].[User]'),
            {Firstname:TextInputFirstname.Text,
                Surname:TextInputSurname.Text}
        )
);
Patch('[dbo].[Journey]',
    Defaults('[dbo].[Journey]'),
    {UserID:First(AffectedRecords).UserID,
        StartDate:DatePickerJourneyStart.SelectedDate,
        MileageInMiles:Value(TextInputMileage.Text),
        JourneyDesc:TextInputJourneyDesc.Text
    }
)
```

In the formula that's shown here, the first function patches a new record into the user table using the details that the user enters into the surname and firstname text input controls. The patch function returns a table of the affected records and we store this in a collection called AffectedRecords.

The second function retrieves the UserID of the newly added user, and the formula uses this to patch a new record into the journey table. Because the AffectedRecords collection could contain multiple records, the code calls the First function to return the first record.

Patching Associated Records in SharePoint

When patching records, another common task is to patch lookup values. It's simple to patch lookup values with data sources that use numeric IDs or text codes to identify lookup values. But with SharePoint, it's not as simple to patch lookup values. We'll now look at how to carry out this task.

Figure 9-22 shows a reconstruction of our journey table in SharePoint. The Journey list contains a lookup column called User that derives its values from a separate SharePoint list called UserList.

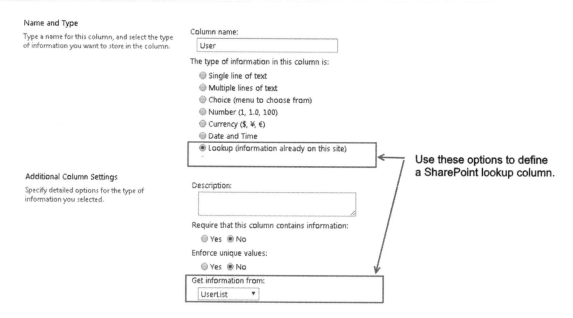

Figure 9-22. *The user column in the journey list looks like this*

Let's suppose that we want to add a new item to the journey list and assign the user item that matches the id value of 2. The fragment of code that returns the user item that we can pass to the patch function is shown beneath.

```
User:{'@odata.type':
            "#Microsoft.Azure.Connectors.SharePoint.SPListExpandedReference",
    Id:2, Value:""
}
```

This code might seem quite obscure, in particular, the reference to the property @odata.type. What is this and where does it come from? To explain this, the method to patch a lookup value is to supply a record to the patch function that represents the lookup value. To determine the fields that this lookup record contains, we can examine the Value1 drop-down for the default property in an auto-generated edit screen, as shown in Figure 9-23. This reveals that the lookup record includes three fields: @odata.type, Value, and Id. So to build a valid record that we can pass to the patch function, the record should contain these three fields.

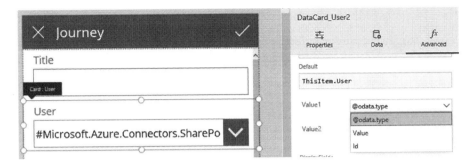

Figure 9-23. *Determining the Odata type property of a SharePoint drop-down*

For SharePoint lookup values, the value of @odata.type will always be #Microsoft.Azure.Connectors. SharePoint.SPListExpandedReference. We can determine this by changing the value of Value1 to @odata.type and running our app. When we return to designer, the value that we require (#Microsoft. Azure.Connectors.SharePoint.SPListExpandedReference) will appear in the drop down box. The content of the user drop down in Figure 9-23 illustrates this.

An interesting thing about the lookup record that we built is that it isn't necessary to provide a value for the value property. Just the Id value is sufficient enough. So to patch a record to the journey list in SharePoint, the full formula we would use is shown below.

```
Patch(Journey,
    Defaults(Journey),
    { StartDate:   "2017-01-01",
       VehicleID:   1,
        MileageInMiles:   3,
        EndDate:   "2017-01-01",
        User:{'@odata.type':
            "#Microsoft.Azure.Connectors.SharePoint.SPListExpandedReference",
              Id:2, Value:""
            }
      }
)
```

Patching Associated Records into a CDS Data Source

With CDS data sources, the code is more straightforward because we don't need to build a lookup record that includes the odata.type field. Instead, we can just specify the Id and Value properties as shown beneath. Like the SharePoint example, we can leave the Value property blank.

```
Patch(Journey,
    Defaults(Journey),
    {StartDate:   "2017-01-01",
       VehicleID:   1,
       MileageInMiles:   3,
       EndDate:   "2017-01-01",
       User:{ Id:2, Value:""}
     }
)
```

Deleting Data

There are two functions that we can call to delete data: Remove and RemoveIf. The Remove function requires us to supply the record that we want to delete. A typical way to call this function is to provide it with the selected record in a gallery control. As an example, here's the formula from the delete icon on the details screen from an auto-generated app that's based on the Journey table:

```
Remove(Journey, BrowseGallery1.Selected);
```

In contrast, the RemoveIf function enables us to specify the records that we want to delete. This enables us to delete a single record by Id value, or to delete multiple records. For example, we could add the following formula to a button to delete all journey records that are older than 3 years old.

```
RemoveIf(Journey, JourneyDate < DateAdd(Now(), -3, Years));
```

One thing to note is that like in the case of the budget tracker sample app (see Chapter 7, 'Displaying a Delete Confirmation Screen'), we need to delete any related records before we delete the main record. Note that the delegation issue applies, and that the RemoveIf function operates against the first 500 records only.

Setting Default Screen Values

To help users more easily create new records, we can set default field values for a record. Here's how to modify the edit screen on an auto-generated app for the journey table. We'll default the start date to today's date when a user creates a new record. To do this, open the edit form and find the card that corresponds to the start date field, as shown in Figure 9-24. Unlock the card and set the default property of the data card to the formula shown below:

```
If (EditForm1.Mode = FormMode.New, Now(), ThisItem.StartDate)
```

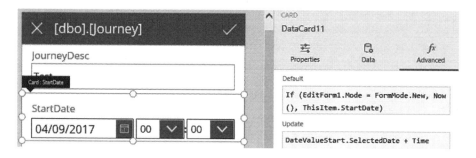

Figure 9-24. *Setting default screen values*

This formula detects the form mode, which can be one of two modes - new or existing. If the form is in new mode, the formula returns today's date. Otherwise, the formula returns the start date of the exiting record.

Validating Form Values

With data sources such as SharePoint and SQL Server, PowerApps provides data type and data length validation. Sometimes, it's necessary to apply additional validation rules, and in this section, we'll look at how to add this feature to our auto-generated journey app. To demonstrate a technique that we can use, here's how to ensure that users enter end date values that are greater than the start date.

To add this validation rule, open the edit screen and find the start date card. Unlock the card and rename the start date picker and time controls to `DateValueStart`, `HourValueStart`, and `MinuteValueStart`. Next, unlock the end date card and rename the end date picker and time controls to `DateValueEnd`, `HourValueEnd`, and `MinuteValueEnd`. Beneath the date and time controls, add a label control, and set the color to red, as shown in Figure 9-25. Set the text property of the label control to the formula that's shown below.

```
If((DateValueStart.SelectedDate +
      Time(Value(HourValueStart.Selected.Value),
          Value(MinuteValueStart.Selected.Value),
          0)
  )
    >
  (DateValueEnd.SelectedDate +
    Time(Value(HourValueEnd.Selected.Value),
        Value(MinuteValueEnd.Selected.Value),
        0)),
  "End date must be greater than start date",
  ""
)
```

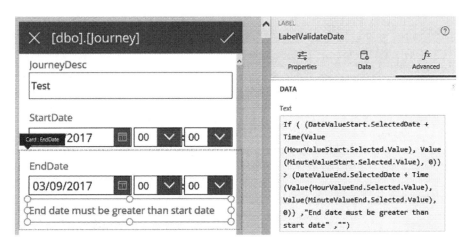

Figure 9-25. *Adding a validation message that compares two fields*

This formula calls the `if` function to test if the end date value exceeds the start date. If a user enters valid data, the label shows an empty string. Otherwise, it shows a message that indicates the error to the user.

To configure the label so that it doesn't take up any space when the data is valid, set the `AutoHeight` property to true. Note that we can only resize the height of the card control to hide the label when the label text is empty.

To complete this example, it's a good idea to also apply this rule to the save icon. This would prevent the form calling the submit form function when the data is invalid. The formula we would use is shown beneath:

```
If((DateValueStart.SelectedDate +
        Time(Value(HourValueStart.Selected.Value),
            Value(MinuteValueStart.Selected.Value),
            0)
    )
    >
    (DateValueEnd.SelectedDate +
        Time(Value(HourValueEnd.Selected.Value),
            Value(MinuteValueEnd.Selected.Value),
            0)),
    false,
    SubmitForm(EditForm1)
)
```

▓ **Tip** A great way to validate data is to call the `IsMatch` function. We can call this function to check that users enter data in the correct format. For example, we can call this function to validate the format of email addresses or telephone numbers.

Checking Validation Rules

With data sources that support validation rules such as SharePoint or SQL Server, we can test whether input data adheres to the rules by calling a function called `Validate`. This is ideal during occasions when we want to build custom data entry screens.

The validate function can validate a single field or an entire record. To demonstrate this function, Figure 9-26 shows a custom screen for adding journey records. Our SQL database imposes a maximum of 50 characters on the journey description field. To validate the journey description value that a user enters, we can use the formula that's shown beneath:

```
Validate( '[dbo].[Journey]', "JourneyDesc", TextInputJourneyDesc.Text )
```

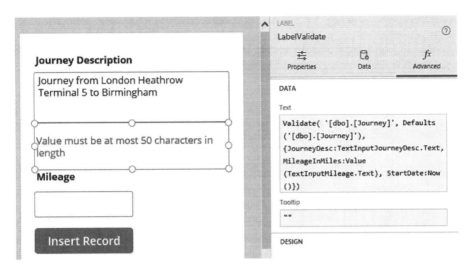

Figure 9-26. *Using the validate function to validate a single field*

The validate function returns a string and a natural place to show the result of this function is in a label. If there are no errors, the function returns an empty string.

To validate an entire record rather than a single field, we can pass an existing record and the intended changes to the validate function. The formula beneath shows how to validate a new record.

```
Validate('[dbo].[Journey]',
        Defaults('[dbo].[Journey]'),
        {JourneyDesc:TextInputJourneyDesc.Text,
           MileageInMiles:Value(TextInputMileage.Text),
           StartDate:Now()
          }
)
```

Because the intention here is to validate a new record, we call the Defaults function to return a base record that we can pass to the validate function. If we were validating an existing record, we would provide the existing record to the validate function instead.

■ **Tip**   A good way to force users to enter numeric data is to use a text input control and to set the format property to TextFormat.Number. This technique can help us avoid writing specific code to validate numeric input data.

Sending Notifications

For Android and iOS users, we can alert users through the notifications area of the mobile operating system. When a user receives an alert, the user can click the message to open the specific app that's associated with the message.

We can send notifications from any app or from Microsoft Flow. To send a notification from an app, we would add a data connection to the PowerApps Notification Provider. We would then use this data connection to send our notifications. The notifications that we send must be targeted at specific users and the method we use to identify users is by email address.

To demonstrate this feature, here's how to modify our auto-generated journey app so that it sends a notification to a manager whenever a user creates a new record.

Because the messages that we send are associated with an app, the first step is to determine the unique identifier for our app. To do this, find the app in the web portal and navigate to the details section, as shown in Figure 9-27. A quick way to go to the approximate place in the portal is to click the share menu item in PowerApps Studio.

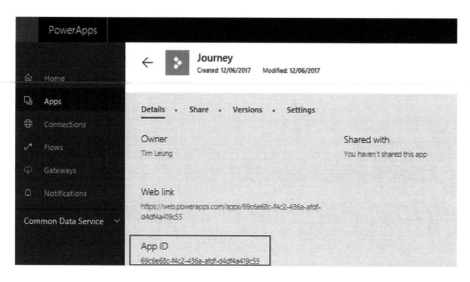

Figure 9-27. *Determining the id of an app*

The next step is to add a data source to the PowerApps Notification Provider. When we add the data source, the designer will prompt us to enter the AppID or Web link.

To avoid any confusion, note that there is a similar data connector called Notifications, as shown in Figure 9-28. The purpose of this connector is to send email notifications, rather than mobile device alerts.

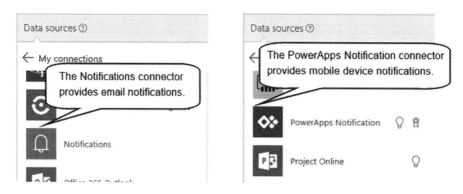

Figure 9-28. *Adding a data source to the PowerApps Notifications Provider*

The next step is open the edit form and to modify the formula for the save icon. Modify the `OnSelect` property as shown below:

```
If(EditForm1.Mode=FormMode.New,
    SubmitForm(EditForm1);
        PowerAppsNotification.SendPushNotification(
            {recipients:["tim@timleung.co.uk"],
             message:"A new journey record was created",
             openApp:true}
        ),
    SubmitForm(EditForm1)
)
```

This formula uses the value of `EditForm1.Mode` to test if the user is entering a new record. If this is true, the formula calls the `SubmitForm` function to save the record and then calls the function to send the notification. If the user is not entering a new record, the code calls the `SubmitForm` function only.

A piece of behavior that catches some users out is that when a user enters a new record, the value of `EditForm1.Mode` changes to edit mode immediately after the call to the `SubmitForm` succeeds. Therefore, if we want to use the value of `EditForm1.Mode` to test that a user is entering a new record, we need to carry out this test before we call `SubmitForm`.

At this point, we can run our app. When we add a new record, the app will send a notification to the mobile device of the recipient, as shown in Figure 9-29.

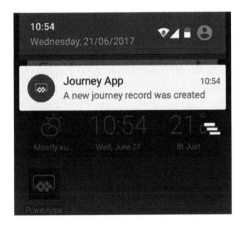

Figure 9-29. *Example of the actual sent message*

There are two useful features about the `SendPushNotification` function that are worth mentioning. The first is that we can specify multiple recipients by providing a comma-separated list. The second is that we can specify a table of parameters. When the user starts the app by clicking the notification message, the parameter values will be available to the target app. Here's an example formula to illustrate these concepts.

```
PowerAppsNotification.SendPushNotification({
        recipients:["tim@timleung.co.uk","administrator@timleung.co.uk"],
        message:"A new journey record was created",
        openApp:true,
        params:Table({key:"JourneyID",
                       value: EditForm1.LastSubmit.JourneyID }
                     )
      }
)
```

This code illustrates the formula to retrieve the journey id of the newly created record. On the assumption that the data source is an SQL Server table and that the JourneyID field stores an identity value that the server generates, we can use the LastSubmit property of the form to retrieve any values that have been generated by the server.

In our app, we could then use the code Param("JourneyID") to retrieve the parameter value. We could then apply the technique in Chapter 8 to open the specified record directly in the app.

Summary

There are two very important points to understand when working with data. The first is that PowerApps imposes a 500 row limit when it retrieves data from a data source. The impact of this is that PowerApps might fail to retrieve the records that we expect. The second point is delegation. When filtering data, we can use delegable operators against data sources that support delegation. With delegable operators, the data source filters the data and returns the results to the client device. With non-delegable data sources or operators, the data source returns all the data to the client and the client performs the filtering. Non-delegable operations are slower and if the source data exceeds 500 rows, the filter result will not include any records beyond the base data of 500 rows. When we build formulas that filter data in a non-delegable way, the formula bar underlines the formula with a blue line. This feature is very useful because it warns us against these potential problems.

The two most useful functions to search for records include Filter and LookUp. Both of these functions accept a data source and a formula that defines a successful match. The main difference between the two functions is that the Filter function returns multiple records, whereas the LookUp function returns the first record.

The browse screen in an auto-generated app provides basic search capabilities. We looked at how to build a search screen that enables users to filter records by drop-down lists and by date picker controls. This technique calls the filter function to filter the source data by data entry controls. We looked at how to address some difficult issues. To offer the choice in a drop-down control to return all records, one option is to add a 'show all records' item to the top of the drop-down list. This requires us to combine a 'show all records' row with the items in the drop-down. The technique we learned here also enables us to combine (or union) multiple sets of data together. This technique adds each data set that we want to combine to a separate row in a single column table. We then call the Ungroup function to combine all the data sets into a single table.

A typical requirement is to offer a search facility that returns records by date. If the records that we want to match against contain both date and time elements, it's necessary to create a filter operation that returns records that fall between midnight and 23:59 of the target date. To find records that match a list of items, we can filter the source records with a formula that utilizes the in function.

When displaying data, a common requirement is to join or to show the details of a related record. PowerApps provides no specific join operator so instead, we use the LookUp function to carry out this task. We learned how to return distinct records and to how to check for non-matching records across a set of tables. The method to return distinct records is to group our records by the column that contains the data where we want to find distinct values.

The typical example of why we might want to find non-matching records across a set of tables is to search for customers without any order records. We can accomplish this by filtering the source records with a formula that applies the not and in functions.

A useful topic that we explored was how to carry out data operations with formula. The function that updates and inserts records is called a patch. We found out how to carry out nontrivial data creation tasks, including how to retrieve auto-generated data from the data source, and how to insert records into multiple tables. The patch function accepts a data source, the record to update, and the field values to set. To create a record, we would define a new record with a function called Defaults. We would then pass this to the patch function to create the record in the underlying data source. The patch function returns the records that were updated, including any server-generated values. We can use this to find any server-generated primary key values.

To simplify the entry of new records, we can configure the form control to provide default values. To do this, we would apply a formula to the default property of the data card. This formula would return a default value if the form is in new mode, or return the existing value if the form is in edit mode.

In the final part of this chapter, we learned how to show messages in the notifications section of a mobile device. We can configure the system to open the associated PowerApp when a user clicks the message. To build this type of functionality, we would utilize the PowerApps Notification connector. This connector enables us to target messages at specific users. It also enables us to attach parameter values to the message. This is a useful feature because it enables us to configure the startup behavior of an app when a user clicks the notification message.

CHAPTER 10

Working with Images

With PowerApps, we can build apps to take advantage of the cameras that are built into smartphone and tablet devices. In this chapter, we'll discover how to take photos and how to perform image-related activities such as scanning barcodes and receiving pen input.

We'll start by building a simple auto-generated app that can store and retrieve images. Later in this chapter, we'll find out how to build an image gallery screen by exploring how the site inspection template app implements this feature.

The useful topics that we'll cover in this chapter will include the following:

- How to configure a data store. To store images with an Excel data store, it's necessary to set up our spreadsheet in a specific way. We'll find out exactly how.

- We can use a file selection control or a camera control to select images. It can be tricky to work with these controls because depending on circumstances, the control value can return binary data, or a pointer to a file in a private storage area. We'll clarify exactly the data that these controls return.

- We'll find out how to scan barcodes and how to use the pen control. The pen control is especially useful because we can use it to capture signatures, and to convert handwritten annotations to text.

Choosing Where to Store Images

PowerApps supports the storage of image data in Excel, CDS, and SQL Server data sources. Other data sources are not yet supported: the most notable one being SharePoint. With SharePoint, PowerApps doesn't support the 'Hyperlink or Picture' column types. It isn't able to display the images that are stored in these columns and it also doesn't support file attachments.

To work around this limitation, a hack that some app builders carry out is to store the base 64 text representation of the image in a text field. The main issue with this approach is that it's not straightforward to retrieve the image data from controls such as the camera or to add picture control. These controls often expose an identifier rather than the actual image data, and we'll explore this in more detail as the chapter progresses.

Tip　The PowerApps blog provides a detailed guide on how to store images in Azure Blob Storage. This is quite an involved technique and you can find out more here:

`https://powerapps.microsoft.com/en-us/blog/custom-api-for-image-upload/`

Setting Up a Data Source

To store image data, we need to configure our data source to store data of this type. In this section, we'll look at how to set up an Excel spreadsheet, CDS entity, or SQL Server table to store image data.

Storing Images in Excel

With Excel data sources, PowerApps stores image files in a subfolder where the Excel spreadsheet resides. The Excel file stores the path and name of the file. The benefit of Excel is that it's easy to work with the image data. We can easily download and view the image files from within the cloud storage.

To set up an Excel file to store images, create a spreadsheet as shown in Figure 10-1. Use the Insert ➤ Table menu item in Excel to configure the data range as a table.

Figure 10-1. *Creating a spreadsheet to store image data*

In our example, the purpose of this spreadsheet is to store the photos and signatures of users. The PhotoData column stores the image path file name and the Description column enables the user to provide some descriptive text. Note that any image columns must end with the word [image]. This enables the designer to recognize the column as an image field. We'll use the UserSignature column later in this chapter to demonstrate the use of the pen control.

We can store our Excel spreadsheet on all the supported file-based data stores such as OneDrive or Dropbox. Out of these two providers, Dropbox works better than OneDrive. This is because OneDrive has a problem that occurs when you share your app with other users. If other users are logged into their personal OneDrive accounts, PowerApps saves the image files incorrectly into the OneDrive account that is associated with the user, rather than the OneDrive account that is associated with the data connection in the app.

Storing Images in CDS and SQL Server Databases

With the CDS, it's simple to set up an entity to store image data. In the designer, simply add a field and set the type to image, as shown in Figure 10-2.

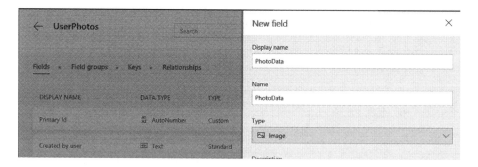

Figure 10-2. *Creating an image field for a CDS entity*

With SQL Server, it's just as easy. In SQL Server Management Studio, simply create a table, and add a new column of data type image, as shown in Figure 10-3.

Column Name	Data Type	Allow Nulls
🔑 UserID	int	☐
Description	nvarchar(MAX)	☐
PhotoData	image	☑
UserSignature	image	☑

Figure 10-3. Setting up an SQL field to store image data

One note of caution is that Microsoft plans to remove the image data type in future releases of SQL Server and therefore recommend the use of the varbinary data type instead. The disadvantage of the varbinary data type is that when we build auto-generated apps against fields of this type, PowerApps will not detect these as image fields and will not provide the option to use image controls on the default cards.

Creating an Image App

The quickest way to build an app to store images is to create an auto-generated app. Let's build an auto-generated app and examine the image-related features.

In an auto-generated app, the edit screen includes an 'Add picture' control, which is a control that the user can use to upload a file from the local device (Figure 10-4). The file extensions that PowerApps supports include .jpg, .jpeg, .gif, .png, .bmp, .tif. .tiff, and .svg.

Figure 10-4. The edit screen in an auto-generated app includes an 'add picture' control

211

The detail screen provides a picture control to display the image that the user has uploaded.

Let's run our app and add a new record. Click the Add Picture control and upload an image file. Now save the record and examine the contents of the spreadsheet. As Figure 10-5 shows, PowerApps inserts the image path and location into the PhotoData field.

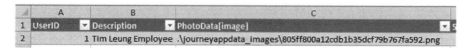

Figure 10-5. *The Excel file contains a link to the image file.*

In the location where the spreadsheet resides, PowerApps creates a subfolder to store the image files. The name of the folder matches the name of the spreadsheet with the word "_images" appended to the end, as shown in Figure 10-6.

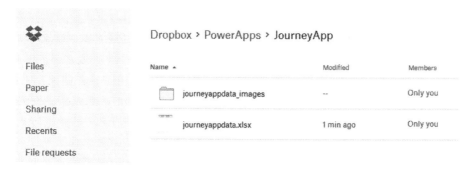

Figure 10-6. *Folder view in Dropbox, showing the image folder*

With Excel data sources, one thing to note is that when you delete a record, PowerApps does not delete the image that is associated with the record.

Viewing Records in the CDS

Let's examine what we would see with a CDS data source. As Figure 10-7 shows, the data section of the entity designer shows the records in the entity. However, this view doesn't show images, or even indicate whether an image is associated with the record. The 'Open in Excel' feature also does not show the image data. This highlights a potential difficulty when we store images in the CDS. It can be difficult to extract our image data from the CDS, and this can make it difficult to migrate away from the CDS if we choose to do this at a future point in time.

Figure 10-7. *The data view in the CDS*

Using the Add Picture Control

The 'Add Picture' control integrates very well with the form control and enables us to easily add pictures to a data source. But if we want to use this control in isolation, it's not simple to retrieve the actual image data from the control. Let's explore this in a bit more detail.

The 'Add Picture' control is a composite control that consists of an 'add media button' control and an image control. The image control displays the image that the user adds. The media property of the 'add media button' returns the image data.

If we were to insert an 'Add Picture' control and display the contents of the media property in a label control, the media property would return a unique identifier that references a unique identifier. Figure 10-8 illustrates how this would look in the Windows version of PowerApps Studio.

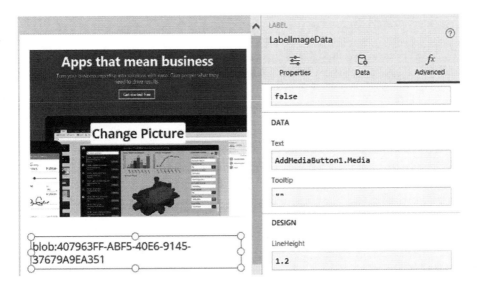

Figure 10-8. *The media property of the 'add picture' control*

If we were to run the app in the browser or Android versions, the value of the media property would appear in the following format:

- Browser version- `https://us.create.powerapps.com/60ca5079-ef7d-4b10-95b2-96a4ceb3c0c6`

- Android version - `http://127.0.0.1:49428/60ca5079-ef7d-4b10-95b2-96a4ceb3c0c6`

The important point here is that we can't easily retrieve the binary content from the 'Add Picture' control. The conversion from a blob address to the binary content occurs when an app connects to a data source and calls an operation on the data source (such as a save operation). If we were to write a custom API method that receives image data, we could call the method from PowerApps and retrieve the binary data from our API code.

Using the Camera Control

The camera control enables us to build apps to capture photos. To demonstrate the use of this control, here's how to replace the Add Picture control in an auto-generated app with a camera control.

As an introduction, the camera control provides a property called photo. This property returns the image from the camera at the moment when we read the property. The standard behavior on most mobile apps is to provide a method for the user to take a snapshot and to review the image before saving it. This is the feature that we'll build in this section.

To begin, open the edit screen and select the default card for the photo data field. Unlock the card and delete all the controls on the card. We can use the screen explorer view on the left-hand side of the designer to quickly delete all the controls. Add a camera control and insert an image control adjacent to it. Name these controls CameraUserPhoto and ImageUserPhoto, as shown in Figure 10-9.

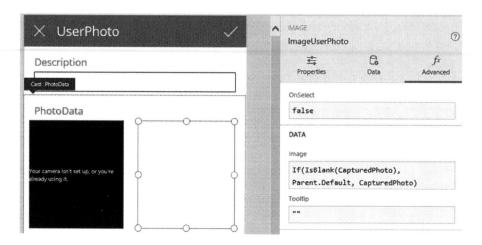

Figure 10-9. *Add a camera control and an image control*

The next step is to build the feature that allows the user to take a snapshot. The method we'll use is to store the photo in a variable when the user taps the camera control. To do this, add the following code to the OnSelect property of the camera control:

```
UpdateContext({CapturedPhoto: CameraUserPhoto.Photo})
```

An important step is to clear this variable when the user navigates away from the screen. If we fail to do this, the captured image will remain when the user reopens the screen. To clear the variable, set the OnHidden property of the screen to the following formula:

```
UpdateContext({CapturedPhoto: Blank()})
```

The next step is to configure the image control so that it shows the image when a user opens an existing record, or to show the image that the user captures with the camera. To do this, set the image property of the image control to the formula beneath:

```
If(IsBlank(CapturedPhoto), Parent.Default, CapturedPhoto)
```

Finally, we need to set up the form to save the photo to the data source. To do this, set the Update property of the card to ImageUserPhoto.Image.

At this point, we can run our app and use the camera control to capture and save photos.

Retrieving the Camera Data

In the previous section, we saw how the Media property of the Add Picture control returns a unique identifier that begins with the text "blob:". Does the camera control behave in the same way? The answer is that it varies.

On browser, iPhone, and Android devices, the Photo property of the camera control returns a base64 encoded representation of the image. Figure 10-10 shows the result on Android when we display the photo property of the camera control in a label. The photo property returns a string that begins "data:image/jpeg;base64," followed by a long base64 encoded representation of the image. This is useful because we can store the result in a text field in a data source. Outside of PowerApps, a simple way to convert this text representation to an image is to strip off the preceding "data:image/jpeg;base64," text and to enter the remaining characters into an online base64 to image converter. You can find plenty of these online converters by searching the web.

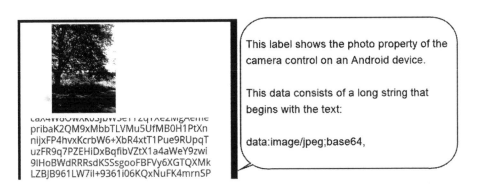

Figure 10-10. *The Photo property of the camera control returns base64 encoded text on some devices*

However, in PowerApps Studio and on Window devices (such as Surface tablets), the photo property does not return the base64 representation of the image and instead returns a string that looks like this: "blob:60ca5079-ef7d-4b10-95b2-96a4ceb3c0c6".

The important point to take from this is that when we build custom features with the camera control, it's important to exercise some caution because the photo property returns different results depending on the device.

Switching Between Cameras

Many mobile devices provide at least two cameras - a rear camera and a front-facing camera. We can set the camera id property to choose which camera to use. Here's how to add a control to allow the user to switch cameras.

First, add a slider control and name it SliderCameraId. Set the max property to 1 and the default value to 0. Next, set the camera property of the camera control to SliderCameraId.Value, as shown in Figure 10-11. You can now run your app and use the slider control to change the camera.

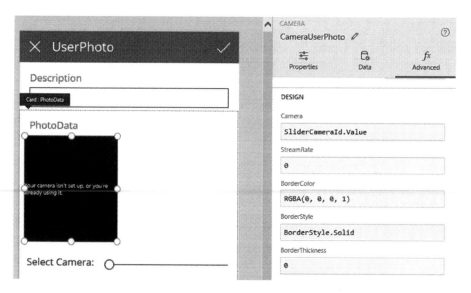

Figure 10-11. *Add a slider control to enable the user to switch cameras*

Setting Brightness, Contrast, and Zoom Levels

We can use the same technique as above to enable users to set the brightness, contrast, and zoon levels of the camera. Simply add slider controls and set the Zoom, Brightness, or Contrast properties of the camera control to the value of the slider control. Table 10-1 shows the details of these properties.

Table 10-1. *Camera Control Properties*

Property	Property Description
Zoom	The percentage by which an image from a camera is magnified.
Brightness	How much light the user is likely to perceive in an image.
Contrast	How easily the user can distinguish between similar colors in an image.

■ **Note**   There's no way to configure the resolution of the picture that the camera control captures. Users with high-resolution cameras may find that the camera control captures images with insufficient resolution.

Creating a Gallery

The template apps provide some sophisticated image and photo-taking techniques that we can reuse in our own apps. The best app that uses the camera control is the site inspection app. This app provides a screen that adds photos to a site inspection record. This screen contains a camera control that allows a user to attach up to seven photos at a time, as shown in Figure 10-12. The middle of the screen contains a gallery control that displays images that have been captured. The 'done' button at the bottom part of the screen saves the images to an Excel data source.

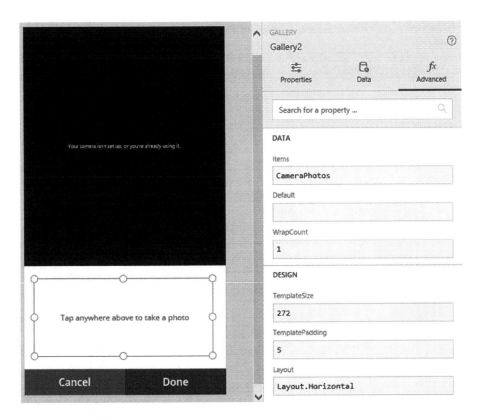

Figure 10-12. *The photo entry screen*

There are two places in the app where a user can reach this photo entry screen. The first is through a screen called 'new inspection screen'. This is the screen that a user can use to add a new site inspection record. The second is through a screen called 'image screen'. This screen enables users to view the photos that are associated with an existing site inspection record.

Let's take a closer look at the photo capture screen. How exactly does this screen work? When the user taps the camera control (the name of this control is Camera1), the control runs the formula that's shown beneath.

```
If(CountRows(CameraPhotos) <=7,
    Collect(CameraPhotos,
            {Note:"",
             Photo:Camera1.Photo,
             PhotoId:CountRows(CameraPhotos)
            }
    )
)
```

This formula captures the images into a collection called CameraPhotos. The first part of this formula checks that there are fewer than seven items in the collection. The app only collects photos when this condition is true. Each record in the collection includes a field called PhotoId. The collect function sets the PhotoId value of a record to the count of records when it adds a record to the collection. This technique assigns a sequential PhotoID value to each record.

The 'done' button calls the patch function to save the photos to the Excel data source. An excerpt of this code is shown in Listing 10-1.

Listing 10-1. Patching the data to the data source

```
If(NewRecord,
    Navigate(NewInspectionScreen,ScreenTransition.Fade),
    If(CountRows(CameraPhotos)>=1,
        UpdateContext(
                {AddPhoto:Patch(SitePhotos,
                                Defaults(SitePhotos),
                                {PhotoId:Max(SitePhotos,PhotoId)+1,
                                 Photo:Last(FirstN(CameraPhotos,1)).Photo,
                                 ID:Gallery3.Selected.ID,
                                 Note:Text(Last(FirstN(CameraPhotos,1)).Note)
                                })
                }
        )
    );
    If(CountRows(CameraPhotos)>=2,
        UpdateContext(
                {AddPhoto:Patch(SitePhotos,
                                Defaults(SitePhotos),
                                {PhotoId:Max(SitePhotos,PhotoId)+1,
                                 Photo:Last(FirstN(CameraPhotos,2)).Photo,
                                 ID:Gallery3.Selected.ID,
                                 Note:Text(Last(FirstN(CameraPhotos,2)).Note)
                                })
                }
        )
    );
```

The main purpose of this formula is to update the photos for an existing site inspection record. The first part of this formula checks the value of the NewRecord variable. If the user is adding a new site inspection record, the formula navigates the user to the 'new inspection screen'. If the user is editing an existing record, the formula calls the patch function to insert a record into a table called SitePhotos. This table stores the photo data and Figure 10-13 shows the data structure. The PhotoId field uniquely identifies each record, and the ID field refers to the primary key value of the parent site inspection record.

	A	B	C	D
1	**PhotoId** ▾	**Photo[image]** ▾	**Note** ▾	**ID** ▾
2	1	./data_images/1-100.jpg	Built in 1980 with signific	1
3	2	./data_images/1-101.jpg		1
4	3	./data_images/1-102.jpg		1
5	4	./data_images/1-103.jpg		1
6	5	./data_images/1-104.jpg		1
7	6	./data_images/2-100.jpg	Parking lot has two acces	2
8	7	./data_images/2-101.jpg		2
9	8	./data_images/2-102.jpg		2
10	9	./data_images/2-103.jpg		2
11	10	./data_images/3-100.jpg	Outdoor spaces have bee	3
12	11	./data_images/3-101.jpg		3
13	12	./data_images/3-102.jpg		3
14	13	./data_images/3-103.jpg		3
15	14	./data_images/3-104.jpg		3
16	15	./data_images/4-100.jpg	Smoking pavillion added	4
17	16	./data_images/4-101.jpg		4
18	17	./data_images/4-102.jpg		4
19	18	./data_images/5-100.jpg	Zoned commercial	5
20	19	./data_images/5-101.jpg		5
21	20	./data_images/5-102.jpg		5
22	21	./data_images/5-103.jpg		5
23	22	./data_images/5-104.jpg		5

Figure 10-13. *SitePhotos data source*

The code that patches each image follows the same pattern. Listing 10-1 illustrates the code to patch the first two images and omits the remaining code for brevity. The pertinent code that patches the first image is shown beneath.

```
Patch(SitePhotos,
     Defaults(SitePhotos),
     {PhotoId:Max(SitePhotos,PhotoId)+1,
      Photo:Last(FirstN(CameraPhotos,1)).Photo,
      ID:Gallery3.Selected.ID,
      Note:Text(Last(FirstN(CameraPhotos,1)).Note)
      }
)
```

The first interesting thing is the excerpt of code that generates the PhotoId value. The formula calls the max function to return the highest photo id value from the site photos data source, and adds one. This is the code that generates a sequence of sequential photo id values.

Another interesting part of this formula is the logic that retrieves an individual photo from the CameraPhotos collection. As an example, the formula to retrieve the forth record from a collection would look like this:

```
Last(FirstN(CameraPhotos,4)).Photo
```

219

This formula calls the FirstN function to return the first four records from the CameraPhotos collection. The outermost call to the Last function returns the last record from the result of the FirstN function, which equates to the fourth record in the collection.

The code we've seen adds photos to an existing site inspection record. In the case where a user is adding a new site inspection record, it's not possible to use this code because there isn't a parent site inspection record to relate the photos to. In this instance, the formula returns the user to the new inspection screen. This screen provides a form control to add a new site inspection record. When a user adds a new record, the code in the OnSuccess property of the screen adds the photos in the CameraPhotos collection to the SitePhotos table. The OnSuccess formula looks almost identical to the code in the photo capture screen, as shown in Figure 10-14.

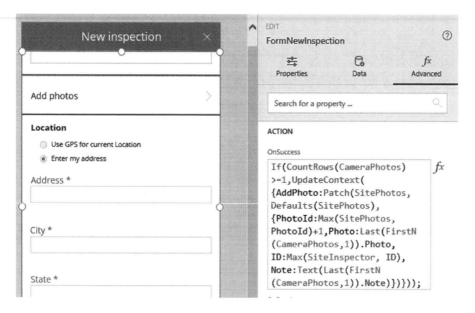

Figure 10-14. Adding photos to a new site inspection record

To summarize, the code in this section provides some excellent learning points. The first is the technique that captures the photos into a collection and defers the save operation to a later point in time. This code demonstrates how we can use the patch function to insert multiple records at a time. The code also demonstrates the syntax we can use to generate a sequence of numbers, and how to retrieve a record by ordinal number (for example, the second, third, fourth record, etc)

■ **Note**   The code in this section provides an excellent example on how to generate sequences of numbers, and how to retrieve records by ordinal number.

Using the Pen Control

PowerApps provides a pen control that is ideal for capturing annotations or signatures. This control generates images in png format and we can easily assign this control to the image fields on a form. To do this, set the control type to 'Add Notes', as shown in Figure 10-15.

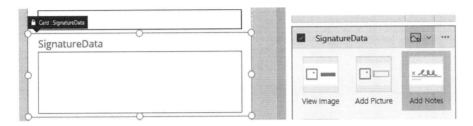

Figure 10-15. *Change the control type from Add Picture to Add Notes*

We can now run our app and use the pen control to enter text, as shown in Figure 10-16. When we save our record and examine the folder that contains our Excel spreadsheet, we'll find a png file in the images folder that contains the note.

The pen control provides an image property that allows us to access the annotation. Just like the add picture control, this property returns a blob address. We would need to save the record, or to pass the image property value to a data source to obtain the image data.

Figure 10-16. *Using the pen control at runtime*

Erasing Text

To allow users to correct any mistakes, there are a couple of techniques we can use. We can set the pen mode to erase, or we can completely clear the contents of the control.

With the pen mode set to erase, the user can erase individual pen strokes by drawing over the annotation. Let's look at how to implement this feature. The mode property allows us to switch between the pen modes. To enable users to alter the pen mode, we can add a toggle control and write formula to set the mode property of the pen control depending on the value of the toggle control, as shown in Figure 10-17.

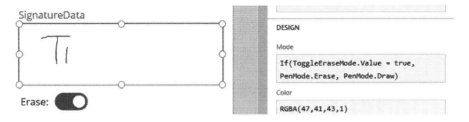

Figure 10-17. *Switching the pen mode to erase*

Alternatively, we can use the reset property technique from Chapter 8 to completely clear the contents of the pen control. To demonstrate this technique, here's how to add a button to clear the contents of the pen control.

First, add a button and add formula to set the value of a variable to true, and then back to false. In this example, we'll name our variable ResetPenControl and the formula would look like this:

```
UpdateContext({ResetPenControl: true});
UpdateContext({ResetPenControl: false})
```

Figure 10-18 illustrates the view in the designer. The next step is to set the Reset property of the pen control to ResetPenControl. We can now run our app and click the button to clear the contents of the pen control.

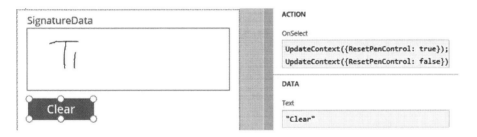

Figure 10-18. *Adding a button to clear the contents of the pen control*

Converting Annotations to Text

A great feature of the pen control is the ability to convert annotations to text. This feature is simple to implement because the pen control exposes a property called RecognizedText. We can read this property to retrieve the pen control's attempt to convert the annotation to text. The accuracy of the text recognition can vary and will not be perfect. Figure 10-19 demonstrates the text recognition feature by setting the text of a label to the recognized text property of a pen control. The value of the recognized text changes following the entry of each letter in the pen control.

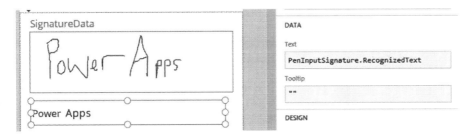

Figure 10-19. *Recognizing annotations*

Scanning Barcodes

PowerApps provides a control to capture barcodes. In this section, we'll explore how to use this control to scan and extract barcode numbers. This control supports six common barcode types, and these are shown in Figure 10-20.

Figure 10-20. *Supported barcode types*

The notable barcode type that is not supported is the QR (quick response) barcode. QR barcodes often appear in adverts, and you can scan these barcodes with a smart phone to open an associated web page.

To demonstrate the barcode control, we'll build a simple screen that enables a user to scan a barcode and to extract the barcode number. The first step is to insert a barcode control and label control onto a screen. Name these controls BarcodeControl and LabelBarcodeNumber, as shown in Figure 10-21. To configure the control so that it scans the barcode when the user taps the control, set the OnSelect property of the barcode control to the formula shown below:

```
UpdateContext({CapturedBarcode: BarcodeControl.Value})
```

Next, set the 'barcode type' property to the barcode type that we want to detect. A useful feature we can enable is the 'show live barcode detection' option. With this feature enabled, the control displays a rectangular overlay when it detects a barcode. This makes it easier for the user to scan the barcode.

223

Figure 10-21. *Configuring the barcode control*

The final step is to set the text property of the label control to the variable CapturedBarcode. At this stage, we can run our app and use the control to scan a barcode. When the control scans the barcode successfully, the number will appear in the label control.

To learn more about this control, the PowerApps blog contains a detailed article that describes this control in detail. You can find this article here:

https://powerapps.microsoft.com/en-us/blog/make-barcode-scanning-apps-in-minutes/

Summary

In this chapter, we looked at ways to capture, store, and retrieve image-related data. The main data sources that support image are the CDS, SQL Server, and Excel data sources.

To store image data in an Excel spreadsheet, the important step is to define a column with a name that ends with [image]. The next step is to save the spreadsheet to a cloud storage provider. When we build an auto-generated app and save a record that includes an image, PowerApps saves the image to a subfolder of the folder that contains the Excel spreadsheet and stores the file location of the image in the spreadsheet.

Auto-generated apps allow users to upload images to image fields through the Add Picture control. This control enables users to select a file from the local file system.

PowerApps provides a camera control that is useful when we want to build apps where users can capture photos. The typical way to use this control is to capture an image when a user taps the camera control. The photo property of the control returns the image data, and we can store this in a variable, prior to saving the image to the data source. Many mobile devices include multiple cameras, and it's possible to choose which camera the control uses. We can also configure the brightness, contrast, and zoom properties of the camera.

The example site inspection app provides an excellent example of how to use the camera control. This app allows the user to take up to seven photos at a time. The screen collects the images to a collection, and calls the patch function to add the multiple images to the Excel data source. This app includes some useful code snippets that we can reuse. This includes formula to retrieve a record by ordinal number, and code to generate numeric field sequences.

A very useful control is the pen control. Users can use this control to enter signatures or annotations. With auto-generated apps, you choose to use this control against an image field by choosing this control type in the card settings of a form.

Finally, PowerApps provides a barcode control and we can use this to scan and retrieve the barcode numbers for a range of common barcode types.

CHAPTER 11

■ ■ ■

Mapping Data

PowerApps is designed for mobile devices and therefore works naturally with location services. Although we can easily retrieve location details from within an app, there are various intricacies that we need to be aware of, especially when we want to save location details to a data store. In this chapter, we'll examine these issues and focus on the following topics:

- Retrieving GPS data. We'll find out how to retrieve values such as longitude, latitude, compass bearing, and acceleration details.

- Saving location details. We'll create an auto-generated app and go through the steps to provide the capability for users to retrieve and save location details on the edit form.

- Integrating with mapping services. We'll find out how to use mapping services to pinpoint locations. We'll cover two of the most popular services - Google Maps and Bing Maps.

Introduction to GPS

PowerApps can integrate with the location services that are provided by mobile device operating systems. These services can provide the device location based on GPS or cellular information. From within an app, we can use formula to determine the longitude, latitude, or compass bearing of a device.

For readers who are unfamiliar with longitude and latitude values, here's a brief introduction. Longitude and latitude values are measured in degrees, and we can use these readings to locate a specific location on Earth. These values can be positive or negative. Locations in the Southern hemisphere have a negative longitude, and locations in the Western hemisphere have a negative latitude. Figure 11-1 illustrates this in the form of a diagram.

© Tim Leung 2017
T. Leung, *Beginning PowerApps*, https://doi.org/10.1007/978-1-4842-3003-9_11

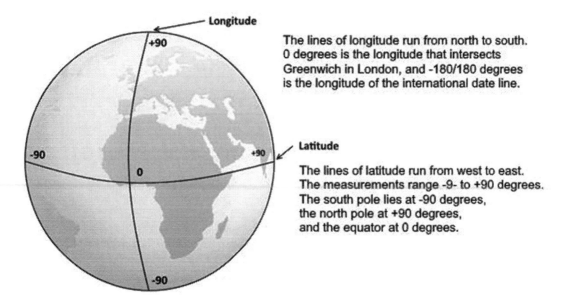

The lines of longitude run from north to south.
0 degrees is the longitude that intersects
Greenwich in London, and -180/180 degrees
is the longitude of the international date line.

The lines of latitude run from west to east.
The measurements range -9- to +90 degrees.
The south pole lies at -90 degrees,
the north pole at +90 degrees,
and the equator at 0 degrees.

Figure 11-1. *Longitude and Latitude measurements*

When we retrieve a location from a mobile device, the accuracy of the reading can vary. If the user has only just switched on the GPS, there may be insufficient time for the device to lock onto sufficient satellites to give an accurate reading. In this situation, devices have a tendency to return the last known location.

In the case of PowerApps, an important point is that when a user starts an app with the GPS turned on and turns off the GPS at a later point, any subsequent attempt to retrieve the location will return the last known location.

Retrieving Location Details

With PowerApps, we can very easily retrieve the current location of a device. PowerApps provides functions to obtain the longitude, latitude, and compass bearing of a device. To demonstrate this topic, we'll build an app that can retrieve and store location details.

Introducing Signals

PowerApps provides objects called signals. The signals that are of interest in this section are the location, compass, and acceleration signals. A key characteristic of a signal is that its value can constantly change. In the case of the location signal, the value of this signal can change regularly to reflect the current location.

We can treat signals as though they are records. In the case of the location signal, we can treat this as a record that contains three fields: longitude, latitude, and altitude. If we want to retrieve the longitude or latitude in formula, we would use the syntax Location.Longitude or Location.Latitude respectively.

The location signal returns longitude and latitude.readings in degrees, and altitude readings in the number of feet above sea level.

Freezing the Location Details

In the vast majority of cases, it's good practice not to work directly with a signal. In many cases, we want to work with a snapshot of a location at a single moment in time. Let's imagine that we've built an app that captures photos and stores the location where the photos were taken. In this scenario, it wouldn't be accurate to retrieve the location at the point when the user saves the record. If the user were traveling in a car, there could be a considerable difference in distance between the time when the user takes the photo and the time when the user saves the record. Therefore, it's common practice to save locations to a variable and to work with the variable value. This is the technique that we'll adopt in this chapter.

Obtaining Longitude and Latitude.Readings

To demonstrate how to retrieve locations, we build a screen to retrieve the location details into a variable and to display the values on screen. To build this example, add a screen and insert three labels. Name these controls LabelLongitude, LabelLatitude, and LabelAltitude. Now add a button and name it GetLocation (Figure 11-2). Set the OnSelect property of the GetLocation button to the formula beneath:

```
UpdateContext({CurrentLocation: Location})
```

This code stores the result of the Location signal to a context variable called CurrentLocation. The next step is to set the Text properties of the LabelLongitude and LabelLatitude labels to the values CurrentLocation.Longitude.and CurrentLocation.Latitude respectively.

At this point, we can run our app to test this functionality. To make sure that the location signal returns data when we run our app in PowerApps Studio, make sure to turn on location services in the settings of Windows. In Windows, we can specify a default location. The location signal in PowerApps returns the default location if our computer cannot detect a more precise location.

Figure 11-2. *Layout of sample screen*

At runtime, the GetLocation button may fail to retrieve the location and the app will appear to do nothing. To improve this behavior, we can show a message that indicates this condition. We can accomplish this by amending the formula in the GetLocation button so that it stores a message in a variable when location services are not available. The formula beneath illustrates this technique.

```
UpdateContext({CurrentLocation: Location});
UpdateContext({LocationMessage:If(IsBlank(Location.Longitude),
                                   "Location Unavailable",
                                   "")
            }
)
```

To explain this formula in more detail, when PowerApps fails to retrieve a location, it returns blank longitude and latitude.readings. We can test for the presence of a blank longitude to determine when a device has failed to retrieve the location. In this example, the formula stores the message "Location Unavailable" in a variable called LocationMessage when the location details are not available. When location details are available, the formula sets the value of this variable to an empty string. We can then display this message through a label on a screen.

Saving Location Details

A typical task is to store the location values to a data source. In this section, we'll walk through the steps to create an auto-generated app to store these details. Figure 11-3 shows the source data that we'll use. Just like our previous example, we'll add a button that retrieves the location. We'll then use the location details to populate the data entry controls on the edit form.

Figure 11-3. *Layout of sample data*

The first step is to create an auto-generated app based on this data source. Next, add a button and name it GetLocation. Set the OnSelect property of the GetLocation button to the same formula as before, as shown beneath:

```
UpdateContext({CurrentLocation: Location})
```

Unlock the card for the longitude.field and change the default property of the text input control to the formula shown beneath:

```
If(IsBlank(CurrentLocation.Longitude),
   Parent.Default,
   CurrentLocation.Longitude
)
```

This formula shows the longitude.value that the user obtains by clicking the GetLocation button. If this value is blank, the formula returns the existing longitude value for the record.

The next step is to modify the update property of the card so that it updates the data source with the desired value. Select the card for the longitude.field and set the Update property to the formula shown beneath:

```
If(IsBlank(CurrentLocation.Longitude),
   Parent.Default,
   CurrentLocation.Longitude
)
```

230

Now repeat the same process for the latitude values. Set the default property of the latitude text input control and the update property of the latitude card to the formula shown beneath.

```
If(IsBlank(CurrentLocation.Latitude),
   Parent.Default,
   CurrentLocation.Latitude
)
```

The final step is to clear the CurrentLocation variable when the user leaves the screen. Here's the code to add to the OnHidden property of the screen.

```
UpdateContext({CurrentLocation: Location})
```

Figure 11-4 shows the layout of the screen in the designer. At this stage, you can run your app and save the updated location details to a data store.

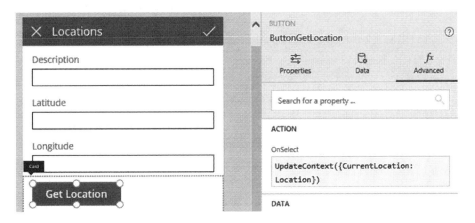

Figure 11-4. *Layout of the sample screen*

Switching the Signal On/Off

Apps that use location services can quickly drain the battery of a device. It's not just the GPS that causes the power drain. If an app includes formulas that refer to the location signal, those formulas will recalculate whenever the location changes. This behavior adds an additional overhead to the battery drain.

One way to conserve battery life is to turn off the location signal when it's not needed. To turn off the location signal, we can add a button to our screen and add the following code:

```
Disable(Location)
```

Here's the formula to turn the signal back on again:

```
Enable(Location)
```

A piece of behavior that's worth noting is that a user may start an app with the GPS of the device switched off. In the case of an Android device, if a user turns on GPS through the icon in the notification bar or through any other quick access icon, the location signal from PowerApps might continue to return no data. One way to force the location signal to refresh and return data is to minimize PowerApps to the background and to switch back to the app. One technique to force PowerApps to the background is to call the launch function to launch a webpage that contains instructions for the user to switch back to PowerApps.

Other Signals

There are two other signals that might be of use when you're building a location-based app - the Compass and Acceleration signals. The Compass.Heading function returns the heading value, measured in degrees.

The Acceleration signal returns the acceleration in X, Y and Z planes, measured in g units (this is the standard unit of measurement of acceleration, equivalent to 9.8 meters per second squared). Figure 11-5 shows this in the form of a diagram.

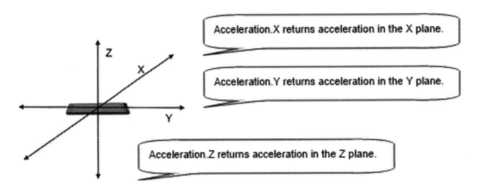

Figure 11-5. *Measuring Acceleration*

Displaying Maps

We can display locations much more meaningfully through the use of maps. Two common online mapping services we can use are Google Maps and Bing Maps and in this section, we'll look at both.

Both these services provide a static map API that returns an image of a map based on arguments that we provide through the web address. To show the output, we can use an image control to display the map that the service returns.

Google and Bing provide free plans for commercial use. With Google, the free standard plan provides a maximum of 25,000 map loads during each 24-hour period. The maximum resolution of the maps that we can retrieve through the standard plan is 640x640 pixels. With Bing, we can register for a free 'Basic Bing Maps key' and this offers up to 125,000 map views per calendar year for commercial use.

Both Google and Bing offer the same basic mapping features through the static map APIs. This includes the ability to center a map based on longitude and latitude, or by address or other search terms. Additional basic features include the ability to display markers, and to switch the presentation between aerial or road map views. An added feature of Bing Maps is that it provides the ability to show traffic flow and routing details between two points.

Using Google Maps

With Google Maps, the format of the web address that returns an image from the static maps API is shown below.

```
https://maps.googleapis.com/maps/api/staticmap?center=51.51128434,-0.11915781&zoom=12&size=400x400
```

The two important values that we need to provide are the latitude and longitude. We provide these as comma-separated latitude and longitude values through the center argument. Technically, we should use the key parameter to specify the API key value that we generate after registering for the Google Maps service. For test purposes, the API appears to work without needing a key, but this may change in the future.

To demonstrate how to show a Google map on a screen, let's modify the detail form from the auto-generated app that we created earlier in this chapter. Open the details form and add a custom card. Insert an image control and set the image property to the following value:

```
"https://maps.googleapis.com/maps/api/staticmap?center="& ThisItem.Latitude & "," &
ThisItem.Longitude & "& zoom=12&size=500x400"
```

Figure 11-6 shows the view of the screen in the designer. We can now run our app and the details screen will display a map that corresponds to the latitude and longitude of the current record.

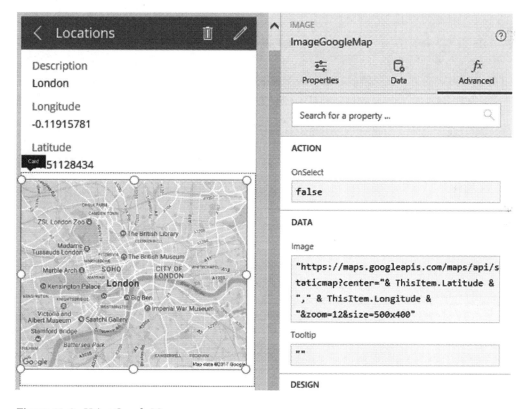

Figure 11-6. *Using Google Maps*

For more information on how to use this API, including how to change the view and how to add markers, visit the Google Static Maps API website through the link below:

```
https://developers.google.com/maps/documentation/static-maps/intro
```

Bing Maps

Bing Maps provides a static map API that works similarly to Google Maps. The example Site Inspector uses this method, and we can refer to this app to find out more. The Bing service requires us to register and to obtain an API key to access the service. Here's the website to register for a key.

```
https://www.bingmapsportal.com/
```

For development purposes, a quick way to obtain an API key is to run the example Site Inspector app and to use the API key that's embedded in this app. The format of the web address that returns an image from the API is shown below:

```
http://dev.virtualearth.net/REST/v1/Imagery/Map/Road/51.51128434,-0.11915781/15?mapSize=500,
500&key=wg9mvoY3hN6AVoUPutnZ~y8lVN1szjh6d5E8Vs8h48A~AtTHu5h2www6JiWYy5l3eKT8Cfl7SDg4f4jJUiwV
L9beAGFEPcLyCe2iBvkF--_9
```

The values that we need to provide here are the location and the key. The web address above specifies the comma-separated latitude and longitude value of 51.51128434 and -0.11915781.

Here's how to modify the detail form from our auto-generated app to use Bing Maps to display the location of the current record. Like the Google Maps example, open the details form and add a custom card to the form. Insert an image control and set the image property to the following value:

```
"http://dev.virtualearth.net/REST/v1/Imagery/Map/Road/"& ThisItem.Latitude & "," & ThisItem.
Longitude & "/15?mapSize=500,500&key=wg9mvoY3hN6AVoUPutnZ~y8lVN1szjh6d5E8Vs8h48A~AtTHu5h2www
6JiWYy5l3eKT8Cfl7SDg4f4jJUiwVL9beAGFEPcLyCe2iBvkF--_9"
```

Figure 11-7 shows the view of the screen in the designer. We can now run our app and the details screen will use the Bing Maps API to display a map that corresponds to the latitude and longitude of the current record. For more information on how to use the Bing Maps API, here's the link to the help site.

```
https://msdn.microsoft.com/en-us/library/ff701724.aspx
```

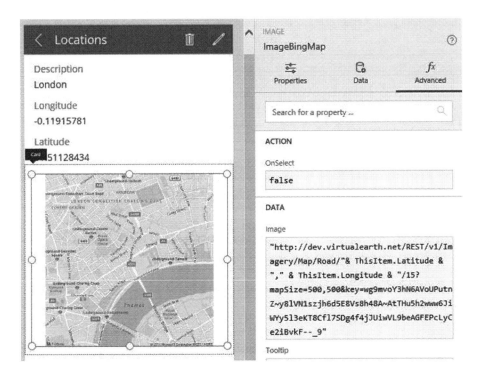

Figure 11-7. *Using the Bing Maps API*

Summary

In this chapter, we looked at how to work with location services. PowerApps provides signals to help us determine the location, compass, and acceleration values of the current device. The main characteristic of a signal is that it returns a value that constantly changes. A signal returns a record of information, and the location signal returns three fields: longitude, latitude, and altitude.

The compass signal enables us to retrieve the current heading using the formula Compass.Heading. The acceleration signal returns the acceleration of the device in the X, Y, and Z planes.

The best way to save the current location is to store the location value to a local variable and to use the variable to update the data source. This technique enables us to take a snapshot of a location and to avoid any inaccuracy that might occur if we choose instead to retrieve the location during the time when we save the record.

Apps that use location services can quickly drain the battery of a device. We can help preserve the battery life by calling a function to disable the location signal.

In the final part of this chapter, we looked at how to show Google and Bing Maps on our screens. Both these services provide a service that returns an image of a map based on arguments that we provide through the web address. To display the map, we would use an image control to display the result from the mapping service.

CHAPTER 12

Using Charts

To help users visualize data, PowerApps offers a range of chart controls. Although these are simple to use, a difficult challenge is to work out how to convert a set of raw data into a format that enables the chart control to display our desired view of the data.

For example, a common business requirement is to show how figures change over a given time, for planning and measurement purposes. However, this type of data aggregation can be difficult to implement so in this chapter, we'll find out how to carry out these steps. We'll also cover a range of useful topics that will include the following:

- Using and configuring charts. We'll find out what chart controls are available and how to configure settings such as the legend text, colors, and labels.

- Aggregating data. We'll look at how to group and sum data by date, or by some other column. To help users compare data, we'll find out to show multiple series on a single chart.

- Filtering data. We'll find out how to configure the data on a chart to change dynamically, depending on criteria that a user enters through screen controls. This technique provides users with more flexibility to visualize data in ways that can better aid decision making.

Introduction

PowerApps provides three different chart types – bar, line, and pie. To explore the capabilities of charts in PowerApps, a great place to begin is to examine the Budget Tracker App. This app features a pie chart, as shown in Figure 12-1.

© Tim Leung 2017

T. Leung, *Beginning PowerApps*, https://doi.org/10.1007/978-1-4842-3003-9_12

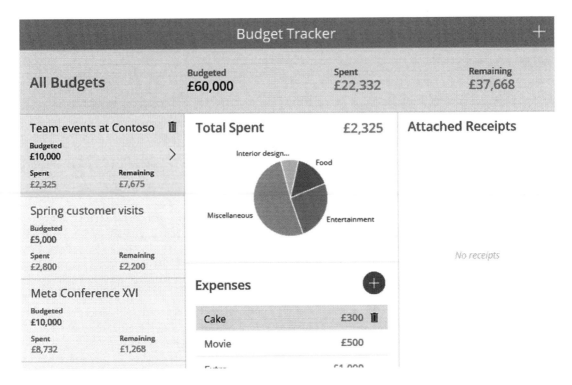

Figure 12-1. *Budget Tracker Application*

Because PowerApps is designed for non-developers, the chart controls are intuitive to use. We can simply add a chart control to a screen and use the designer to set our data source. However, transforming data into a format that works with the chart controls can often be difficult. So in the first section, we'll examine techniques to group and aggregate data. Figure 12-2 shows the layout of the example data that we'll use.

JourneyID	StartDate	User	MileageInMiles
1	2017-02-01	Tim	30
2	2017-02-01	John	15
3	2017-02-06	Tim	10
4	2017-02-10	Tim	16
5	2017-02-14	John	4
6	2017-02-06	Sally	10
7	2017-02-10	Sally	16
8	2017-02-14	Tim	4

Figure 12-2. *Example Data for this chapter*

This is a simplified version of the journey data from earlier in this book, and highlights more clearly the users and mileages. This data includes the date of a journey, the name of the person that traveled, the vehicle that was used, and the mileage that was covered.

Aggregating Data

Taking our example data, let's start by building a column chart that shows the total mileage traveled by user. Our target chart will show users along the x axis and the mileage along the y-axis. Figure 12-3 illustrates how such a chart would look in Excel.

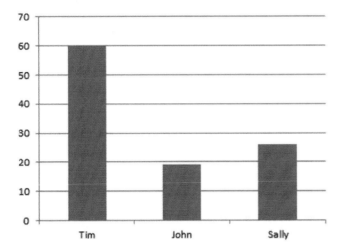

Figure 12-3. *Illustration of desired result in Excel*

To build this chart, we first need to aggregate our source data. To show the total mileage by user, it's necessary to build a data set that resembles the format that's shown in Figure 12-4.

User ▼	SumMileage ▼
Tim	60
John	19
Sally	26

Figure 12-4. *Desired format of aggregated data*

With PowerApps, it's not possible to aggregate data with a single command like we would with SQL. Instead, it's necessary to apply a series of formulas to gradually transform our data, step by step. In our example, we would carry out two steps to aggregate our data, as shown in Figure 12-5.

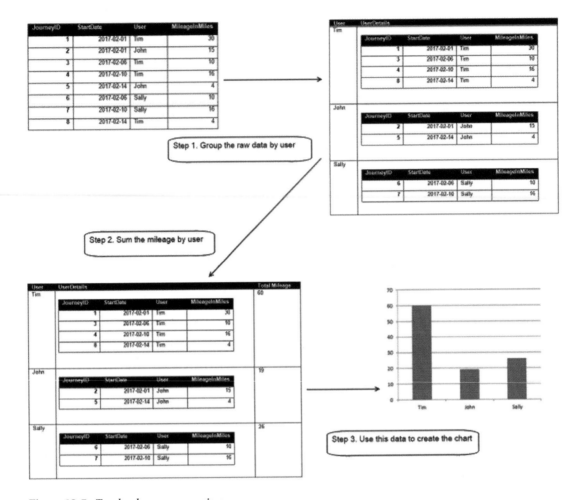

Figure 12-5. *Top-level process overview*

The first step is to group the data into two columns. The first column contains the user and the second column contains the remaining columns of data. The second step is to add a third column to store the data that we want to sum.

Column Chart

Let's now walk through the steps to add a column chart that displays the data that we discussed above. To carry out this task, we'll add the journey data to an app and create a new screen. We'll then add a button and attach the formula to aggregate the data line by line. The purpose of this is to enable us to more closely examine and understand the actions of the formula.

Once we add the journey data and create a screen, add a button and set the text to 'Show chart'. Next, set the OnSelect property of the button to the formula beneath:

```
ClearCollect(
  JourneysByUser,
  GroupBy(Journey, "User", "JourneyDetails")
)
```

This formula calls the GroupBy function to group the journey data into two columns. The result of this function returns a table with two columns. The first column contains the user name and the second contains the remaining rows. The ClearCollect function stores the output in a collection called JourneysByUser.

Let's now run our app and click the button. After we click the button, we can return to the designer and view the result through the collections menu, as shown in Figure 12-6.

Figure 12-6. *Viewing the collection in the designer*

From here, we can select the JourneysByUser collection and view the two-column result of the GroupBy function. A useful feature is the ability expand the JourneyDetails cell, as shown in Figure 12-7. We can use this to check our data and to make sure that our formula produces the correct values.

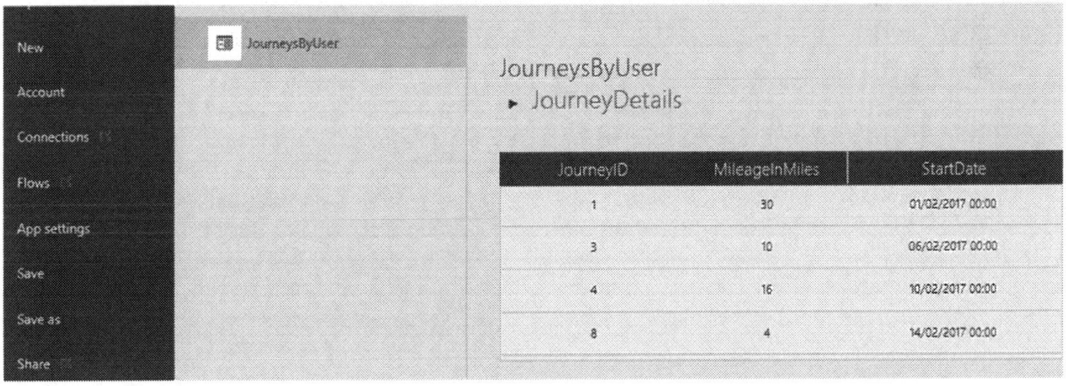

Figure 12-7. *View the collection*

Let's complete our formula so that it returns the total mileage by user. Select the button and modify the OnSelect property to include an additional line to calculate the total, like so:

```
ClearCollect(
  JourneysByUser,
  GroupBy(Journey, "User", "JourneyDetails")
);

ClearCollect(
  MileageByUser,
  AddColumns(JourneysByUser,
             "Total Mileage",
             Sum(JourneyDetails, MileageInMiles)
             )
)
```

We can now run our app and click the button once again. Like before, we can return to the designer afterward and view the result in the collections menu, as shown in Figure 12-8.

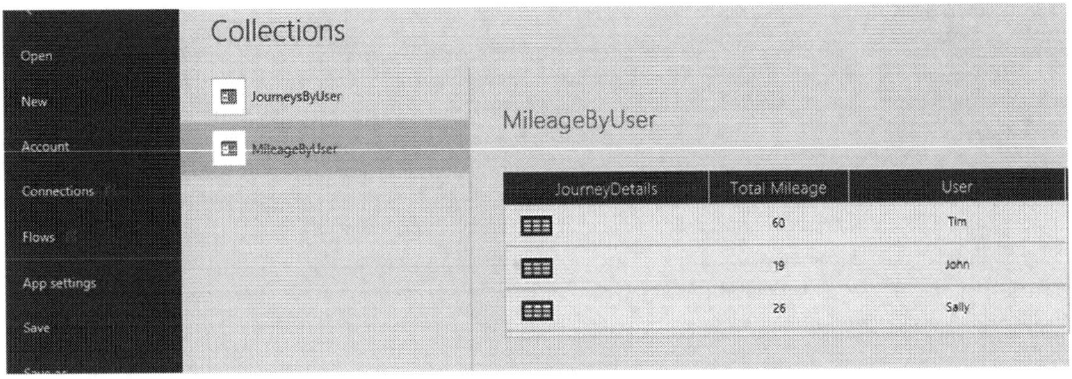

Figure 12-8. *View the collection*

The additional line in this formula adds a column called "Total Mileage" to the JourneysByUser collection. The third argument to the AddColumns function specifies the value to set for each row. Here, we call the sum function to calculate the sum of the Mileage field for the user.

To clarify the usage of the Sum function, the first argument specifies the source data - JourneyDetails. JourneyDetails is the child table in the JourneysByUser collection that contains the journey details for an individual user.

At this stage, we now have a set of data that we can use to populate a chart.

Creating a Chart

Now that we've built our aggregated source data, let's now examine the steps to create a chart. The first step is to add a new screen; let's call this ChartScreen. Next, use the Insert menu to add a chart control to the screen. The chart control is a composite control that consists of three items: a chart, title, and legend. The items property of the chart object specifies the source data for the chart. Set this to MileageByUser, as shown in Figure 12-9.

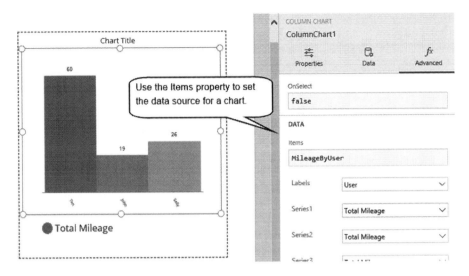

Figure 12-9. *Adding a chart control*

To display a chart that's based on data in a collection, there's a specific process that we need to follow. It's necessary to build the data in the collection before we open the screen that houses the chart control. If we use formula to build the data collection on the same screen that contains the chart control, the chart control won't refresh itself to show the latest data from the collection.

To apply this technique, select the 'Show Chart' button from our previous screen and amend the OnSelect property to add an extra line to open the chart screen, like so:

```
ClearCollect(
  JourneysByUser,
  GroupBy(Journey, "User", "JourneyDetails")
);

ClearCollect(
  MileageByUser,
  AddColumns(JourneysByUser,
          "Total Mileage",
          Sum(JourneyDetails, MileageInMiles)
          )
);

Navigate(ChartScreen,ScreenTransition.Fade)
```

At this point, we can run our app and click the 'Show Chart' button to open the chart screen and to view the column chart.

To enhance our example, let's suppose that we don't want to initiate a chart through the click of a button and to open the result in a new screen. Is that any way to accomplish this? The answer to this is yes, and there are a couple of techniques that we can use. The first is to use the table function, and we'll explore this later in the chapter. The second is to avoid the use of collections and to set the items property of the chart control to the pertinent formula that builds the collections. In our example, we would set the items property of the chart control to the formula shown here:

```
AddColumns(GroupBy(Journey, "User", "JourneyDetails"),
          "Total Mileage",
          Sum(JourneyDetails, MileageInMiles)
)
```

In most cases, it's still very useful to build our initial formula with collections because it enables us to use the collections designer to visualize the actions of our formula.

Setting Legends

A standard practice is to use legends to identify the data in the charts. By default, the chart control includes a legend. However, you'll notice in Figure 12-9 that the legend shows the series name, 'Total Mileage'. While this can be useful in some circumstances, a better use of the legend in this example is to show the user name. To accomplish this, set the items property of the legend to the data source of the chart (MileageByUser), and set the value to user, as shown in Figure 12-10.

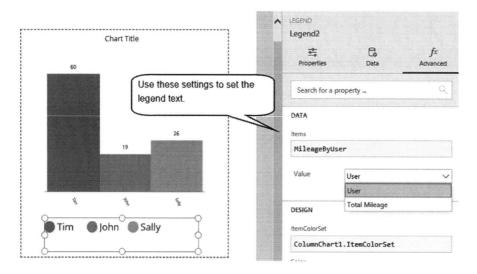

Figure 12-10. *Setting the legend text*

When we now run our screen, the legend will display the user names, rather than the series name.

Setting Label Orientation

By default, the labels on the x axis are slanted by 60 degrees to better accommodate charts with multiple items on the X axis. For charts with fewer items, we can change the angle of the label with the XLabelAngle property, as shown in Figure 12-11.

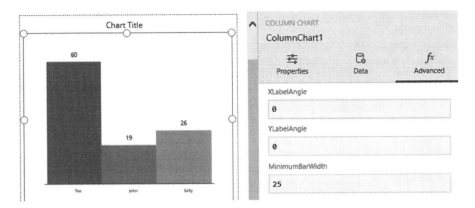

Figure 12-11. *Setting the label orientation*

Applying Colors and Styles

The chart control applies a default set of colors that are defined through the `ItemColorSet` property, as shown in Figure 12-12. This property contains an array of colors, and we can modify these values to change the colors of the items in the chart.

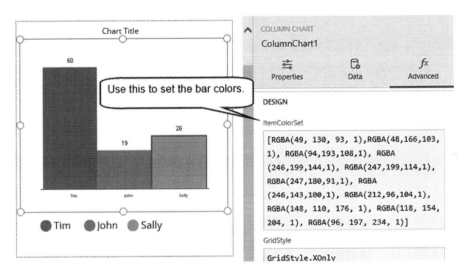

Figure 12-12. *Setting the chart colors*

Other useful properties we can set include the grid style, marker suffixes, the width of the gap between the bars, and the minimum and maximum values in the scale, as shown in Figure 12-13.

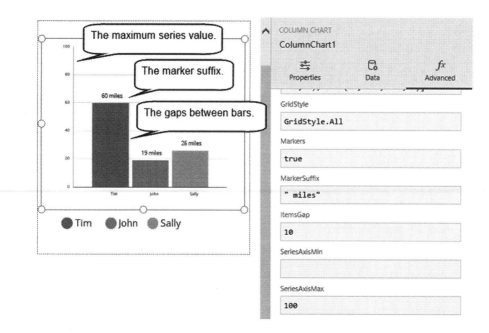

Figure 12-13. *Some of the chart items that we can configure*

Pie Chart

Another type of chart that PowerApps supports is the pie chart. The process of creating a pie chart is mostly identical to the column chart. The pie chart is also a composite control that includes a chart, legend, and title. Like the column chart control, the items property of the chart control defines the data source, and we can also configure items such as colors and legend items in the same way.

Let's look at how to set up a pie chart that displays the same data as before (that is, the total mileage by user). On our chart screen, remove the column chart and insert a pie chart control. Set the items property of the control to the MileageByUser collection, as shown in Figure 12-14.

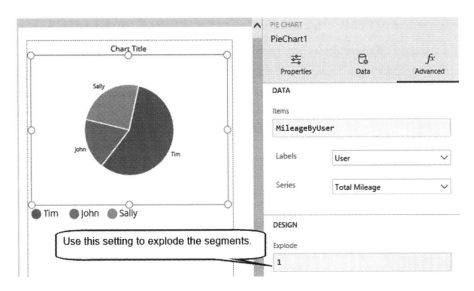

Figure 12-14. *Setting up a pie chart*

We can now run our app and view the pie chart. One useful property we can set is the explode property. This setting explodes the sections of the chart to provide a visual effect that highlights the segments of the chart

Line Charts

The third chart type that we'll look at is the line chart.

Grouping Data by Month

To demonstrate how to create a line chart and to illustrate a common charting requirement, here's how to create a chart that groups data by date. We'll build a line chart that displays the mileage traveled by users by month, and we'll walk through this process step by step.

The line chart control works similarly to the column and pie chart controls. The control requires a data source so the first task is to devise a formula that aggregates our journey data into a structure that shows a sum of mileage by month. The technique that we'll use incorporates the use of the table function. We'll use this function to build a table that contains two columns: month name, and total mileage. This table will contain 12 rows, one for each month of the year. Here's the formula to build this table:

```
Table(
  {Month:"Jan",
   Mileage:Sum(Filter(Journey, Month(StartDate)=1 && Year(StartDate)=2017),
          MileageInMiles)},
  {Month:"Feb",
   Mileage:Sum(Filter(Journey, Month(StartDate)=2 && Year(StartDate)=2017),
          MileageInMiles)},
  {Month:"Mar",
   Mileage:Sum(Filter(Journey, Month(StartDate)=3 && Year(StartDate)=2017),
          MileageInMiles)}
)
```

For brevity, this formula shows only the data for the first three months. However, we can easily adapt the formula to add the remaining rows from April to December. For each additional row, we would need to set the month name and amend the filter function to filter by the relevant month and year values.

The next step is to add a line chart control to a screen and to set the items property to the formula that's shown above. Figure 12-15 illustrates the appearance of this chart control in the designer.

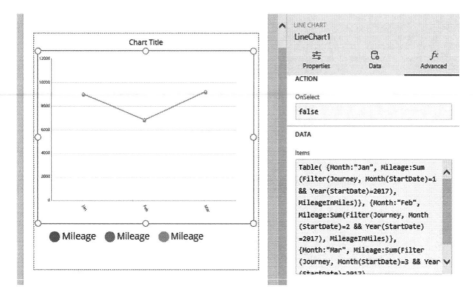

Figure 12-15. *Setting up a line chart*

Showing Chart Data Dynamically

The beauty of setting the items property of a chart control to a formula that uses the table function is that we can reference external controls. We can use this feature to build charts that derive data from user selections. In this example, we could provide a drop-down box of years, and allow the user to filter the chart data by year. To accomplish this, add a drop-down control to your screen and set the items property to an array of year values. Name this control DropdownYear. Now modify the items property of the chart control so that it filters the data by the selected year, as shown below.

```
Table(
    {Month:"Jan",
     Mileage:Sum(Filter(Journey,
                        Month(StartDate)=1 &&
                        Year(StartDate)= Value(DropdownYear.Selected.Value)),
                MileageInMiles)},
    {Month:"Feb",
     Mileage:Sum(Filter(Journey,
                        Month(StartDate)=2 &&
                        Year(StartDate)= Value(DropdownYear.Selected.Value)),
                MileageInMiles)},
```

```
{Month:"Mar",
  Mileage:Sum(Filter(Journey,
                    Month(StartDate)=3 &&
                    Year(StartDate)= Value(DropdownYear.Selected.Value)),
               MileageInMiles)}
)
```

Figure 12-16 shows the appearance of this chart in the designer. We can now run our app and use the drop-down to change the year.

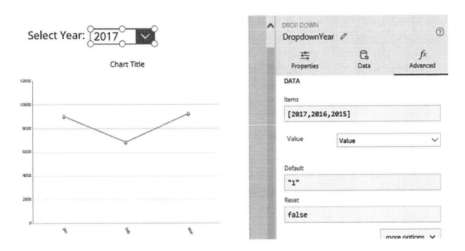

Figure 12-16. *Dynamically changing the data in a chart*

Showing Multiple Series

The chart controls support up to nine series and we can use this feature to display multiple groups of data on a chart. To demonstrate the application of multiple series, here's how to build a line chart that displays the mileage traveled by each user, by month.

This technique requires us to construct a data source that breaks down the mileage by month and user. Figure 12-17 shows the target layout that we're aiming for, based on a larger set of records.

Month	Tim	John	Sally
Jan	3373	2703	2922
Feb	2141	2535	2153
Mar	3124	2658	3431

Figure 12-17. *Example data structure for multiple series*

To build this data structure, we would use the table function as shown beneath.

```
Table(
    {Month:"Jan",
     Tim: Coalesce(
             Sum(Filter(Journey, Month(StartDate)=1 && Year(StartDate)= 2017 &&
                             User="Tim"),
                 MileageInMiles
             ),0),
     John: Coalesce(
             Sum(Filter(Journey, Month(StartDate)=1 && Year(StartDate)= 2017 &&
                             User="John"),
                 MileageInMiles
             ),0),
     Sally: Coalesce(
             Sum(Filter(Journey, Month(StartDate)=1 && Year(StartDate)= 2017 &&
                             User="Sally"),
                 MileageInMiles
             ),0)
    },
    {Month:"Feb",
     Tim: Coalesce(
             Sum(Filter(Journey, Month(StartDate)=2 && Year(StartDate)= 2017 &&
                             User="Tim"),
                 MileageInMiles
             ),0),
     John: Coalesce(
             Sum(Filter(Journey, Month(StartDate)=2 && Year(StartDate)= 2017 &&
                             User="John"),
                 MileageInMiles
             ),0),
     Sally: Coalesce(
             Sum(Filter(Journey, Month(StartDate)=2 && Year(StartDate)= 2017 &&
                             User="Sally"),
                 MileageInMiles
             ),0)
    },
    {Month:"Mar",
     Tim: Coalesce(
             Sum(Filter(Journey, Month(StartDate)=3 && Year(StartDate)= 2017 &&
                             User="Tim"),
                 MileageInMiles
             ),0),
     John: Coalesce(
             Sum(Filter(Journey, Month(StartDate)=3 && Year(StartDate)= 2017 &&
                             User="John"),
                 MileageInMiles
             ),0),
     Sally: Coalesce(
             Sum(Filter(Journey, Month(StartDate)=3 && Year(StartDate)= 2017 &&
                             User="Sally"),
```

```
        MileageInMiles
    ),0)
  }
)
```

The first step is to set the items property of a chart control to this formula. Next, set the 'number of series' property to three, and select the user names from the series drop-downs, as shown in Figure 12-18. At this stage, we can run our app and view the chart.

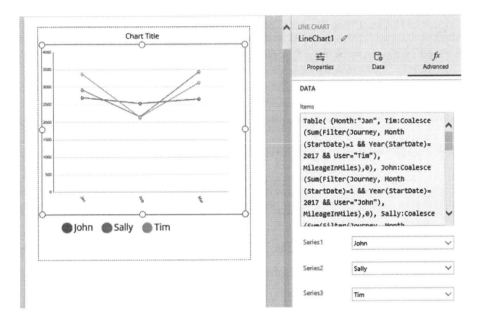

Figure 12-18. *A chart that shows multiple series of data*

Within this formula, one function that we've not come across is the Coalesce function. This useful function accepts any number of arguments, and returns the first non-blank value. We use the Coalesce function here to return 0 rather than a blank value in the case where no records exist when the formula attempts to sum the mileage for a given user during a specific month.

▓ **Caution**   With all the examples in this chapter, remember that unless we use an SQL Server data source and call functions that are delegable, PowerApps will impose a 500-record limit on the data that it returns. If more than 500 rows exist in our source data, any aggregate calculations that we perform may not be accurate.

Summary

PowerApps provides the following three chart controls: bar, line, and pie. In this chapter, we looked at how to use all three of these controls.

The chart controls are straightforward to use. The most difficult part is to aggregate the data in a way that is suitable for the chart control. The typical way to build source data for a chart is to use formulas that call the GroupBy and Sum functions. In this chapter, we saw several examples of how to apply this technique.

The first chart type that we looked at was the column chart. To demonstrate this control, we built a chart to show a summary of miles traveled by user. To transform our source data into a structure that contains the sum of miles traveled by each user, we carried out our actions step by step and used collections to save our progress. The collections section of the designer enables us to view the result of our actions and we can use this to make it easier for us to build complex formula.

When we use a collection as a data source for a chart, it's necessary to build the data in the collection before we open the screen that houses the chart control. To avoid the need to initialize chart data through a button click or user action, we need to avoid the use of collections as the data source for a chart. One technique to accomplish this is to set the data source of a chart to a formula that's based on the table function. When we call the table function, we can refer to controls on a screen, and we can use this technique to build charts that update automatically depending on criteria that the user enters.

In the final part of this chapter, we looked at how to create a line chart. In our example, we looked at how to summarize data by month. We then used the table function to build a formula to transform the data into a structure that the line chart control can use to display multiple series - one line for each user.

CHAPTER 13

■ ■ ■

Securing Apps

The ability to secure apps and data is important, particularly given the ease with which we can build apps that connect to sensitive commercial data. In this chapter, we'll investigate how to keep our apps and data safe. The techniques that we'll cover will include the following:

- How to strengthen the login process. We'll find out how to authenticate users based on one-time SMS text message codes. This provides a higher level of security, compared to using usernames and passwords.

- How to secure data. We'll look at how to grant or deny user access to underlying CDS or SharePoint data sources. We'll also find out how to secure access to individual records. This technique is useful because we can restrict users to viewing only the records that they create. In this section, we'll also look at how to secure access to screens and features.

- How to prevent data leakage. With the help of data loss prevention policies, we'll find out how to stop users from copying data from internal on-premise data sources to external cloud data sources.

Authentication

Let's start by looking at the way that users log into PowerApps. Users use Microsoft Work Accounts to log in into PowerApps. To maintain security, it's important for users to choose strong passwords and to guard their credentials. But is there anything more to further secure the authentication process?

The answer to this question is yes. A great feature that Office 365 offers is multi-factor authentication. With this feature, the system sends an SMS text message to the user during each login attempt. This message includes a code and the login attempt succeeds only when the user enters the correct code. This can protect apps against malicious users who try to guess passwords, or more sophisticated attackers who attempt to carry out brute force dictionary attacks. It can also protect against usernames and passwords that might have been compromised through keystroke loggers or other malware.

We can apply multi-factor authentication to specific users through the Office 365 admin center. To set this up, the first step is to locate the user in the Admin center, as shown in Figure 13-1.

© Tim Leung 2017

T. Leung, *Beginning PowerApps*, https://doi.org/10.1007/978-1-4842-3003-9_13

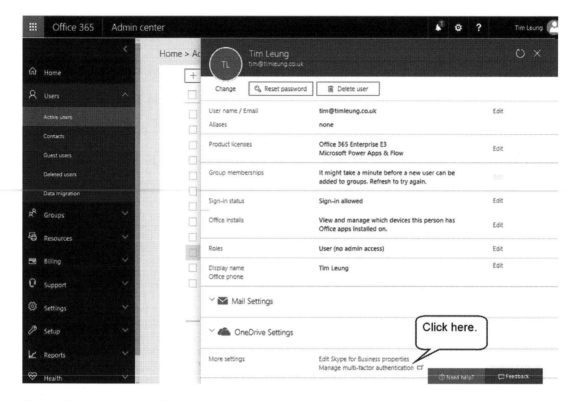

Figure 13-1. *Setting up multi-factor authentication*

The bottom part of this screen shows a link with the title 'manage multi-factor authentication'. This opens a separate page to complete the setup of multi-factor authentication. With this setting enabled, PowerApps will prompt the user to provide a phone number at the next login attempt, as shown in Figure 13-2. From this point onward, the user will be prompted for additional verification on each login.

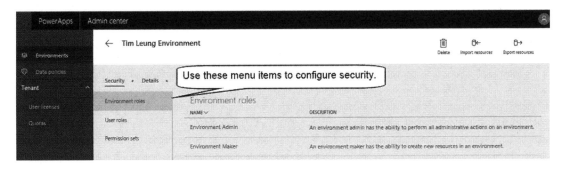

Additional security verification

Secure your account by adding phone verification to your password. View video to know how to secure your account

Step 1: How should we contact you?

| Authentication phone ⌄ |

| Select your country or region ⌄ | |

┌─Method─────────────────────
│ ○   Send me a code by text message
│ ●   Call me
└────────────────────────────

Next

| Your phone numbers will only be used for account security. Standard telephone and SMS charges will apply. |

Figure 13-2. The user will be prompted to provide a phone number

Role-Based Security

In addition to strengthening the authentication process, we can also configure security at the data source level. A common requirement is to apply different sets of permissions to different groups of users. A typical setup is to grant certain users with full edit permissions to data, and to grant other users with read-only access. In this section, we'll look at how to implement user-level permissions in apps with CDS or SharePoint data sources.

Securing the CDS

With CDS data sources, the environment section of the Admin center enables us to configure settings for each individual environment, as shown in Figure 13-3.

Figure 13-3. Security settings that apply to environments

There are three items in the security section - Environment roles, User roles, and Permission sets. Environment roles control the management of the environment and define the users that can create and administer entities in the CDS database. There are two fixed environment roles - Environment Admin and Environment Maker. Users who belong to the Environment Maker role can create and view all apps in an environment, and can carry out tasks in the CDS database. Users who belong to the Environment Admin role have full control over the environment.

The User roles and Permissions sets options control runtime access to the content in the CDS database.

Granting Read and Write Access to Entities

Let's walk through how to grant certain users full access to an entity, while restricting other users to read-only access. The objects that define user-level access to entities are user roles and permission sets.

User roles are containers for groups of users, whereas permission sets allow us to define create, read, update, and delete permissions on entities.

To demonstrate, let's imagine that we've built an app that's based on the journey entity and that three active users exist - Tim, Jenefer, and Jill. The aim of this exercise is to grant Tim and Jenefer full access to the data, and to restrict Jill with read-only access.

The first step is to create two permission sets. Name the first permission set 'Maintain Journey Data' and grant create, read, update, and delete permissions for the journey entity, as shown in Figure 13-4.

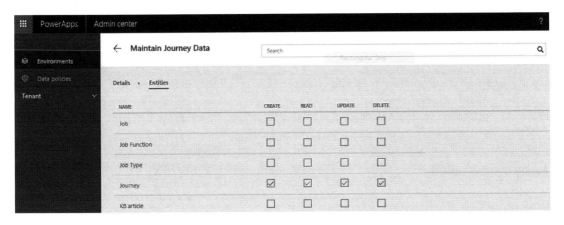

Figure 13-4. *Setting up the 'Maintain Journey Data' permissions set - grant full access to the journey entity*

Now create a second permission set called 'View Journey Data' and grant read access only to the journey entity.

The next step is to create a set of user roles. Let's call these 'Company Managers' and 'Company Viewers'. For the 'Company Managers' role, add the 'Maintain Journey Data' permission set and add the users Tim and Jenefer, as shown in Figure 13-5. For the 'Company Viewer' role, add the 'View Journey Data' permission set and add the user Jill.

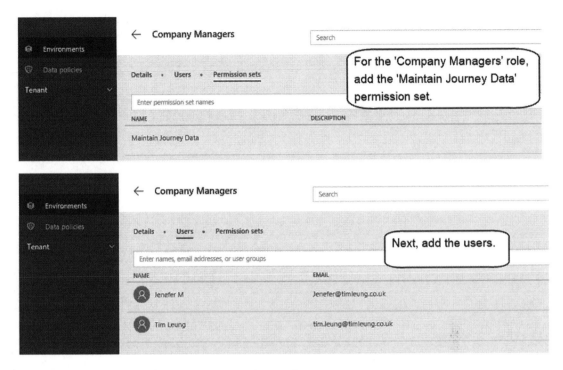

Figure 13-5. *Setting up the 'Company Managers' user role*

The completes the configuration of the data source and later in this chapter, we'll look at how to use formula to verify these permissions.

Securing SharePoint Lists

Let's now look at how to implement role-level access for a list in SharePoint Online. SharePoint security is a large topic, so we'll cover just the basic steps of granting certain users full edit access to a list, while restricting other users to read-only access.

SharePoint provides groups that are defined at a site level. Groups are containers for users. Against each group, we can assign a permission level. The permission level defines the actions that are permitted, and we can use this to grant read, edit, or delete permissions on list items.

To demonstrate, let's set up SharePoint groups for 'Company Managers' and 'Company Viewers,' just like our CDS example. To create a group, use the cog icon to open the 'Site Settings' page. From here, click the 'Site Permissions' link. Click the 'Create Group' button in the ribbon bar (Figure 13-6) to create the new groups.

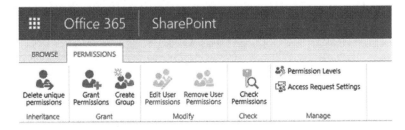

Figure 13-6. *Creating a new SharePoint group*

When we create a new group, we can associate a permission level with the group. In the case of our 'Company Managers' group, we can set the permission level to Edit, as shown in Figure 13-7. This permission level provides members with the ability to add, update, and delete list items. We can set the permission level of our 'Company Viewers' group to Read, to provide read-only access to list items.

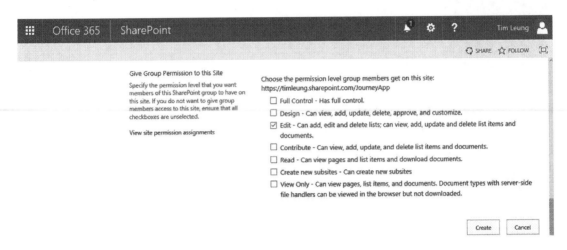

Figure 13-7. Specifying permissions of a group

After creating the 'Company Managers' and 'Company Viewers' groups, we can open the group and add members, as shown in Figure 13-8.

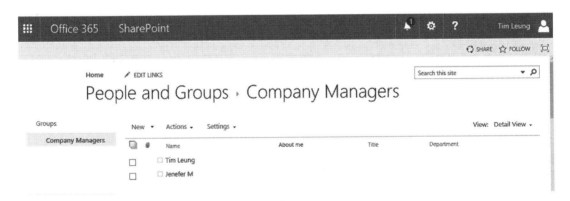

Figure 13-8. Adding users to the 'Company Managers' group

By default, the lists in SharePoint will inherit the site-level permission settings. It's possible to define a custom set of permissions for each list. To do this, open the SharePoint list that you want to protect and use the gear icon to open the list settings page. From this page, click the link that's titled 'permissions for this list'. When this page opens, click the 'stop inheriting permissions' button. We can then use this page that's shown in Figure 13-9 to assign permission levels against each group.

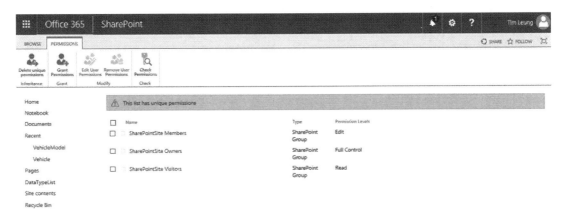

Figure 13-9. *Assigning custom permissions for a SharePoint list*

A very useful feature on this screen is the Check Permissions button. Because a user can belong to multiple groups, it can be difficult to determine the exact permissions that a user has. The Check Permissions button allows us to easily see the effective permissions of a user.

The built-in permission levels that we've used are adequate for most scenarios. For more granular control, we can create custom permission levels. For example, the built-in edit permission level enables members to add, update, and delete list items. If we want to allow members to add and update but not delete list items, we would need to create a custom permission level. The place to create a custom permission level is through the Site Settings ➤ Site permissions menu item at the root level. From here, we can click the permission levels button in the ribbon bar to open the page that enables us to create a custom permission level.

On-Premises SharePoint

For on-premise SharePoint data sources, we can use the same procedure to set up role-level security. Note that PowerApps does not share SharePoint data connections. When a user runs an app with a SharePoint data source, the initial screen prompts the user to enter their SharePoint credentials. Therefore, the connection to SharePoint will take place under the security context of the credentials that the user enters.

Verifying Permissions Within an App

All apps will enforce the permissions at the data source level. When we build an auto-generated app against a data source with user-level permissions, the app disables any features that the user does not have access to. For example, the app disables the icon that opens the record entry screen if the user has insufficient permissions to add records to the data source.

As shown in Figure 13-10, the add record icon includes formula that disables the control in this scenario. This formula relies on a function called DataSourceInfo. This function enables us to verify the permissions of a user. Table 13-1 shows the example usage of this function.

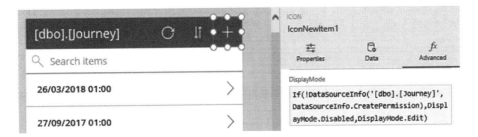

Figure 13-10. *The new record icon refers to the create permission*

Table 13-1. *DataSourceInfo*

Example Call	Description
DataSourceInfo(Journey, DataSourceInfo. ReadPermission)	Returns whether the logged-in user can read journey records
DataSourceInfo(Journey, DataSourceInfo. EditPermission)	Returns whether the logged-in user can edit journey records
DataSourceInfo(Journey, DataSourceInfo. CreatePermission)	Returns whether the logged-in user can create journey records
DataSourceInfo(Journey, DataSourceInfo. DeletePermission)	Returns whether the logged-in user can delete journey records

The DataSourceInfo function expects two arguments - the data source name, and an argument that defines the permission that we want to check. The function returns a true/false value to indicate whether the logged-in user has been granted the specified permission.

Disabling Icons and Buttons

Let's take a closer look at the technique to disable buttons and controls. As Figure 13-10 shows, we can use the DisplayMode property to disable a control. There are actually two places in the designer where we set this property. In addition to the DisplayMode text box in the advanced section of the properties pane, we can also set the display mode through a drop-down in the main properties section, as shown in Figure 13-11.

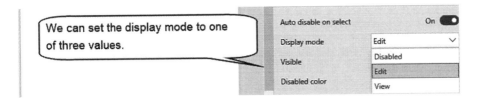

Figure 13-11. *The DisplayMode property of a control*

As you can see, this drop-down can take one of three values: Disabled, Edit, or View. You might be curious as to what the difference is between these three settings. What exactly is the difference between Edit and View? The View setting disables a control and prevents it from running the formula that is attached to the OnSelect property. However, the control will not look disabled to the user - it will appear like a working control. The Edit setting configures a control to be fully functional. The Disabled setting configures a control to look disabled, and it will prevent the control from running the formula that is attached to the OnSelect property.

In cases where we want to set the display mode of a control conditionally, we would add formula to display mode text box, rather than use the drop-down.

Configuring Record-Level Access

PowerApps provides no built-in way to apply security at a record level. However, we can devise our own methods to authorize access at a record level. In this section, we'll look at how to restrict access to individual records in CDS or SharePoint Online data sources. To demonstrate a typical requirement, here's how to build an app where users can create new records and modify their own records, but not edit records that were created by other users.

Setting Up the Data Source

We can easily implement this requirement in apps that are based on CDS and SharePoint Online data sources because these data sources record the created by and last modified user details automatically, as shown in Figure 13-12. In this screenshot, notice how PowerApps use a globally unique identifier (GUID) to identify the created by and last modified users.

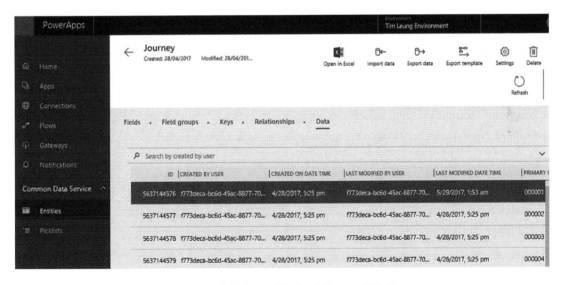

Figure 13-12. *The CDS stores the GUID of the 'created by' and 'last modified' users*

Getting the Logged On User

To apply any type of record-level security, we need to know who the currently logged-on user is. Through the User function, we can obtain the email address and full name of the current user, as shown in Figure 13-13. Note that the user function can return the profile image for the user but at the time of writing, this feature does not work correctly. You can find out more details here:

https://powerusers.microsoft.com/t5/PowerApps-Forum/user-image/td-p/4460

Figure 13-13. *The user function returns the currently logged-on user.*

We can use the email address to uniquely identify the logged-on user. But to retrieve the GUID of a user, we need to carry out an additional step. The step is to add a data source with the Office 365 Users connector, which is a connector that enables us to retrieve and to update Office 365 profiles, as shown in Figure 13-14.

Figure 13-14. *Adding a connection to the Office 365 Users data source*

After we add this data source, we can convert an email address to the GUID value using the formula below:

Office365Users.UserProfile("tim@timleung.co.uk").Id

To convert a user id GUID to an email address, the formula we would use is this:

Office365Users.UserProfile("f773deca-bc6d-45ac-8877-7060cf191398").Mail

Filtering Records by the Logged On User

Now that we have a method to retrieve the GUID of the logged-on user, we can modify the gallery controls in our apps to show only the data that relates to the logged-in user. To filter the gallery control in the browse screen in an auto-generated app that's based on a CDS data source, we would filter the data source by the 'created by user'. It's a good idea to retrieve current user id into a variable to improve performance and to do this, here's the formula we would add to the OnVisible property of a screen.

```
UpdateContext({CurrentUserID:Office365Users.UserProfile(User().Email).Id})
```

We could then apply the filter function to the Items property of our gallery control with the formula shown beneath:

```
Filter(Journey, CreatedBy= CurrentUserID)
```

To clarify why it's more efficient to use a variable when filtering data, Figure 13-15 shows the warning that appears when we apply the formula to look up the current user's id inline. With this syntax, PowerApps cannot delegate the filter expression to the CDS and will filter the data locally.

Figure 13-15. *Filtering a gallery control by the logged-on user*

In situations where we want to refer to the current user id frequently, an alternative is write the formula that looks up the current user id in the StartUp property of the first screen and to store the value in a collection. This makes the value more readily available and saves us from calling the Office 365 data source multiple times. However, one slight awkwardness is that it's not possible to run the StartUp formula in PowerApps studio, and this behavior can make it more difficult to design our apps.

To prevent users from updating records that were created by other users, we can write formula to disable the save icon on the edit screen. To do this, set the value of the CurrentUserID variable in the OnVisible property of the screen. Next, set the display mode property of the icon to the following formula:

```
If(
    If(EditForm1.Mode = FormMode.Edit,
        Not(BrowseGallery1.Selected.CreatedByUser = CurrentUserID),
        false
    ),
    DisplayMode.Disabled,
    DisplayMode.Edit
)
```

This formula ensures that the icon will always be enabled when a user creates a new record, and Figure 13-16 illustrates the view of this screen in the designer.

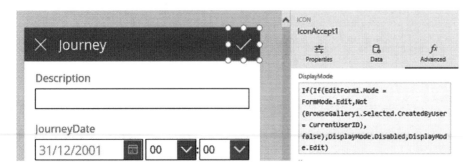

Figure 13-16. *Disabling the save button*

For more granular control, we can create a table to store the users that are permitted to view, update, or delete each individual record in a table. We would also apply a similar technique for data sources other than the CDS or SharePoint online, because these data sources do not automatically store the record owner.

Whenever we customize record-level access, we should consider whether the user can circumvent the rules in our app by accessing the data source outside of PowerApps. If the user can access the data outside of PowerApps, this can undermine the efforts that we make in PowerApps to secure our data.

Creating Data Loss Prevention Policies

With the help of DLP (Data Loss Prevention) policies, we can prohibit users from copying sensitive company data to unintended destinations. To give an example, some companies might want to prevent users from copying on-premise SQL Server data to a spreadsheet that's hosted in OneDrive. DLP policies protect data by grouping data sources into two groups: business data and non-business data. Policies prevent app builders from mixing data sources from different groups in the same app.

To demonstrate, here's how to build a DLP policy to isolate SQL Server and SharePoint data sources. To create a DLP Policy, select the Data Policies menu item from the Admin Center and click the New policy button at the top of the screen. This opens the screen that's shown in Figure 13-17.

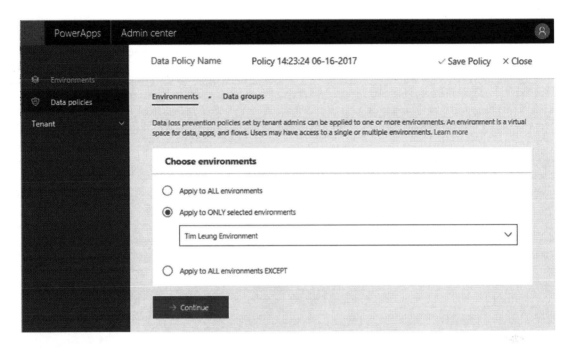

Figure 13-17.   Creating a data loss prevention policy

Note that we can set the name of a policy through the section at the top of the screen. This section might look like a read-only label, but the text is editable.

In the 'Data groups' section, use the add button to add the SQL Server and SharePoint connectors to the 'Business data only' group as shown in Figure 13-18.

Figure 13-18.   Adding connectors to the business data only group

Testing a DLP Policy

Now that we've implemented a DLP policy, let's see what happens when we attempt to build an app that includes SQL Server and OneDrive data sources.

To test our policy, create an auto-generated app based on an SQL Server data source. Now try to add a data source to an Excel spreadsheet from OneDrive. When we attempt to add this connection, PowerApps shows a warning and prevents us from adding the data source, as shown in Figure 13-19. This confirms that our DLP policy has worked.

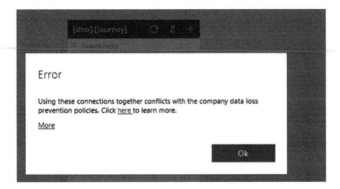

Figure 13-19. *Data loss prevention policy warning*

An interesting question is, can PowerApps apply policies retrospectively? For instance, if we have an existing app that contains both SQL Server and OneDrive data sources, would any new policy that we create apply to the existing app? The actual behavior is interesting. If we were to apply a policy retrospectively, the existing app will still run. However, PowerApps Studio will hang when we attempt to open the app and this behavior will prevent us from editing existing apps.

Summary

In this chapter, we looked at techniques to secure our apps and data. Users log on to PowerApps using a Microsoft Account, and therefore, the security of an app relies on these credentials. To further secure accounts, administrators can configure multi-factor authentication. With this setting enabled, users will only be able to log on after entering an SMS code.

With CDS and SharePoint data sources, we can apply role-based security to restrict the actions that specific users can carry out. For instance, we can grant certain groups of users full access, while restricting other groups of users to read-only access. With CDS databases, we use permission sets to grant create, edit, read, and delete permissions on entities. We then associate permission sets with user roles. User roles are containers for users. With SharePoint, we can also group users and to apply custom permissions.

For data sources that don't natively support role-based security, we can implement a custom approach to permissions. Such an approach relies on us knowing who the logged-in user is and we can determine this by calling the User function. This function returns the email address and we can use this to uniquely identify the logged-on user.

There is no built-in method to apply record-level permissions so once again, we would need to build our own scheme. CDS and SharePoint make this task slightly easier because these data sources automatically store the user id of the user that created the record, and the user id of the user that last modified the record. To interpret these user ids, we can use the Office 365 Users connector to convert user ids to email addresses, and email address to user ids.

Finally, we can protect data with the use of data loss prevention policies. DLP policies group data sources into business and non-business groups. A DLP policy prevents users from creating a single app that includes data sources from both the business and non-business groups.

PART III

Maintaining Your Application

CHAPTER 14

■ ■ ■

Importing and Exporting Data

Getting data in and out of PowerApps is useful because it enables apps to integrate with wider business processes.

Exporting data is particularly useful for reporting and backup purposes. Importing data can be very useful for data migration purposes, or for setting up apps for first-time use.

The are several ways to import and export data from PowerApps. These techniques may appear straightforward, but beyond the simple task of working with a single table of data, there are some difficult challenges that we can face. To import sets of related data, how do we maintain the linkages between parent and child records? If we import data to a system that contains existing records, how do we build a synchronization process to add nonexistent records and to update the existing records? This chapter will answer these questions. Other topics of specific interest will include the following:

- How to provide import and export capabilities to end users. We can add import and export controls to screens; however, it's not obvious how these controls work. In this chapter, we'll find out exactly how to use these controls.

- How to work with CDS data sources. We'll find out how to use an administrative feature in the portal to import and export data. We'll also examine tips that can help us resolve import failures.

- How to work with Excel. With the help of an Excel add-in, we can view, copy, and edit CDS data directly from a spreadsheet. We'll find out exactly how this works.

Using the Import and Export Controls

To enable users to import and export data from within an app, PowerApps provides two controls - an import control and an export control. We can add these controls through the Controls menu, as shown in Figure 14-1.

© Tim Leung 2017

T. Leung, *Beginning PowerApps*, https://doi.org/10.1007/978-1-4842-3003-9_14

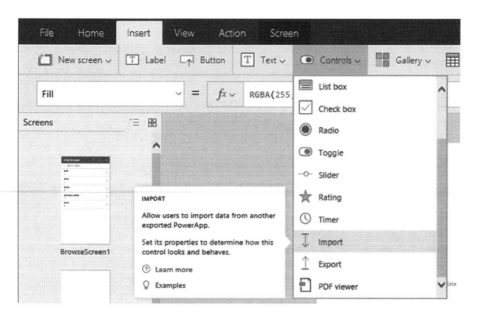

Figure 14-1. *Adding the Import and Export controls to a screen*

These controls provide a simple way for end users to back up, and restore data and to demonstrate this feature, we'll build a screen that users can use to import and export records from our sample data. For simplicity, we'll base our examples on an Excel data source.

As a brief overview, the export control displays a button that the user can click. The user can click this button to download and save an export file to the local file system. The export control produces a compressed zip file that contains data in XML format. We can specify the data that we want the control to export. This could include all records from a data source, or a filtered subset of data.

The import control displays a button. When a user clicks the button, the control prompts the user to select an export file. From within an app, we can write custom formula to work with the data that the user uploads. We can patch this input data to a data source, or we can carry out other custom tasks with this data.

Exporting Data

To demonstrate the import and export controls, we'll build an app to export and import data from the table of vehicle makes. The first step is to create an app and to add a connection to the data source. Next, create a new screen and insert an export control. Use the data property to specify the data to export, as shown in Figure 14-2. In this example, the name of the data source is `VehicleMake`.

Figure 14-2. *Specifying the data*

The Data property of this control defines the data to export. We can set the value of this to a table or we can call functions like Filter, Search, or Lookup to limit the export data.

At this point, let's run our app and examine what happens. When we click the export button, PowerApps opens a save dialog and prompts us to save the output to a local file location. We can use this file later with the import control.

The export file that PowerApps produces is a compressed zip file that contains three separate files, as shown in Figure 14-3. The main file that contains the data is called data.xml. It's possible to modify the contents of this file in a text editor. If we were to modify the contents manually, we would need to recompress the file with the header and schema files before importing it into PowerApps.

Name	Date modified	Type	Size
data	19/06/2017 23:10	XML Document	2 KB
header	19/06/2017 23:10	JSON File	1 KB
schema	19/06/2017 23:10	JSON File	5 KB

Figure 14-3. *The extracted contents of the export file*

■ **Note** Note that the Export button does not work when PowerApps runs in a browser.

Importing Data

Let's now examine the import control. This control allows us to import the data that we exported with the export control, and there are two broad ways for us to handle the input data. The first is to add the input data as new rows in the target data source. The second is to add only the records that don't exist in the destination data source and to update the records that do exist. For both approaches, the initial step is to add an import control to our screen. By default, the name of the control that we add to a screen is Import1.

Importing New Records

To configure the import control to add new records to the data source, add the following formula to the OnSelect property.

```
ClearCollect(ImportedData, Import1.Data);
Collect(VehicleMake, ShowColumns(ImportedData, "MakeID", "Name")
```

Figure 14-4 shows this control in the designer.

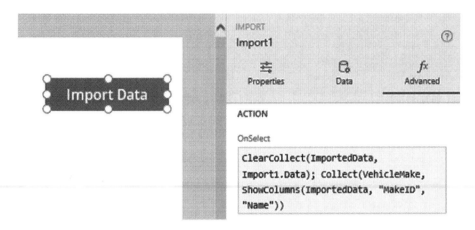

Figure 14-4. The import control

The initial line in this formula calls the ClearCollect function to store the imported data in a collection called ImportedData. The data property of the import control (Import1.Data) returns the contents of the input file. The second line calls the Collect function to insert the records from the ImportedData collection into the VehicleMake data source.

In cases where the destination data source is an Excel spreadsheet, it's important to call the ShowColumns function to define strictly the fields to import. The reason for this is because our export file contains the entire VehicleMake table. Because of this, the export file also includes data from a system field called ' __PowerAppsId__ '. If we were to call the collect function directly against this data, the save operation would fail silently when it attempts to insert values for the ' __PowerAppsId__ ' field. Therefore, we must exclude the ' __PowerAppsId__ ' field by calling either the ShowColumns or DropColumns functions.

If the destination data source were a database table with server-generated fields such as auto-incrementing identity values, we would also apply the same technique to exclude these fields during an import.

At this point, we can run our app and import our export file. If all goes well, the operation will append the input data into the target data source.

■ **Caution**   When calling the Collect function, be very careful to spell the data source correctly. If you spell the data source incorrectly, the function collects the data to a new local collection that matches the incorrect spelling. At this point, it's easy to spend ages trying to work out why the function didn't add the records to the desired data source.

Inserting and Updating Data

Let's now configure the import control to add only the records that don't exist in the destination data source and to update the records that do exist. We can accomplish by calling the patch function to the update the existing records, followed by the collect function to add the nonexistent records. This example works on the basis that the MakeID field uniquely identifies each record. Here's the formula that we would add to the OnSelect property of the import control. This formula contains comments to aid clarity. To avoid errors, it's important to remove these comments from your actual app.

```
'Setup the collections of data
ClearCollect(ImportedData, VehicleMake);
ClearCollect(RecordsToUpdate,
            ShowColumns(Filter(ImportedData,
                            (MakeID in ShowColumns(VehicleMake, "MakeID")))
                    , "MakeID", "Name"
            )
);

ClearCollect(RecordsToAdd,
            ShowColumns(Filter(ImportedData,
                            Not(MakeID in ShowColumns(VehicleMake, "MakeID")))
                    , "MakeID", "Name"
            )
);

'Update the existing records
ForAll(RecordsToUpdate,
            Patch(VehicleMake,
                LookUp(VehicleMake, RecordsToUpdate[@MakeID]=MakeID),
                {Name:RecordsToUpdate[@Name]}
            )
);

'Insert the new records
Collect(VehicleMake, RecordsToAdd)
```

The first part of this formula creates collections that contain the records to update and the records to add. These formulas utilize the in function to return the matching and non-matching records from vehicle make and import tables, based on the MakeID. The collection that contains the records to update is called RecordsToUpdate, and the collection that contains the records to add is called RecordsToAdd.

To update the records, the formula calls the ForAll function to loop through the collection of records to update. For each record in this collection, the formula calls the Patch function to update the data source. The final part of this formula calls the Collect function to add the nonexistent records.

To clarify this technique, the reason why we initially add the records to add and update to local collections is for reliably. If we call the patch or update functions on the direct result of an inline filter operation, the save operation can fail due to the complexity of the expression.

The formula to update the records calls the ForAll function. This function expects two arguments: the data source to loop over and the action to apply to each row.

The patch function expects three arguments - the data source to update, the source record, and the destination record. In this example, we call the Lookup function to locate the source record to update. Notice the use of the disambiguation syntax to distinguish between the MakeID fields in the VehicleMake and RecordsToUpdate data sources.

One final point to mention is that the patch function can update multiple records, and it's possible to call this function in the format that's shown beneath:

```
Patch(DataSource, SourceRecords, RecordsToUpdate)
```

We can use this method to avoid calling the ForAll function and calling the Patch function for each record. To update the multiple records with the patch function, the data source must have a primary key so that the function can identify the records to update. Therefore, this technique does not work on Excel data sources where it's not possible to define primary key fields, and this is the reason why we use the ForAll function in this example.

Understanding Import Errors

The process of importing data can be highly susceptible to error. Let's look at this in more detail.

When a user clicks the import button, the control checks that the file is valid. If the file does not match the format that PowerApps expects (that is, a compressed file with XML content), PowerApps will display the error that's shown in Figure 14-5.

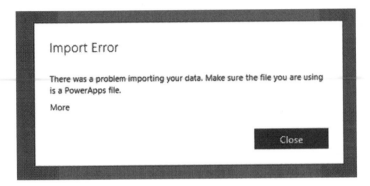

Figure 14-5. *Error when a user attempts to import an invalid file*

Beyond this, the import control does not carry out any additional validation. In our example, it's possible for a user to upload a file of journey records when our import feature expects vehicle make records. Therefore, one reason why we initially import the data into a collection is to provide us with an opportunity to cleanse or to transform the data before we save it to the target data source. We can call the Validate function to verify the data in the collection before we attempt to save it to the data source.

When we develop screens to import data, a good tip is to call the Errors function to display any errors that might have occurred during the save operation. The formula below returns the first error in the data source.

```
First(Errors('[dbo].[VehicleMake]')).Message
```

Figure 14-6 demonstrates the type of information the we can return when we attempt to import data into an SQL Server data source. Without the help of this technique, it can be very difficult to determine the cause of an import failure.

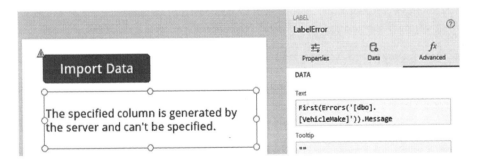

Figure 14-6. *Viewing the errors*

Importing and Exporting Related Data

We'll now look at how to export and import multiple sets of data. The way to achieve this is to add the sets of data to a parent collection and to export this single collection. This process can be particularly useful in data migration scenarios.

To demonstrate this technique, here's how to export the vehicle make and vehicle model tables from an Excel data source and to import the data into a CDS database. Figure 14-7 shows the example Excel data that we'll export.

MakeID	Name
1	Audi
2	Ford
3	Lexus
4	Mercedes-Benz
5	BMW

ModelID	MakeID	Name	Year
1	1	A4	2008-2015
2	1	A5	2007-2015
3	2	Fiesta	2002-2008
4	2	Grand C-Max	2010-2017
5	2	Modeo	2014-2017
6	3	GS	2012-2017
7	3	IS	2013-2017
8	4	SLK	2004-2010
9	4	C Class	2007-2014
10	4	E Class	2009-2016
11	5	1 Series	2004 – 2011
12	5	3 Series	2011-2017
13	5	3 Series	2003-2010

Figure 14-7. *Design of the Excel tables*

To export our data, the key step is to build a collection that includes both tables. Here's the formula that we can attach to the OnVisible property of the screen that contains the export control.

```
ClearCollect(MakeModelCollection, {Makes:VehicleMake, Models:VehicleModel})
```

It may seem more obvious to add this formula to the OnSelect action of the export control. However, this will not work due to timing. The export control exports the data before it runs the formula in the OnSelect action.

The formula above creates a collection that contains a single record that contains the vehicle make and vehicle model tables, as illustrated in Figure 14-8.

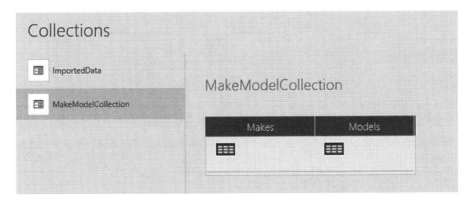

Figure 14-8. *Exporting Collections of data*

The next step is to add an export control and to set the data property to MakeModelCollection.

Importing the Data

Figure 14-9 shows the design of the destination tables in the CDS. To adhere to the standard naming convention that the CDS designer applies, the primary key field of both the vehicle make and vehicle model entities is PrimaryID. The PrimaryID field is an auto number field, and a feature of this example is to show how to migrate the old MakeID and ModelID identifiers to new PrimaryID values that the CDS generates.

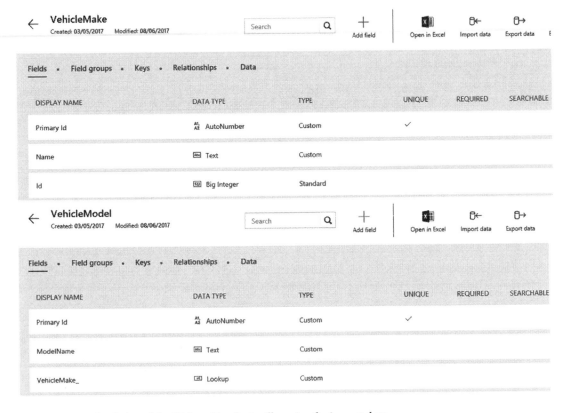

Figure 14-9. *The design of the CDS entities that will receive the import data*

In this example, the field name of the CDS vehicle model entity that stores the model name is called ModelName, in contrast to the field name in the Excel data source that was called Name. The reason for this difference is to demonstrate how to map data when destination field names differ from the source field names.

To build the import feature, the first step is to add the CDS vehicle make and vehicle model entities to a new app. Next, add a new screen and insert an import control. Next, set the OnSelect action to the formula that's shown beneath. Note that like before, you should remove the comments that are shown in this formula.

```
'Import the data
ClearCollect(ImportedData, Import1.Data);
ClearCollect(VehicleMakesImport, First(ImportedData).Makes);
ClearCollect(VehicleModelsImport, First(ImportedData).Models);

'Add the vehicle make records
Clear(VehicleMakesAdded);
ForAll(VehicleMakesImport,
        Collect(VehicleMakesAdded,
                {MakeIDOriginal:VehicleMakesImport[@MakeID],
                MakeRecordCDS:Patch(VehicleMake,
                                    Defaults(VehicleMake),
                                      {Name:VehicleMakesImport[@Name]}
                                )
                }
        )
);

'Prepare the vehicle model records to add
ClearCollect(VehicleModelsToAdd,
            AddColumns(VehicleModelsImport,
                        "VehicleMake_",
                        LookUp(VehicleMakesAdded,
                        VehicleModelsImport[@MakeID]=VehicleMakesAdded[@MakeIDOriginal]).
                        MakeRecordCDS
                        )
);

Collect(VehicleModel,
        ShowColumns(RenameColumns(VehicleModelsToAdd, "Name", "ModelName"),
                "ModelName","Year", "VehicleMake_"
        )
)
```

Here's an explanation of this formula. The first part of the formula stores the import data into working sets of collections. It stores the vehicle makes and models into collections called VehicleMakesImport and VehicleModelsImport respectively.

Next, the formula loops through the input table of vehicle makes. For each input record, the formula patches a new record into the CDS vehicle makes entity. It stores the original MakeID value and the new CDS record in a collection called VehicleMakesAdded. The formula utilizes the return value from the patch function to retrieve the new CDS record. The reason it's important to retrieve this is because it provides us with the new PrimaryId value that corresponds to the MakeID of the original data. We need this later when we add the related vehicle model records.

Note that PowerApps restricts the functions that we can call from inside the ForAll function. For example, we can't set variable values with UpdateContext or collect data with ClearCollect. This is one reason why this part of the formula relies on the Collect function. To improve performance, PowerApps can carry out the actions within the ForAll function in parallel. As a result, PowerApps might not add the records to the CDS in a sequential sequence that matches the import data.

Figure 14-10 shows the result of this part of the formula in the designer.

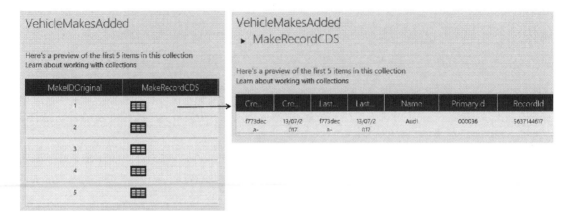

Figure 14-10. *The collection of newly added records and the original MakeID values*

The next part of the formula builds a collection that contains the vehicle models that we want to add to the CDS. This collection is called VehicleModelsToAdd and contains the model name and year values from the input data, and the matching CDS vehicle make record. The formula calls the Lookup function on the VehicleMakesAdded collection to retrieve this record. Figure 14-11 shows how this collection appears in the CDS.

VehicleModelsToAdd

Here's a preview of the first 5 items in this collection
Learn about working with collections

MakeID	ModelID	Name	VehicleMake_	Year
1	1	A4		2008-2015
1	2	A5		2007-2015
2	3	Fiesta		2002-2008
2	4	Grand C-Max		2010-2017
2	5	Modeo		2014-2017

Figure 14-11. *The collection of vehicle make records to append*

The final part of the formula calls the Collect function to add the vehicle model records to the CDS. Notice the use of the RenameColumns function to enable the formula to add the source field "Name" to the destination field "ModelName". To specify the vehicle make lookup value, we specify the field name "VehicleMake_".

Importing and Exporting CDS Data

Another way to the import and export data from the CDS is to use an administrative feature in the entity designer. This feature enables us to import and export data in Excel format. We'll now explore this feature in greater detail.

Importing Data

There are two relevant buttons that relate to the import of data - the Export template and Import data buttons. The Export template button generates an empty spreadsheet that we can complete and import into the CDS. The template generation screen provides the option to choose the fields that appear in the spreadsheet and it provides the option to generate a spreadsheet that contains only the required fields for the entity.

Let's walk through the steps to import vehicle model data from an Excel spreadsheet. First, click the Export template button to generate a template spreadsheet, as shown in Figure 14-12.

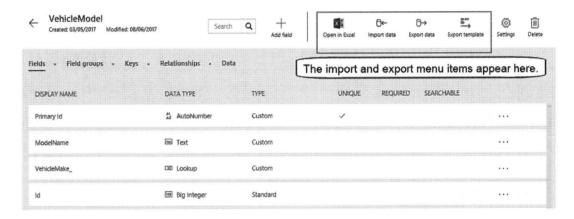

Figure 14-12. *Importing data*

Next, complete the template spreadsheet and save the file to your local machine. Figure 14-13 illustrates an example of this spreadsheet. This screenshot highlights the method to import lookup values. To set the vehicle make, we would supply the primary ID value of the associated vehicle make record. So in this example, we would enter the "VehicleMake_PrimaryID" value.

	A	B	C	D
1	PRIMARYID	MODELNAME	VEHICLEMAKE__PRIMARYID	YEAR
2		Mustang	000037	2005-2014
3		Taurus	000037	2010-2017

Figure 14-13. *Complete the Excel spreadsheet with data*

The next step is to return to the entity designer and to click the Import data button. This opens a screen to upload our Excel spreadsheet and to select the worksheet that contains our data. From this screen, we can open the field mapping settings, as shown in Figure 14-14. If our source spreadsheet did not originate from the system-generated template, we can use this screen to map the fields from the source Excel spreadsheet to destination entity fields.

Field mappings for VehicleModel

IMPORT FILE (SOURCE)	VEHICLEMODEL (TARGET ENTITY)
PRIMARYID	PRIMARYID
MODELNAME	MODELNAME
VEHICLEMAKE_PRIMARYID	VEHICLEMAKE_PRIMARYID
YEAR	YEAR

Figure 14-14. Configuring the field mappings

Once we complete these settings, we can click the import button to finalize the import process.

Resolving Error Conditions

In practice, the import process can fail, especially when we attempt to import large quantities of data. There are many reasons why failures can occur and one main reason is invalid data. For example, the data type of a source value might not match the data type of the destination field. Also, failures can occur when a data value exceeds the maximum length of the destination field, or when a data value causes a duplicate in a destination field that is designed to store unique values. When the import process fails, the screen displays an error message like the one that's shown in Figure 14-15.

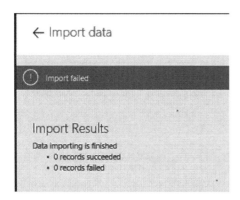

← Import data

ⓘ Import failed

Import Results

Data importing is finished
- 0 records succeeded
- 0 records failed

Figure 14-15. Import failure message

Unfortunately, the message often provides little to diagnose import errors. Sometimes, the process can generate an error report that appears in the notifications section. Sadly, the error report can often be blank.

In some cases, the import process can fail if the data range of the source spreadsheet contains empty rows. Therefore, it can help to copy the rows into a new spreadsheet and to import the new spreadsheet. Alternatively, it can also help to save the spreadsheet in CSV format and to import the CSV file instead. One final thing that can help is to split the contents of a large spreadsheet into multiple smaller spreadsheets and to import each spreadsheet individually. The benefit of this technique is that it can help us more easily identify the exact rows that cause the failure.

Exporting Data

The entity designer provides a button to export data to CSV or Excel formats. There are two ways to access this feature. We can export the data for a single entity by opening the entity in the designer and clicking the 'export data' button. Alternatively, we can click the 'export data' button from the main entities list. This opens the screen that's shown in Figure 14-16. We can use this screen to export multiple entities in one go. When we select this option, the export feature generates a ZIP file that contains separate files for each entity.

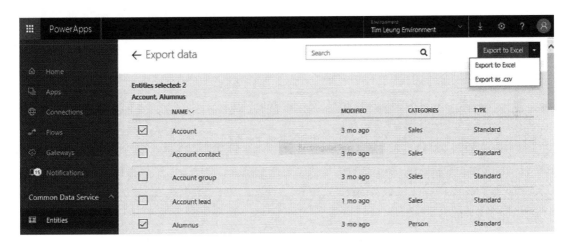

Figure 14-16. *Exporting data to Excel*

Using the Excel Add-In

A useful tool that that can help us work with CDS data is the PowerApps Office Add-in. We can use this to view, edit, and delete rows in entities. A big benefit of the add-in is that it allows us to take advantage of the copy and paste features in Excel, and we can use this to quickly add and manipulate data. This add-in works with Excel 2016 and Excel Online only. To use the add-in with the desktop version of Excel 2016, a prerequisite is to install the add-in. We can obtain this through the Office Store via the link beneath:

`https://store.office.com/en-001/app.aspx?assetid=WA104380330`

To demonstrate how to use the add-in, we'll walk through the steps to open our vehicle make entity in Excel Online. First, open the entity designer and click the 'open in Excel' button. This button initiates the download of an Excel file. Save this file locally and upload it to OneDrive for Business. The reason why we choose OneDrive for Business is because this service uses Microsoft Work Accounts for authentication. The PowerApps add-in authenticates to the CDS with a Microsoft Work Account and by running Excel Online under the same security context as the add-in, we can avoid potential problems where the add-in fails to connect to the CDS.

After uploading our spreadsheet to OneDrive for Business, we can open our spreadsheet directly from our browser. The add-in appears in the right-hand side of the screen, as shown in Figure 14-17. We can click the new icon to add a new row to our entity. If we make any changes to existing rows, we can click the publish icon to save our changes.

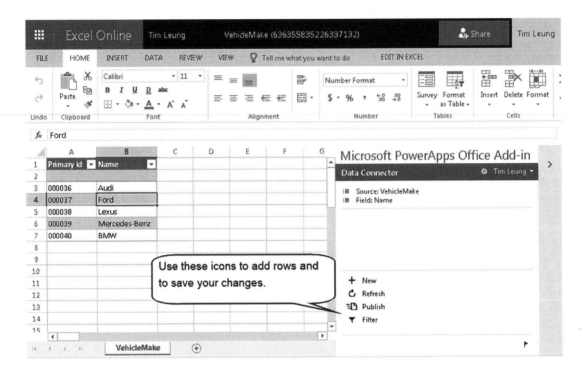

Figure 14-17. *Use the Office Add-In*

Importing Static Data

In cases where we want to access static read-only data, we can import Excel data directly into an app. To import an Excel file, the first step is to define the data as a table and to give it a meaningful name, just like we would for any other Excel data source.

The next step is to click the 'add static data to your app' item from the data sources list, as shown in Figure 14-18. This opens a file dialog that we can use to select our Excel file. Once the import process completes, we can access the data just like any other Excel data source. The only difference of course is that we cannot update or add rows to this data.

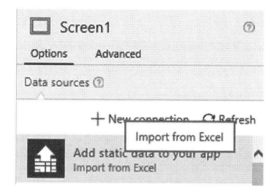

Figure 14-18. *Select the Add static data to your app option*

Summary

There are several ways to import and export data from PowerApps. The main set of controls that carry out this task are the import and export controls. Unlike some other import and export methods, one benefit of using these controls is that we can provide import and export capabilities to the end users of our apps.

To export data with the control, we specify the data that we want to export. This could be any type of data including a collection, a table, or a filtered set of data. At runtime, a user would click the export control to download an export file. The file contains a compressed copy of the data in XML format.

We can use the import control to import data that users have exported with the export control. To utilize this control, we would add it to screen and attach formula to the OnSelect property to define the actions to carry out. Typically, we would add formula to add the data to a collection. We can then cleanse, validate, and transform the data prior to saving it to a data source. We would call functions like Patch and Update to save the data.

To export and import sets of related data, we would export a collection that contains a nested set of tables. We would then use the import control to import these records and to patch the parent records, followed by the child records.

With CDS databases, we can use the import and export options in the entity designer to export data. The import and export features can work with data in Excel and CSV formats.

A useful tool is the PowerApps Office add-in. This enables us to add, edit, and delete CDS records from inside Excel 2016 or Excel Online. The entity designer provides a button to download an Excel file that we can use with the add-in.

Finally, it's possible to import static read-only data for use in our apps. We can find the option to do this through the 'data sources' menu in the designer.

CHAPTER 15

Using Flow

By integrating our apps with Microsoft Flow, we can build more rounded and complete solutions. Microsoft Flow fills the gaps that PowerApps leaves behind and enables us to perform tasks beyond the limits of PowerApps.

With Microsoft Flow, we can access records from all the same data sources that we can access in PowerApps. To filter records, we use operators that are based on a protocol called OData. And to carry out other programming tasks such as program control, string manipulation, and date formatting, we can use a language called workflow definition language. Sometimes, it's necessary to mix OData operators and workflow definition language. An example is where we want to filter records by a programmatic expression. The challenge here is that we need to escape expressions in a way that might not be obvious. Within this chapter, we'll find out how to address these tricky syntactical issues.

At the start of this chapter, we'll cover basic concepts such as what we can do with flows and how to call flows from apps. Next, we'll walk through practical examples of how to use flow, which will include the following:

- How to carry out file operations. We'll find out how to use the on-premises gateway to copy files from OneDrive (or any other cloud storage provider), to a location on our internal network.

- How to send email notifications. A typical use of flow is to send notifications and we'll find out how to send emails. We'll populate the email body with data from a database. We'll also find out how to conduct row-by-row processing, and how to call SQL Server stored procedures. Stored procedures can help improve performance and to overcome some of limitations that delegation imposes.

- How to develop approval processes. We'll learn how to build workflows that require approval from other users. Such flows can react differently depending on the approval outcome. We'll find out how to configure a flow that requires approval from multiple users, or approval from a single user out of a list of possible approvers.

What Is Flow

To start this chapter, let's examine the following question - what is Flow and what can we do with it? Microsoft Flow is a service that carries out processes and workflows independently of PowerApps. Just like PowerApps, Microsoft Flow is designed for non-developers and provides the ability to build workflows without any coding skills. With Flow, we can design workflows through a simple to use, graphical web-based designer. Because the designer is web based, there isn't a need to install any custom software.

A key characteristic of 'workflow' is the ability to respond to events. An example of this is for Flow to detect when a user creates a new record, and to respond by sending an email to a manager. In more complex scenarios, Flow also offers the ability to add conditional and looping constructs into your workflow.

To feed our Flows with data, we can connect to a wide range of data sources. Most of these are data sources that we've seen in PowerApps already, such as SharePoint, OneDrive, Dropbox, and SQL Server. It's also possible to connect to CDS databases and to use the on-premises gateway to access internal SharePoint and SQL Servers.

In addition to these standard data sources, we can also connect to third-party web services. Flow supports REST (Representational State Transfer) based web services that use JSON (JavaScript Object Notation), and it also supports most of the common authentication methods.

An important thing to note is that the use of Flow isn't unlimited. The number of Flows that we can run is limited through PowerApps licensing. As a rough indication, each Office 365 user can run up to 2,000 Flows per month. Plan 1 users can run up to 4,500 Flows per month, whereas Plan 2 users have an allowance of 15,000 Flow runs. As with all licensing guidelines, it's very possible that these limits will change over time.

What Can We Do with Flow?

The typical use of Flow usually features notifications. and approvals. A simple example is a Flow that checks when a tweet arrives and sends an email notification to a manager if the content of the message includes a specific word. An example of a Flow that features an approval process is a vacation request system. It's possible to build workflows that require approval from single or multiple approvers, and we'll examine this later in this chapter.

Flow enables us to carry out some practical tasks and here are some examples.

- File handling - we can create, copy, and carry out file operations on files in OneDrive, Dropbox, and other supported cloud storage providers. We can also transfer files through FTP. A great feature is the ability to access the files in internal networks through the on-premises gateway.

- SQL tasks - we can connect to on-premise and Azure databases to insert, update, and retrieve rows from tables. A very helpful feature is the ability to call stored procedures. This can help overcome some of the bugs and problems that exist in PowerApps, and can also help us improve the performance of our apps.

- SharePoint - we can carry out tasks that are not supported in PowerApps, such as accessing files that are stored in SharePoint.

- Looping - PowerApps doesn't include any looping constructs, besides the limited ForAll function (there are certain functions that we cannot call within a ForAll loop). We can overcome this limitation with Flow to carry out actions repeatedly until a condition becomes true.

- Scheduling - we can schedule Flows to run at predetermined times. We can use this to carry out tasks such as data archiving, backup, or overnight reporting.

Creating a Flow

To demonstrate how to create a flow, we'll start by building a flow that copies a file from OneDrive to a location on our internal network. A prerequisite is to install the on-premises gateway (see Chapter 5). Once we install and configure a gateway, we can create a flow by visiting the flow website:

```
https://flow.microsoft.com/
```

Another way to reach this page is to click the File ➤ Flows menu item from PowerApps Studio. Figure 15-1 shows the page to create a flow. This page offers us the choice to create a blank flow, or to create a flow from a template.

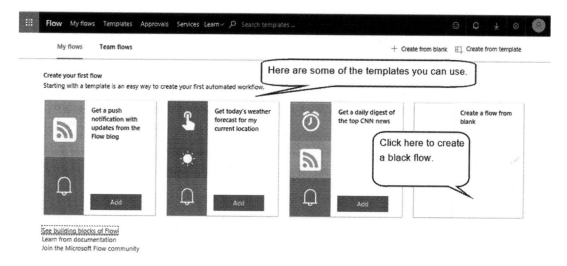

Figure 15-1. *The Microsoft Flow website*

Copying Files

To build our flow, choose the option to 'create a flow from blank'. This opens the page that's shown in Figure 15-2. A flow provides two basic objects - connectors and triggers. Connectors allow us to access data sources such as the CDS, SQL Server, Excel, and many more. From within Flow, we can access the same connectors that are available in PowerApps.

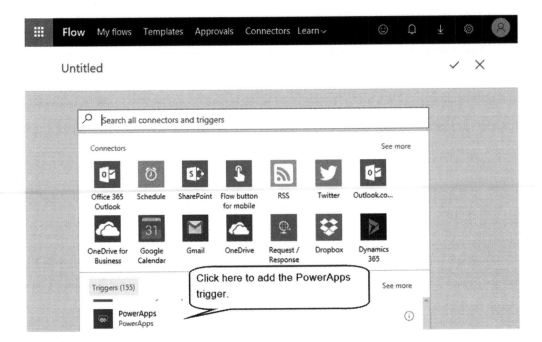

Figure 15-2. *Creating our first flow*

Triggers define events that we can react to. An example of a trigger is the occurrence of a user adding a new item to a SharePoint list. We can respond to triggers with actions. An example of an action is to send an email message to a manager.

To build flows that users can call from PowerApps, the initial step in the flow must be the PowerApps trigger. Besides the PowerApps trigger, another common trigger is the schedule trigger. We can use this trigger to run flows at specified times, or to repeat flow runs at intervals.

Once we add our initial trigger, we can append additional steps. Figure 15-3 shows the steps that we can add after the PowerApps trigger. This includes actions, conditions, switch cases, or loops.

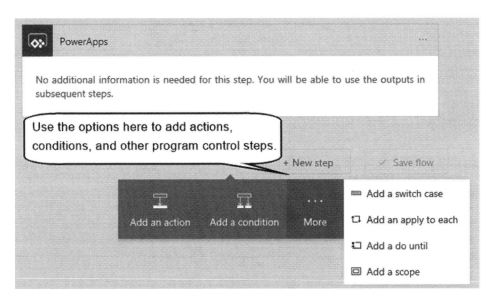

Figure 15-3. *Adding a step to a flow*

To select the source file for our file copy operation, click the 'Add an action' option and choose the OneDrive connector. Select the 'Get file content' action and select the source file with the file browser. To configure the OneDrive connector, including the account name and authentication credentials, click the icon with the three ellipses in the title bar of the step to access additional menu items.

To configure the destination location for the file copy operation, add an additional step and choose the 'Create file' action. We can click the icon with the three ellipses to configure the connector. This enables us to set the root destination location. This can be a location on the machine that runs the on-premises gateway (for example, C:\GatewayFiles) or it can be a network share (for example, \\server\share).

The next step is to enter the destination folder and file name. To select the file content, click the 'file content' input control. This prompts the designer to show a list of available options, and one of these will be the output from the OneDrive connector. This step highlights the method to pass results between actions. Figure 15-4 shows the appearance of our flow.

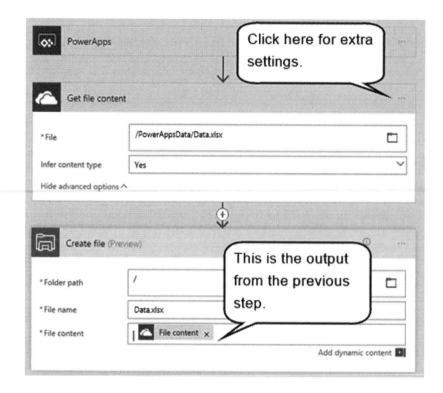

Figure 15-4. *Flow to copy a file from OneDrive to a location inside our network*

At this point, we can save our work. For the purposes of this demonstration, we'll name our flow 'BackupExcelData.'

Calling Flows from Apps

Now that we've created our flow, let's build a screen to enable users to call the flow from within an app. This process is straightforward. Simply add a button to a screen and click the flows button from the Action menu, as shown in Figure 15-5. This opens a list of flows that we can add to our app. Once we add a flow, we can refer to it in formula and call the Run method to execute the flow.

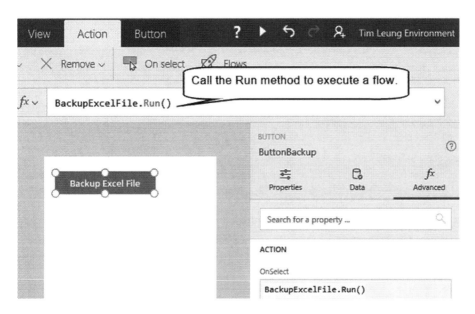

Figure 15-5. *Calling Flow from a screen*

We can now run our app and click the button to test our flow. If the flow succeeds, we'll find a copy of the file in the destination folder.

An important piece of behavior is that the Run method does not return a result to PowerApps. This is slightly limiting because it prevents us from using flow to process data and to return rows or single values to our calling app. The way to work around this problem is to save the result to a data source from within flow. After running the flow in PowerApps, we can add additional formula to retrieve the result from the data source.

Sending Notifications

To demonstrate a more complex example, here's how to build a flow to send email notifications. We'll create a screen with the option to specify a user, year, and month. A button on this screen will initiate a flow that produces an email summary of journey records that match the specified criteria.

Although the idea of composing an email might seem simple, it requires us to carry out several tasks, and some of these can be quite complex. Figure 15-6 illustrates the result of this exercise, and highlights the technical topics that we'll cover.

Key topics that we'll cover in this section:

1. How to create a flow that accepts input parameters.

2. How to retrieve and filter data by parameter values, and how to pass the results to other actions in a flow.

3. How to compose HTML email messages.

(This is the screen that calls the flow.)

4. How to use variables and to calculate the sum of records.

5. How to loop through records and to show the output in an HTML table.

6. How to format datetime values with workflow definition language.

7. How to carry out more complex calculations with workflow definition language.

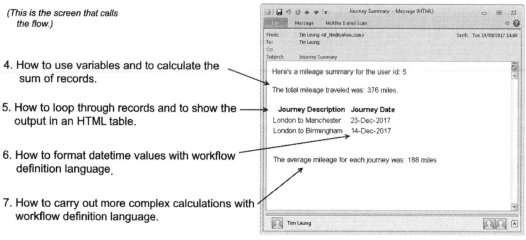

(This is the email message that the flow creates.)

Figure 15-6. *The key topics that we'll cover in this section*

The topics in this section will be useful because they play a key role in enabling us to build flows that can fulfill real life, nontrivial business requirements.

This example uses an on-premise SQL Server database as the data source, and Figure 15-7 illustrates the journey table that we'll use.

	JourneyID	StartDate	UserID	VehicleID	MileageInMiles	EndDate	Text
1	1	2018-04-23 00:00:00.000	10	10	116	2018-04-23 00:00:00.000	NULL
2	2	2017-12-23 00:00:00.000	7	8	189	2017-12-23 00:00:00.000	NULL
3	3	2017-06-02 00:00:00.000	8	6	219	2017-06-02 00:00:00.000	NULL
4	4	2017-12-14 00:00:00.000	10	6	9	2017-12-14 00:00:00.000	NULL
5	5	2017-11-28 00:00:00.000	1	4	105	2017-11-28 00:00:00.000	NULL
6	6	2018-04-26 00:00:00.000	2	2	237	2018-04-26 00:00:00.000	NULL
7	7	2018-02-14 00:00:00.000	2	2	33	2018-02-14 00:00:00.000	NULL
8	8	2018-03-02 00:00:00.000	10	3	185	2018-03-02 00:00:00.000	NULL
9	9	2017-09-27 00:00:00.000	7	10	172	2017-09-27 00:00:00.000	NULL
10	10	2018-03-26 00:00:00.000	7	2	313	2018-03-26 00:00:00.000	NULL
11	11	2018-02-26 00:00:00.000	8	2	5	2018-02-26 00:00:00.000	NULL
12	12	2017-07-03 00:00:00.000	4	8	316	2017-07-03 00:00:00.000	NULL

Figure 15-7. *The SQL Server data source that we'll use*

Like our previous example, the first step is to create a flow and to add the PowerApps trigger as the initial step.

Filtering Data

The next step in our flow is to access our on-premises SQL database and to retrieve the journey records that match the user id, month, and year arguments that the user provides from PowerApps.

The first step is to add a new action and select the "SQL Server - Get rows" action. Through the settings of the action, we can use a drop-down control to specify the source table, as shown in Figure 15-8.

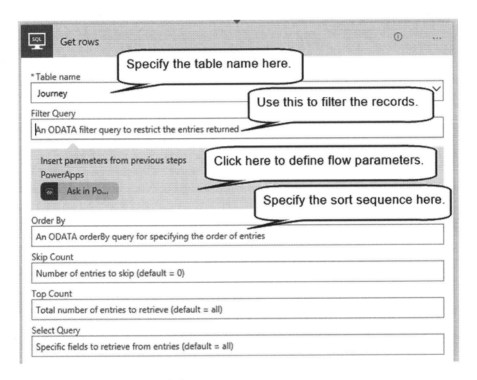

Figure 15-8. *Getting rows with the SQL connector*

To filter the data that the 'Get rows' action returns, it's not possible to use a SQL WHERE clause, as you might imagine. Instead, the way to filter data in a flow is to provide OData filter expressions. OData stands for Open Data Protocol. This protocol provides a standard way to query data from web services. The benefit of this is that we can learn a single query language and use that with all the data connectors that are available in flow. For example, if we were to use a SharePoint data source rather than an SQL data source, we could use the same OData syntax to perform a query. As Figure 15-9 shows, the 'get items' action for a SharePoint connection provides the same ability to filter by an OData expression.

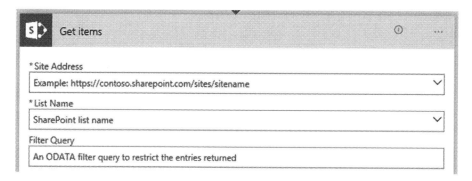

Figure 15-9. SharePoint provides the same ability to filter by OData expressions

Table 15-1 shows a list of common OData operators. As this table shows, there are mathematical, string, and date operators that we can use.

Table 15-1. OData filter expressions

Description	Operator	Example
Equal	eq	UserID eq 8
Not equal	ne	JourneyDesc ne 'London'
Greater than	gt	JourneyID gt 8
Greater than or equal	ge	JourneyID ge 10
Less than	lt	JourneyID lt 8
Less than or equal	le	JourneyID le 8
Logical and	and	JourneyID ge 10 and UserID eq 8
Logical or	or	UserID eq 8 or UserID eq 3
Logical negation	not	not UserID eq 8

To configure the 'get rows' step to filter the journey records by parameter values that the user supplies through PowerApps, we can compose an OData query and click the 'Ask in PowerApps' button in the places where we want to accept user input. Figure 15-10 shows the appearance of this in the designer. Notice how we can use OData operators to define the sort sequence of the results also.

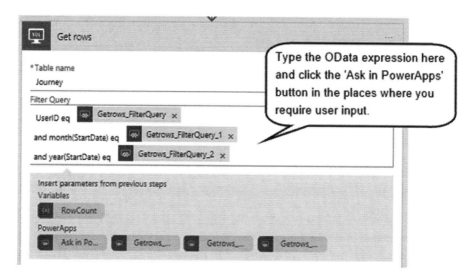

Figure 15-10. *Specifying filter operators*

One slight limitation is that for SQL Server data sources, we can compose OData expressions to filter by text and character values only. It's not possible to filter datetime values with an expression that looks like this:

JourneyDate eq ''2017-01-25T05:13:40.1374695Z'

Instead, we need to utilize the OData month and year functions to extract and filter by the relevant parts of the date, as demonstrated in this example. For reference, the OData function to return the day is called day.

Working with Variables

Now that we've retrieved a set of data, let's look at how to work with the results. To demonstrate how to use loops, variables, and to perform simple calculations, here's how to sum the mileage field of the data that we retrieved.

To calculate the sum, we'll declare a variable. Next, we'll loop over the rows and increment the variable by the mileage value.

To declare a variable, insert a step at the start of the flow immediately after the initial PowerApps trigger. Select the "Variables - Initialize variable" action and create a new variable called MileageRunningTotal. Set the data type to float, and set the initial value to 0, as shown in Figure 15-11.

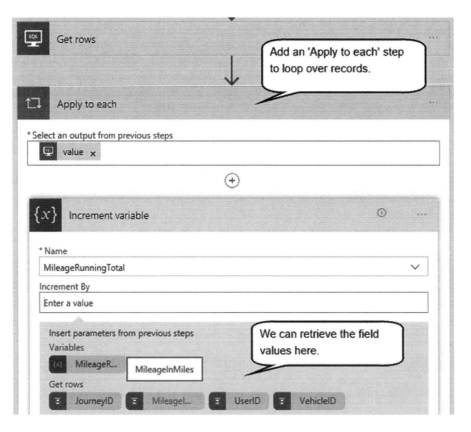

Figure 15-11. Initializing a variable

Next, add an "Apply to each" step after the "Get Rows" action, and set the input of the step to the result of the "Get Rows". Within the "Apply to each" step, add an "Increment variable" action and select the option to increment the MileageRunningTotal variable by the MileageInMiles field, as shown in Figure 15-12.

Figure 15-12. Incrementing a variable

With the "Apply to each" step, there are a couple of points to be aware of. First, with Excel data sources, the designer doesn't show the Excel column headings so it's not possible to use this same technique with Excel. Second, it's not possible to add an "Apply to each" step inside another "Apply to each" step. Therefore, this can be a challenge if we need to build a flow with nested loops.

■ **Tip**　You can move steps in a flow by dragging and dropping with the mouse. This is particularly useful if you configure a step inside an 'Apply to each' loop and want to move it outside at a later point in time.

Sending the Email

To send an email, add a connector to an email service. Flow provides connectors for a range of email connectors, including SMTP (Simple Mail Transport Protocol), Gmail, Office 365 Outlook, and Outlook.com.

For the purposes of this example, choose the Outlook.com connector and select the "Send an email" action. With all email connectors, we can use static values or parameter values to set the message recipient and subject fields of the message. We can also combine static text and parameter values when composing the message body, as shown in Figure 15-13.

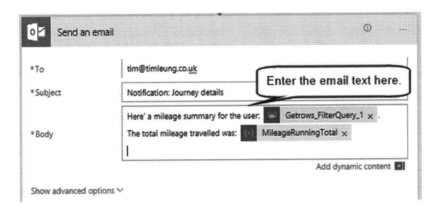

***Figure 15-13.**　Composing email messages*

A useful thing we can do is to set the message type to HTML in the advanced settings. We can use HTML to produce emails that contain formatted text, images, and colors.

■ **Note**　Note that connectors are shared with owners of a flow only. With SMTP, a user who is not the owner of a flow will need to enter valid SMTP settings when the PowerApps app loads. These settings are not simple for end users to enter because it will include values such as server name and port number, as well as the username and password.

Manipulating Data

In addition to variables, Flow provides other ways to manipulate data and we'll now explore these in more detail.

Constructing HTML Tables

Flow provides the ability to convert rows of data to HTML or CSV strings. These are useful techniques because they enable us to convert raw rows of data into a flattened format that users can interpret. To demonstrate this technique, we'll modify our email example to additionally show the journey records that relate to the user.

The connector that enables us to carry out this task is the "Data Operations" connector. As Figure 15-14 illustrates, this connector provides seven useful actions, including the operations to create CSV and HTML tables.

Data Operations - Parse JSON

Data Operations - Compose

Data Operations - Filter array

Data Operations - Select

Data Operations - Create CSV table

Data Operations - Create HTML table

Data Operations - Join

Figure 15-14. *Data operations connector*

The "Create HTML table" action accepts an input and converts all the rows and columns to an HTML table. Often, it's necessary to filter the rows and columns before we carry out the conversion to HTML and we can accomplish this by using the "Select" and "Filter array" actions.

In our example, it's not necessary to convert all the columns in our journey table to HTML. Therefore, we can call the Select action to filter the columns before outputting the result to an HTML table. Figure 15-15 shows the two steps to output the journey table to HTML.

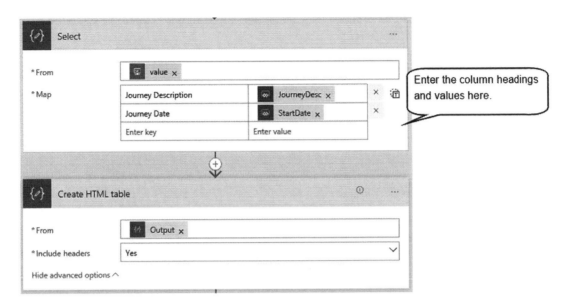

Figure 15-15. *Converting rows to HTML*

As this illustration shows, the select action enables us to rename the columns with descriptions that are more meaningful. In this example, we've renamed the `JourneyDesc` and `StartDate` fields with friendlier names.

At this stage, we can insert the output the of "Create HTML table" into the body of our email message. The designer will show this item as a selectable option when we click into the email message input control. Figure 15-16 shows the HTML output that appears in the email.

Journey Description   **Journey Date**

London to Manchester 2017-12-23T00:00:00Z

London to Birmingham 2017-12-14T00:00:00Z

Figure 15-16. *The HTML content that appears in the email*

Introducing Workflow Definition Language

Flow provides a language called workflow definition language. We can use this to cater for scenarios that require more programmatic control. Here are some practical ways for us to use workflow definition language.

- String manipulation - We can convert the casing of strings with the `toLower` and `toUpper` functions. We can call the `length` function to return the length of a string, and we can perform string manipulation with the `substring` and `replace` functions. We can also call the `startswith` and `endswith` functions to check if a string starts or ends with a specified piece of text.

- Date handling - The `utcnow` function returns the current date and time in UTC format. This is very useful because we can use this expression in filter operations to return records for the current date. There are also functions to carry out date arithmetic such as `addhours`, `addminutes`, and `adddays`. We can also format dates with the `formatDateTime` function.

- Math - We can carry out addition, subtraction, multiplication and division with the functions add, sub, mul, and div.

- Program Control - The if function works like the if function in PowerApps. This is useful because it provides a way to test a condition and to return values depending on the result. We can utilize the if function directly in user definable settings within individual actions. Other functions include and, or, not, greater, greaterOrEquals, and lessOrEquals.

Table 15-2 shows the example usage of some of most useful functions.

Table 15-2. *Example workflow definition functions*

Description	Example Use	Result
Length of a string	length('tim')	3
Length of an array	length(['tim','tom'])	2
Concatinate strings	concat('hi ', 'world')	hi world
Get a substring	substring('hi world',3,5)	world
Replace text	replace('the dog', 'the', 'a')	a dog
Uppercase text	toUpper('Tim')	TIM
Lowercase text	toLower('tim)	tim
Maths Functions		
Add two numbers	add(3,2)	5
Subject two numbers	sub(10, 3)	7
Multiply two numbers	mul(4,2)	8
Divide two numbers	div(10/2)	5
Date Functions		
Get current UTC date/time	utcnow()	2017-07-14T13:30:00Z
Get current UTC date/time	utcnow('yyyy/MM/dd')	2017/07/14
Format a date/time	formatDateTime(utcnow, 'dd mmm yy')	14 Jul 2017
Add minutes	addminutes('2017-07-14T13:30:00Z', 35)	2017-07-14T14:05:00Z
Add days	adddays('2017-07-14T13:30:00Z', 10)	2017-07-24T13:30:00Z
Add months	addmonths('2017-07-14T13:30:00Z', -2)	2017-05-14T13:30:00Z
Logic Functions		
Equals	equals(1, 1)	True
Greater than	greater(15,20)	False
And	and(greaterOrEquals(5,5), equals(8,8))	True
If, and	if(equals(6, 6), 'yes', 'no')	Yes

This is just a small subset of the most useful string, number, date, and logic functions. Workflow definition language provides many extra powerful functions, including functions to carry out XML operations, complex date time calculations, data type conversions, and set operations such as unions and joins.

Note that Microsoft Flow is a service that's built ontop of Azure Logic Apps. Azure Logic Apps is a workflow service that's very similar to Flow, and shares the same graphical workflow designer. The main difference is that Azure Logic Apps contains additional developer features, such as security and support for source control and testing. Therefore, a good place to find help with workflow definition language is through web resources that are targeted at Azure Logic Apps. For example, here's a useful page on the Microsoft Azure website that contains a list of all workflow definition language commands.

```
https://docs.microsoft.com/en-us/azure/logic-apps/logic-apps-workflow-definition-language
```

One caveat is that it's important to exercise some caution because subtle differences exist between Azure Logic Apps and Flow, and the syntax that we use with these two services are not always identical.

Applying Workflow Definition Language

Where exactly can we use workflow definition language? The answer is that we can use workflow definition language in almost all places where we can enter some text. However, one very versatile place is the "Data Operations - Compose" action. This action enables us to calculate output values that we can use in other parts of a flow.

To demonstrate this technique, here's how to configure a 'Get Rows' action to return Journey records for today's date.

The first part of this flow includes three compose actions to retrieve the day, month, and year of the current date. The compose actions call the utcnow function to retrieve the date components. When we compose expressions with workflow definition language, it's important to enclose commands with double quotes. It's also necessary to prefix commands with the @ symbol. The @ symbol enables Flow to recognize the proceeding text as workflow definition language, rather than literal text.

Figure 15-17 shows the layout of these actions. To make it easier to refer to output of these actions, it's a good idea to rename the actions that we create. In this example, these three actions are renamed to CurrentDay, CurrentMonth, and CurrentYear.

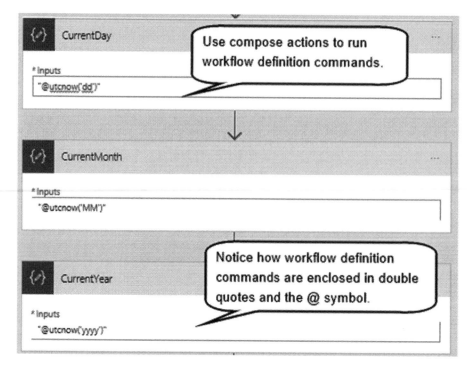

Figure 15-17. *Using compose actions to retrieve the current day, month, and year*

To complete this flow, the final step is to incorporate the output of these actions into an OData query expression for the 'Get Rows' action, as shown in Figure 15-18.

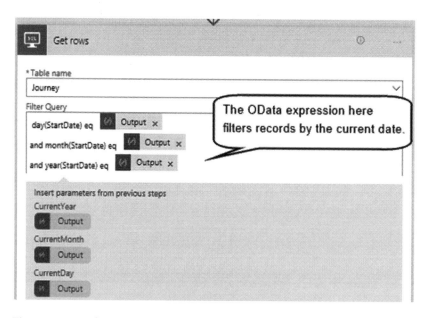

Figure 15-18. *Filtering records by today's date*

Using Output Values in Workflow Definition Commands

It's not possible to use the visual designer to add the results of actions to a workflow definition command. Instead, we need to access the function outputs with special syntax. It can be difficult to work out what this is so in this section, we'll look at a tip that can help us.

To demonstrate this technique, here's how to modify our flow to include a calculation of the average mileage for the rows that we return. Our flow already stores the total mileage in a variable called MileageRunningTotal. To calculate the average, we need to divide the MileageRunningTotal value by the number of records that the 'get rows' action returns. To retrieve the number of records that the 'get rows' action returns, we need to call the length function and to provide the output of the 'get rows' action. Figure 15-19 shows visually what we're attempting to do.

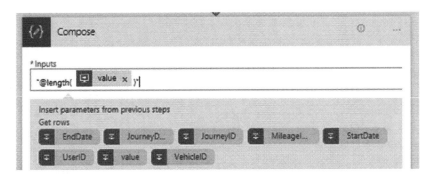

Figure 15-19. *Attempting to retrieve a count of the rows returned*

The expression that's shown in Figure 15-19 is not valid because it mixes a value from the visual designer with a workflow definition language expression. So in this example, what workflow definition language expression would we use to reference the visual 'value' object that we see in Figure 15-19?

To way to work this out is to save the flow and to use the error message to determine the correct syntax. If we attempt to save this action, flow returns the error that's shown in Figure 15-20.

Figure 15-20. *Finding the names of output parameters by examining errors*

By inspecting this error message, we can see that following identifier refers to the output from the 'Get rows' action.

```
body('Get_rows')?['value']
```

As a point of reference, the ? operator enables us to access null values without triggering a runtime error. By using this same technique, we can work out the syntax to return the value of the MileageRunningTotal variable. The result looks like this:

```
variables('MileageRunningTotal')
```

Now that we know the syntax to access the `MileageRunningTotal` variable and the row count from the 'get rows' action, we can create a compose action and add code to divide these two values. Figure 15-21 shows the syntax we would use. We can then incorporate this result into the email message that we send to the user.

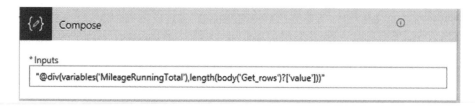

Figure 15-21. Calculating an average value

Referring to Items in Loops

Within "Apply to each" steps, we can use the `item` function to refer to the current item in the loop. As an example, here's how to amend the flow so that it formats the journey dates more neatly. Figure 15-22 shows the change that we would make to our 'Data Operations - Select' action.

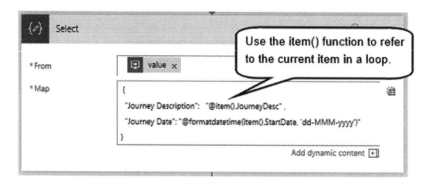

Figure 15-22. Converting rows to HTML and applying a format

An important point that this highlights is that with the 'Data Operations - Select' action, we must use the icon in the body of the action to switch the action to text mode. If we don't switch to text mode, the action outputs the literal command instead of parsing the workflow definition language.

Calling SQL Stored Procedures

For SQL Server data sources, we can call stored procedures with flow. For app builders who work with SQL Server, this opens many possibilities. We can use this to improve performance or to overcome some of the delegation limitations in PowerApps.

To demonstrate this technique, here's how to delete all journey records for a user in a specified month. In Chapter 9, we saw how to do this with the `RemoveIf` function. The problem with this technique is that it performs very slowly. Second, this technique removes only the first 500 records. By deleting the records directly through a stored procedure, we can overcome these problems.

Writing stored procedures is large topic and beyond the scope of this book. Therefore, the intention here is to create an awareness that this technique exists.

To demonstrate, Listing 15-1 shows the definition of a stored procedure to delete journey records that match a specified user, month, and year. To create this procedure, we require access to SQL Management Studio and suitable permissions for the server.

Listing 15-1. An example stored procedure to delete records

```
CREATE PROC DeleteJourneyForUser
        @UserID int,
        @MonthNum int,
        @YearNum int

AS

        DELETE FROM [Journey]
        WHERE
        UserID= @UserID
        AND Month(StartDate)=@MonthNum
        AND Year(StartDate)=@YearNum
```

Once we add the stored procedure, we can call it from flow using the 'Execute stored procedure' action, as shown in Figure 15-23. When we create the action, we can map the stored procedure parameters to flow parameters. This enables us to supply the parameter values from within PowerApps.

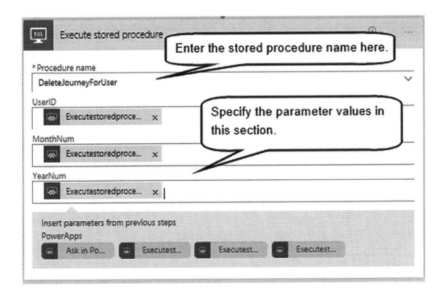

Figure 15-23. *Calling a stored procedure*

It's worth noting that for simple deletions and updates of records in SQL Server, we can use the 'Delete' and 'Update' actions, and provide OData expressions to specify the records to update.

Approving Actions

A powerful feature that flow provides is action approval. This feature is powerful because we can configure actions to occur following approval from a single approver, multiple approvers, or a single approver from a list of approvers.

Examples of how we could use this feature include building processes to request approval from managers before publishing a document to SharePoint. We could use this same mechanism to request approval before a user posts a message to social media, or to update records from a data source. The Microsoft flow website provides an example of how to build a SharePoint-based system to approve vacation requests.

To demonstrate this feature, here's how to build a flow to only allow the deletion of journey records following approval from a manager.

To first step is to add an approval action, as shown in Figure 15-24. The 'start an approval' action enables us to target the request at individuals by an email address. We can define multiple approvers by entering a list of semicolon-separated email addresses into the 'Assigned to' text box. The approval types that we can select are 'Anyone from the assigned list', and 'Everyone from the assigned list'. We can also attach additional details to the approval request, including a title, description, and link.

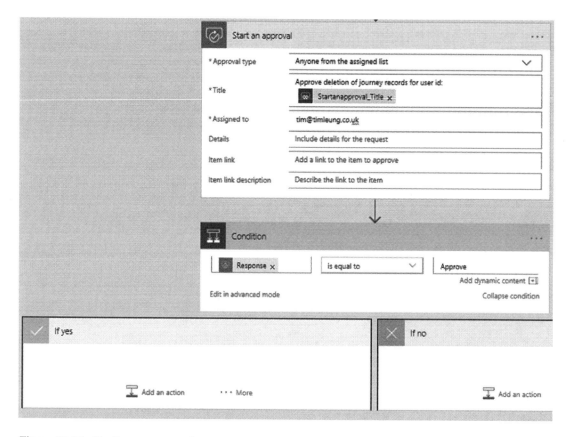

Figure 15-24. *Starting an approval*

Immediately after the 'start an approval' step, we can add a condition to test whether the response matches the value 'Approve'. We can then add the actions that we want to carry out to the 'if yes' section of the condition step. This would include the action to carry out the record deletion.

How exactly does an approver authorize an approval request? After the flow runs, the request will show up in a dedicated section on the flow website, as shown in Figure 15-25. The approver can use this to approve or reject requests.

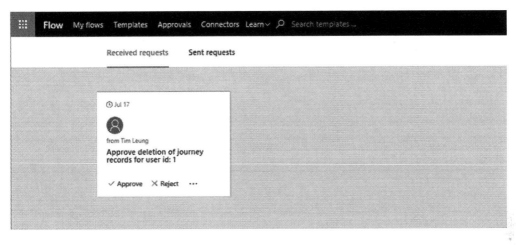

Figure 15-25. *Approving a flow*

To configure a flow to require approval from multiple users, we would chain together 'start an approval' actions. We would then configure conditions to test the responses, and to carry out actions depending on the result.

Managing Flows

To complete this chapter, let's look at the section on the flow website that enables us to manage flows. The 'My flows' part of the website shows a list of flows, and we can use the options on this page to edit or delete a flow. Figure 15-26 shows the page that appears when we view the details for a flow. On this page, we can view the run history of the flow, as well as the connectors and the owners.

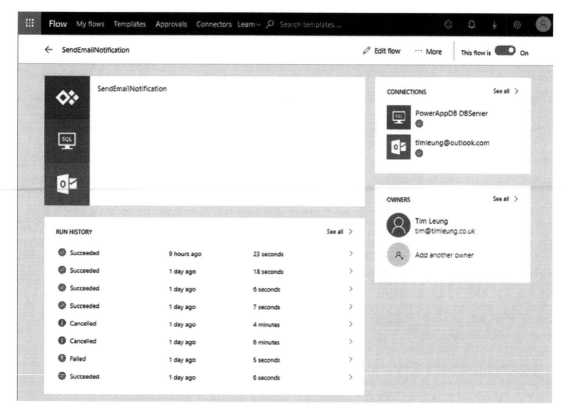

Figure 15-26. *Viewing the status of a flow*

We can use the run history section to open a specific run and to view the results of each step, as shown in Figure 15-27. This feature is very useful because it enables us to debug and diagnose any problems that arise during a flow run.

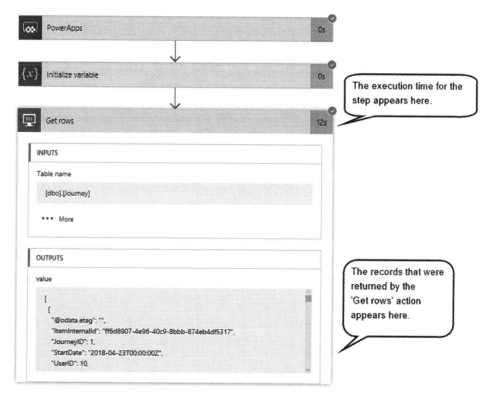

Figure 15-27. *Viewing the data that was returned during a flow run*

Here are a couple of points that are worth noting. When we update a flow and add additional 'Ask PowerApps' parameters, an existing app will not recognize these changes. We need to delete the flow from our app and re-add it for PowerApps to recognize our new parameters.

The second point is that there's no way to back up flows, or to move flows between environments. Therefore, we should apply some caution. We can consider taking screenshots of flows to help us re-create our work, in case we accidently delete steps that we later want to restore.

Summary

In this chapter, we looked at how to use Flow. Flow allows us to carry out tasks independently of PowerApps. Flow provides us with the ability to carry out certain tasks that are not possible with PowerApps. Practical examples of the types of things we can do with Flow include sending notifications, copying files, and carrying out data tasks by connecting more directly with SQL Server or SharePoint.

Flow provides a browser-based graphical designer that caters for non-developers. It offers the ability to build processes that include loops, conditions, and schedules without the need for code. With these features, we can build solutions to automate repetitive processes.

The core components of Flow are triggers and actions. A trigger defines an event, for example, "when a new document is added to SharePoint". In response to a trigger, we can carry out an action, for example, "send an email to a manager".

We can connect to a wide range of data sources, including all the connections that are available from within PowerApps. We can even use the on-premises gateway to connect to SQL Server or SharePoint. With the help of this connector, we can call SQL stored procedures and directly add, update, or delete the data in tables. We can therefore utilize Flows to help overcome delegation limitations and to improve the performance of our apps. The on-premises gateway provides an additional benefit because it enables us to access files in our internal networks. In this chapter, we saw an example of how to use flow to copy files from OneDrive to an internal file share.

We can use variables to help us better accomplish tasks in Flow. For example, we can use variables to carry out calculations. We can also use workflow definition language to carry out programmatic tasks, and we saw several examples of how to apply this to an app.

Workflow definition language provides functions that can carry out string manipulation, and date formatting, and other programatic tasks. We can insert workflow definition commands in most places where we can enter text. The "Data Operations - Compose" action provides a handy place for us to execute and to return values from workflow definition commands. Calls to workflow definition commands must begin with the @ symbol. This indicates that the preceding content is workflow definition command, rather than literal text. We can pass the output of other actions to a function and in such cases, it's necessary to use special syntax to refer to other objects in a flow. An easy way to work out the correct syntax is to deliberately cause an error and to the use the error message to determine the correct syntax.

Finally, Flow provides an approval framework that can help us carry out workflow processes. We can configure actions to occur after approval from one or more individuals. Approvers visit a special section on the flow website to approve or reject approval requests.

PART IV

Extending Your Application

CHAPTER 16

Working Offline

PowerApps is designed for mobile devices, and there are times when these devices lose connectivity with the Internet. The ability for users to continue working during these times can be extremely useful. This is especially true for field workers, users that work outside regularly, or users that travel often.

To cater for these scenarios, PowerApps provides the ability to cache data on the local device. We can use this feature to build apps that can work offline. However, building an app that works completely offline is a manual task and it introduces a very difficult challenge - how to synchronize data and to resolve conflicts.

If an offline user modifies a record that another user modifies during an offline session, who wins? Can we merge changes from two users together? And how do we cope with situations where an online user deletes the record that an offline user modifies? In this chapter, we'll find out the answers to these questions. The specific topics that we'll cover in this chapter will include the following:

- What happens when a device becomes offline? We'll examine the behavior of a standard app when it becomes offline.

- How to view data offline. We'll look at how to cache data to the local device, and how to detect offline conditions. When an app becomes offline, we'll find out how to display the cached data.

- How to add and update records while offline. We'll develop a system to enable the offline update of data. We'll find out how to build a conflict resolution screen. When conflicts occur, users can use this screen to retain the offline record, or to revert to the most recent server version of the record.

What Happens Offline?

To begin, let's examine what happens when a device becomes disconnected from the Internet. In the case of a running auto-generated app that becomes offline midway through a session, the app will continue to be mostly functional. The browse screen will continue to show the data that existed before the app became offline, and the search and sort buttons on this screen will continue to work. Individual records will still open in the display screen and we can even open records in the edit screen to view the data.

As we would expect, the refresh button on the browse screen will not work. Also, the save button on the edit screen will not work because both of these actions require an active Internet connection. In cases where PowerApps fails to carry out an action due to a lack of connectivity, it displays an error message like the one that's shown in Figure 16-1.

© Tim Leung 2017
T. Leung, *Beginning PowerApps*, https://doi.org/10.1007/978-1-4842-3003-9_16

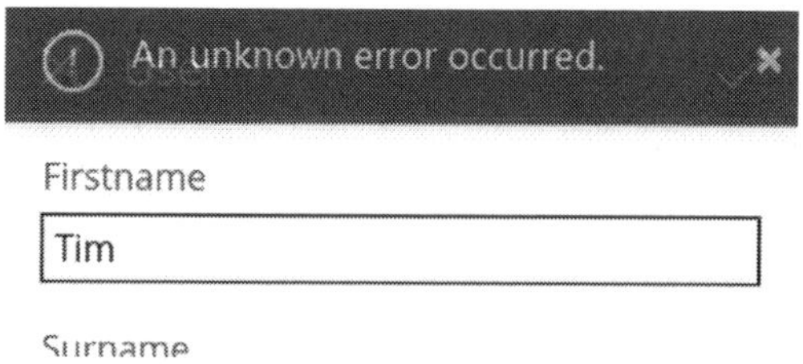

Figure 16-1. *The error that occurs when we attempt to save a record while offline*

In cases where a user starts PowerApps while disconnected from the Internet, the user can only run apps that have previously run on the device. When an app loads while offline, it can't retrieve an initial set of data from the data source and therefore won't show any data.

▓ **Note**   A simple way to test how an app behaves offline is to run your app on a mobile device and to enable 'airplane mode'.

Techniques to Enable Offline Working

To build apps that can work offline, there are two key features that can help us: the connection signal, and the SaveData and LoadData functions.

We can use the connection signal to detect the connection status of an app. Table 16-1 illustrates the formula we can use to utilize this signal.

Table 16-1. *The connection signal*

Formula	Result
Connection.Connected	true when the device is connected to a network
Connection.Metered	true when a device is connected to a metered network

This signal can detect whether the active connection is a metered connection. The cellular connection is usually configured as a metered connection on smartphones. The ability to detect a metered connection is useful because we can adapt our app to use less data when the device is connected to a metered connection. For instance, we can write formula to hide images in this scenario.

Saving and Retrieving Local Data

A key feature that enables us to build offline apps is the ability to store collections of data into a private area on the local device. The functions to save and retrieve local data are called SaveData and LoadData respectively.

The SaveData function expects two parameters - the collection of data to save, and a file name. Here's an example of how to store the data from a collection called LocalJourney into a file called OfflineJourneyFile.

SaveData(LocalJourney, "OfflineJourneyFile")

The SaveData function stores and encrypts the data in an area that is isolated from other users and other apps. To retrieve the file data, we would call the LoadData function like so:

LoadData(LocalJourney, " OfflineJourneyFile", true)

The first parameter specifies the target collection for the data and the second parameter specifies the file name from which to retrieve the data. The third parameter configures the LoadData function to continue without error if the file doesn't exist.

We can only call LoadData to retrieve the data that we saved with SaveData from the same app. It's not possible to load data from other apps.

Making an App Available Offline

Let's now walk through the process of adapting an auto-generated app to work offline. Our app will be based on a CDS data source. The modification that we'll apply will enable users to view, update, and add records while offline. We'll base this example on our journey entity. Figure 16-2 shows an overview of how this process will work.

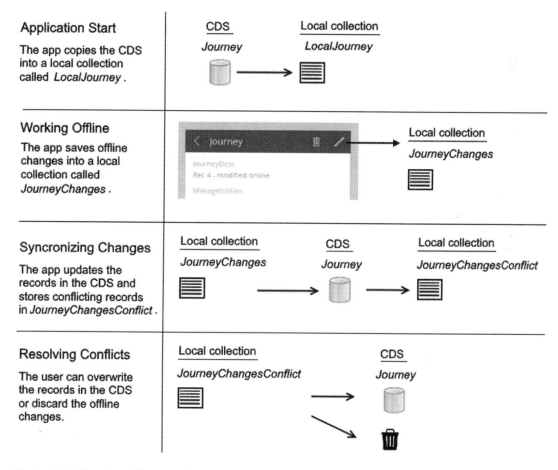

Figure 16-2. *Overview of how to adapt an app to work offline*

When the app starts, it loads the data from the CDS data store into a local collection. We'll adapt all the screens in the app to work against the local collection rather than directly against the CDS table. When a user edits or adds a new record, the app will save any changes to the underlying CDS table if the device is online. If the device is offline, the app saves the changes to a holding table (JourneyChanges in our example).

During any data refresh or update operation, the app will cache the changes to the local device by calling the SaveData method. If the device is offline when the app starts, it attempts to load the data from a local file rather than the CDS.

The app will include a screen that shows the records in the holding table, as shown in Figure 16-3. When the device becomes online, the user can use this screen to synchronize the changes to the CDS data store.

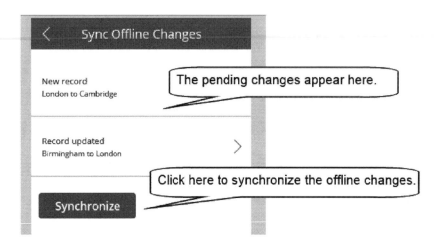

Figure 16-3. *Synchronization screen*

In cases where the user disconnects from the network for an extended period, other users might modify the same records. To prevent users from overwriting each other's changes, the app will check that no changes have been made before synchronizing the data. If data conflicts exist, the user can choose to keep or to discard the offline changes using the screen that's shown in Figure 16-4.

Figure 16-4. *The user can choose to keep or discard changes.*

The prerequisite for this example is to build an auto-generated app that's based on the journey table that's shown in Figure 16-5. The two important fields that our app relies on are the Primary Id and Last Modified Datetime fields. We will use the primary id field to uniquely identify records and we'll use the Last Modified Datetime to check whether changes have occurred during the offline session. The data type of the Primary Id field is a server-generated auto number field.

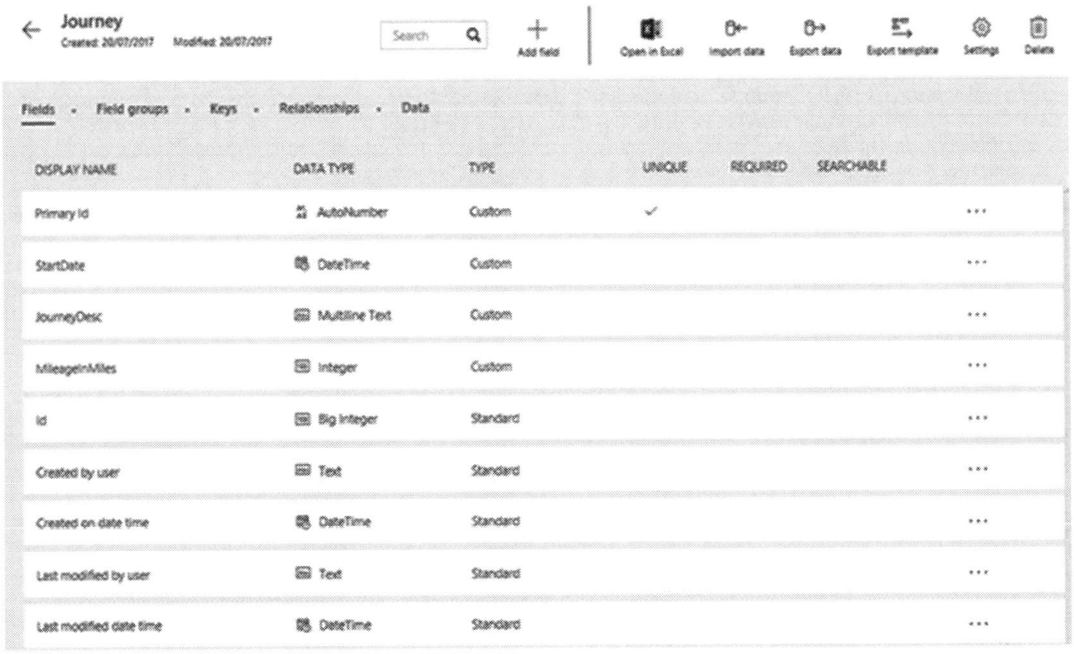

Figure 16-5. *CDS Data source*

To keep this example simple, we won't include any lookup data. To make lookup data available offline, we would need to extend our app to load the lookup data in a local collection.

Note that building an offline app is a highly customized process. Therefore, the main purpose of this example is to provide an insight into the challenges that exist and to provide a broad structure that we can adapt to build offline apps.

Setting the Data Source to a Local Collection

When the app loads, the main task is to load the source data from the CDS to a local collection, in addition to several other data initialization tasks. Listing 16-1 shows the code to add to the OnStart property of the browse screen.

Note that throughout this chapter, the code listings will include boldified comments for additional clarification. It's important to remove these lines in our actual app because the comments will cause errors in the formula.

Listing 16-1. Loading the data to a local collection

```
If(Connection.Connected,
    ClearCollect(LocalJourney, Journey),
    LoadData(LocalJourney, "OfflineJourneyFile", true)
);

UpdateIf(LocalJourney, IsBlank(JourneyDesc), {JourneyDesc:""});
SaveData(LocalJourney, "OfflineJourneyFile");
LoadData(JourneyChanges, "OfflineJourneyChangesFile", true);
```

319

```
'Initialize collections that we'll use elsewhere (Optional)
'JourneyChangesReview is a collection we'll use later to help synchronize records
ClearCollect(JourneyChangesReview,
                     {OfflineRecord:BrowseGallery1.Selected,
                       CurrentRecord:BrowseGallery1.Selected
                     }
);
Clear(JourneyChangesReview);

'JourneyChangesConflict is a collection we'll use later to store data conflicts
ClearCollect(AddColumns(JourneyChangesReview, "Status", ""));
Clear(JourneyChangesConflict)
```

The first part of this formula checks if the device is connected to the Internet. If so, it copies the data from the CDS entity (called Journey) into the local collection. If not, it retrieves the saved data from the file on the device and copies that data to the local collection.

The UpdateIf function replaces all null instances of the JourneyDesc field to an empty string. The purpose of this is to fix a bug that affects edit forms that bind to local collections that contain null values. A card on a form will not update the value of a field in a local collection if the original value is null. Therefore, the fix is to initially replace all null values with empty strings.

The next section in the formula caches the data to a local file by calling the SaveData function. This provides the app with data if a user subsequently starts the app later while offline. Next, the formula calls the LoadData function to load any unsynchronized data modifications that might have taken place during a previous offline session.

The formula that appears next is optional. This section of code initializes the collections that we'll use later with random values and immediately clears the values afterward. The purpose of this is to prime the designer with the schema of the local collections. By doing this, the IntelliSense in the formula bar can recognize the fields in the collections and the designer won't underline any unrecognized fields in red.

The next step is to reconfigure all the screens in the app to use the LocalJourney collection. On the basis that the CDS data source is called Journey, the step is to rename all references of the Journey data source to LocalJourney. The places in the app to modify are these:

- BrowseScreen1 ➤ BrowseGallery1 ➤ Items

- DetailsScreen1 ➤ DetailForm1 ➤ DataSource

- EditScreen1 ➤ EditForm1 ➤ DataSource

Finally, we need to modify the Refresh icon on the browse screen so that it saves the data to the offline file after a refresh. Listing 16-2 shows the formula.

Listing 16-2. Refreshing the Data

```
If(Connection.Connected,
   Refresh(Journey);
   ClearCollect(LocalJourney, Journey);
   UpdateIf(LocalJourney, IsBlank(JourneyDesc), {JourneyDesc:""});
   SaveData(LocalJourney, "OfflineJourneyFile")
)
```

Handling Offline Deletions

For an app to be fully functional offline, it should handle the offline deletion of data. The display screen provides a delete icon. Listing 16-3 shows how to adapt the formula in this icon to support the offline deletion of data.

Listing 16-3. Formula to delete records

```
RemoveIf(LocalJourney, BrowseGallery1.Selected.PrimaryId = PrimaryId);
If(Connection.Connected,
   RemoveIf(Journey,
            LookUp(Journey,BrowseGallery1.Selected.PrimaryId = PrimaryId)
   ),
   Collect(JourneyChanges, {Record:BrowseGallery1.Selected, Status:"D"});
   SaveData(JourneyChanges, "OfflineJourneyChangesFile");
);
Back()
```

The first line of this formula removes the record from the LocalJourney collection. If the device is connected to the Internet, it also removes the record from the main Journey data source. If the device is offline, the formula stores the data in a collection called JourneyChanges. This collection keeps track of all offline changes and Figure 16-6 shows the layout of this collection. The status field indicates the type of modification that has taken place. The values we'll use are "D" for a deleted record, "A" for a new record, and "U" for an updated record.

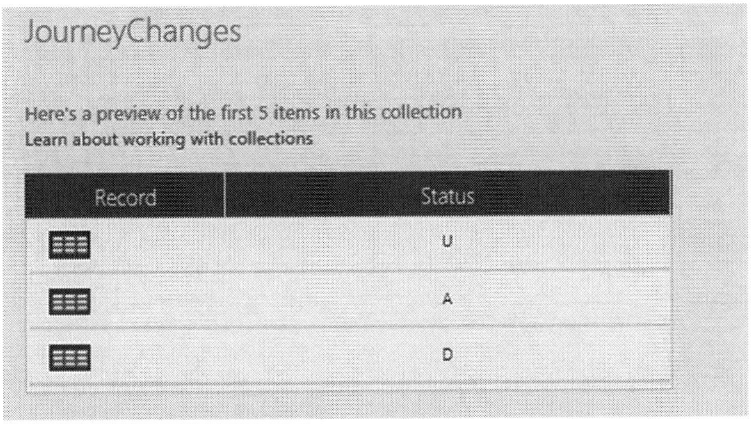

Figure 16-6. *The JourneyChanges data collection to store offline changes*

The next section in the formula calls the SaveData function to save the data to the offline file. This enables the app to retain the data modifications if a user quits an offline session and starts another offline session.

Deleting Records from Local Collections

Note that the most reliable way to remove an item form a local collection is to remove the item by a unique identifier, rather than to reference the item itself with formula like so:

```
Remove(LocalJourney, BrowseGallery1.Selected)
```

Although this syntax looks correct, it only works with connected data sources. This is the reason why the formula in this section calls the RemoveIf function, rather than the Remove function. You can find out more about this behavior here:

```
https://powerusers.microsoft.com/t5/PowerApps-Forum/Method-to-Remove-items-from-local-
Collection/m-p/27157
```

Handling Offline Record Updates

To provide offline data edit and data entry capabilities, there are several changes that we need to make to the save icon on the edit screen. Figure 16-7 shows the high-level process.

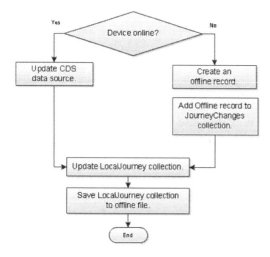

Figure 16-7. *The JourneyChanges data collection to store offline changes*

A key modification is to adapt the edit form to avoid the use of the SubmitForm function to save the record to the LocalJourney collection. The reason for this is to enable us to generate a temporary primary id value when the device is offline. Usually, the CDS would generate this value but this would not happen if the device is offline. We need to allocate a temporary primary id value to enable us to edit or delete records that were created offline.

Listing 16-4 shows the formula to add to the OnSelect property of the save icon.

Listing 16-4. Formula to save a record

```
'1. Collect values for use later in the formula.
UpdateContext(
   {EditForm1Mode: If(EditForm1.Mode = FormMode.New, "A", "U")}
);

' 1.1 Get the form values that the user enters.
UpdateContext(
   {EditForm1Record: EditForm1.Updates}
);

'1.2 Calculate the next available temporary id.
UpdateContext(
   {PrimaryIdNew: If(Min(LocalJourney, PrimaryId) > 0,
                      -1,
                      Min(LocalJourney, PrimaryId) - 1)
   }
);

'2. If the device is online, update the CDS data source
'   JourneyRecordCDS stores the return record from the patch operation.
If(Connection.Connected,
   If(EditForm1Mode="A",
      UpdateContext(
         {JourneyRecordCDS:Patch(Journey,
                                 Defaults(Journey),
                                 EditForm1Record)
         }
      ),
      UpdateContext(
         {JourneyRecordCDS:Patch(Journey,
                        LookUp(Journey,
                           BrowseGallery1.Selected.PrimaryId = PrimaryId),
                        EditForm1Record)
         }
      )
      )
   ,
   '3 If the device is offline, build a journey record to patch to
     the JourneyChanges collection. JourneyRecordOffline is the record that
     we build here If the user is adding a new record, set the primary id
     value to the temporary value that we calculated earlier.

   If(EditForm1Mode="A",
      UpdateContext(
         {JourneyRecordOffline:{JourneyDesc:EditForm1Record.JourneyDesc,
                                StartDate: EditForm1Record.StartDate,
                                MileageInMiles: EditForm1Record.MileageInMiles,
                                PrimaryId: Text(PrimaryIdNew)
                                }
         }
      ),
```

```
    UpdateContext(
        {JourneyRecordOffline:{JourneyDesc:EditForm1Record.JourneyDesc,
                            StartDate: EditForm1Record.StartDate,
                            MileageInMiles: EditForm1Record.MileageInMiles,
                            LastModifiedDateTime:
                                BrowseGallery1.Selected.LastModifiedDateTime
                            }
        }
    )

    )
);
```

**'4 Now synchronize the LocalJourney collection. If online, patch the
the JourneyRecordCDS to the LocalJourney collection. Otherwise, patch
the JourneyRecordOffline record.**

```
If(Connection.Connected,
    If(EditForm1Mode="A",
        Patch(LocalJourney,
                Defaults(LocalJourney),
                JourneyRecordCDS
        ),
        Patch(LocalJourney,
                LookUp(LocalJourney,
                    BrowseGallery1.Selected.PrimaryId = PrimaryId),
                JourneyRecordCDS
        )
    ),
    If(EditForm1Mode="A",
        Patch(LocalJourney,
                Defaults(LocalJourney),
                JourneyRecordOffline
        ),
    Patch(LocalJourney,
            LookUp(LocalJourney,
                BrowseGallery1.Selected.PrimaryId = PrimaryId),
            JourneyRecordOffline
    )
);
```

**'5. If the user edits a record that was created offline, remove and re-add the record in
JourneyChanges**
```
RemoveIf(JourneyChanges, Record.PrimaryId = JourneyRecordOffline.PrimaryId);

If(Value(JourneyRecordOffline.PrimaryId) < 0,
    Collect(JourneyChanges, {Record: JourneyRecordOffline,Status:"A"}),
    Collect(JourneyChanges, {Record: JourneyRecordOffline,Status:"U"})
    )
);
```

'6. Save the updated data to the offline file
```
SaveData(JourneyChanges, "OfflineJourneyChangesFile")
```

324

The first section of the formula stores whether the user is adding or editing a record into a variable called EditForm1Mode. The next line retrieves the form values to a variable called EditForm1Record. The Updates property provides access to the form values. The ability to access the values that a user enters into a form can be very useful in many other scenarios.

If the app is online, the next part of the formula calls the patch function to save the record to the CDS data source. The patch function returns the CDS record that was added or updated. In the case of a new record, the result from the patch function will include the server-generated primary id value. We retain this record in a variable called JourneyRecordCDS so that we can update the LocalJourney collection later on.

If the device is offline, the code builds a journey record that we can patch into the LocalJourney collection. In the case of a new record, we allocate a temporary primary id value. This enables the app to uniquely identify records that were created offline. Without this temporary primary id value, we would not be able to remove or edit records that were created offline. To avoid the possibility of generating duplicate primary id values, the formula allocates primary id values that are negative. For data updates, the offline journey record includes the last modified date time value. We need this to check for conflicts during the synchronization process.

Merging Records

The formula that builds the JourneyRecordOffline record effectively merges a source record with the updates that a user enters through the edit form. It might seem a good idea to call the patch function to merge the two records using syntax like this:

```
Patch(BrowseGallery1.Selected, EditForm1.Updates)
```

In practice, this technique isn't reliable and it's better to merge records with the more verbose syntax that we used earlier. You can read more about the problems of merging records with the patch function here.

```
https://powerusers.microsoft.com/t5/PowerApps-Forum/Bug-report-Patch-function-not-working-
as-expected-when-merging/m-p/29156
```

Building the Synchronization Screen

The next stage is to build the sync screen. The main part of this screen shows a sync button. Figure 16-8 shows what should happen during the synchronization process.

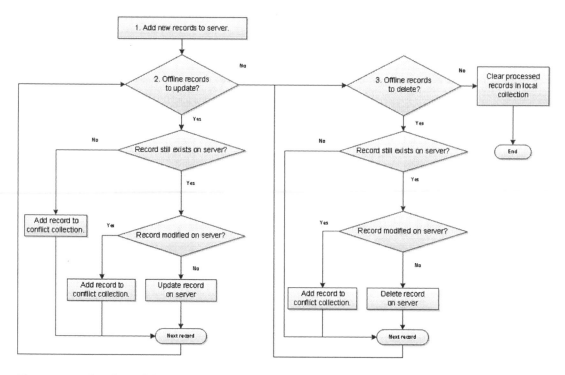

Figure 16-8. *Flowchart of the synchronization feature*

To build the synchronization feature, the first step is to add a new screen. Next, add a gallery control and set the items property to the JourneyChanges collection. To display a field from the offline record, we can use the syntax ThisItem.Record.<Fieldname>, as shown in Figure 16-9.

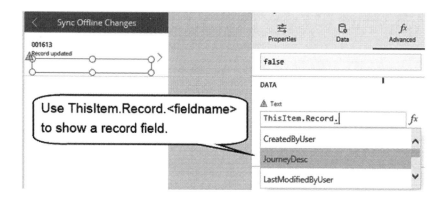

Figure 16-9. *Appearance of the synchronization screen*

At this point, we can add an icon on the browse screen to navigate to the synchronization screen, as shown in Figure 16-10.

Figure 16-10. *Opening the Sync screen*

Returning to the synchronization screen, add a button to synchronize the data. Set the OnSelect property of the button to the formula that's shown in Listing 16-5. This formula carries out the process that's shown in the flowchart at the start of this section (Figure 16-8). There are three logical parts to this formula that consists of code to add the new records, code to synchronize the updated records, and code to synchronize the deleted records.

Listing 16-5. Synchronizing the records

```
'1 Save the records that were added
ForAll(Filter(JourneyChanges, Status="A"),
      Patch(Journey,
            Defaults(Journey),
            {JourneyDesc:Record.JourneyDesc,
             StartDate:Record.StartDate,
             MileageInMiles:Record.MileageInMiles
             }
      )
);

RemoveIf(JourneyChanges, Status="A");

Clear(JourneyChangesReview);
Clear(JourneyChangesConflict);

'2 Refresh the CDS data source. For records updated offline, retrieve the corresponding
current record
Refresh(Journey);
ForAll(Filter(JourneyChanges, Status="U"),
      Collect(JourneyChangesReview,
            {OfflineRecord:Record,
             CurrentRecord:LookUp(Journey, PrimaryId = Record.PrimaryId)
             }
      )
);
```

'3 If the source record is not found, add the record to the conflict collection

```
If(CountRows(Filter(JourneyChangesReview,IsEmpty(CurrentRecord))) > 0,
    Collect(JourneyChangesConflict,
            AddColumns(Filter(JourneyChangesReview,IsEmpty(CurrentRecord)),
                    "Status",
                    "Update failed - source record deleted"
            )
    )
);
RemoveIf(JourneyChangesReview, IsEmpty(CurrentRecord));
```

'4 Process the records that have not been modified on the server

```
ForAll(Filter(JourneyChangesReview,
            CurrentRecord.LastModifiedDateTime=
                        OfflineRecord.LastModifiedDateTime),
    Patch(Journey,
        CurrentRecord,
        {JourneyDesc:OfflineRecord.JourneyDesc,
         StartDate:OfflineRecord.StartDate,
         MileageInMiles:OfflineRecord.MileageInMiles
         }
    )
);
RemoveIf(
    JourneyChangesReview,
    CurrentRecord.LastModifiedDateTime=OfflineRecord.LastModifiedDateTime
);
```

'5 The remaining rows in JourneyChangesReview are conflicting records

```
If(CountRows(JourneyChangesReview) > 0,
    Collect(JourneyChangesConflict,
            AddColumns(JourneyChangesReview,
                    "Status",
                    "Update failed - source record modified by other user"
            )
    )
);
Clear(JourneyChangesReview);
```

'6 Collect the records that were deleted offline into JourneyChangesReview

```
ForAll(Filter(JourneyChanges, Status="D"),
        Collect(JourneyChangesReview,
                {OfflineRecord:Record,
                 CurrentRecord:LookUp(Journey, PrimaryId = Record.PrimaryId)
                 }
        )
);
```

'7 Remove records that have also been deleted on the server

```
RemoveIf(JourneyChangesReview, IsEmpty(CurrentRecord));
```

'8 Process the records that were deleted offline
```
ForAll(Filter(JourneyChangesReview,
               CurrentRecord.LastModifiedDateTime=
                   OfflineRecord.LastModifiedDateTime),
       Remove(Journey, CurrentRecord)
);
RemoveIf(JourneyChangesReview,
           CurrentRecord.LastModifiedDateTime=
           OfflineRecord.LastModifiedDateTime
);
```

'9 The remaining rows in JourneyChangesReview are conflicting records
```
If(CountRows(JourneyChangesReview) > 0,
   Collect(JourneyChangesConflict,
           AddColumns(JourneyChangesReview,
                      "Status",
                      "Delete failed - source record modified by other user"
           )
   )
);
```

```
Clear(JourneyChanges);
```

'9 Update the offline file
```
SaveData(JourneyChanges, "OfflineJourneyChangesFile");
```

'10 Build a message that we can show to the user
```
If(CountRows(JourneyChangesConflict) > 0,
   UpdateContext(
      {ConflictMessage:
          Text(CountRows(JourneyChangesConflict)) & " conflicting record(s)"}
   ),
   UpdateContext(
      {ConflictMessage: ""}
   )
);
```

This formula works by processing the offline data modifications from the JourneyChanges collection. When all the records have been processed, this collection will be empty.

As the formula processes the records, it stores working copies in a collection called JourneyChangesReview. For each record that was modified offline, the process retrieves the up-to-date record and stores the result in the JourneyChangesReview collection. Figure 16-11 shows the schema of this collection.

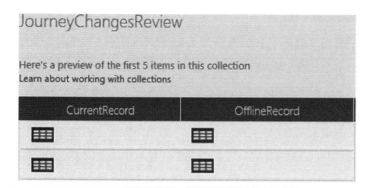

Figure 16-11. *The JourneyChangesReview collection*

If the process cannot locate an up-to-date record, this indicates that the source record was deleted. If the up-to-date record shows a different last modified datetime, this indicates that the source record was modified by another user. In both these cases, the formula stores the conflicting records in a collection called JourneyChangesConflict. Figure 16-12 shows the schema of this collection

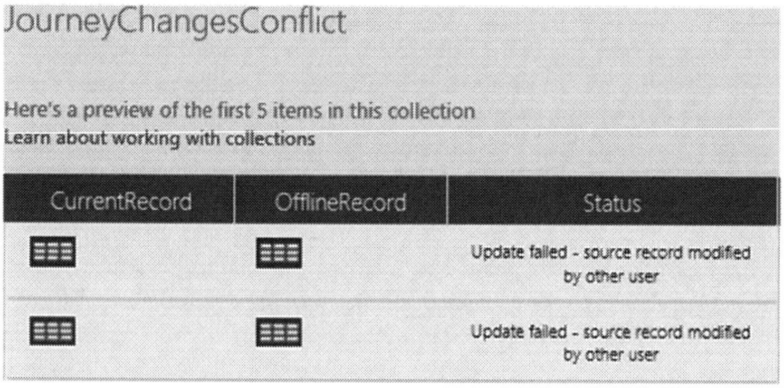

Figure 16-12. *The JourneyChangesConflict collection*

During this process, the formula will add the new records to the data source, and update the records that are not in a conflicting state. At the end of this process, we'll be left with only the records in the JourneyChangesConflict collection.

Disabling Icons and Buttons

With all the controls that are associated with the synchronization process, we can disable a control based on the state of the app. As we saw earlier in this book, the DisplayMode property provides the means to disable a control. This can take one of three values: Disabled, Edit, or View. The main difference between the View and Disabled modes is that in View mode, the control will be disabled but visually appear as though it's not disabled.

In our example, we can use the formula below to disable the synchronization button when the device is offline.

```
If(Connection.Connected,
    DisplayMode.Edit,
    DisplayMode.Disabled
)
```

Figure 16-13 shows how this appears in the designer.

Figure 16-13. *The DisplayMode property of a control*

Building the Conflict Resolution Screen

If the synchronization process returns records that are in a conflicted state, we can provide a means for users to resolve these data conflicts. This will allow users to retain the offline changes, or to revert to the most recent server version of the record. To build this feature, the first step is to create a screen and to add a gallery control. Name this control GalleryConflict and set the items property to JourneyChangesConflict. We can configure the gallery control to show the fields that we desire using the syntax OfflineRecord.<Fieldname>.

The next step is to add the controls that users can click to retain or discard the offline changes. Add two buttons to item of the gallery control, as shown in Figure 16-14.

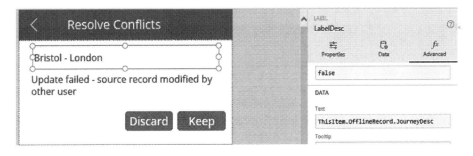

Figure 16-14. *Creating a conflict resolution screen*

The process to retain the server version of a record is to simply remove the offline version of the record. Here's the formula that we would add to the OnSelect property of the button to discard the offline change:

```
RemoveIf(JourneyChangesConflict,
        OfflineRecord.PrimaryId =
        GalleryConflict.Selected.OfflineRecord.PrimaryId)
```

331

It's useful to note that although the syntax beneath may seem valid, the formula will not remove the selected record. Therefore, it's better to use the former syntax that references the record to remove by primary id.

```
Remove(JourneyChangesConflict, GalleryConflict.Selected)
```

To retain the offline version of the record, we would patch the offline record to the data source. Here's the formula to add to the OnSelect property of the button to retain the offline version:

```
Patch(Journey,
      GalleryConflict.Selected.CurrentRecord,
      {JourneyDesc: GalleryConflict.Selected.OfflineRecord.JourneyDesc,
        StartDate: GalleryConflict.Selected.OfflineRecord.StartDate,
        MileageInMiles: GalleryConflict.Selected.OfflineRecord.MileageInMiles
      }
);
RemoveIf(JourneyChangesConflict,
            OfflineRecord.PrimaryId =
               GalleryConflict.Selected.OfflineRecord.PrimaryId
)
```

Finally, to enable users to open the conflict resolution screen, we can provide a button on the synchronization screen as shown in Figure 16-15. As this screenshot shows, we can write formula to disable or hide this button if there are no conflicting records.

Figure 16-15. *Opening the Conflict screen*

Summary

In this chapter, we examined what happens when an app becomes offline and we walked through the steps to develop an app that works offline.

When an auto-generated app becomes offline, the browse screen continues to show the data that existed before the app became offline. Not surprisingly, the refresh and save functions will not work. When an app is disconnected from the Internet, users can start apps that they have run previously. However, an auto-generated app that starts offline will not show any data. PowerApps does not automatically retain app data for future offline sessions.

To cater for these offline scenarios, PowerApps provides two useful features that can help. First, it provides the ability to save and retrieve data from files on the local device. Second, it can detect whether the device is connected to the Internet, and it can also detect if the connection is a metered connection.

To build an app that can edit, create, and delete records while offline, the general technique is to call a function called SaveData to cache the data to a local file. If a user starts an app while offline, we can call a function called LoadData function to load the contents of the local file into the app.

To support offline data modifications, we can save the offline data changes to a local collection and call the SaveData function to store the changes in a locale file. When the app becomes online again, we can patch the offline changes to the data store.

Providing offline editing capabilities is not a trivial task. The main difficulty is that other users can modify or delete source records during an offline session. During the data synchronization process, we need to check for conflicting records. We looked at how to write formula to detect data conflicts by examining the last modified time of the source record. In the event of a data conflict, we developed a process to move the offending record to a conflict collection. At the end of the synchronization process, the user can review the conflicting records and choose whether to apply or to discard the offline changes.

■ ■ ■

CHAPTER 17

Creating Custom Data Connectors

PowerApps supports a wide range of data sources through its built-in data connectors. But what if we want to access data sources that are not natively supported - is this possible? The answer is yes. By building a custom data connector, we can connect to any data source that is accessible through a web service. And if our required data source doesn't include a web service interface, we can overcome this by building our own web service (although this falls outside the scope of this book).

For non-developers, however, this topic can involve lots of confusing jargon. This includes words such as Restful services, JSON, and Swagger. To make this task as simple to understand as possible, we'll walk step by step through a practical example of how to call a postcode lookup service. The purpose of this exercise is to provide a means for users to enter data more quickly and easily. By the end of this chapter, you'll be able to apply the same techniques to add similar valuable features to your apps. The key features that we'll cover in this chapter will include the following:

- What we can accomplish through web services and how the Web works. This chapter explains the technical jargon that surrounds this topic and describes how web requests and responses work. This will provide useful background knowledge for later parts of this chapter and beyond.

- How to build a custom connector. We'll walk through the steps to build a custom connector. This will include how to create a web service description file and how to register the service with PowerApps.

- How to use a custom connector. This chapter will explain the most important task of all - how to call the web service from an app, and how to display the results on screen controls. We'll also find out how to save these results to a data source by adapting an auto-generated app.

What Can We Accomplish with Web Services?

There are thousands of web services that we can call. All modern social media sites provide access features through web services. These include sites such as Twitter, YouTube, and many more.

For business purposes, practical uses can include looking up stock prices, currency conversion rates, or converting IP addresses to locations. In fact, the list is almost endless. If you have some idea of what you want to do, you can probably find a service that fulfills your requirement by searching the web. If no such service exists, you can write your own web service, or find a developer to build a web service for you.

Overview of Steps

Here's an overview of the steps to call a web service from PowerApps. To accomplish this, we need to build a custom connector. This is a connector that we can use inside an app, just like the built connectors such as SharePoint, Excel, and SQL Server. Once we build a custom connector, we can add a data source in our app that uses the custom connector. We can then write formula that references the data source to call the web service methods.

Here's a high-level overview of how to make a web service available in PowerApps:

- Find or build a web service.

- Document the web service and produce a contract.

- Define a custom connector through the PowerApps admin website.

- From within an app, add a data source that's based on the custom connector.

- Write formula to call the web service.

The most difficult part of this process is to document the web service and to produce a contract. This part is crucial because the custom connector requires this to know exactly how a web service works and behaves. This includes details such as the address, method names, parameters, and return values.

To define this contract, there are two formats that we can use: The 'Open API' (also known as Swagger) format, or the Postman format. To create these files, we would use the Swagger and Postman programs. Both of these are fully fledged API documentation tools that provide a feature set way beyond what we need to create a custom connector.

Swagger is the de facto tool for documenting web services. With Swagger, we use a language called YAML (Yet Another Markup Language) to document a web service. Once this is complete, we save the output in JSON format because this is the format that PowerApps expects.

Because the target output format is JSON, we can avoid the use of Swagger and Postman and build a contract file directly with a text editor. For beginners, this can be easier because it avoids the need to register for a Swagger account and to learn how to use an additional tool. Later in this chapter, we'll look at Swagger and Postman but before that, we'll go through some basic web concepts such as HTTP requests, responses, and verbs. This is important because the configuration pages for a custom connector refer to these concepts.

Understanding How the Web Works

For non-developers, some of the terminology can be confusing. The documentation refers to REST, JSON, and other acronyms. Another term we frequently hear is 'RESTful API'. But what do all these terms mean?

REST stands for Representational State Transfer and it describes a common characteristic of a modern web service. With REST, every call to a web service must provide all the data that the service needs to fulfill a request. We can provide this data through arguments in the web address, or the body or headers of the request.

A purpose of REST is to avoid the storage of session data on a specific server and in doing so, it avoids the need to tie down the communication between a client and a service to a specific web server. This enables infrastructure teams to more easily load balance, replace, or scale up a service by adding more servers. When each request contains all the state data, it makes it possible to cache results on any intermediary device between the client and server, and this can help speed up performance.

API stands for application programming interface. Through an API, one system can call functionality or access data from another system through programmatic means. Therefore, a RESTful API describes something that we can use to access a system through web calls that are REST based.

Another aim of a REST service is to provide addresses that are descriptive and understandable. For example, here's the format of a typical REST-based URL.

```
http://myserver.com/journeys/item/1729
```

Due to the format of this URL, we can guess that the purpose of this request is to return a journey record that matches journey id 1729.

Making HTTP Web Requests

Web devices communicate with web servers through HTTP (Hypertext Transfer Protocol). With this protocol, the communication between a client device and a server consists of isolated requests and responses. When a client requires data from a web server, it makes a request to the server. The server replies with a response and at this point, the communication finishes. A web session between a device and a server consists of a series of isolated requests and responses.

Every HTTP request includes a verb. This describes the type of request that the client is making and it can be one of four types: GET, POST, PUT, and DELETE.

In all instances where a client wants to retrieve data from a server, it issues an HTTP request with the GET verb. The client can provide arguments through the path, like so. In this example, the URL specifies a journey id of 1729.

```
http://myserver.com/journeys/item/1729
```

HTTP requests can also specify arguments through query string parameters. Here's the format of a URL that uses a query string parameter. The parameters values appear after the ? symbol in the address, and consist of name-value pairs that are separated with the = sign.

```
http://myserver.com/journeys.aspx?id=1729
```

When a client calls a web service to add or submit data, it typically issues an HTTP request with the POST verb. The data that the client posts will be attached to the body of the request.

Understanding HTTP Responses

A web server replies to HTTP requests with responses that include a status code. Perhaps the most common status code that people are aware of is the 404 status code. A web server returns this status code when the user requests a page that doesn't exist. Another status code is 500, and this is the error code that a server returns when it encounters an error that the caller cannot resolve.

When we call a web service, the status code that we want to receive is 200. This is the status code that indicates success. Another success code is 201, and this is a code that indicates a successful POST or a PUT request.

The response from a web service method might include data that will usually be in XML or JSON format. Modern web services tend to return data in JSON format because this format is more lightweight. Listing 17-1 shows an example of a successful HTTP response that includes JSON data.

Listing 17-1. How a 200 response with JSON data looks like

```
200 OK
Content-Type: application/json

{
  "post code": "90210",
  "country": "United States",
  "country abbreviation": "US",
  "places": [
    {
      "place name": "Beverly Hills",
      "longitude": "-118.4065",
      "state": "California",
      "state abbreviation": "CA",
      "latitude": "34.0901"
    }
  ]
}
```

This structure will look familiar because we've seen this notation used throughout this book. JSON encloses a data set in curly brackets and separates field items with commas. For each field item, JSON separates the field name from the field value with a colon.

In contrast, XML format wraps data items with start and end tags. In general, it takes more data to express the same thing with XML and this is one reason why JSON is the format of choice for web services.

Documenting a Web Service

Now that we have an understanding of web protocols, let's walk through the process of building a custom connector that connects to a postal code lookup web service.

The first step is to find a web service that provides this functionality. The simplest way to find a service is to carry out a web search on the phrase 'zipcode api'. This type of search returns numerous web services that we can use. This example uses a service called Zippoptam.us, but we can just as easily use any other web service.

Figure 17-1 shows the home page of this service. The description here provides simple instructions on how to call this service. For example, to search for the zipcode '90210', we would use the following web address:

```
http://api.zippopotam.us/us/90210
```

Figure 17-1. Zippopotam home page

To test this service, Figure 17-2 shows the response when we enter this address into a web browser. As this screenshot shows, the service returns a result in JSON format.

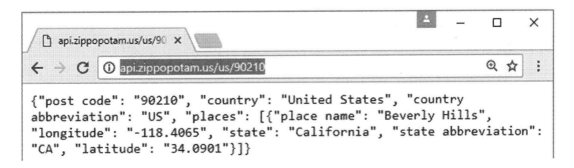

Figure 17-2. The JSON result from the Zippopotam service

Creating a Web Service Description

The next step is to build a document or contract that describes the Zippopotam web service. This is important because it enables PowerApps to understand the methods, parameters, and return values of the service.

For this example, we'll produce an 'Open API' document in JSON format. We'll examine two tools that can help us document web APIs: Postman and Swagger.

Using Postman

Postman is a desktop program that runs on Windows and Mac. To use Postman, we first need to download and install the application. The web address for Postman is: `https://www.getpostman.com/`

Figure 17-3 shows a screenshot of the app.

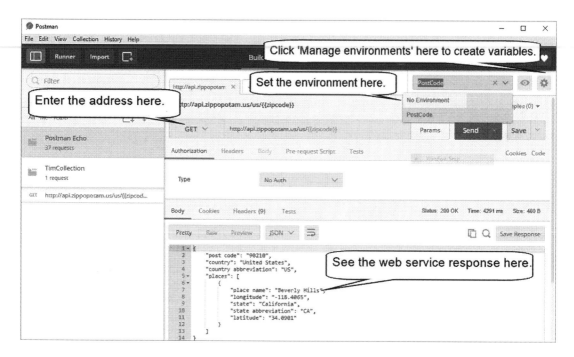

Figure 17-3. *The Postman app*

The best approach with Postman is to create an environment in which to work in. An environment provides a container where we can define variables. We can use the designer to call the web methods and to see the response of the server. Variables enable us to provide parameter values for web requests.

The save feature in Postman saves a collection of files where each file represents a web request. PowerApps can natively create a custom connector based on a collection of Postman files.

Using Swagger

Unlike Postman, Swagger is a web-based tool. To use Swagger, we first need to visit the Swagger website and to create an account. Swagger offers a range of subscription plans that includes a free individual plan. This free plan provides enough functionality to document a web service for use with PowerApps. Here's the website for Swagger:

`https://app.swaggerhub.com/`

To use Swagger, create an account, log in, and select the option to 'Start a new API project.' Swagger provides the option to create a project based on a template. A helpful template is the PetStore API template. This template is designed for learning purposes and demonstrates lots of useful syntax.

For basic purposes, the easiest option is to build a project based on a blank template. Once we create a project, we can use the left-hand section to define our web service. Figure 17-4 shows the YAML that we would use to describe the postcode lookup service.

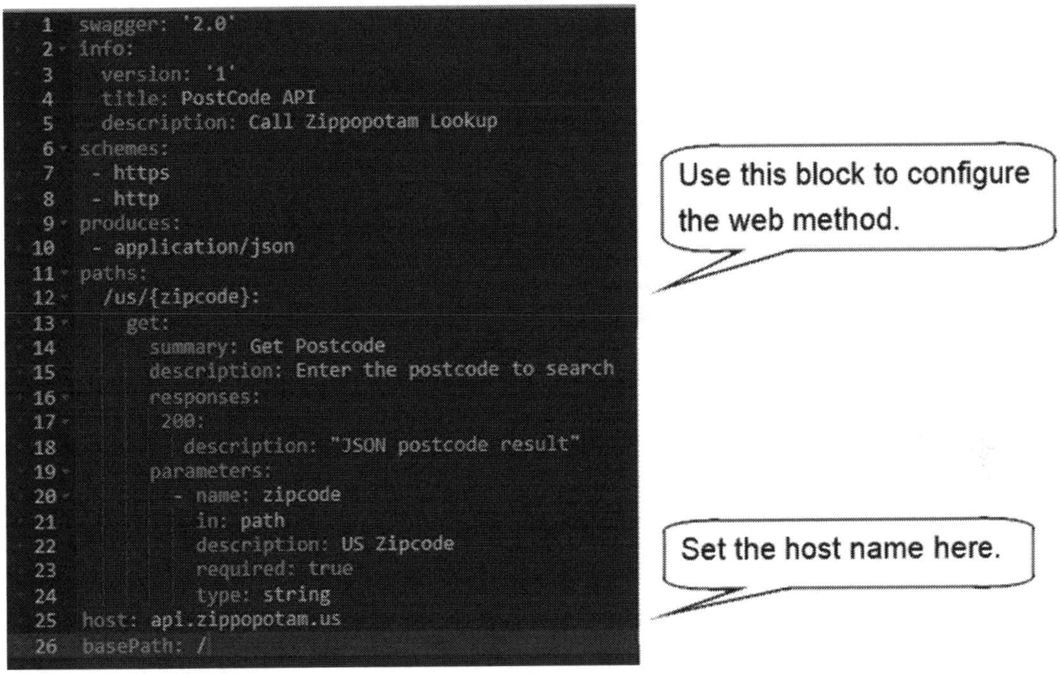

```yaml
1   swagger: '2.0'
2 ▾ info:
3     version: '1'
4     title: PostCode API
5     description: Call Zippopotam Lookup
6 ▾ schemes:
7     - https
8     - http
9 ▾ produces:
10    - application/json
11 ▾ paths:
12 ▾   /us/{zipcode}:
13 ▾     get:
14         summary: Get Postcode
15         description: Enter the postcode to search
16 ▾       responses:
17 ▾         200:
18             description: "JSON postcode result"
19 ▾       parameters:
20 ▾         - name: zipcode
21             in: path
22             description: US Zipcode
23             required: true
24             type: string
25 host: api.zippopotam.us
26 basePath: /
```

> Use this block to configure the web method.

> Set the host name here.

Figure 17-4. *Creating YAML*

The code in this illustration provides a template that we can use to describe simple web services. To reuse this YAML for a different web service, the most crucial parts to modify are the host and basePath settings. These define the base URL for the service.

The paths entry that begins on line 12 defines the web method that returns an address based on a zipcode. Within a path definition, we can define parameter placeholders by enclosing the parameter names in curly brackets (for example, /us/{zipcode}).

Within the designer, we can use the feature in the right-hand section to call our web service and to view the result from the server, as shown in Figure 17-5. Once we complete our work in Swagger, the final step is to click the icon in the top-right section to download the document in JSON format.

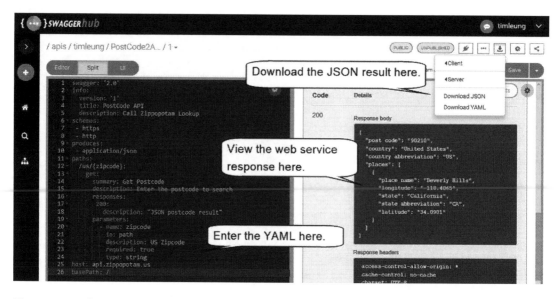

Figure 17-5. *The Swagger designer*

Examining an Open API Document

Listing 17-2 shows the JSON output that Swagger produces. The structure of this code looks very similar to the YAML that we entered into Swagger.

This listing is useful because we can use it as a template to define other web services. Just as before, the crucial sections are the host and the paths settings. We can import this JSON content directly into PowerApps when we create our custom connector. Therefore, this is the code that we would author manually if we were to choose not to use Swagger or Postman.

Listing 17-2. JSON Output

```
{
  "swagger": "2.0",
  "info": {
    "version": "1",
    "title": "PostCode API",
    "description": "Call Zippopotam Lookup"
  },
  "schemes": [ "https", "http" ],
  "produces": [ "application/json" ],
  "paths": {
    "/us/{zipcode}": {
      "get": {
        "summary": "Get Postcode",
        "description": "Enter the postcode to search",
        "responses": { "200": { "description": "JSON postcode result" } },
```

```
      "parameters": [
        {
          "name": "zipcode",
          "in": "path",
          "description": "US Zipcode",
          "required": true,
          "type": "string"
        }
      ]
    }
  }
},
"host": "api.zippopotam.us",
"basePath": "/"
}
```

Creating a Custom Connector

Now that we've built an Open API document, the difficult part is over. The next step is to create a custom connector and we can do this easily through the PowerApps admin site. From the admin site, click the Connectors menu item on the left-hand menu and click the 'Manage custom connectors' item that appears in the top menu. When the Custom connectors screen opens, click the 'Create Custom Connector' item.

The page to create a custom connector consists of four sections: general, security, definition, and test. Figure 17-6 shows the first screen, the general screen. To upload our Open API file, select the 'Upload an OpenAPI file' radio option and click the file browse button to select the file. Other options include the ability to specify an OpenAPI URL or to upload a Postman collection.

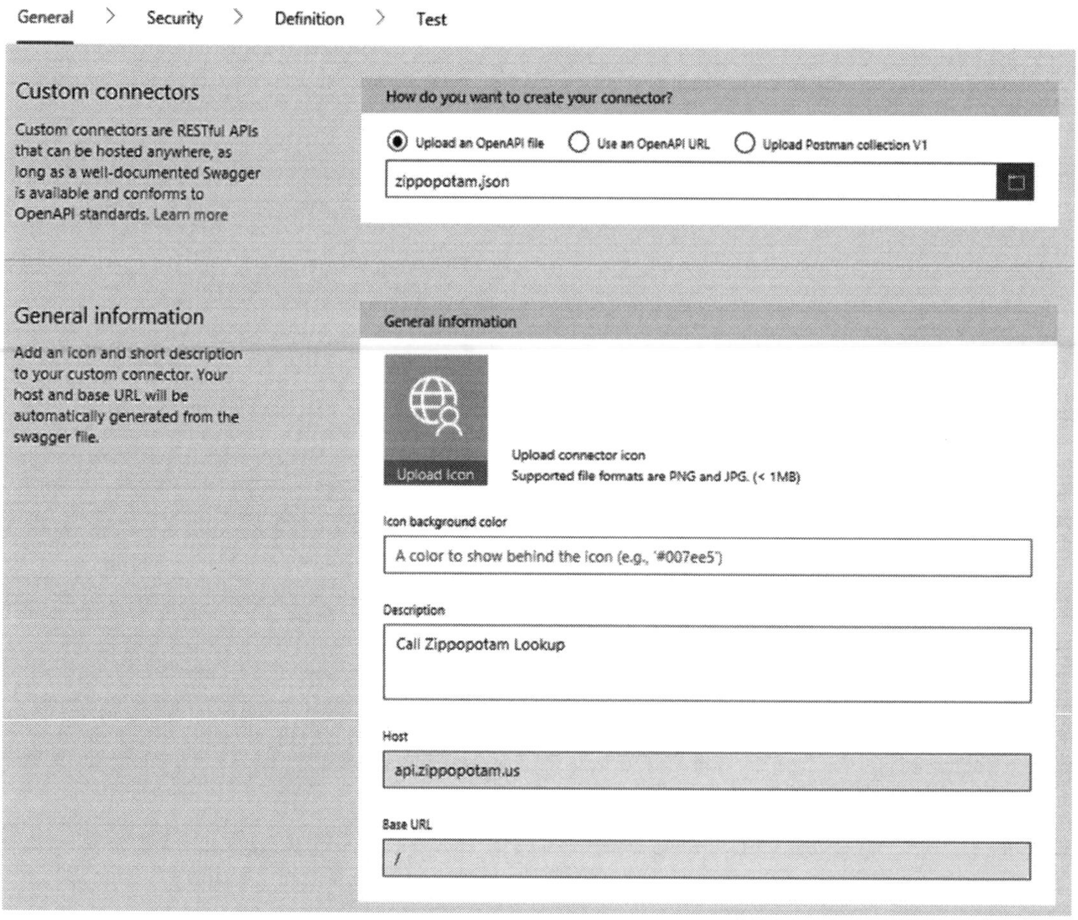

General > Security > Definition > Test

Custom connectors

Custom connectors are RESTful APIs that can be hosted anywhere, as long as a well-documented Swagger is available and conforms to OpenAPI standards. Learn more

How do you want to create your connector?

(•) Upload an OpenAPI file   ( ) Use an OpenAPI URL   ( ) Upload Postman collection V1

zippopotam.json

General information

Add an icon and short description to your custom connector. Your host and base URL will be automatically generated from the swagger file.

General information

Upload icon

Upload connector icon
Supported file formats are PNG and JPG. (< 1MB)

Icon background color

A color to show behind the icon (e.g., '#007ee5')

Description

Call Zippopotam Lookup

Host

api.zippopotam.us

Base URL

/

Figure 17-6. *Creating a custom connector*

Creating a custom connector with one of these options will populate the general section in the lower part of the screen. This section includes the host and base URL settings. These two settings are not editable, but it's crucial that these settings are correct. If not, we need to correct the entries in the OpenAPI file and re-upload the file through this screen.

The next screen enables us to configure the security of the web service. The Zippopotam web service does not require authentication, but many other web services do. To connect to a web service that requires authentication, use the settings that are shown in Figure 17-7. This screenshot shows the text boxes to enter a username and password with basic authentication.

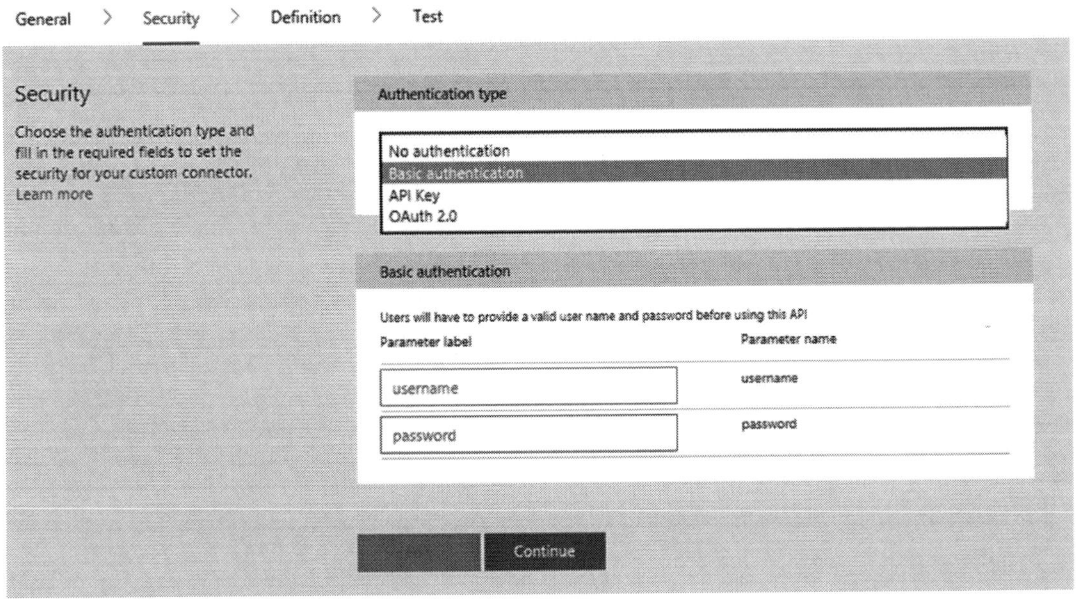

General > Security > Definition > Test

Security

Choose the authentication type and fill in the required fields to set the security for your custom connector. Learn more

Authentication type

No authentication
Basic authentication
API Key
OAuth 2.0

Basic authentication

Users will have to provide a valid user name and password before using this API

Parameter label

Parameter name

username	username
password	password

Continue

Figure 17-7. Configuring authentication

The next page enables us to define the web service method. The settings here derive their values from the contents of the Open API file that we uploaded. The URL setting defines the endpoint of the web service. This setting is not editable, but it's very important to make sure it is correct. The combined values of the host, root path, and URL settings should make up the correct web service address.

The parameters from the Open API file appear lower down in the screen. Figure 17-8 shows the zipcode parameter. We can click this entry to view and to further configure the parameter.

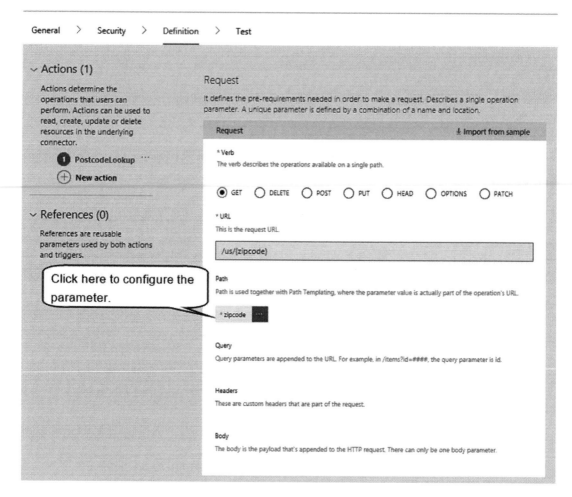

Figure 17-8. *Configuring the web service definition*

The next step is to define the JSON result that the web service returns. This enables PowerApps to understand the structure of the data and to provide suitable IntelliSense in the formula bar. Click the '200' response entry that appears lower in the page. In the page that opens, click the 'import from sample' button to reveal the panel that's shown in Figure 17-9.

Figure 17-9. *Configuring the web service response*

Because our web service returns JSON, enter `'content-type application/json'` into the headers text box. For the body section, enter JSON data that matches the data structure that the web service returns. We can call the web service from a browser and paste the output into this box. When we click the import button, the output data fields from the web service will appear, as shown in Figure 17-10.

Response   ⬇ Import from sample

* Name

200

Headers
These are custom headers that are part of the response.

NAME	DESCRIPTION	TYPE
Content-Type	Content-Type	string ⌄

References Used
The following are the references used by this entity

The output data fields appear here.

Body
The payload that is available on the response. These are the tokens that will show up as the outputs in designer.

| country ··· | country abbreviation ··· | latitude ··· | longitude ··· | place name ··· |

| state ··· | state abbreviation ··· | post code ··· |

Figure 17-10. *Configuring the web service response*

The next page enables us to test the connector. If the test succeeds, a success message appears, as shown in Figure 17-11. If the test fails, it can be difficult to diagnose the exact cause because the error message that comes back is not particularly helpful. In such cases, the first thing to check are the host and URL values. Incorrect values here are a likely cause of errors.

Figure 17-11. *Testing the web service method*

Using the Custom Connector

Now that we've added our custom connector, we can use it in our apps. The connector will appear in the add data source menu as shown in Figure 17-12. Once we add a data source, we can use it in our formulas.

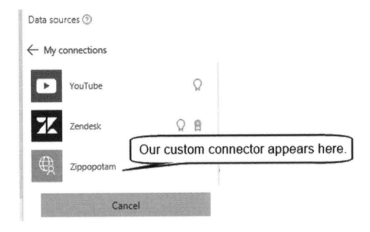

Figure 17-12. *Adding a data source for a custom connector*

To show how to populate data controls on a screen with results from a web service, here's how to adapt the edit screen from an auto-generated app. We'll add a text box for users to enter a ZIP code and a button that retrieves the associated data from the Zippopotam service.

In this demonstration, we'll use an app that's based on the location table from Chapter 11. The button will retrieve the longitude and latitude values for the zipcode, and populate the text input controls on the form. An important feature of this modification is that it retains the save feature of the form. As a reminder, Figure 17-13 shows the structure of the location table.

Figure 17-13. *Layout of the location table*

To create this example, the first step is to build an auto-generated app that's based on this data structure. On the edit screen, add a card and on this card, insert a text input control called TextinputZipcode. Next, add a button called GetLocation and set the OnSelect property of the button to the formula beneath:

```
UpdateContext(
    {AddressResult: PostCodeAPI.Zippopotam(TextinputZipcode.Text)}
)
```

Unlock the card for the longitude field and change the default property of the text input control to the formula shown beneath:

```
If(IsBlank(First(AddressResult.places).longitude),
    Parent.Default,
    First(AddressResult.places).longitude
)
```

349

The purpose of this formula is to show the longitude value that the user obtains by clicking the GetLocation button. If this value is blank, the formula returns the existing longitude value for the record.

The next step is to modify the update property of the card so that it updates the data source with the desired value. Select the card for the longitude field and set the Update property to the same formula, as shown beneath:

```
If(IsBlank(First(AddressResult.places).longitude),
    Parent.Default,
    First(AddressResult.places).longitude
)
```

Now repeat the same process for the latitude values. Set the default property of the latitude text input control, and then update the property of the latitude card to the formula shown beneath.

```
If(IsBlank(First(AddressResult.places).latitude),
    Parent.Default,
    First(AddressResult.places).latitude
)
```

The final step is to clear the longitude and latitude values that are associated with the AddressResult variable when the user leaves the screen. Here's the formula to add to the OnHidden property of the screen.

```
UpdateContext({AddressResult:
{
  places: [
    {
      longitude: "",
      latitude: ""
    }
  ]
}
})
```

Note that it's not possible to set a variable to a null value using the syntax that's shown below. This is the reason why it's necessary to use the verbose syntax that is shown above to set the AddressResult variable to a blank value.

```
UpdateContext({AddressResult: Blank})
```

Figure 17-14 shows the layout of the screen in the designer. At this stage, we can run our app and save the updated location details to the data store.

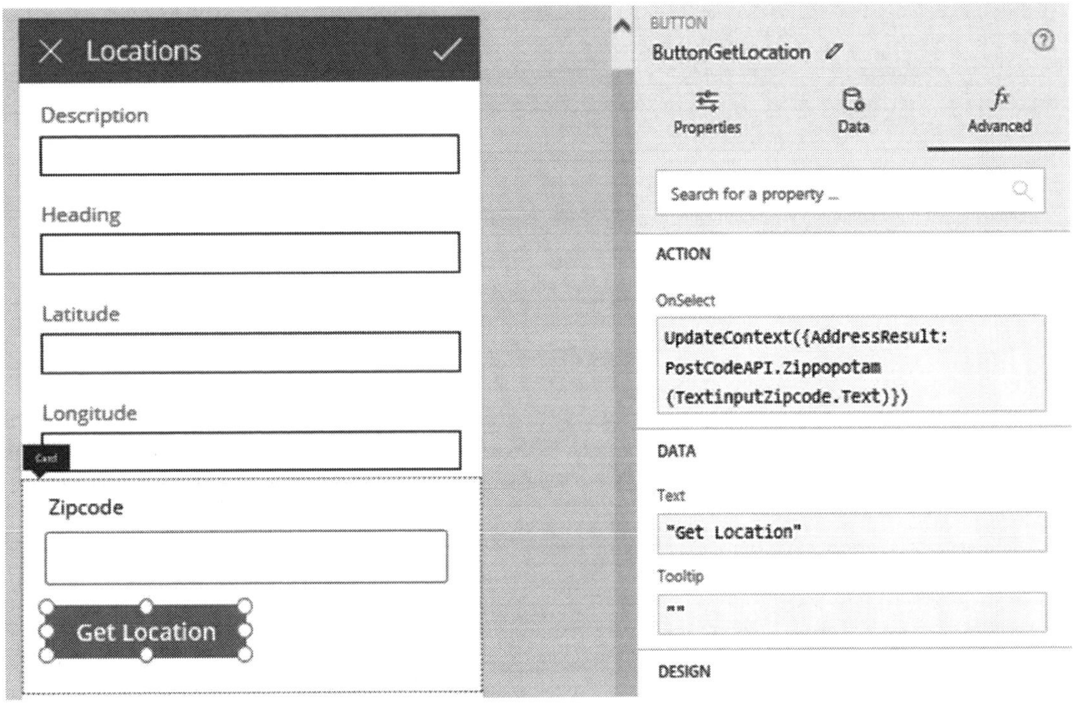

Figure 17-14. *Layout of the sample screen*

Summary

In this chapter, we looked at how to build a custom connector. This enables apps to call web services. This provides an enormous benefit because it extends widely the systems and data sources that apps can integrate with. Examples of what we can do include connecting to social media sites, retrieving stock prices, or converting currency values.

After we build or find a web service that we want to use, the first step is to document the web service and to produce a contract. Two tools that we can use to do this are Swagger and Postman. With Swagger, we can generate an Open API file in JSON format that describes the web service. The contents of this file would include the address, expected parameters, and expected output of web methods.

Once we produce this contract, we can upload it through the PowerApps admin website and use it to create a custom connector. During this stage, we can configure authentication settings, the parameters of web methods, and the data structures that they return. When this process is complete, we can use the connector to add a data source to an app, and write formula to call the web method.

To show how to save the results from a web service, we adapted the edit screen from an auto-generated app. We saved the result of the web service to a local variable and modified the default and update properties of the form cards to refer to the variable values.

To create custom connectors, it's useful to understand the technology behind web services. To call a web method, a client device uses HTTP to communicate with a server. To retrieve data, it issues an HTTP request to the server. The response from the server can include a payload of data, and a common format for the return data is JSON. HTTP responses include a status code and the code that we generally seek is 200 - this is the code that indicates success.

■ ■ ■

Data Models

The built-in standard entities in the CDS support many common business scenarios. However, it can often be difficult to find the entities to cater to a specific requirement because there are more than 90 standard entities, and it's difficult to know where to start. To bring some clarify, this appendix offers an overview of the standard entities and provides a summary of the names, fields, and relations between the entities.

The final part of this appendix summarizes the structure of the example journey app that we've seen throughout this book.

Overview of CDS Entities

The standard entities are organized into the eight groups: Foundation, Person, Group, Sales, Customer Service, Organization, Purchase, and Human Resources. To begin this section, we'll examine the purpose and relationships between the entities in each group.

Foundation Entities

The foundation entities allow us to store fundamental details about a business. This group contains seven entities, which are Business unit, Business unit contact, Cost center, Product, Product category, Product category assignment, and Unit of measure conversion.

Figure A-1 shows the relationships between these entities, and it also illustrates relationships with entities that fall outside of this group. This diagram indicates the direction of the one-to-many relationship between pairs of entities.

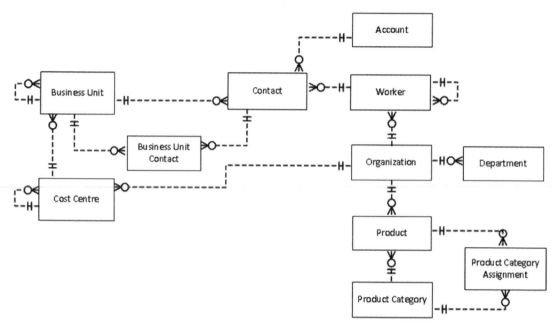

Figure A-1. *Foundation Entities*

The business unit, cost center, and organization entities store the contact details and descriptions for each record. A notable entity is the product entity. This entity stores the description, price, and image for each record. The product entity includes a lookup field that stores the product category for each record. For additional flexibility, we can choose not to use this lookup field and to use the Product category assignment entity instead. This enables us to set multiple product categories for each product record, as shown in Figure A-1. The same concept applies to the Contact and Business unit entities. We can associate a contact with a single business unit, or alternatively, associate a contact with multiple business units with the help of the Business Unit Contact entity.

Another notable feature is that for each business unit and cost center record, we can associate the record with a parent record. This theme of self-joins and many-to-many relationships extends throughout many of the entities in the CDS.

Person Entities

The entities in the person group store details about people. There are eight entities in this group, which include Alumnus, Application user, Application user contact, Constituent, Contact, Person, Tenant, and Worker.

These entities are very similar and store details such as the name, address, and social media identifiers for each record. The Application user entity includes a field that stores the application id of a user. This field is perfect for storing the Office 365 GUID of a user.

The worker entity provides fields to store the hire date and the manager of the worker. Most of the entities in the person group include fields to store taxation details. The exceptions are the contact, alumnus, and application user entities.

One highlight of the contact entity is that it includes a marital status field. None of the other entities provide this field.

As Figure A-2 shows, we can associate an application user record with multiple contact records though the help of the Application user contact entity.

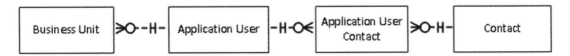

Figure A-2. *Person Entities*

Group Entities

There are entities that we can use to define groups of people. This includes the Application User Group, Team, Household, and Family entities. These entities include fields that store the description and primary contact details of the group.

The Person entity stores details about individuals, and we can use the Team Member, Household Member, and Family Member entities to associate single individuals with multiple teams, households, or families. Figure A-3 illustrates the relationships between these entities.

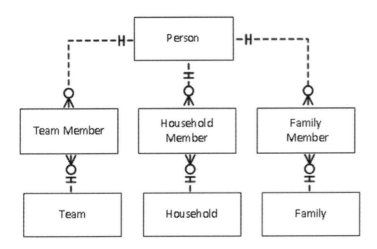

Figure A-3. *Group Entities*

Sales Entities

The sales group provides entities to help build apps for sales purposes. We can use the entities in this group to record the details of accounts, leads, opportunities, competitors, and orders.

The Account entity stores account information that includes the name, shipping address, payment terms, and credit limit of each account. The account entity plays a pivotal role and many other entities refer to this entity. This includes entities that record sales details such as leads, orders, case management, quotations, and invoices. Figure A-4 illustrates the main entities that relate to the account entity. With the help of these entities, we can associate accounts with the multiple organizations using the Account Group entity. We can use the Account Contact entity to associate a contact with multiple accounts.

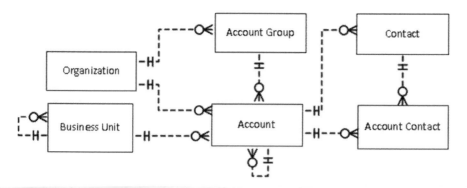

Figure A-4. *Account Entities*

Another notable feature about the Account entity is that it includes a lookup field to store the parent account for each record.

Figure A-5 shows the entities that we can use to store leads, opportunities, and competitors.

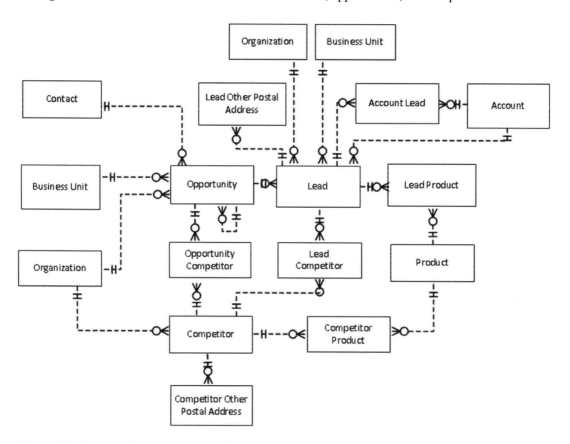

Figure A-5. *Opportunities, Competitor, and Lead Entities*

Figure A-6 shows the entities that store quotation details, and Figure A-7 shows the entities that store sales invoice details.

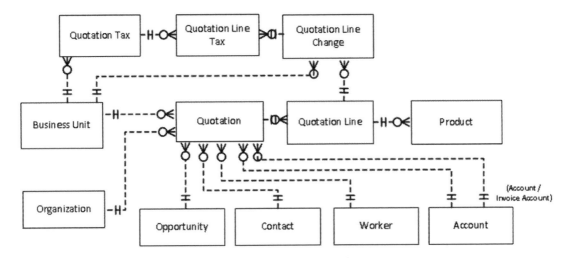

Figure A-6. *Quotation Entities*

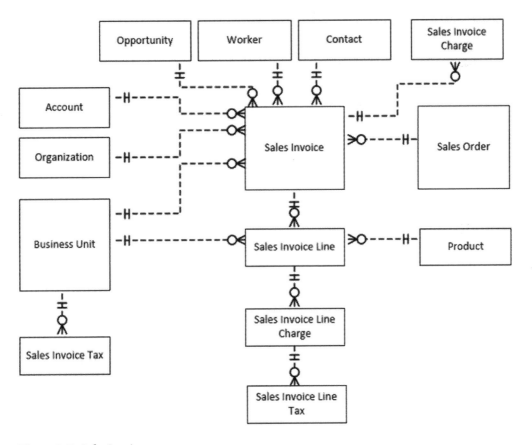

Figure A-7. *Sales Invoice*

Figure A-8 shows the entities that store sales order details.

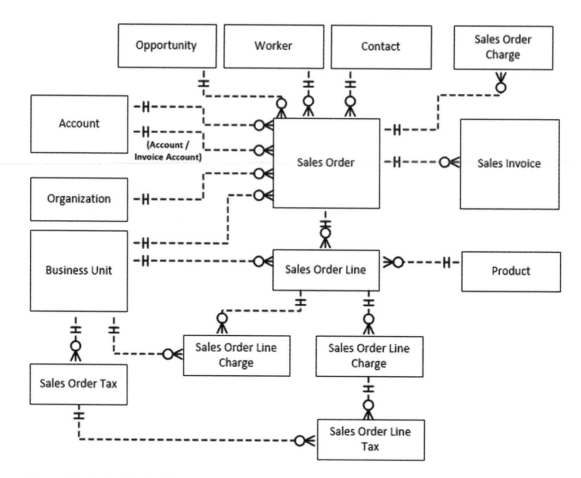

Figure A-8. *Sales Order Entities*

Purchase Entities

The purchase group provides entities to help build apps for purchasing operations. We can use the entities in this group to record vendors, purchase orders, and invoices from vendors. Figure A-9 shows the main entities that are related to the Vendor entity.

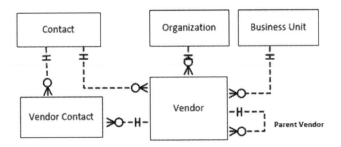

Figure A-9. *Vendor Entities*

Figure A-10 shows the entities that relate to purchase orders, while Figure A-11 shows the entities that relate to vendor invoices.

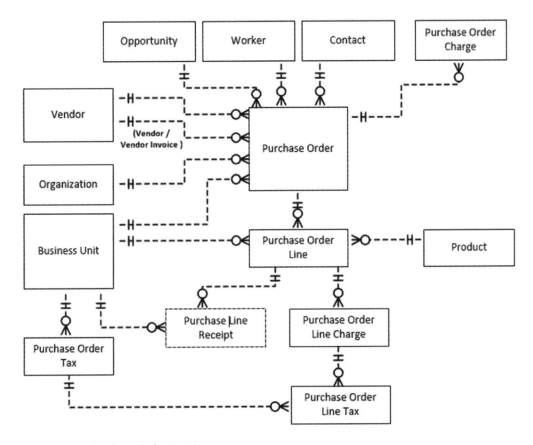

Figure A-10. *Purchase Order Entities*

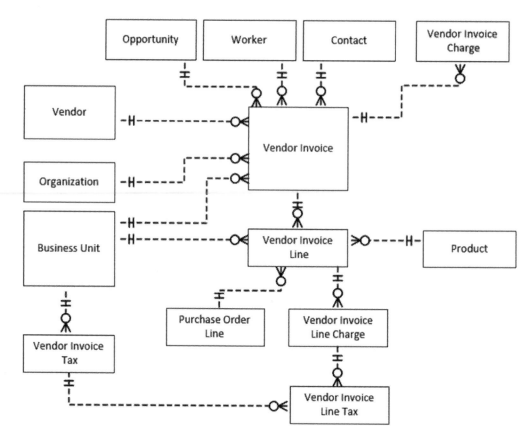

Figure A-11. *Vendor Invoice Entities*

Customer Service Entities

The customer service group provides entities to help build apps for customer service purposes. Figure A-12 shows the entities in the customer services group. For each case record, we can create multiple case activity records. We can use the KB Article entity to store knowledgebase records, and we can associate multiple KB Articles with each Case Activity record with the use of the Case Activity KB Article entity.

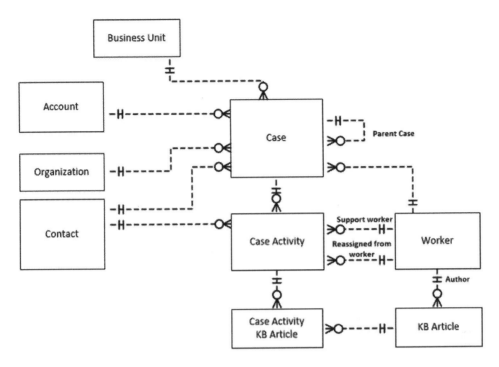

Figure A-12. *Customer Service Entities*

Human Resources Entities

The human resources group provides entities to help build apps to support human resource departments. Figure A-13 shows the entities in this group. We can use the entities in this group to store leave request details, and details about jobs, workers, and positions.

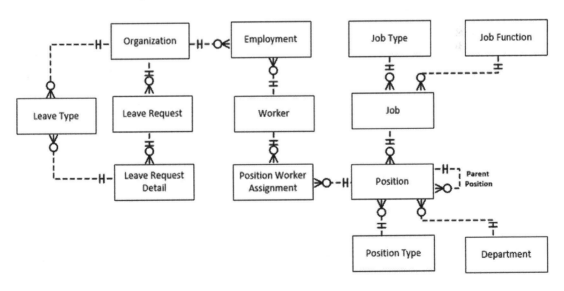

Figure A-13. *Human Resources Entities*

CDS Field Names

This final part of this appendix lists the fields in each standard entity.

Foundation Entities

Listing A-1 shows the fields for each entity in the foundation group.

Listing A-1. Foundation Entities

```
Business Unit ( BusinessUnitId, Costcenter_CostcenterId, Description, EmailAlternate,
EmailPrimary, Fullname, Image, IsDefaultForOrganization, IsEmailContactAllowed,
IsPhoneContactAllowed, MailingPostalAddress, OfficeGraphIdentifier, Organization_
OrganizationId, OrganizationName, OtherPostalAddress, OwnedByUser, ParentBusinessUnit_
BusinessUnitId, PartyType, Phone01, Phone02, Phone03, PhonePrimary, SatoriId,
ShippingPostalAddress, Source, Status, TaxIdentificationIssuer, TaxIdentificationNumber,
WebsiteURL)

Business Unit Contact (BusinessUnit_BusinessUnitId, Contact_ContactId, Datasource,
Description, OwnedByUser)

Cost Center (CostcenterId, Description, Name, Organization_OrganizationId, OwnedByUser,
Parentcostcenter_Costcenterid)

Product (ProductId, DefaultBuyingUnitOfMeasure, DefaultSellingQuantity,
DefaultStockingUnitOfMeasure, Description, Image, IsStocked, Name, Organization_
OrganizationId, OwnedByUser, Productcategory_CategoryId, Producttype, SellingUnitprice,
StandardCostAmount, Status, UnitOfMeasureScale)

Product Category (CategoryId, Description, Name, Organization_OrganizationId, OwnedByUser,
Parentprodcutcategory_Categoryid)

Product Category Assignment (Product_ProductId, Productcategory_CategoryId, OwnedByUser)

Unit of measure conversion (FromUnitOfMeasure, ToUnitOfMeasure, FromToConversionRate,
OwnedByUser, ToFromConversionRate)
```

Person Entities

Listing A-2 shows the fields for each entity in the person group.

Listing A-2. Person Entities

```
Alumnus (AlumnusId, BirthDate, BusinessPostalAddress, Description, EmailAlternate,
EmailPrimary, FacebookIdentity, Fullname, Gender, Generation, GraduationClass,
GraduationDate, HomePostalAddress, Image, IsEmailContactAllowed, IsPhoneContactAllowed,
LinkedinIdentity, Name, OfficeGraphIdentifier, OwnedByUser, PartyType, PhoneBusiness,
PhoneCell, PhoneHome, PhonePrimary, Profession, ShippingPostalAddress, SocialNetwork01,
SocialNetwork02, SocialNetworkIdentity01, SocialNetworkIdentity02, Source, Status,
TwitterIdentity, WebsiteURL)
```

Application User (AaduseroId, ApplicationuserId, BirthDate, BusinessPostalAddress, BusinessUnit_BusinessUnitId, Description, EmailAlternate, EmailPrimary, FacebookIdentity, Fullname, Gender, Generation, HomePostalAddress, IsAdmin, IsEmailContactAllowed, IsPhoneContactAllowed, LinkedinIdentity, Name, OfficeGraphIdentifier, OwnedByUser, PartyType, PhoneBusiness, PhoneCell, PhoneHome, PhonePrimary, Profession, ShippingPostalAddress, SocialNetwork01, SocialNetwork02, SocialNetworkIdentity01, SocialNetworkIdentity02, Source, Status, TwitterIdentity, WebsiteURL)

Application User Contact (Applicationuser_AaduseroId, Contact_ContactId, Datasource, Description, IsOwner, OwnedByUser)

Constituent (ConstituentId, BirthDate, BusinessPostalAddress, Description, EmailAlternate, EmailPrimary, FacebookIdentity, Fullname, Gender, Generation, HomePostalAddress, Image, IsEmailContactAllowed, IsPhoneContactAllowed, IsSecurityPrincipal, LinkedinIdentity, Name, OfficeGraphIdentifier, OwnedByUser, PartyType, PhoneBusiness, PhoneCell, PhoneHome, PhonePrimary, Profession, SatoriId, ShippingPostalAddress, SocialNetwork01, SocialNetwork02, SocialNetworkIdentity01, SocialNetworkIdentity02, Source, Status, TaxIdentificationIssuer, TaxIdentificationNumber, TwitterIdentity, WebsiteURL)

Contact (ContactId, BirthDate, BusinessPostalAddress, BusinessUnit_BusinessUnitId, Department, Description, EmailAlternate, EmailPrimary, FacebookIdentity, Fullname, Gender, Generation, Governmentidentifier, HomePostalAddress, Image, IsEmailContactAllowed, IsPhoneContactAllowed, IsPostalMailAllowed, LinkedinIdentity, MaritalStatus, Name, OfficeGraphIdentifier, Organization_OrganizationId, OwnedByUser, PartyType, Personinformation, PhoneBusiness, PhoneCell, PhoneHome, PhonePrimary, Primaryaccount_AccountId, Primaryaccountrole, Profession, ShippingPostalAddress, SocialNetwork01, SocialNetwork02, SocialNetworkIdentity01, SocialNetworkIdentity02, Source, Status, TwitterIdentity, WebsiteURL, WorkerResponsible_WorkerId)

Fan (FanId, BirthDate, BusinessPostalAddress, Description, EmailAlternate, EmailPrimary, FacebookIdentity, FanSince, FavoritePlayer, Fullname, Gender, Generation, HomePostalAddress, Image, IsEmailContactAllowed, IsPhoneContactAllowed, IsSecurityPrincipal, LinkedinIdentity, Name, OfficeGraphIdentifier, OwnedByUser, PartyType, PhoneBusiness, PhoneCell, PhoneHome, PhonePrimary, Profession, SatoriId, ShippingPostalAddress, SocialNetwork01, SocialNetwork02, SocialNetworkIdentity01, SocialNetworkIdentity02, Source, Status, TaxIdentificationIssuer, TaxIdentificationNumber, TwitterIdentity, WebsiteURL)

Person (PersonId, BirthDate, Description, EmailAlternate, EmailPrimary, FacebookIdentity, Fullname, Gender, Generation, Image, IsEmailContactAllowed, IsPhoneContactAllowed, IsSecurityPrincipal, Linkedinapiurl, LinkedinIdentity, MailingPostalAddress, Name, OfficeGraphIdentifier, OtherPostalAddress, OwnedByUser, PartyType, Phone01, Phone02, Phone03, PhonePrimary, Profession, SatoriId, ShippingPostalAddress, SocialNetwork01, SocialNetwork02, SocialNetworkIdentity01, SocialNetworkIdentity02, Source, Status, TaxIdentificationIssuer, TaxIdentificationNumber, TwitterIdentity, WebsiteURL)

Tenant (TenantId, BirthDate, BusinessPostalAddress, Description, EmailAlternate, EmailPrimary, FacebookIdentity, Fullname, Gender, Generation, HomePostalAddress, Image, IsEmailContactAllowed, IsPhoneContactAllowed, IsSecurityPrincipal, LinkedinIdentity, OfficeGraphIdentifier, OwnedByUser, PartyType, PersoName, PhoneBusiness, PhoneCell, PhoneHome, PhonePrimary, Profession, SatoriId, ShippingPostalAddress, SocialNetwork01,

SocialNetwork02, SocialNetworkIdentity01, SocialNetworkIdentity02, Source, Status, TaxIdentificationIssuer, TaxIdentificationNumber, TwitterIdentity, WebsiteURL)

Worker (WorkerId, Alias, BirthDate, Building, BusinessPostalAddress, BusinessUnit_ BusinessUnitId, Description, EmailAlternate, EmailPrimary, Externalreference, FacebookIdentity, Fullname, Gender, Generation, HomePostalAddress, Image, IsEmailContactAllowed, IsPhoneContactAllowed, LinkedinApiUrl, LinkedinIdentity, Manager_ WorkerId, Name, OfficeGraphIdentifier, Organization_OrganizationId, OriginalHireDate, OwnedByUser, PartyType, PhoneBusiness, PhoneCell, PhoneHome, PhonePrimary, Profession, Room, SatoriId, ShippingPostalAddress, SocialNetwork01, SocialNetwork02, SocialNetworkIdentity01, SocialNetworkIdentity02, Source, Status, TaxIdentificationIssuer, TaxIdentificationNumber, TwitterIdentity, Type, WebsiteURL)

Group Entities

Listing A-3 shows the fields for each group entity.

Listing A-3. Group Entities

Application User Group (ApplicationUserGroupId, BusinessUnit_BusinessUnitId, Description, EmailAlternate, EmailPrimary, Fullname, Groupname, IsSecurityPrincipal, MailingPostalAddress, OfficeGraphIdentifier, OtherPostalAddress, OwnedByUser, PartyType, PhonePrimary, ShippingPostalAddress, Source, Status, WebsiteURL)

Family (FamilyId, Description, EmailAlternate, EmailPrimary, Fullname, Groupname, Image, MailingPostalAddress, OtherPostalAddress, OwnedByUser, PartyType, Phone01, Phone02, Phone03, PhonePrimary, ShippingPostalAddress, Source, Status, WebsiteURL)

Family Member (Family_FamilyId, Person_PersonId, Description, OwnedByUser, PrimaryRole, Status)

Household (HouseholdId, Description, EmailAlternate, EmailPrimary, Fullname, Groupname, Image, MailingPostalAddress, OtherPostalAddress, OwnedByUser, PartyType, Phone01, Phone02, Phone03, PhonePrimary, ShippingPostalAddress, Source, Status, WebsiteURL)

Household Member (Household_HouseholdId, Person_PersonId, Description, OwnedByUser, PrimaryRole, Status)

Team (TeamId, Description, EmailAlternate, EmailPrimary, Fullname, Groupname, Image, MailingPostalAddress, OtherPostalAddress, OwnedByUser, PartyType, Phone01, Phone02, Phone03, PhonePrimary, ShippingPostalAddress, Source, Status, WebsiteURL)

Team Member (Team_TeamId, Person_PersonId, Description, OwnedByUser, PrimaryRole, Status)

Sales Entities

Listing A-4 shows the fields for each entity in the sales group.

Listing A-4. Sales Entities

Account (AccountId, AccountGroup_AccountGroupId, BirthDate, BusinessUnit_BusinessUnitId, CreditLimitAmount, Description, DunsNumber, EmailAlternate, EmailPrimary, Employeecount, FacebookIdentity, FreightTerms, Fullname, Gender, Image, Industrycode, IsEmailContactAllowed, IsPhoneContactAllowed, LinkedinIdentity, MailingPostalAddress, MaritalStatus, OfficeGraphIdentifier, Organization_OrganizationId, OrganizationName, OtherPostalAddress, OwnedByUser, Parentaccount_AccountId, PartyType, Paymentterms, Personinformation, PersonName, Phone01, Phone02, Phone03, Phonefax, PhonePrimary, Primarycontact_ContactId, Salescurrencycode, SatoriId, ShippingMethod, ShippingPostalAddress, SocialNetwork01, SocialNetwork02, SocialNetworkIdentity01, SocialNetworkIdentity02, Source, Status, StockExchange, StockTicker, TaxIdentificationIssuer, TaxIdentificationNumber, TwitterIdentity, WebsiteURL)

Account Contact (Account_AccountId, Contact_ContactId, Datasource, Description, OwnedByUser)

Account Group (AccountGroupId, Description, Name, Organization_OrganizationId, OwnedByUser)

Account Lead (Account_AccountId, Lead_LeadId, OwnedByUser)

Competitor (CompetitorId, Description, DunsNumber, EmailAlternate, EmailPrimary, FacebookIdentity, Fullname, Image, Industrycode, KeyProductName, LinkedinIdentity, MailingPostalAddress, OpportunityDescription, Organization_OrganizationId, OrganizationName, OtherPostalAddress, OverviewDescription, OwnedByUser, PartyType, PersonName, Phone01, Phone02, Phone03, Primarycontact_ContactId, Referenceinfourl, ReportedAnnualRevenue, ReportingQuarter, ReportingYear, ShippingPostalAddress, SocialNetwork01, SocialNetwork02, SocialNetworkIdentity01, SocialNetworkIdentity02, Source, Status, StockExchange, StockTicker, StrengthDescription, ThreatDescription, TransactionCurrency, TwitterIdentity, Weaknesses, WebsiteURL, WinPercentage)

Competitor other postal address (AddressId, Competitor_CompetitorId, Description, OtherPostalAddress, OwnedByUser)

Competitor Product (Competitor_CompetitorId, Product_ProductId, CompetitorProductId, OwnedByUser)

Contact Lead (Contact_ContactId, Lead_LeadId, OwnedByUser)

Lead (LeadId, Account_AccountId, AnnualRevenue, BirthDate, BudgetAmount, BudgetStatus, BusinessUnit_BusinessUnitId, Description, DunsNumber, EmailAlternate, EmailPrimary, EstimatedAmount, EstimatedCloseDate, FacebookIdentity, Fullname, Gender, Generation, Image, IndustryCode, IsDecisionMaker, IsEmailContactAllowed, IsInterestConfirmed, IsPhoneContactAllowed, IsSecurityPrincipal, LastCampaignDate, LeadRating, LeadSource, LinkedinIdentity, MailingPostalAddress, OfficeGraphIdentifier, Organization_OrganizationId, OrganizationName, OtherPostalAddress, OwnedByUser, PartyType, PersonName, Phone01, Phone02, Phone03, PhonePrimary, PreferredContactMethod, Profession, PurchaseTimeLine, QualificationDescription, QualifyingOpportunity_OpportunityId, SatoriId, ScheduleFollowUpProspect, ScheduleFollowUpQualify, ShippingPostalAddress, Sic, SocialNetwork01, SocialNetwork02, SocialNetworkIdentity01, SocialNetworkIdentity02, Source,

Status, StockExchange, StockTicker, TaxIdentificationIssuer, TaxIdentificationNumber, TwitterIdentity, WebsiteURL)

Lead Competitor (Competitor_CompetitorId, Lead_LeadId, OwnedByUser)

Lead Contact (Lead_LeadId, Contact_ContactId, Datasource, Description, OwnedByUser)

Lead Other Postal Address (AddressId, Description, Lead_LeadId, OtherPostalAddress, OwnedByUser)

Lead Product (Lead_LeadId, Product_ProductId, OwnedByUser)

Opportunity (OpportunityId, ActualCloseDate, ActualValueAmount, BudgetAmount, BusinessUnit_BusinessUnitId, CloseProbability, CompetitorsIdentified, Contact_ContactId, CreatedDate, CurrentSituationDescription, CustomerContactsIdentified, CustomerNeedDescription, CustomerPainPointsDescription, Description, DiscountAmount, DiscountPercentage, EstimatedCloseDate, EstimatedValueAmount, FollowUpProspectDate, FollowupqualifyDate, Industrycode, Isdecisionmaker, Name, NextfollowupDate, Organization_OrganizationId, OriginalEstimatedValueAmount, OriginatingLead_LeadId, OwnedByUser, ParentOpportunity_OpportunityId, ProposalMeetingDate, ProposedSolutionDescription, PurchaseProcess, PurchaseTimeframe, QualificationDescription, RatingCode, SalesStage, SalesTeamIdentified, Source, Status, Timeline)

Opportunity competitor (Competitor_CompetitorId, Opportunity_OpportunityId, OwnedByUser)

Opportunity product (Opportunity_OpportunityId, Product_ProductId, Description, DiscountAmount, IsPriceOverridden, LineAmount, OwnedByUser, Quantity, Sequence, TotalTaxAmount, Unitprice)

Partner (PartnerId, BusinessUnit_BusinessUnitId, Description, DunsNumber, EmailAlternate, EmailPrimary, FacebookIdentity, Fullname, Image, Industrycode, IsEmailContactAllowed, IsPhoneContactAllowed, IsSecurityPrincipal, LinkedinIdentity, MailingPostalAddress, Organization_OrganizationId, OrganizationName, OtherPostalAddress, OwnedByUser, Parentpartner_PartnerId, PartyType, Phone01, Phone02, Phone03, PhonePrimary, Primarycontact_ContactId, SatoriId, ShippingPostalAddress, SocialNetwork01, SocialNetwork02, SocialNetworkIdentity01, SocialNetworkIdentity02, Source, Status, StockExchange, StockTicker, TaxIdentificationIssuer, TaxIdentificationNumber, TwitterIdentity, WebsiteURL)

Quotation (QuotationId, Account_AccountId, Accountcontact_ContactId, BillingAddress, BusinessUnit_BusinessUnitId, CustomerPurchaseOrderReference, DeliveryAddress, Description, DiscountAmount, Discount Discountpercent, ExpectedShipDate, ExpirationDate, FreightTerms, InvoiceAccount_AccountId, Name, Opportunity_OpportunityId, Organization_OrganizationId, OwnedByUser, Paymentterms, QuotationDate, Quotationtype, RequestedDeliveryDate, SalesOrderReference, SalesPersonworker_WorkerId, ShippingMethod, Status, StatusReason, TotalAmount, TotalChargeAmount, TotalDiscountAmount, TotalDiscountPercent, TotalTaxAmount)

Quotation Charge (Quotation_QuotationId, Chargetype, Amount, BusinessUnit_BusinessUnitId, Description, Name, OwnedByUser)

Quotation Line (Quotation_QuotationId, Sequence, BusinessUnit_BusinessUnitId, DeliveryAddress, Description, DiscountAmount, DiscountPercent, ExpectedShipDate,

LineAmount, MostRecentActualShipDate, Name, OwnedByUser, Product_ProductId, Productname, PromisedShipDate, Quantity, RequestedDeliveryDate, Status, StatusReason, TotalChargeAmount, TotalTaxAmount, UnitPrice)

Quotation Line Charge (QuotationLine_Quotation_QuotationId, QuotationLine_Sequence, Chargetype, Amount, BusinessUnit_BusinessUnitId, Description, Name, OwnedByUser)

Quotation Line Tax (QuotationLine_Quotation_QuotationId, QuotationLine_Sequence, TaxType, Amount, BusinessUnit_BusinessUnitId, Description, Name, OwnedByUser, RateCode)

Quotation Tax (Quotation_QuotationId, TaxType, Amount, BusinessUnit_BusinessUnitId, Description, Name, OwnedByUser, RateCode)

Sales Invoice (SalesInvoiceId, Account_AccountId, Accountcontact_ContactId, BillingAddress, BusinessUnit_BusinessUnitId, CustomerPurchaseOrderReference, Description, DiscountAmount, Discount FreightTerms, InvoiceDate, Name, Opportunity_OpportunityId, Organization_OrganizationId, OwnedByUser, PaymentTerms, SalesOrder_SalesOrderId, SalesPersonworker_WorkerId, ShippingMethod, Status, TotalAmount, TotalChargeAmount, TotalDiscountAmount, TotalTaxAmount)

Sales Invoice Charge (SalesInvoice_SalesInvoiceId, Chargetype, Amount, BusinessUnit_BusinessUnitId, Description, Name, OwnedByUser)

Sales Invoice Line (SalesInvoice_SalesInvoiceId, Chargetype, Amount, BusinessUnit_BusinessUnitId, Description, Name, OwnedByUser)

Sales Invoice Line Charge (SalesInvoiceLine_SalesInvoice_SalesInvoiceId, SalesInvoiceLine_Sequence, ChargeType, Amount, BusinessUnit_BusinessUnitId, Description, Name, OwnedByUser)

Sales Invoice Line Tax (SalesInvoiceLine_SalesInvoice_SalesInvoiceId, SalesInvoiceLine_Sequence, TaxType, Amount, BusinessUnit_BusinessUnitId, Description, Name, OwnedByUser, RateCode)

Sales Invoice Tax (SalesInvoice_SalesInvoiceId, TaxType, Amount, BusinessUnit_BusinessUnitId, Description, Name, OwnedByUser, RateCode)

Sales Order (SalesOrderId, Account_AccountId, Accountcontact_ContactId, BillingAddress, BusinessUnit_BusinessUnitId, CustomerPurchaseOrderReference, DeliveryAddress, Description, DiscountAmount, Discount ExpectedShipDate, FreightTerms, InvoiceAccount_AccountId, Name, Opportunity_OpportunityId, OrderDate, Organization_OrganizationId, OwnedByUser, Paymentterms, RequestedDeliveryDate, SalesPersonworker_WorkerId, ShippingMethod, Status, TotalAmount, TotalChargeAmount, TotalDiscountAmount, TotalTaxAmount)

Sales Order Charge (SalesOrder_SalesOrderId, Chargetype, Amount, BusinessUnit_BusinessUnitId, Description, Name, OwnedByUser)

Sales Order Line (SalesOrder_SalesOrderId, Sequence, BusinessUnit_BusinessUnitId, DeliveryPostalAddress, Description, DiscountAmount, ExpectedShipDate, LineAmount, MostRecentActualShipDate, Name, OwnedByUser, Product_ProductId, ProductName, PromisedShipDate, Quantity, RequestedDeliveryDate, Status, TotalChargeAmount, TotalTaxAmount, UnitPrice)

Sales Order Line Charge (SalesOrderline_SalesOrder_SalesOrderId, SalesOrderline_Sequence, Chargetype, Amount, BusinessUnit_BusinessUnitId, Description, Name, OwnedByUser)

Sales Order Line Shipment (SalesOrderline_SalesOrder_SalesOrderId, SalesOrderline_Sequence, Sequence, ActualShipDate, BusinessUnit_BusinessUnitId, Description, OwnedByUser, Quantity, Status)

Sales Order Line Tax (SalesOrderline_SalesOrder_SalesOrderId, SalesOrderline_Sequence, TaxType, Amount, BusinessUnit_BusinessUnitId, Description, Name, OwnedByUser, RateCode)

Sales Order Tax (SalesOrder_SalesOrderId, TaxType, Amount, BusinessUnit_BusinessUnitId, Description, Name, OwnedByUser, RateCode)

Customer Service Entities

Listing A-5 shows the fields for each entity in the customer service group.

Listing A-5. Customer Service Entities

Case (CaseId, Account_AccountId, ArrivalDate, BusinessUnit_BusinessUnitId, Category, CloseDate, Comment, CurrentAssignedSupportWorker_WorkerId, CurrentContact_ContactId, CustomerSatisfactionCode, Description, Name, Organization_OrganizationId, OriginCode, OwnedByUser, ParentCase_CaseId, Severity, SolutionType, Status)

Case Activity (SupportCase_CaseId, Sequence, BeginDate, BusinessUnit_BusinessUnitId, CaseSeverity, CaseStatus, Comment, Contact_ContactId, ContactType, Description, EndDate, HasKbArticle, Image, IsReassignment, IsSeverityChange, IsStatusChange, OwnedByUser, PriorCaseSeverity, PriorCaseStatus, ReassignedComment, ReassignedFromCaseworker_WorkerId, ReassignedReason, SupportWorker_WorkerId, Type)

Case Activity Kb Article (CaseActivity_SupportCase_CaseId, CaseActivity_Sequence, KbArticle_KbArticleId, ArticleValue, Description, KbArticleName, OwnedByUser)

Kb Article (KbArticleId, ArticleScore, Author_WorkerId, Description, LinkToArticle, OwnedByUser, Synopsis)

Organization Entities

Listing A-6 shows the fields for each entity in the organization group.

Listing A-6. Organization Entities

Organization (OrganizationId, Description, DunsNumber, EmailAlternate, EmailPrimary, FacebookIdentity, Fullname, Image, IndustryCode, IsEmailContactAllowed, IsInternal, IsPhoneContactAllowed, LinkedinIdentity, MailingPostalAddress, OfficeGraphIdentifier, OrganizationName, OtherPostalAddress, OwnedByUser, Parentorganization_OrganizationId, PartyType, Phone01, Phone02, Phone03, PhonePrimary, Primarycontact_ContactId, SatoriId, ShippingPostalAddress, SocialNetwork01, SocialNetwork02, SocialNetworkIdentity01, SocialNetworkIdentity02, Source, Status, StockExchange, StockTicker, TaxIdentificationIssuer, TaxIdentificationNumber, TwitterIdentity, Type, WebsiteURL)

Organization Contact (Organization_OrganizationId, Contact_ContactId, Datasource, Description, OwnedByUser)

Purchase Entities

Listing A-7 shows the fields for each entity in the purchase group.

Listing A-7. Purchase Entities

Purchase Order (PurchaseOrderId, ApprovalStatus, BillingAddress, BusinessUnit_
BusinessUnitId, ConfirmedDeliveryDate, DeliveryPostalAddress, Description, DiscountAmount,
ExpectedDeliveryDate, ExpectedShipDate, FreightTerms, OrderDate, Organization_
OrganizationId, OwnedByUser, Paymentterms, PriceIncludesSalesTax, PromisedDeliveryDate,
PromisedShipDate, RequestedDeliveryDate, ShippingAddress, ShippingMethod, Status,
TaxRegistrationNumber, TotalAmount, TotalChargeAmount, TotalDiscountAmount, TotalTaxAmount,
Vendor_VendorId, Vendorcontact_ContactId, VendorForInvoice_VendorId, VendorInvoice,
VendorReference, WorkerBuyer_WorkerId)

Purchase Order Charge (PurchaseOrder_PurchaseOrderId, Chargetype, Amount, BusinessUnit_
BusinessUnitId, Description, Name, OwnedByUser)

Purchase Order Line (PurchaseOrder_PurchaseOrderId, Sequence, BusinessUnit_
BusinessUnitId, ConfirmedDeliveryDate, DeliveryPostalAddress, Description, DiscountAmount,
ExpectedDeliveryDate, ExpectedShipDate, LineAmount, MostRecentActualReceiptDate,
MostRecentActualShipDate, Name, OwnedByUser, PriceUnitQuantity, ProcurementCategory,
Product_ProductId, ProductName, PromisedDeliveryDate, PromisedShipDate, Quantity,
RequestedDeliveryDate, Status, TotalChargeAmount, TotalTaxAmount, UnitPrice,
VendorProductName)

Purchase Order Line Charge (PurchaseOrderline_PurchaseOrder_PurchaseOrderId,
PurchaseOrderline_Sequence, ChargeType, Amount, BusinessUnit_BusinessUnitId, Description,
Name, OwnedByUser)

Purchase Order Line Receipt (PurchaseOrderline_PurchaseOrder_PurchaseOrderId,
PurchaseOrderline_Sequence, Sequence, ActualReceiptDate, BusinessUnit_BusinessUnitId,
Description, OwnedByUser, Quantity, Status)

Purchase Order Line Tax (PurchaseOrderline_PurchaseOrder_PurchaseOrderId, PurchaseOrderline_
Sequence, TaxType, Amount, BusinessUnit_BusinessUnitId, Description, Name, OwnedByUser,
RateCode)

Purchase Order Tax (PurchaseOrder_PurchaseOrderId, TaxType, Amount, BusinessUnit_
BusinessUnitId, Description, Name, OwnedByUser, RateCode)

Vendor (VendorId, BirthDate, BusinessUnit_BusinessUnitId, Description, DunsNumber,
EmailAlternate, EmailPrimary, FacebookIdentity, Fullname, Gender, Image, IndustryCode,
IsDisabledOwned, IsEmailContactAllowed, IsMinorityOwned, IsNativeamOwned,
IsPhoneContactAllowed, IsWomanOwned, LinkedinIdentity, MailingPostalAddress,
OfficeGraphIdentifier, Organization_OrganizationId, OrganizationName, OtherPostalAddress,
OwnedByUser, ParentVendor_VendorId, PartyType, PersonName, Phone01, Phone02, Phone03,
PhonePrimary, Primarycontact_ContactId, SatoriId, ShippingPostalAddress, SocialNetwork01,
SocialNetwork02, SocialNetworkIdentity01, SocialNetworkIdentity02, Source, Status,
StockExchange, StockTicker, SupplierApprovalStatus, TaxIdentificationIssuer,
TaxIdentificationNumber, TwitterIdentity, WebsiteURL)

Vendor Contact (Vendor_VendorId, Contact_ContactId, Datasource, Description, OwnedByUser)

Vendor Invoice (VendorInvoiceId, BillingAddress, BusinessUnit_BusinessUnitId, Description, DiscountAmount, FreightTerms, Organization_OrganizationId, OwnedByUser, PaymentTerms, PurchaseOrder_PurchaseOrderId, ShippingAddress, ShippingMethod, Status, TotalAmount, TotalChargeAmount, TotalDiscountAmount, TotalTaxAmount, Vendor_VendorId, VendorContact_ContactId, VendorInvoiceDate, WorkerBuyer_WorkerId)

Vendor Invoice Charge (Vendorinvoice_VendorInvoiceId, ChargeType, Amount, BusinessUnit_BusinessUnitId, Description, Name, OwnedByUser)

Vendor Invoice Line (VendorInvoice_VendorInvoiceId, Sequence, BusinessUnit_BusinessUnitId, Description, DiscountAmount, LineAmount, Name, OwnedByUser, Product_ProductId, ProductName, PurchaseOrderline_PurchaseOrder_PurchaseOrderId, PurchaseOrderline_Sequence, Quantity, Status, TotalChargeAmount, TotaltaxAmount, UnitPrice, VendorProductName)

Vendor Invoice Line Charge (VendorInvoiceLine_VendorInvoice_VendorInvoiceId, VendorInvoiceline_Sequence, ChargeType, Amount, BusinessUnit_BusinessUnitId, Description, Name, OwnedByUser)

Vendor Invoice Line Tax (VendorInvoiceLine_VendorInvoice_VendorInvoiceId, VendorInvoiceLine_Sequence, TaxType, Amount, BusinessUnit_BusinessUnitId, Description, Name, OwnedByUser, RateCode)

Vendor Invoice Tax (VendorInvoice_VendorInvoiceId, TaxType, Amount, BusinessUnit_BusinessUnitId, Description, Name, OwnedByUser, RateCode)

Human Resources Entities

Listing A-8 shows the fields for each entity in the human resources group.

Listing A-8. Human Resources Entities

Employment (Worker_WorkerId, Organization_OrganizationId, ValidFrom, AdjustedWorkerStartDate, EmployerNoticeAmount, EmployerUnitOfNotice, EmploymentEndDate, EmploymentStartDate, LastDateWorked, OwnedByUser, TransitionDate, ValidTo, WorkerNoticeAmount, WorkerStartDate, WorkerType, WorkerUnitOfNotice)
Job (JobId, AllowUnlimitedPositions, DefaultFulltimeEquivalent, Description, Jobfunction_JobfunctionId, Jobtype_JobtypeId, MaximumNumberOfPositions, Name, OwnedByUser, Title, ValidFrom, ValidTo)
Job function (JobfunctionId, Description, OwnedByUser)
Jobtype (JobtypeId, Description, ExemptStatus, OwnedByUser)
Leave Request (LeaveRequestId, Comment, Organization_OrganizationId, OwnedByUser, RequestDate, Status, Worker_Workerid)
Leave Request Detail (LeaveRequest_LeaveRequestId, LeaveType_LeaveTypeId, LeaveDate, Amount, OwnedByUser)

LeaveType (LeaveTypeId, Description, Organization_OrganizationId, OwnedByUser)
Position (PositionId, Activation, AvailableForAssignment, Department_DepartmentId,
Description, FullTimeEquivalent, Job_JobId, OwnedByUser, ParentPosition_PositionId,
PositionType_PositionTypeId, Retirement, Title, ValidFrom, ValidTo)
Position Type (PositionTypeId, Classification, Description, OwnedByUser)
Position Worker Assignment (Position_PositionId, ValidFrom, OwnedByUser, ValidTo, Worker_
Workerid)

Retail Entities

The retail group contains just one single entity, as shown in Listing A-9.

Listing A-9. Retail Entities

Retail Channel Worker (Retailchannel_RetailchannelId, Worker_WorkerId, OwnedByUser, Status)

Data Structure of the Sample 'Journey' Application

For reference, this section summarizes the data structure for the journey app that this book uses. Figure A-14 shows the table names and the relationships between the tables. Figure A-15 shows some example data from these tables.

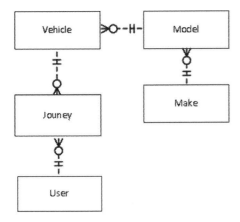

Figure A-14. *Table names and relationships*

Journey table.

JourneyID	StartDate	UserID	JourneyDesc	VehicleID	MileageInMiles	EndDate
1	2018-04-23	10	London - Bristol	10	116	2018-04-23
2	2017-12-23	7	Sheffield - Derby	8	189	2017-12-23
3	2017-06-02	8	Penzance - Reading	6	219	2017-06-02
4	2017-12-14	10	Norwich - Manchester	6	250	2017-12-14
5	2017-11-28	1	Birmingham - Manchester	4	105	2017-11-28

User table.

UserID	Firstname	Surname	Gender	Address1	Address2	City	Postcode	Country	Telephone	Mobile	Active
1	Tim	Leung	Male	3 Forest Run Circle		London		England	20-(915)361-6099		
2	Tom	Thompson	Male	4087 Daystar Way		New York		United Stat	358-(866)328-8478		
3	Lou	Thomas	Female	12 Mozzarella Cherry Way		Penzance		England	44-(731)100-0291		
4	Sunny	Stump	Male	57874 Red Cloud Street		Surenavan		Finland	374-(344)829-6202		
5	Em	Comelli	Male	3438 Schmedeman Road		Geoktschai		Mongolia	994-(116)563-3094		
6	Gwenni	Lathey	Female	22 Maryland Terrace		Chikushino-shi		Egypt	81-(336)169-7418		

Vehicle table.

VehicleID	ModelID	Registration	Color	FuelType	Seats	InsuranceEnd	Transmission	ComfortLevel
1	3	DA12 CJM	Green	P	4	2018-05-22T10:00:00Z	A	5
2	5	OX14 ACU	Red	P	4	2018-05-08T11:00:00Z	A	5
3	8	GV60 YAH	Blue	P	2	2018-04-21T12:00:00Z	M	4
4	12	HV55 REF	White	D	4	2018-05-04T11:00:00Z	M	3
5	4	NI17 HTA	Black	D	7	2018-05-08T11:00:00Z	M	3

Make table.

MakeID	Name
1	Audi
2	Ford
3	Lexus
4	Mercedes-Benz
5	BMW

Model table.

ModelID	MakeID	Name	Year
1	1	A4	2008-2015
2	1	A5	2007-2015
3	2	Fiesta	2002-2008
4	2	Grand C-Max	2010-2017

Figure A-15. *Example values in the sample*

Index

A

Action approval, 308–309
Admin Center, 21–22
App properties
    aspect ratio, 135
    background color, 49–50
    icon, 50
    orientation, 50
App startup behavior/parameters, 123
Assigning permissions, 57
Auto-generated app
    browse screen, 34–35
    creating, 27–29
    detail screen, 36–37
    edit screen, 38, 40–42

B

Barcodes, 209, 223
Buttons
    conditions, 332
    enable/disable, 259–260, 264
    setting actions, 101
    set visibility, 260

C

Cards unlock, 42
CDS entities
    application user, 11
    customer, 360–361, 368
    data types, 72, 74
    fields, 72–73
    foundation, 353–354, 362
    granting read/write access, 256
    group, 355, 364
    human resources, 361, 370
    importing/exporting, 70
    organization, 354, 368
    person entities, 354–355, 362

purchase
    invoice, 358–360
    order, 358–359
    vendor, 358–359
sales
    account, 355–356
    competitor, 355–356
    invoice, 356–357
    opportunities, 356
    order, 358
    quotation, 355–357
    store leads, 356
    service, 360–361, 368
Charts
    column, 239–240, 243, 246–247, 252
    legends, 244
    line, 237, 243, 247–249, 252
    pie, 237, 246–247, 252
Collect (function), 274–275, 279–280
Collections
    data, 114, 116, 241–243, 252
    LoadData function, 318, 320, 332
    SaveData and LoadData, 316, 320
Columns
    adding, 116–117
    dropping, 117
    renaming, 117
    ShowColumns function, 117
Common data service (CDS)
    connecting with Excel, 283
    database creation and deletion, 68–70, 81
    deleting sample data, 81
    entities (*see* CDS entities)
    exporting data, 281, 283
    field groups, 72, 77–78
    importing data, 281–282
    PowerApps, 209
    securing, 253, 255–256
    standard entities, 70–71, 81
    storage limits, 68, 74, 92
    storing images, 210

© Tim Leung 2017
T. Leung, *Beginning PowerApps*, https://doi.org/10.1007/978-1-4842-3003-9

Common data service (CDS) (*cont.*)
  viewing records, 212
  working offline, 317–318
Conditional tests (If function), 100, 120
Controls
  add picture, 209, 211–213, 215, 221, 224
  audio, 173
  barcode, 209, 223–225
  button, 147, 152, 175
  camera, 209, 213–217, 224–225
  chart, 237–238, 242–249, 251–252
  checkbox, 145, 152–153
  date picker, 146, 155–158
  disable, 259
  drop down control, 145, 147, 156, 160,
      164–165, 170
  enable/disable, 260–261
  entity form, 166–168
  export, 271–272, 277
  HTML text, 149–150
  icons, 148, 156
  image, 173–174
  import, 271–274, 276, 278
  labels, 149–150, 156
  list box, 145, 160, 164, 173
  radio, 145–146, 150–152
  setting values, 101
  set visibility, 256, 261
  Shapes, 149, 174
  slider, 146, 150, 153–154
  tab control, 129, 135, 140–142
  table, 145, 151, 164–165, 177
  text input, 145–146, 150–151, 154, 160
  timer, 145, 174–175
  toggle, 150, 152–153
  video, 172
Conversion
  handwriting to text, 209
  numbers to text, 103
  text to dates, 103
  text to numbers, 126
  text to upper/lower/proper case, 104
Custom connector, 335–336, 338, 340,
    342–344, 348, 351

D

Data lists, 113, 118, 126
DataSourceInfo, 259–260
Data sources
  adding/removing/renaming, 32, 34
  collection, 12
  excel, 25
  Microsoft translation services, 90
  MSN weather services, 91

refreshing (updating), 58–59
SharePoint, 84, 86, 88
sharing, 59–60, 259
SQL Server, 84
static data, 284
Data structure, 353, 371
Dates
  arithmetic, 112
  entering dates without times, 155
  entry (date picker control), 155
  formatting, 111
  getting month/day names, 112
  storing, 156
  UTC conversion, 157
Delegation, 180–182, 200, 206
Dialing phone numbers, 95
Disambiguation, 192, 275
Drop down control
  adding values, 182–183, 188, 206
  displaying CDS values, 168–170
  nesting controls, 163–164
  set display items, 147, 161

E

Environments
  CDS data sources, 256
  configuration, 21–22
  moving apps, 57–58
Error handling, 125–126, 282
Errors(function), 276
Excel, 209–210, 212, 216, 218, 221, 224–225,
    289, 299
  add-in, 271, 283–284
  backup Excel file, 292
  preparing spreadsheet for use, 25–26
  storing images, 210
  update records with Patch, 274–275

F

Files copying, 288, 289, 311, 312
Flow, 287–295, 297, 299–301, 303–312
ForAll, 279, 329
Forms
  arrange controls horizontally/vertically, 130,
      134, 141
  default values, 207
  EditMode, 323–325
  FormMode, 200, 263
  null values with collections, 320
  reading data, 42–44
  resetting values, 145, 175–176
  retrieve entered values
        (updates property), 325

saving data, 45–46, 151
securing save button, 263
submitted values, 206
updating data from web service, 351
updating values, 233
validation, 202
Formula
    entering/editing, 95
    running on start, 124, 263
    semi-colon, 96, 113

▓ G

Gallery control, 34–35, 37, 52
    display nested record values, 326
    displaying images, 209, 212–213, 215–216
    layout, 129, 132–134, 136, 141

▓ H, I

HTTP
    request, 336–337, 351
    response, 336–337, 351
    return status, 337, 351
    verb, 336–337

▓ J, K

JavaScript Object Notation (JSON), 288, 335–338,
    340–342, 346–347, 351

▓ L

Location, 227–232, 234–235
LookUp (function), 275, 280, 162

▓ M

Maps
    Bing Maps, 227, 232, 234–235
    Google Maps, 227, 232–234
Mobile players
    installing, 60–61
    system requirements, 10

▓ N

Notifications, 311
    Email, 287, 293
    mobile, 179, 203–205, 207
Null values
    checking, 119
    Coalesce, 251
    JourneyDesc field, 320
    searching, 190

Numbers, 223, 225
    auto-incrementing sequences, 220
    basic arithmetic, 107
    formatting currencies, 109
    formatting zeros, 137
    rounding, 109
    trigonometric functions, 95, 109, 126

▓ O

OData, 287, 295–297, 304, 307
Office, 365
    plans types/pricing, 18
    userId GUID, 262
Offline, 333
On-premises Gateway, 291
    copying files, 287–288, 312
    installing/uninstalling, 82, 84, 86
    overview, 11
    starting/stopping, 83

▓ P, Q

Parent, 97
Patch(function)
    add new record, 196
    merging records, 325
    retrieve auto-generated IDs, 196–198, 279
    return values, 279
    update data, 195
Permissions, 255–259, 266–267
Postman, 336, 340, 342–343, 351
PowerApps Studio
    finding items, 51
    installing, 22–24
    opening apps, 51
    pricing, 10
    saving apps, 51
    system requirements, 8–9
Publishing apps
    runtime language, 61–63
    versioning, 60

▓ R

Records, 212, 217, 220
    aggregating, 237, 239
    average, min, max and sum, 117, 119
    check for non existence, 192
    counting, 118
    creation, 196
    deletion, 179, 200
        confirmation, 129, 139–140
        local collections, 322
    distinct, 193–194, 206

Records (*cont.*)
    filtering by logged on user, 263
    grouping, 185–186, 206
    grouping (by month), 247, 249, 251
    importing, 272–273
    joining, 191, 206
    looping through results, 118
    merging, 325
    retrieve by ordinal number, 220
    retrieving, 194, 196
    row by row processing (ForAll), 275, 327–329
    sorting, 184, 188
    sum, 135, 137–138
    ungrouping, 185–187
    union, 185
    updating, 195–196
        conditional (UpdateIf), 325
        multiple rows, 195
Regular expressions, 105–106, 126
Representational State Transfer
        (REST), 288, 336–337
500 row limit, 179, 206
        overcoming, 306

■ S

Sample apps
    asset checkout, 4
    budget tracker, 5–6, 135–136, 139, 237
    service desk, 6–7
    site inspector, 7–8
Screens
    adding, deleting and rearranging, 33–34
    custom navigation, 95, 127
    Navigation, 121
    navigation, 99
    passing data, 113, 116
    setting layouts, 129, 132–134
    startup screen, 33
Searching data
    by date criteria, 187
    by drop down, 179, 182, 184, 189
    lists, 189–190
    by SSN, 95, 105, 126
    strings, 105
Securing apps, 59
SharePoint
    choice items, 67, 88, 257, 259
    creating lists, 67, 87, 257–259
    securing lists, 257
Signals
    connection, 316
    location, 228–229, 231–232, 235

SQL Server, 67, 82, 84–85, 209–211, 224, 287–289,
        294–295, 297, 306–307, 311–312
    filtering data, 297
    preventing Data Loss (DLP Policy), 264, 266
    storing images, 210
    stored procedures, 287–288, 306–307, 312
SubmitForm, 39, 45–46
Subscription
    Community edition, 15, 18
    features, 19
    flow–limits, 288
    pricing-office 18, 365
    pricing-standalone, 13–14
    registration, 20
Swagger, 335–336, 340–342, 351

■ T

Tables, 95, 98, 102, 113–114, 116, 118–119, 126–127
Text
    concatenation, 103, 164
    hashtags, 103
    input control, 150–151, 188, 203
    label and HTML text control, 149–150
    line breaks, 96, 101, 126
    replacing values, 107
Themes, 129, 142–143
ThisItem, 97, 114, 119
Translating Data, 90
Troubleshooting, on-premises Gateway
        service, 67, 83

■ U

User management
    adding users, 55–56
    authentication, 253–254, 266
    getting logged on user, 262
    Logging on, 21
    Microsoft personal account, 16–18
    Microsoft work account, 16–18

■ V

Validation, 42, 87, 182, 201–202
Variables
    context, 98–99, 101–102, 114, 121, 125–126
    global, 102, 124, 126
    NavigationContext, 168

■ W, X, Y, Z

Workflow, 287–288, 301–303, 305–306, 312

Get the eBook for only $5!

Why limit yourself?

With most of our titles available in both PDF and ePUB format, you can access your content wherever and however you wish—on your PC, phone, tablet, or reader.

Since you've purchased this print book, we are happy to offer you the eBook for just $5.

To learn more, go to http://www.apress.com/companion or contact support@apress.com.

Apress®

All Apress eBooks are subject to copyright. All rights are reserved by the Publisher, whether the whole or part of the material is concerned, specifically the rights of translation, reprinting, reuse of illustrations, recitation, broadcasting, reproduction on microfilms or in any other physical way, and transmission or information storage and retrieval, electronic adaptation, computer software, or by similar or dissimilar methodology now known or hereafter developed. Exempted from this legal reservation are brief excerpts in connection with reviews or scholarly analysis or material supplied specifically for the purpose of being entered and executed on a computer system, for exclusive use by the purchaser of the work. Duplication of this publication or parts thereof is permitted only under the provisions of the Copyright Law of the Publisher's location, in its current version, and permission for use must always be obtained from Springer. Permissions for use may be obtained through RightsLink at the Copyright Clearance Center. Violations are liable to prosecution under the respective Copyright Law.

① initiate a phone call from within a phone app that shows a phone number

OnSelect → Launch("tel://" & [insert na of data field])

② initiate an email message from withi a phone app that shows an email address:

On Select → Launch ("mailto:" & [insert nam of data field])

note
With the above 2 tips, do not use the brackets; just the name of the data field that contains the phone # or th email address.

_____

③ initiate a text message from within a phone app that shows a phone #:

On Select → Launch ("sms:" & [insert name of data field that stores a phone #])

ple pp. 123

(cont.)

④ Open a web page from within a phone app where "webPage" is a data field:

On Select → Launch ("https://" &WebAddress)

73465863R00226

Made in the USA
San Bernardino, CA
06 April 2018